€37.50

THE FUNCTIONS OF THE
MEDIEVAL PARLIAMENT OF ENGLAND

THE FUNCTIONS OF THE
MEDIEVAL PARLIAMENT
OF ENGLAND

G.O. SAYLES

THE HAMBLEDON PRESS

LONDON   AND   RONCEVERTE

Published by The Hambledon Press, 1988

102 Gloucester Avenue, London NW1 8HX (U.K.)

309 Greenbrier Avenue, Ronceverte, WV 24970 (U.S.A.)

ISBN 0 907628 92 3

British Library Cataloguing in Publication Data

The Functions of the medieval parliament of
    England.
    1. England, *Parliament* — History —
    Sources   2. Great Britain — Politics
    and government — 1154–1399 — Sources
    I. Sayles, G.O.
    328.42'09   JN515

Library of Congress Cataloging-in-Publication Data

Sayles, G. O. (George Osborne), 1901–
The functions of the medieval Parliament of
England.

    Includes index.
    1. England. Parliament — History — Sources.
2. Great Britain – Politics and government — 1066–1485 —
Sources.   I. Title.
JN505.S29   1988   328.42'09   87-26678

Printed in Great Britain by Billing & Sons Ltd, Worcester

Contents

To Hilary

Foreword

From the sixteenth century to the present day studies of the medieval parliament have mainly focused their attention on its composition, especially on the personnel of the house of commons. To such volumes there is no end: from Dugdale to the 'Official History of Parliament', which is itself misnamed because it is not a history of parliament but only of the commons in parliament. Perhaps the approach to the subject would have been different if Thomas Madox had not left out of his *History of the Exchequer* the material he had gathered on the medieval parliament. He meant to use it for a separate book which never got written. His manuscript has now been printed by Miss C. S. Sims in the *Huntington Library Quarterly* (1959) for all to see how far his re-creation of the medieval parliament disagrees with what became the accepted version.

Parliament is a political institution, the contemplation of which induces strong emotional reactions. For its history has suffered from the common tendency to find in the past the features of contemporary institutions. English historians were proud of the English parliament, which was universally admired, especially in the nineteenth century, in the belief that parliamentary democracy was to be seen at work from the thirteenth century onwards. Two fallacious assumptions were involved: that a political institution might be good in itself, irrespective of time and circumstance, and that historical continuity implied identity of function. In consequence, the essential question was set aside: it was not who composed parliament, but instead what powers did it have and how did it use them in relation to the needs of contemporary society. A mass of detailed information survived to answer this question, but most of it was either ignored or put on one side as irrelevant, and only those select portions of the evidence, mainly writs of summons, were studied or cited which seemed to support an *a priori* conception about the commons. And it is still difficult, if not painful, even for professional historians, to realise that in origin parliament was a feudal court and that certain features of the modern English parliament can be understood only if its feudal origin is realised. The place occupied by the baronage in the scheme of parliaments under the Provisions of Oxford in 1258, and again after Edward II's failure to continue the system established by Edward I, is peculiarly English. A succession of kings in the thirteenth century, skilful in warfare and adroit in politics, might have given England a very different constitution. Of what it might have been we may form an idea from the parliaments of the first half of Edward I's reign, so like those of contemporary France. The deep recurrent mistrust of the king, the repeated efforts for baronial control of the administration, can be traced to John and his ultimate incapacity to rule. It was the expedients, devised by the barons in his reign and under Henry III and Edward II and Richard II, that contributed most to the shaping of the English parliament. Though they were informed by a continuous tradition reaching back to Runnymede, the barons built better than they knew, for there was no conscious pursuit of political or constitutional ideals.

This selection of documents is intended to redress the balance. Fifty years ago Professor A. E. Levett, in pleading for a 'source book' to illustrate the early history of parliament, declared that 'few books would be more difficult to make, few more destructive of claptrap' (*History*, January 1931). The scheme here adopted is simple: each of the 130 or so parliaments that met between 1258 and 1350 has been furnished with documents, mainly official, showing what it did. Thus a general picture of the institution at work is provided. The year 1258, though it does not indicate the beginning of parliament, marks the time when it was incorporated in the first written constitution of England, that is the Provisions of Oxford, whereby it was arranged that three parliaments were to be convoked every year at specified times. Parliament thereby ceased to be an indeterminate 'occasion'. The year 1350 has no particular significance except convenience and, indeed, no proper point at which to stop occurs until 1529 with the Long Parliament of the Reformation.

The single aim of this volume is to allow those interested in the origins and early development of parliament to have easy access to the relevant documents. Since these are written in Latin or Old French, to produce them in their original form would confine their use to the diminishing number of those versed in these languages. Therefore the habit of a life-time has been abandoned and they have been translated for wider consultation. This can be done nowadays with good conscience, for ours is the age of the camera: if the rendering of any document is regarded as suspect, a photographic reproduction can be obtained easily and cheaply. For this purpose the source of each document has been carefully set down. And when one ancient university has for some years been sponsoring a Degree course in 'Latin Literature in Translation, primarily for those without Latin', and a sister university has deliberately and drastically reduced expenditure on its Classics Department and spent elsewhere the money saved, it is evident that Latin and, still more, Old French are on their way to join Greek and Anglo-Saxon as caviare to the general. It has been said that translation is like a woman: if faithful, not beautiful; if beautiful, not faithful. Beauty does not enter into the argument with official documents but an attempt has been made, while remaining faithful to the text, to avoid that wooden form of English which seems to beset translations. It may be added that it is harder to give a translation than to copy the text: for example, we can print the Latin *communitas* or the French *commune* without difficulty, but how do we translate this word into English to give it its proper contemporary meaning?

This book has been maturing since 1924 and in its progress over sixty years it has received innumerable kindnesses from the custodians of manuscripts at the Public Record Office, the then British Museum, Lambeth Palace and the Guildhall in London; at many Oxford and Cambridge colleges; at Canterbury Cathedral archives; the old Advocates and the University Library in Edinbugh; Chetham's Library and John Rylands Library in Manchester. If I do not name those who befriended me it is not because the list would be long but because most of them have passed beyond any expression of gratitude by one approaching his ninetieth year. The details of books, articles and reviews laid under grateful contribution can be very easily obtained from the many bibliographies published and there is no need to burden the text with them.

For the actual production of this volume I am particularly indebted to my daughter Hilary, who has read the proofs with expert eye and apparent enjoyment, and to my friend Martin Sheppard, who has published it with his customary enthusiasm, skill and expedition.

20 April 1987   G.O.S.

Calendar of Parliaments

List of References in Manuscripts

Public Record Office, London

INTRODUCTION

Introduction

The history of any institution must first and foremost be a history of its functions. Since no human institution functions impersonally, the manner in which its functions are performed will depend upon the personality of those who do the work, and it will also be strongly affected by the conditions of everyday life. A society, for example, where ranks and classes are sharply differentiated, such as were all medieval societies in Western Europe, will need different institutions from those of an egalitarian society, the ideal of modern Europe: the institutions may continue to bear the same name but they will serve different purposes and will operate differently. The differences may appear small but, like the differences between man and man, they are nevertheless of great importance. This is true, not only between different countries like England and France in the same age, which both had parliaments from the thirteenth century onwards, but also between different ages in the same country: for example, in our own country a parliament under Edward I meant something very different from a parliament under Edward IV, which in turn differed from one under Edward VI, which differed from one under Edward VII.

We must therefore try to regard the medieval parliament through the eyes of men of the thirteenth, fourteenth and fifteenth centuries. No one living in the twentieth century can achieve this with complete success, however much he may familiarise himself with the ways of thought and speech and life of six or seven hundred years ago, however long the time he may spend with writings made when the hopes and fears they express were unresolved, the folly unchecked, the wisdom undimmed. There comes between him and the parchment the knowledge of so many tens of thousands of days which, one by one, few from deliberate intent and nearly all imperceptibly, have moulded and changed parliament, in common with all institutions, often leaving forms and words scarcely altered but with their content transformed. We must beware of forms and words. We take pride in their antiquity; we are strengthened and comforted if we are persuaded that our thoughts, our liberties, our beliefs, the very fetters we embrace, were those also of our fathers and have come to us in their original integrity. And so we make our ancestors speak our own thoughts, conduct themselves by our own standards, pursue our own ends. But Simon de Montfort, Thomas of Lancaster, the three Edwards, their friends and ministers, are as remote from us in ideas, speech and aims as Innocent III, Thomas Aquinas, Pierre Dubois and John Wycliffe. We may go a long way to understanding and sympathising with these men, but the more we understand them, the less shall we believe that they were modern catholics or modern protestants, modern statesmen or modern politicians, although, like our own contemporaries, they were never overwise nor overfoolish, living and improvising from day to day, ignorant, as we are, of what the morrow would bring forth.

These general propositions are perhaps truisms and the illustrations obvious, nevertheless the generalisations are in constant danger of being forgotten, particularly in England, where institutions have a long and continuous history, in contrast with France or Germany or Italy or other countries where at different points of time there have been attempted breaks with the past and conscious and deliberate efforts to remake political and administrative institutions. In fact, no break with the past can be more than partial, and no reconstruction can fail to build into the new fabric far more old material than is rejected. The great service that Alexis de Tocqueville rendered was to demonstrate this truth in a country where there was a strongly held belief that, for good or ill, the Revolution that began in 1789 marked a chasm, as it were, between old and new. This conception of the Revolution was largely myth, a myth which has unfortunately influenced much subsequent political thought. But there are other myths, not very dissimilar in character, which historians have embraced. There was, for example, the belief that 'the thin red line' of the Norman Conquest caused an abrupt break in English administrative contrivances, a belief that can only be sustained by neglecting the evidence. On the other hand, great changes have occurred that are almost unperceived because they were not marked by wars or political revolutions and therefore, being gradual, escaped the attention not only of contemporaries but of later historians who approached the past with preconceptions drawn from the present.

Our first task is to describe one of these changes, for it determined the structure of government in which the English parliament began to operate. Apart from that structure any discussion of parliament is meaningless, for parliament has not only been conditioned by it but has, in turn, influenced it. These inter-actions, complex and never static, so difficult to disentangle and comprehend, are the stuff of English parliamentary history. But there was a time when parliament was unknown in England and we must begin in that time in order to make the foundation and early growth intelligible.

The Structure of Government, 1066-1258

William the Conqueror seems never to have envisaged the possibility that England and Normandy could continue after his death under a single ruler. Though continued unification must have been in his mind, he could see no means by which it could be maintained: his eldest son Robert was far from being suitable for the task and the conception of impersonal government lay far in the future. He did therefore what seemed best in the light of the circumstances: the duchy he inherited passed to his eldest son Robert and the kingdom he had acquired passed to his second son William Rufus. Had duke Robert displayed any capacity for government in Normandy, the two countries might have been severed finally on the Conqueror's death and England might have pursued without further interruption the political evolution that had been in progress there since the tenth century. For the Conquest itself brought few changes in methods of government, for the Normans had little of their own to contribute to the stock of political ideas they found in the much more sophisticated English kingdom both in central government or in local government, in methods of taxation or of financial control, in administrative processes or legal codes. Norman lords displaced English lords but they entered an English society which, like French society, had already become 'feudal' with the emergence of the hereditary fief, the *beneficium* as it was called in England as in France, and of the service that ran with land. And so a five-hide holding of a Saxon thegn became the five-hide fee of a Norman knight. It is true that English thegn became French baron, English knight French chevalier, but these were merely changes of nomenclature. There was no colonisation of England by the Normans in the sense that they had any intention of abandoning their homeland to settle elsewhere. These ferociously acquisitive men regarded their English possessions as primarily a highly profitable investment abroad. Had England followed its own way as the Conqueror arranged, it would have absorbed 'Normans' into its society by processes of inter-marriage, like that of the Conqueror's third son Henry, as it had undoubtedly absorbed the earlier 'Northmen' from Scandinavia and Denmark. Thereafter it was highly probable that England, separated from Normandy, would have been affected by French feudalism as Western Germany so plainly was: the gradual elevation of the status of knight, or rather the differentiation which raised the wealthier landed knights and depressed the poorer knights into serjeants, and the later further development which, as knighthood became increasingly burdensome, produced the class of English squires who could not, or had no mind to, aspire to the higher ranks of chivalry. But before the reign of Henry I there were no signs that the way in which England was governed had greatly changed: the English language continued to be used in administration as in literature, no documents in French are to be found.

But England was not destined to go its own way. For England and Normandy were joined together again by the battle of Tinchebray in 1106 by which Henry I overcame his brother Robert. That battle determined that the king of England was to be duke of Normandy. In so doing it also determined that French should be dominant in England, the language of court and culture, and it determined further that England should be ruled by cosmopolitan French-speaking administrators and soldiers, who were as much at home in Syria as in Ireland. It was therefore this battle in 1106, not that of Hastings in 1066, which decided that England should fall, for three centuries, within the ambit of French civilisation and our most characteristic institutions should seem to be French and not English. If this seems a paradox, let us reflect that the battle ensured that men would speak of parliament and not witan or folkmoot, of judges and not lawmen, of mayors and not portreeves. And not only is the word 'parliament' French but much else of its nomenclature: its peers and its commons, its bills and its acts, its petitions. Such English words as 'speaker' and 'woolsack' are late upstarts in its secular history. Though Normandy came to be lost to the English king a hundred years later, by then this made little immediate difference. The thirteenth and fourteenth centuries are the period of Simon de Montfort, of the brothers Jean and Geoffrey de Joinville (the one the companion of the French king St. Louis, the other the ruler of Ireland under the English king Edward I), of Jean sire de Pecquigny, vidame de Amiens, who was another servant of king Edward's to be found in John Balliol's parliament and in the parliament of Paris, of Walter de Mauny, Jean le Bel and Jean Froissart, and of many others it would be superfluous to mention.

After his decisive victory at Tinchebray (this and not the variants common in England is the recognised official spelling) Henry I against all expectation had reunited the dominions of his father, and he was set on transmitting both England and Normandy to a single heir. In order to establish a permanent and effective administration of both dominions, he had to devise new methods and create new offices. The problem with which he was confronted was how to carry on the government in each country when he was absent. It is not entirely a new problem, for the Conqueror had had to provide for the administration of England when he was so often away in Normandy. But there is nothing to suggest that he regarded the problem as one that required a settled and lasting solution; after his lifetime there would be, so far as he could foresee, no problem, and there was therefore no need for more than an improvisation. Henry I, however, had not only to improvise for the moment but to build also for the future. In a surprisingly short period of time we find in England the essential features that will distinguish English administration under Henry II and his sons and leave their impress for many centuries. The device adopted was to appoint a minister – the justiciar – who would be head of the administration while the king was present and who would be his representative when he was absent. This explains why the contemporary *Constitutio Domus Regis*, with its lists of honorific members of the king's household and the subordinates who perform the day-to-day tasks, omits altogether the most important minister of all, the justiciar. For he could hardly be a member of a household which, in theory at least, was always with the king, whether he was on one side of the Channel or the other. And when the king was in England, he similarly left behind him in Normandy a justiciar who became identified with the seneschal, with powers like those exercised by the justiciar in England. The history of these justiciar-seneschals in Normandy is very imperfectly known, but what is known of that history shows a very close correspondence with the history of the English justiciars. The important fact is that the English office and the Norman office were complementary and were made necessary by Henry I's scheme for giving his dominions a permanent administration which would function irrespective of his own presence. Later the system was extended to Ireland by his grandson Henry II with the office of justiciar of Ireland, and this confirms the impression that Henry I had a carefully thought-out system of government which could be extended to whatever lands fortune should bring under the sway of the king of England. So he had conceived the revolutionary idea of an impersonal monarchy as known in the days of Rome. The significance of this conception in the twelfth century has not been fully recognised by historians and it explains why in this field England came to be far in advance of continental countries which shared a common culture. Only by this contrivance of government was it possible for Henry I to spend fifteen years, more than half his reign, out of his kingdom and in his duchy. Henry II for his part was absent from England for two-thirds of his reign and twice he spent more than four years at a stretch in Normandy and twice more than two years together elsewhere in France. As for Richard I, his stay in England during his ten years as king can be counted in months.

We are particularly concerned to explain how England was governed in the eighty years between 1154 and 1234. Under Henry I, the justiciar, an official unknown to that French court which the dukes of Normandy had in the past sedulously taken as a model, presided over a court, with competence in judicial and financial matters,[1] to which the name 'exchequer' was given both in England and in Normandy. The anarchy under Stephen and the profound reforms under Henry II created complications but at the end of this period the structure of government had been fashioned in such a way as to last, with some modifications, until the seventeenth century, and a good deal of the structure, in particular the organisation of the courts of common law, persisted into the nineteenth century. The men who came into power in 1154 and the men who transformed the administration in 1234 had, of course, as little prescience as most administrators: they were concerned with the task of making the administrative machine work and all they had to build with, apart from their own capacity for invention, was already fashioned to their hand. The men of 1154 were confronted with a land at peace but one that had not recovered from prolonged civil war, one in which the contestants had made lavish and reckless promises which, if fulfilled, would have endangered the stability of the state. To those who had known intimately the administration of Henry I the simile that occurred was shipwreck, and it was in the first place to the practices of Henry I that they sought to return.

---

[1] The men who held the court, the 'barons of the exchequer' as they were called, decided legal and financial issues indifferently and there is no virtue in the suggestion that the exchequer was primarily a financial tribunal to which it was found convenient to refer matters of law. The legal side of its work was described in the treatise called 'Glanville' and the financial side in the 'Dialogus de Scaccario'.

Looking back to Henry II's grandfather was not without a political motive, for Henry II affected to ignore the grants of King Stephen, a usurper who had ousted the rightful heir to the throne. But administrators had a stronger motive if their master was to govern on both sides of the Channel without continuous personal rule. The consequence was to develop much further the office of the justiciar. By good luck a succession of most able men was found to fill it. The justiciar was provided with a staff by allotting to him some of the clerks of chancery. The division followed a line already established within the king's household: the clerks of the king's chapel and the king's chamber remained with him wherever he might be, but clerks of the *scriptorium*, upon whom the routine tasks of writing fell, were assigned to the justiciar. And continuity of administration was secured by authorising the justiciar to act in the king's name when he was present in his kingdom: when the king was absent the justiciar acted in his own name.[2] Since the clerks of the *scriptorium* were primarily responsible for the business of the exchequer, the headquarters of the justiciar, and since they also wrote the original writs upon which legal actions were founded, the administration of justice was self-contained. There was no need, as later, for a plaintiff to go to the chancery in Chancery Lane in London to obtain his writ and to a court in Westminster to plead his cause. For in term time the writs were obtainable at Westminster as a matter of course and it was unnecessary, save in exceptional circumstances, for a litigant to follow the justiciar when, as often, he was absent from London.

We can distinguish sessions of the court at which the king nominally presides from sessions at which the justiciar nominally presides, but the nearest analogy to any modern conception is that of a court with two divisions and that analogy is incorrect. When a favoured subject is privileged to be impleaded only *coram me vel capitali iusticiario meo*, the reference is not to alternative tribunals but to alternate presidents of one tribunal, staffed by a single corps of

---

[2] Richard of Ely informs us that the writs of the justiciar were of equal authority to those of the king when the king was absent, and the justiciar's seal was then employed to establish the laws of the realm and to summon cases to court so that those who are cited may be condemned or acquitted (*Dialogus de Scaccario*, p. 33). The court over which he presides is the exchequer which, like the court in which the king administers justice in person, has the distinction that neither its records nor the judgements it delivers may be impugned by any man. And it is plain from the records that the barons of the exchequer were sitting as a court to determine criminal (or at least tortious) and civil actions under Henry I (J. A. Robinson, *Gilbert Crispin, abbot of Westminster*, p. 149).

justices. Either the king will preside or his *alter ego*: there will be no justice of inferior rank. But rarely, except for some years under John, do king and justiciar preside simultaneously over separate divisions of the one tribunal. Moreover, so much of the king's time was spent out of England that the justiciar's court, the exchequer, which was for the most part sedentary at Westminster, developed its own methods, remote from any direct personal influence the king must otherwise have exerted. The justiciar and the justices could not be capricious, as the king might perhaps have been. And so the king's court at the exchequer evolved its forms and procedures and became – as the law it administered became – more and more professional and technical. And since the justices who were sent on eyre – or at least those of them who were judges by profession – were also justices at Westminster and were controlled by the justiciar, in all the king's courts throughout the country there was uniform law and uniform procedure. At the close of Henry II's reign, when the time had come to set down the rules of the common law in the treatise commonly known as Glanville,[3] they could be described as the laws and customs observed in pleading in the king's court at the exchequer and before the king's justices (in eyre) wherever they might be. These words have an importance that has not always been given to them. The author is writing of a system which knows a central court at the exchequer and bodies of justices riding their circuits through the counties. Now, all of our available records – and they are many – tell us that the justiciar presided at the central court and that he supervised and controlled the itinerant justices. The system then was coherent and logical. But the coherence and logic depended upon the circumstance that the king was an absentee. So few actions came before the king himself, be it noted, that there is no need for Glanville to mention pleading *coram rege*. So the only royal and central court in twelfth-century England which had a continuous existence and kept records of its existence was the court of exchequer, the court, that is, of the justiciar. There was a corresponding court in Normandy. The existence of these courts did not preclude the king from himself hearing actions, either personally or by delegation to justices attendant upon himself: he

---

[3] Glanville is, above all, a book of procedure and, what is important, it is a product, not of Germanic tradition, not of any form of feudalism, but of two contemporary forces, Anglo-Norman and Roman, both disposed to order, method and the use of written documents. Glanville typifies our law for something like a century, that is until the legislative reforms of Edward I's reign.

remained the fountain of justice, not only a court of ultimate appeal but sometimes at least a court of first instance to those who sought his presence. But since, until John had been driven from Normandy, the king of England was, for the greater part of his time, an absentee ruler, the trial overseas of any action affecting English land or of English concern was scarcely known. Certainly the growing, the vastly growing, volume of judicial business consequent upon the development of the writ system under Henry II came before the exchequer. The common law had by this time departed very ˆır from patriarchal justice. The picture we are given of the French king, St. Louis, dispensing justice under an oak tree, though it comes from the thirteenth century, would have seemed archaic and repellant to the professional justices of Henry II. The English king did not sit in judgement except in the presence of his justices. The evolution of the common law therefore depended upon the creation of a body of professional judges and all that implies in the way of trained assistance and technical processes. We assume, and doubtless rightly assume, that, as the common law evolved and changed, so the newer rules were adopted all over the country. And if we allow for the persistence of some local customs and the occasional survival of some outmoded forms of action, and if we recognise that writs newly devised at Westminster might not be available in a franchise or a palatinate, after we have totalled up all known exceptions to the rule, it still remains true that, in some way or other, the common law was one and the same in all the courts of England. The greatness of Henry II's achievement was for long not appreciated, nor were its enduring consequences recognised. It was not realised that the contrivances of administration, which the abundance of records of John's reign enables us to study, were an inheritance from his father. Historians, engaged in tracing through the ages the fiction of political freedom or, in other words, representative government, have tended to overlook the reality and worth of a greater good and did not pause to consider how, amidst the shifts and chances of succeeding centuries, there stood inviolate the abiding majesty of the common law, of which the Angevin king and his ministers were the principal architects.[4]

---

[4] We may note the stability of the twelfth-century regime from an unusual angle. By 1272 the conception had been formulated that, with the king's death, the functions of his ministers ceased: consequently, actions which were in progress needed, as it were, to be revived by a writ from his successor to continue process. The archaic tradition had survived that, on the king's death, his peace died with him

The loss of Normandy in 1204 which made John a stay-at-home monarch had consequences of the greatest importance, though they were not immediately apparent because, though John was never again to set foot in the duchy, a good many years were to elapse before the hope of recovering Normandy was abandoned. Nevertheless the *raison d'être* of Anglo-Norman administration disappeared. With the king but occasionally absent from his kingdom, the whole conception of government, which had led to the creation of the justiciarship and the exchequer, gradually crumbled away. The duchy and the kingdom had been the twin-halves of the system: now one half had gone. A king who was normally resident in the kingdom had no need for an *alter ego* to replace him, and institutions, however firmly based like the exchequer on the assumption that, as often as not, the king would be absent, were now out of place. A court *coram rege*, that is, in the technical and sometimes physical presence of the king, an ambulatory court, was established with its own staff of justices and its own series of records, a court that threatened the existence of the sedentary court at Westminster, a court of delegated authority which was, from the king's point of view, no longer necessary. So, though John did not abolish the justiciarship, he did suppress the court at Westminster, to the great inconvenience of his subjects who insisted in the Great Charter of 1215 upon its re-instatement. The logical course might therefore have been to suppress the court *coram rege*, but the question never arose. The death of John in 1216 and the minority of Henry III ensured that this court should be in abeyance and that the court at Westminster should be the only 'great court' (*magna curia*) and that pleas before the king should again be a rarity until 1234.

and that there was then no law to bind and to hold, a tradition that had led to the garrisoning of castles and to a state of almost civil war. But it should be observed that there was no such lapse of government after the death of Richard I during the very considerable interval before John was crowned and while there was no king in England. The justiciar continued in office, the court at Westminster remained open and justice was administered in the name of John, duke of Normandy and king of England. There should be, so it seems to us, but a short step to the conception of the crown as an undying corporation, unaffected by the mortality of the natural man in whom kingship was transiently resident. If the dilemma was not thoroughly resolved in the Middle Ages, we may recall that it was only last century that the final logical consequences of the doctrine of a never-dying king were worked out and a statute of as recent a date as 1867 was necessary to obviate the inconvenience of the dissolution of parliament with the dissolution of what is mortal in the sovereign (Representation of the People Act, 30 and 31 Victoria, c. 102, §51).

In that year occurred a dramatic overhaul of the administration of the country. The office of justiciar was suppressed and there was in consequence a re-shaping of institutions. The 'exchequer' and the 'bench', which had at one time been alternative names for a common administration, had by a process which worked itself out over many years become quite distinct and independent organisations and the first had concentrated on finance and the second on law. Even so it is worth noting that a connexion remained between them as a reminder of their common historical origin because the treasury, which was subordinate to the exchequer, was the place of deposit not only of the financial but also of the judicial records of the kingdom. And a court *coram rege*, the ambulatory court of king's bench, was re-instated and from 1234 its history is continuous. The court at Westminster was continued as the common bench, a sedentary court which was to be particularly concerned with the affairs of private persons rather than those of the king. And there came into existence a third court of common law: the exchequer had jurisdiction not only over its own servants but also over the sheriffs, and its special concern with the revenue and the problems arising therefrom involved a very wide sphere of interest and endowed it with common law jurisdiction.[5]

What history, what reasons, lie behind the repartition of judicial business between the three courts of common law: king's bench, common bench and exchequer? In other countries in Western Europe, in France above all, which shared a common civilisation, there was no development in any way parallel. By comparison the English system involves a superfluity, a re-duplication of tribunals, which would always be mutually jealous and competitive. This touch of the illogical and the absurd was, we may be sure, no piece of deliberate planning. Rather, we may suppose, a plan devised for one set of circumstances had been overtaken by the march of events, and it had been but ill-adjusted to a changed environment.

So from 1234 to 1258 the main lines in the development of the English judicial system had been laid down and consolidated: there were three courts of common law, a well-developed writ system, a growing professionalism which is placing trained lawyers on the bench and at the disposal of litigants. In the last few years of this period Bracton is putting together the great treatise which will be

---

[5] Changes seem also to have been made in the chancery; the ancient connexion between the staffs of the chancery and the exchequer was broken by the appointment of a chancellor of the exchequer.

supplemented but not superseded until the Middle Ages have passed away.

It is also during these years that 'parliament', mentioned for the first time in an official legal record in 1236, enters into the scheme of government to supervise the departments of state and the courts of law, to settle problems that arose within them and between them, and to consider all complaints that the machinery of government was not working satisfactorily. Now the Norman and Angevin kings had had their courts to which their barons owed suit. They were expected to be in attendance on the king when he wore his crown on the three great Feast Days of the year, Christmas, Easter and Whitsunday, and weighty matters might then be discussed. But we have little knowledge of what was done on these occasions and, with the king's many absences from his kingdom, the crown-wearing ceremonies grew less frequent and came almost to an end when Richard I was such a short time in England. There were, of course, other times when the king thought it advisable to convene a council of bishops and barons to deliberate upon major issues of the day: not much is known about them either, but it is clear that the magnates – to use an ugly ghost-word[6] – gave their counsel on political and administrative questions to the king when he asked for it, they were present when suggestions of unusual taxation were raised, and they delivered judgements, as in the *cause célèbre* of the trial at Northampton of archbishop Thomas Becket. Their rights and duties were intermixed. Some of the councils were notable, like those that approved the 'assizes' of Henry II, even though for the most part we can recover the legislative acts as no more than shadows reflected in the form of the legal actions they authorised. But it would be misleading not to point out that the bishops and barons were never full of ardent zeal to leave their homes when bidden: we need only call to mind how often in the fourteenth century parliaments and councils had to be postponed or even abandoned because not enough nobles had bothered to attend. If the king could refrain from burdensome financial demands and govern without creating irritation, they were well content. And it is certain that these councils and assemblies had no definite constitution and formed no regular organ of government. They were afforced, that is enlarged, meetings of the king's court, 'great councils' in the

---

[6] An attempt has been made to avoid the use of this term by the substitution of 'grandees' (C. S. Terry, *The Financing of the Hundred Years' War, 1337-60*) but, somewhat naturally, it has met with no favour.

phraseology of the day. Furthermore, we must remember that the 'king's council' as a recognisable institution was the creation of the thirteenth century and had no place in the twelfth century. The king, of course, had always had his ministers, his *curiales*, in whom he reposed his confidence, who acquired experience in administration and who are often found at the exchequer engaged in one or other of its functions. But the office of justiciar was incompatible with administration by council. The reins of government were in the hands of a man, not of a group: if the king was present, that man was the king: if the king were absent, that man was the justiciar. It is true that experiments were made with associate justiciars, just as Henry II made a disastrous experiment with an associate king in his eldest son; and under Richard I the ineffective Walter of Coutances seems to have been surrounded by a group of associates who presumably acted in some sort as a council. But these were experiments and nothing else: king and justiciar ruled with such counsel as they thought fit to take. It was not until the loss of Normandy resulted in the constant presence of the king in England and the diminished authority of the justiciar that there came into existence something that was less amorphous than the *curia regis*, the 'king's court', and which emerged as the 'king's council' to take on the responsibilities that had so long lain with the justiciars. It had the king's ministers and judges as its hard core, though bishops and barons could, when convenient or if necessary, join in its deliberations. It existed day by day to deal with the routine matters of government and it formed the pivot on which the machine of government will turn for many centuries to come. We have only to read the records of such periods as 1216–1227 or 1242–1243 or 1253–1254, when the king was a minor or abroad, to realise how the council, presided over by a keeper of the realm, had come to occupy the place the justiciar had vacated. And we have now more information about the casual times when the king's council was for some reason or other 'afforced' by the presence of a few or of many others: much depended on the needs of the day, and the 'king's council' was left a large discretion in the matter so that there is an infinite variety of meetings, all of which are quite rightly called 'councils' by contemporaries. But, of course, some were known to be more important than others and when, for example, probably just before Michaelmas 1229 it was advised that justices should not be sent away from headquarters on circuit 'before the assembly and meeting of the magnates at London at Michaelmas, for they may then provide many things for the welfare of the realm that are not yet provided',[7] it is evident that 'great councils' are well-known if haphazardly used instruments of government.

After the reforms in the structure of administration and law in 1234 these 'great councils' continued to be utilised as occasions when serious business could be discussed and a more considered and influential decision be reached on some important point, when ministers and judges could as it were 'pass the buck' and obtain a ruling on matters which they hesitated to decide on their own initiative. In 1236 such a 'great council' is already being officially called a 'parliament',[8] where the king's servants had their place side by side with the magnates and where was represented the highest wisdom, the collective wisdom, of the land in legislation, taxation and judicial matters. We may stay awhile with this particular council, for it presents features that have been regarded as characteristic of parliaments as they evolved under Edward I, and they are indeed features of some of them. We can add too that, as in these parliaments, minor grievances were considered at this council, for the king, with the advice of his magnates, dealt with a dispute regarding the services due to the honor of Peveril in Northampton-shire.[9] One further characteristic of Edwardian parliaments should be noted, for in at least one instance judicial doubts were resolved: an assize of darrein presentment brought by the sub-dean of Salisbury was adjourned to this council. The terms of this adjournment should be particularly remarked: 'in octabis sancti Hillarii apud Westmonasterium ad parliamentum'.[10] There is, so far as we are aware, no earlier reference to 'parliament' in any official document. On this occasion no other minister, apart from the clerk responsible for the essoin roll of the king's bench, calls this council a parliament; but the judge who ordered the adjournment presumably used this word in court and the clerk did no more than translate the judge's French into Latin. 'Parliament' is still an inelegant vernacular word, but here we have proof that it was applied to a meeting which others have termed a great or general council, a council that had, as we have said, the

---

[7] Ancient Correspondence, VI. 128. See also the *Vetus Registrum Sarisburiense*, ii. 86f., for a note that a writ, issued to the sheriffs in 1228, was written 'immediately after the colloquy at London at the Octaves of Hilary'.

[8] Originally the word 'parliament' – or rather the French word *parlement*, from which the latin *parliamentum* appears to have derived – had no administrative political connotation. It meant merely a parley, a conversation, a discussion, and in this general sense it continued in use throughout and long after the Middle Ages.

[9] *Close Rolls, 1234-1237*, p. 399.

[10] Richardson and Sayles, *The English Parliament in the Middle Ages*, article II.

characteristics of an Edwardian parliament. This entry on the essoin roll will tell us something further: as an interested party in the sub-dean's action, the bishop of Salisbury is required to be present at the parliament – he may be summoned in any case in another capacity – and not only the bishop but the defendant and all the recognitors of the assize, who will be conducted there by the sheriff. We have no reason to suppose that the case of the honor of Peveril and the case of the sub-dean of Salisbury were the only minor matters dealt with at this parliament, and we have but to multiply these cases very moderately in order to assemble quite a crowd of people who are in attendance, not because of any great issue but because they are caught up in petty matters that for some reason can be determined only in parliament. But before 1258, though the name of parliament is more and more freely given to assemblies of this kind,[11] we cannot draw a clear distinction between them and other afforced meetings of the council. That distinction can be seen only when parliament is made a recognised and organised part of the machinery of government. That point was reached as a result of the eventful proceedings at Oxford in June 1258.

By this time the king's financial needs had carried him to the verge of bankruptcy and on 2 May 1258 he bowed to the demand for reform in the hope that an aid would extricate him from his difficulties. A group of Twenty-Four, made up of twelve of the king's council and twelve elected by the magnates, was to meet at Oxford. No reference was made to parliament, but simultaneously or very soon afterwards writs of summons must have been issued so that the meeting of the Twenty-Four should be combined with a parliament. The writs have not survived but it cannot be a coincidence that the date on which parliament was to meet, St. Barnabas's Day, 11 June, allows the customary interval of forty days from 2 May. We can construct no calendar of the session, for we have but fragments of information. We know that the barons met in an atmosphere of distrust and exasperation, for they were apprehensive of the king's intentions as they saw around them the display of armed force when troops were brought to Oxford, ostensibly in preparation for a military campaign in Wales. In May the Twenty-Four had thought that they would require until at least Christmas to complete the wide programme of reform that had been

---

[11] There still survive letters of excuse for not obeying the king's summons to attend the parliament he had convoked at London in 1248 (Parliamentary Proxies, file I, nos. 1-4).

envisaged. This was an optimistic estimate, based upon the facile assumption that the baronial reformers would remain united and would receive the willing co-operation of the king's friends. But before June was out it was clear to all but the self-deluded that the path of reform would not only be long but difficult and that the assistance of the king's friends was the last thing that could be counted on. For though all the Twenty-Four were bound by oath to accept a majority decision, the members of the king's immediate circle – his first-born the Lord Edward, his half-brothers the Lusignans, and his nephew the earl of Gloucester – had no intention of keeping their pledged word. Therefore the Twenty-Four, or rather the majority of them, decided to halt and demand a fresh oath that the decisions so far taken would be given a formal and final acceptance. The demand was met with evasions and refusals and they felt it necessary to obtain letters of indemnity to protect them from the king's indignation. We know that the parliament broke up abruptly, apparently on the 28th, when the Lusignans refused to submit to decisions that affected them personally and withdrew to Winchester. Nevertheless the proceedings of less than three weeks at Oxford changed the whole current of events.

In their work of constitutional reconstruction the Twenty-Four resurrected the office of justiciar, and he was to be at the head of the judiciary and concentrate on the eradication of mis-doings, no matter by whom perpetrated, from the operation of justice throughout the whole kingdom. Central officials like the treasurer and the chancellor, and local officials like the sheriffs, were to be appointed for only one year at a time and then answer for their conduct in office. A council of Fifteen, chosen from the king's friends as well as the barons, was to continue the work of the Twenty-Four, operating with the regular civil servants and judges. It is worth noting that no effort was made to coerce the king to observe the oath he had sworn at his coronation: he was simply ignored and pushed aside, and everybody knew that what was done was not done in his name.[12] We who are familiar with the concept that a king may reign but not govern are apt to forget how rarely such a concept had been accepted in practice. How repugnant the alternative prescribed at Oxford must have seemed to Henry III is not hard to imagine and the king complained, not without reason, that those who were agreeable to him and whom he found loyal, true and knowledge-

---

[12] The letter announcing the scheme for redressing the wrongs of the people came, not from the king, but from the Council of Fifteen.

able, had been removed from him.

We need not dally with details of what happened in 1258 and the seven years thereafter, a period which seemed to end in frustration with the king's victory at the battle of Evesham. But they mark the beginning of a new era in the history of parliament, the formulation of legislation, and the dispensation of justice, and to these our comments must be confined.

Parliament as an afforced session of the council was given a status superior to all other afforced sessions. It received definition when it was ordered to assemble three times a year at stated dates, for those who summoned such parliaments with such periodicity must have known what they meant by parliament. Its membership was outlined: the Fifteen were to be present, and the baronage in general were to be represented by twelve of their number in order to save them inconvenience and expense. And though it was taken for granted that civil servants and judges would be there to give their skilled assistance, parliament remained, as it had been before 1258, an assembly of magnates. The English parliament has ceased to be an 'occasion' and is established as an organised institution which henceforth has a continuous and coherent history. We have put behind us the uncertainties of the years of development from the crown-wearings of the Norman and Angevin kings to the councils and colloquies of the 1240's and 1250's to which the name of 'parliament' had been sometimes tentatively applied. Parliament assumed now a distinctive and unmistakable shape. The point of issue came to be whether a parliament could meet irrespective of the king's wishes. The barons contended that it could do so in consonance with the Provisions of Oxford – and acted accordingly. Contemporary chroniclers highlighted the fundamental dispute when they spoke of 'the parliament of the barons'.[12a]

Out of parliament's supervisory authority issued a striking and permanent development which added a new dimension to English law: a body of legislation that was to be unmatched throughout the rest of the Middle Ages. For the outcome of the deliberations at Oxford and later parliaments was the Provisions of Westminster 1259 which, after the Barons' War, were largely embodied in the Statute of Marlborough 1267, which in turn formed the basis of the First Statute of Westminster 1275 under Edward I. Thus was heralded that remarkable outburst of legislation which added statute

---

[12a] *Annales Monastici* (Dunstable), iii. 125, 221.

to statute until it came almost to its end after the death of the chancellor Robert Burnell in 1290. Notable additions are few thereafter and it may be observed here that most of the legislation of the fourteenth and fifteenth centuries, while impressive in bulk, is by comparison jejune, ill-considered and badly drafted. However, this is to look too far ahead: what concerns us here is to note that Bracton, when compiling his treatise on the law of England, paid little heed to statutes and did not realise their potent future. The reformers of 1258 introduced the statute book well and truly to the courts of common law and foreshadowed its dominance as they set the pattern for the great Edwardian legislation.

To the people in general the main achievement at Oxford lay in the initiation of a procedure for remedying their grievances, especially at the hands of the government officials, and giving a practical effect to the time-honoured formula that the Great Charter and its provisions should be observed. In every feudal monarchy the right was recognised of an appeal to the king from the injustice of his vassals or ministers. But the king could not be everywhere and the men he employed were not always trustworthy: in any case, he had to rely very largely upon men drawn from the same class as the owners of privileged franchises and men living in the localities where their duties lay. The inevitable abuses led very early to special measures for their correction. The Inquest of Sheriffs of 1170 was a nationwide attempt at the control and punishment of local officers of the crown, and the machinery of the general eyre – under which judges went on circuit throughout the country – was subsequently used intermittently for like purpose. It was a device for securing that those who had grievances could present them locally to the king's representatives and obtain the punishment of the offenders. But the general eyre had the defect that, besides being an instrument of justice, it was also an instrument of revenue, and if it punished offenders it punished equally the commonalty of the county for technical offences, which were important principally because the penalties took the form of money payments to the crown. The eyre therefore was an unpopular institution despite the benefits it conferred. The result was that a great many grievances were never brought forward at all and there was much unchecked oppression. There were occasions after 1234 when it seemed as though the king was aware of the abuses in his realm, the resentment of his subjects, and the need to assert his authority. It was the sheriffs who particularly needed supervision and in a lecture he gave them at Michaelmas 1250 when they were assembled at Westminster in the exchequer to render their accounts, he stated *inter alia* that sheriffs were not to place the control of hundreds and other offices in the hands of men who would not do justice to the people.[13] Why at this juncture the king was moved to act in this way we do not know, though there was perhaps an unusual recrudescence of lawlessness. In 1254, the year when his own brother warned him that, if he failed to take some positive steps to ensure that the stipulations of the Great Charter were observed, he could expect no financial aid from the laity, some articles were added to the list of investigations that the justices in eyres were required to conduct, articles that may have been an attempt to remedy popular grievances as well as to prevent sheriffs from making illicit profits through the misuse of their office. If so, it was a feeble gesture and there is no real evidence that the king appreciated the significance of the warnings or saw any over-riding need to bring justice to his people. Let us glance briefly at some contemporary complaints. A formulary contains model letters, supposed to be exchanged between the highest ranks of society.[14] One purports to be from Henry III to his earls and barons, demanding an aid for the marriage of his sister (as he did in 1235). The imagined reply protests that the king must not vex his faithful subjects with undue exactions and urges that it is from his own resources that the marriage should be financed since it is not a recognised occasion for an aid. The next model letter is from the bishops and prelates to the earls, barons and knights, proposing common action to oppose the demand: 'The community of subjects is mightier than the dignity or lordship of any lord set over his subjects'.[15] What the king proposes is inequitable and they must strive to bring it to naught. If he goes on as he has begun with scutage and other aids, who is wealthy enough to bear the burden? The subject matter of another letter from a knight is the king's attempt to introduce new and unwonted customs and to marry the children of gentle folk to his favourites, who were cobblers and swineherds in their own country, and again there is a proposal for joint action to resist an invasion of the rights of the subject. A notable phrase claims that it is the law of the realm and not of the king that is to be observed, and there is a pertinent reference to the

---

[13] Prynne, *Brief Animadversions* (1669), p. 53. For a discussion of the text see M. T. Clanchy in *History*, liii (1968) 215ff.

[14] B.L., Add. MS. 8167.

[15] *Ibid.*, fo. 105*b*: Major eciam est universitas subditorum quam sit alicuius domini super subditos constituti dignitas aut dominium.

chapter in Magna Carta against the disparagement of heiresses. The unknown clerks who compiled this formulary are men of no importance but they mirrored the sentiments of their age and there is an assumption that the king will violate the law and that he is to be resisted. There is little kinship of thought between lords and commoners. But there was a bond to unite them: a common mistrust of the king, be he John, Henry III, the three Edwards, Richard II or the Lancastrian dynasty. It is the universality of this spirit that explains, as nothing else will, the appeal of Simon de Montfort to high-born and lowly alike and the popular 'beatification' of him after his death, and the popular award of the crown of martyrdom to the repulsive Thomas of Lancaster in Edward II's reign. This deep-seated and widespread suspicion of royal power in England must be stressed because, in the history of English domestic politics and the English constitution, it seems as significant as the equally deep-seated and widespread suspicion of institutional religion and the pope in the history of the medieval Church. The mistrust is intermittent, it springs now from one cause, now from another, but, if it is stilled from time to time, it seems always ready to emerge. This community of spirit between noble and peasant is something different from the bald expression that there was an alliance between barons and commons to resist the aggressive policy of the crown.

Those deliberating at Oxford were honestly and honourably desirous of putting an end to the manifest and manifold oppressions that the lack of royal justice and the growth of seignorial jurisdictions had occasioned. But if great lords as well as the king were to be assailed, it was to be indirectly and their faces were to be saved: the procedure evolved at Oxford and in subsequent parliaments was directed against the bailiffs, the agents, of the great men of the realm, who were held to have exercised unjustly the jurisdiction delegated to them.

In redressing grievances the justiciar was to be the principal agent. Ever since the office had been suspended in 1234 the baronial opposition had wanted it back again, not however to fulfil its ancient purpose but in the expectation that a justiciar would act as a curb upon the king's authority and show him the way he should go. The justiciar appointed, Hugh Bigod, was active but the pressure for collecting complaints for determination before him in the eyres necessarily took time to get into action, and in any case the volume of judicial work to be done was beyond the capacity of any single man, however energetic. To assist him several commissions were appointed and grievances in every county were collected by four knights of each shire and reduced to writing for submission to them. From some counties, if not from all of them, the knights were summoned to the Michaelmas parliament of 1258 to give an account of their doings and to receive further instructions. It is not, however, the office of justiciar or commissioner that is important[16] but the fact that all over England plaints were being heard that did not require any stereotyped and formal writ and could be put forward in an informal bill or petition (the terms are interchangeable). Though the procedure was not novel in 1258 it was now given an immense stimulus. There will be no connexion between such bills and parliament as yet: only ministers and judges and men of good standing could bring their problems before parliament for its consideration, for it had, as we have seen, been arranged that all others must seek their redress locally. But for some reason about which we can only speculate petitioners were allowed very early in Edward I's reign to address their bills, not only locally to the justices in eyre but directly to the king and council in parliament. The arrangements, set on foot soon after Edward's return from abroad in 1274, to start investigations all over the country into wrongdoing were not completed until 1278, and it may have been thought expedient in the mean time to allow complainants, disappointed at the delay in sending justices in eyre to them in the localities, to bring their grievances directly to the headquarters of government. However that may be, this all-important and highly popular piece of parliamentary procedure certainly had its roots in the events of 1258.

The parliament of England had no architect. To suggest that Simon de Montfort or Edward I had a claim to that title is as grotesque as to suggest that Henry VIII was the father of toleration. The first two did, all unwittingly, contribute to the process that gave England representative institutions, while the third, by loosening the ties with Rome, ensured the emergence of an English protestant church, from which he himself would have recoiled in horror. Politicians, like the rest of us, rarely know where their paths will lead.

We can give some sort of rough list of matters which demanded the attention of parliament in its sessions in the latter part of Henry III's reign. Trial of a judge for corruption,[17] complaints of Gascons

---

[16] The revived justiciarship proved transient and the office lapsed finally in 1265.
[17] Matthew Paris, *Chronica Majora*, v. 233.

against Simon de Montfort,[18] assize of bread and ale in London,[19] payment by poor religious of a subsidy for the Holy Land,[20] a claim to take a whale as wreck,[21] assize of wine in London,[22] lease of crown lands to the nuns of Aconbury,[23] a dispute whether a manor was of ancient demesne,[24] exactions from the men of Byfleet and Weybridge to Guy de Lusignan,[25] a fine exacted by the same Guy de Lusignan on giving seisin of the manor of Sheen to the second husband of a divorced woman,[26] a complaint that an amercement had been twice exacted,[27] a dispute between the abbot and the men of Faversham as to customs and services,[28] an arbitration between the king and Simon de Montfort,[29] a claim of the earl Marshal to the custody of prisoners,[30] the differences between the king and the baronial council,[31] restoration of franchises to Londoners,[32] reprisals against the Flemings.[33] With few exceptions these are law-suits presenting no extraordinary features:[34] only one or two are political disputes which do not take the form of a legal action. Yet politics in a general sense was inevitably among the activities of parliament. Happily we know what Henry III regarded as the functions of parliament from a letter he sent from France to the council in England in February 1260. He refused his consent to the holding of a parliament in his absence but added that the justiciar, to whose keeping the kingdom had been committed, might with its counsel dispense his highest justice (*justitia communis*) provided that no new departure or law (*nova mutatio sive ordinatio*) was made in the

---

18 Bémont, *Simon de Montfort*, pp. 339ff.
19 *Liber de Antiquis Legibus*, p. 21.
20 *Cal. Patent Rolls, 1247-1258*, p. 399.
21 Ehrlich, *Proceedings against the Crown*, p. 218.
22 *Liber de Antiquis Legibus*, p. 26.
23 *Cal. Patent Rolls, 1258-1266*, pp. 47-8.
24 Assize Roll, no. 873, m. 6: below, p. 81.
25 Assize Roll, no. 873, m. 6: below, p. 81, n. 5.
26 Assize Roll, no. 873, m. 7: below, p. 81f.
27 Assize Roll, no. 362, m. 8d: below, p. 82.
28 Curia Regis Roll, no. 167, m. 10: below, p. 91.
29 Curia Regis Roll, no. 167, m. 26: below, p. 92.
30 Assize Roll, no. 911, m. 6: below, p. 96.
31 *Annales Monastici*, iv. 130: below, p. 98.
32 *Liber de Antiquis Legibus*, p. 142.
33 *Ibid.*, p. 142.
34 They have been collected somewhat haphazardly and no attempt has been made to gather all cases of which some record may survive. The cases cited are doubtless a small fraction of those occurring in this period, but there is no reason to suppose that the sample is not representative.

kingdom without the king's presence and consent.[35] Here we have the judicial aspect of parliament sharply distinguished from the deliberative, the legislative, the political aspect of parliament. But this distinction is largely a matter of accident, the accident of an ill-advised and suspicious king, and it will not be seen in normal times. To Englishmen in general who lived under Edward I the judicial aspect of parliament came, as we shall see, to overshadow any other. The book known by the name of *Fleta*, the first English lawbook to mention parliament, was written in his reign and it ascribed to parliament the functions of a high court of law: the determination of judicial doubts, the provision of new remedies for new wrongs, the dispensation of justice to everyone according to his merits. No special emphasis is laid by it upon politics.

Justice and Politics in Parliament

Under Edward I it was formally stated as early as 1275 that there would be two parliaments a year, every Easter and every Michaelmas, and that they would meet at Westminster. If parliament was required to assemble at a different time or a different place or if a specially large attendance was essential for a special purpose, then writs of summons were issued. Otherwise they were not needed. The people at large knew when and where to come with their petitions for the redress of their ills, especially those caused by the misconduct of the king's servants, and come they did in their hundreds as soon as permission had obviously been given them some time before 1278. Clearly so great an upsurge of petitions demanded a constant revision and rearrangement of the way in which this mass of judicial work was to be handled. About this same year John Kirkby became the first man we hear of to fulfil the duties of clerk of the council and thus be closely connected with parliamentary business.[36] The petitions might be dealt with in

[35] Close Roll, no. 76, m. 3d: see below, p. 87f.

[36] Ancient Petition, no. 1589: a petition to the king's council 'and particularly to John Kirkby, bishop of Ely', complaining of a lord who had refused to redress the grievances of his tenants. Some of the responses to the petitions, presented at the Easter parliament of 1278, seem to imply that there was already in existence a roll very like that of the Hilary and Easter parliaments of 1290 (*Rot. Parl.*, i. 8, 9: Responsio est in rotulo. Iniunctum est Radulpho de Sandwico quod committat domicellam in bona custodia, prout irrotulatur). The memoranda of 1279 (below, pp. 157–62) refers to itself as constituting a roll. However, the compiler of the Vetus Codex seems not to have known of any rolls earlier than 1290, but then he ignores later rolls that have survived to our day.

accordance with their place of origin, be it England, Ireland, the Channel Isles, Gascony or, for a time, Scotland, for it should be remembered that parliaments in England were never less specifically national than under Edward I, a Frenchman who cared at least as much for his lands on one side of the Channel as on the other.[37] In 1280 it was decreed that the petitions should be sorted out in such a way that the chancery, the exchequer, the courts of law and the justices of the Jews could deal with those that concerned them, and only difficult matters were to be allowed to filter to the king's council for decision there.[38] Similar divisions of business were maintained in the revised regulations of 1293.[39] Out of such arrangements evolved the standardised procedure which lasted as a formal anachronism until the nineteenth century: the petitions had to be handed in by a specified day to the government clerks who acted as receivers of petitions, and they weeded out those that ought not to have been brought to parliament – some from the mentally unstable – and passed the rest to tribunals of auditors. These heard all they could or dared to hear and they transmitted the others to a committee of the council – usually a few members but augmented in number if necessary – and such as were then thought to need the king's personal consideration were forwarded to him. No better illustration is to be found of the close association of parliament with the departments of state and the courts of law and the highly technical work done by professionals – ministers and civil servants, judges and lawyers.[39a] The actual participation of prelates and barons, the traditional counsellors of the king, could not have been frequent in business of this kind.[40] In any case there is no evidence that at many of the parliaments there was a large attendance of the nobility – it will be remembered that twelve were adequate to represent them in parliament according to the Provisions of Oxford – whilst the presence of representatives of the people was very rarely

---

[37] Edward spent from 13 May 1286 to 12 August 1289 in France without any thought that he was not at 'home'.

[38] Below, p. 172.

[39] Below, p. 209.

[39a] For a splendid collection of documents illustrating the many stages in procedure on a single petition, see Exchequer Miscellanea, 4/43.

[40] In Edward I's early years it was not thought that the magnates should necessarily be present in parliament: in 1277 two Welsh barons were told by the king that 'it is our will and intention that they and their heirs should come to our parliaments, as do other earls and barons, when it is necessary and when they have a special mandate thereon' (*Foedera*, I. ii. 544).

demanded. So when the council sat in parliament it often found greater wisdom than greater numbers. But, of course, certain matters will not, on mere grounds of prudence, be dealt with when very few counsellors were present, and any question of great importance was by tradition one requiring universal advice, the 'common counsel' of the realm: matters touching the state of the kingdom such as war and peace, legislation and taxation. There is no disagreement here. But what is not properly appreciated is that, nevertheless, such matters could be and indeed were discussed and decided in other assemblies that were not parliaments and, because they were not parliaments, did not provide the people with an opportunity to petition and the expectation of an answer.

It is therefore right that we should consider the place of justice and of politics in parliament. For an objection has been raised to the argument that the essence of parliamentary business under the first two Edwards was the dispensation of justice and that this continued to be the distinctive characteristic of parliament in and after Edward III's reign. It is contended that more important than the dispensation of justice was the consideration of public affairs, the high politics of the realm.[41] This objection seems to be founded on a misapprehension of politics in workaday practice when means of communication were not simple. A parliament is an afforced meeting of the king's council, but it is just one council in a series of councils, an infinite variety of councils, which are not parliaments. The bishop of Exeter expressed this point clearly when he termed the parliament at Winchester in 1330 'a royal council' (*regium concilium*); two years earlier he had asked to be excused attendance at 'parliaments and assemblies of your council'.[42] At any of these meetings the problems of state, the weighty affairs of the realm, will be discussed and often they take the form of proceedings at law, and whether a particular piece of business is transacted at any particular meeting must depend upon many factors: its urgency, its documentation (which may take much time in preparation), the presence or absence of particular councillors. We must not imagine that the business of rebellious Irish, marauding Scots or aggrieved Gascons, of the French king or the Roman pope, could wait until a long and formal summons had been served throughout the country to convene a parliament for their discussion. Indeed, if public affairs

---

[41] J. G. Edwards, 'Justice in Early English Parliaments' in *Bull. Inst. Hist. Research*, xxvii (1954), 33–53.
[42] *Register of John de Grandisson*, i. pp. 179, 245.

had been reserved for treatment in parliament, they would have been sadly neglected in the latter years of Edward I and the middle years of Edward III. Doubtless, provided time permitted it, there were matters which would be more suitably considered in parliament, like legislation and taxation, but even here it was many years, as we shall see, before they became monopolised by parliament. And often in the event public affairs were crowded out of parliament and the king had to apologise that he had not the leisure to deal with them and referred them to commissioners or postponed them to another meeting of his council, not necessarily in parliament.[43] The king had so many pressing affairs concerning so many of his dominions that there was always far more on the agenda than it would be possible to deal with adequately in parliament unless – a point to be emphasised – parliament had been in permanent session. When the king was urged in 1314 to assemble parliament to consider the crisis in Scottish affairs, he pointed out that the business demanded the utmost speed and therefore a parliament could not be awaited.[44] Indeed, as it was recognised in 1360, the 'community of the realm' could not be brought together in one place in a short time and therefore local councils were summoned instead.[45] And it is so often evident that parliaments were not best suited for confidential talks, delicate negotiations and secret bargaining.

Let us then turn to examine in detail the non-parliamentary assemblies, the afforced councils other than parliaments, before which came the affairs of the king and his kingdom. Such afforced councils have a long history in England, but we need not go back before the arrangements made in 1258 which allowed for meetings in addition to the three regular parliaments. The minutes of the proceedings at Oxford are not as explicit as we could wish, though they were doubtlessly perfectly intelligible to those concerned. The twelve men chosen to represent the magnates as a whole were to come not only to parliaments but at other times, when it was necessary, on summons by the king or the council. The conclusion to be drawn is that parliament was one form of the king's council which could manifest itself in other forms on other occasions. And, indeed, that this was so is amply evidenced: there came to be too many such councils and the recalcitrant earl of Gloucester refused in

[43] *Rot. Parl.*, ii. 117ff. (1340); cf. n. 32 below.
[44] Malmesbury, *Gesta Regum*, p. 200f.
[45] *Cal. Patent Rolls, 1358-1361*, p. 404.

1269 to attend any more of 'the conferences or parliaments of the king and nobles'.[46] The kind of conference he had in mind is shown by the writ, dated 24 November 1270, informing Nicholas of Yettenden, a long-serving royal justice, that 'for certain most important business concerning us and our realm we have caused some of our magnates and faithful subjects to be summoned to Winchester, to be there by 7 December at the latest, to discuss this business with us', and commanding him to be present.[47] This was not a parliament, though the writ uses phraseology with which we are familiar in parliamentary writs of summons. And then under Edward I the king's council sat, outside parliament, in solemn conclave with prelates and magnates as the occasion demanded, holding deliberations in February 1286 with envoys from the French court,[48] making a speedy grant of taxation in 1294,[49] discussing the war with the Scots in May 1298.[50] How many times the king's council met in this way we do not know, and so often, when we hear of these meetings, we know little or nothing of their business.[51] For example, in the period between Michaelmas 1302 and Lent 1305 when no parliament was summoned, a council was held at Odiham early in January 1303 and the prior of Christ Church, Canterbury, was paid his no light expenses of £8.10s. for attending it,[52] but what it did is hidden from us. It is against such a background that John Balliol, king of Scotland, was compelled to attend 'parliaments and councils',[53] and that an inventory of records refers to 'rolls and memoranda of ordinances made in various parliaments and councils' held by Edward I.[54]

---

[46] *Annales Monastici*, iv. 227f.; below, p. 125.

[47] Chancery Miscellanea, 3/7/18, and cf. no. 21.

[48] John de Oxenedes, *Chronica*, p. 267.

[49] *Parl. Writs*, i. 26f.

[50] *Ibid.*, i. 65.

[51] As, indeed, in the case of the so-called Model Parliament of 1295, which has, curiously enough, left scarce a sign of its activities.

[52] Lambeth MS. 242, m. 231, where the assembly is termed 'parliament' (Item in expensis ad parliamentum de Odiham); cf. *Cal. Chancery Writs*, i. 197: an order on 9 December 1303 to call a council and issue summons to attend.

[53] Walter of Hemingford, *Chronicon*, ed. H. C. Hamilton (Eng. Hist. Soc.), ii. 205, a statement which is not in H. Rothwell's edition of this chronicle.

[54] Palgrave, *Kalendars*, i. 102. For these ordinances in council, see the decree in 1280 which permitted a sheriff henceforth to hold only one tourn a year (*Cal. Close Rolls, 1279-1288*, p. 109); the protection given to clerics in February 1297 who agreed to pay the price to avoid outlawry (L.T.R. Memoranda Roll, no. 68, m. 23: De ordinacione facta pro proteccionibus clericorum faciendis in scaccario); the committal of benefices held by aliens during the war with France in 1295 to the custody of bishops (*ibid.*, no. 69, m. 20); the postponement in 1300 of assizes of novel

Under Edward II there was a notable increase in the number of non–parliamentary councils and the reason is perhaps not far to seek. The barons revolted against his father's bureaucratic form of government, especially in his later years.[54a] His delusions of grandeur had brought him to bankruptcy, and no administration, no matter its talents and its expertise, could hope to survive when it could no longer keep financial records of its spending. In such circumstances the irritation of the nobles, the natural-born counsellors of the king, found expression in the Ordinances of 1311 which put the professional bureaucrats in their place as subordinates: never again would they run the country as it were off their own bat. The barons asserted their own control instead. Within parliaments they constituted themselves as the 'great council', great by the rank of its members and by the importance of the business it transacted.[55] And outside parliament their advice and assent had to be sought more and more frequently 'at other great assemblies',[56] held here and there throughout the land. They had insisted that their voice should be heard and they were required to pay the price, for they were summoned into the king's presence where and when he chose.

disseisin against those setting out on a campaign against the Scots (*Cal. Charter Rolls, 1300-26*, p. 66). Note also the references to the ordinance 'de statu religiosorum de potestate regis Francie' (Chancery Parl. and Council Procs., 2/22); the 'Provisio facta per consilium regis de clericis vicecomitum puniendis' (L.T.R. Memoranda Roll, no. 69, m. 44d: *Stat. Realm*, i. 213); the 'Forma ordinacionis facte de minera regis in comitau Devonie' (*ibid.*, no. 69 (1298), m. 51); the 'Forma convencionis inter regem et mecatores de Florencia facte super dimissione minere Devonie (*ibid.*, no. 70, m. 34: a very carefully drawn document in 1299).

[54a] The comment of the author of the *Mirror of Justices*, a book about which Maitland was too facetious, is worth remembering: 'It is an abuse that, whereas parliament ought to be held for the salvation of the souls of trespassers twice a year and at London, they are now held but rarely and at the king's will for the purpose of obtaining aids and collection of treasure. And whereas ordinances ought to be made by the common assent of the king and his earls, they are now made by the king and his clerks and by aliens and others who dare not oppose the king but desire to please him and to counsel him for his profit, albeit their counsel is not for the good of the community (*comun*) of the people, and this without any summons of the earls or any observance of the rules of right so that divers ordinances are now founded rather upon will than upon right' (p. 155f.).

[55] It is at this time that the term 'privy council' came into use (*Chronica de Melsa*, ii. 332: per suum privatum consilium absque majorum consensu (1314); *Cal. Patent Rolls, 1313-1317*, p. 437: the chief justice was retained as a member of the privy council (1316); *Rot. Parl.*, ii. 50*b*: a petition in 1330 to the king and his privy council; Ancient Petition, no. 4051: devant le roi et son prive conseil au prochein parlement (1318-1320: printed in Sayles, *King's Bench*, i. p.cxlv).

[56] *Foedera*, II. ii. 733 (1328).

We can sympathise with the bishop of Rochester when he was ordered to attend a meeting of the council at Windsor on 23 July 1320 and begged leave to be absent 'because it would be difficult, arduous and expensive for a poor bishop of Rochester to find his way to the king's parliaments and councils wherever they were in the kingdom, for his bishopric had not the wherewithal to do this, and so it is enough for him to come to parliament at London'.[57] And when the archbishop of Canterbury was summonèd to attend the king's council in London in 1341, he excused himself, 'stating that he would willingly come to the king's parliament but not to councils'.[58] This is why we must realise that in the thirteenth, fourteenth and fifteenth centuries men did not think solely of 'parliaments' but of 'parliaments and councils' or 'parliaments, councils and conferences'. Whether or not the council met in parliament often made little practical difference.

The references in contemporary records to 'parliaments and councils' are legion and our illustrations must be selective, but the lesson must be driven home. In 1304 Edward I was stressing the duty of the archbishop of York to attend 'his councils and parliaments'.[59] Early in the fourteenth century the earl of Oxford claimed a right of accommodation in Westminster Abbey such as his ancestors had enjoyed 'for themselves, the members of their household, and their horses all the time the king's parliaments and councils lasted'.[60] The New Temple bridge must not be closed or fall into disrepair, for this would hinder the lords and others who came from London to parliaments and councils at Westminster.[61] And such men going to such meetings protested against other inconveniences: the bishop of Ely and others in 1377 implored the king not to allow Smithfield to be polluted with the smell of entrails thrown into the street but order the beasts to be disembowelled at Knightsbridge.[62] Sheriffs were to see to the provisioning of councils as well as parliaments.[63] Archbishops were to carry their crosses before them without molestation when they attended parliaments

---

[57] Historia Roffensis, f. 52.

[58] *Ibid.*, f. 87*b*.

[59] *Foedera*, I. i. 969 (*Cal. Close Rolls, 1302-1307*, p. 312).

[60] Ancient Petition, no. 12992.

[61] *Cal. Close Rolls, 1337-1339*, p. 218 (1337), *1354-1356*, p. 10 (1354), *1374-1377*, p. 27 (1374).

[62] Ancient Petition, no. 5403: cf. *Rot. Parl.*, iii. 87.

[63] *Foedera*, III. ii. 733.

and councils outside their provinces.[64] The clerks of the chancery in person served the king and his people in his 'parliaments, councils and conferences',[65] and knights, citizens and burgesses were paid their expenses for attending such meetings.[66] The clergy sent their proctors to 'parliaments and councils',[67] and litigents sought redress there,[68] despite being postponed 'from parliament to parliament, from council to council'.[69] Grants of exemption from attending 'the king's parliaments and councils' for earls and barons, and for judges too ill or too old to travel, or for abbots and priors who sought to avoid the costs involved, are too many for separate notice, though it may be observed that the bishop of Bath and Wells was instructed by his metropolitan in 1339 not to stay away from 'parliaments and councils' but to go on attending in order to further the public good.[70] James Audley was in 1353 excused attendance at parliaments and councils and specifically 'assemblies of magnates and nobles'.[71] The duties of the Lord High Constable in 1338 included that of 'coming to the king's parliaments and councils'[72]; the newly created duke of Lancaster in 1351 was to send knights and burgesses to parliaments and councils;[73] the regent appointed in 1372 was required to hold 'both parliaments and councils within the realm and to deal, with the assent of parliaments and councils, with the essential business touching the king and his realm'.[74]

A very long list of such councils could be drawn up, but our concern is particularly with the 'great councils' attended by prelates and nobles.[75] An idea of their number and their composition can be

[64] *Cal. Close Rolls, 1327-1330*, p. 219.
[65] *Registrum Brevium*, fo. 261–261*b*: apparently to be dated 1330.
[66] *Cal. Close Rolls, 1341-1343*, p. 109.
[67] *Cal. Patent Rolls, 1340-1343*, p. 278.
[68] *Rot. Parl.*, ii. 263 (1354).
[69] Ancient Petition, no. 7327.
[70] *Register of Ralph of Shrewsbury*, p. 357f.
[71] *Foedera*, III. i. 257.
[72] *Foedera*, II. ii. 1042.
[73] *Cal. Patent Rolls, 1350-1354*, p. 60f.
[74] *Foedera*, III. i. 2.
[75] It should be observed that the term 'great council' was occasionally used to indicate that the king's council responsible for day-to-day administration was to seek wider professional advice in matters of more than routine importance. So at Michaelmas 1310 the chancellor, treasurer, justices, barons of the exchequer and other councillors were to assist in considering Gascon petitions (Ancient Correspondence, XLV. 149: printed in Davies, *Baronial Opposition to Edward II*, p. 592).

obtained readily enough from C. H. Parry's *Parliaments and Councils*,[76] though it should be added that it by no means supplies an exhaustive list, if in fact our resources are adequate to supply one. We may be permitted to cite a few examples of the evidence that can be garnered from widely different sources. The king's treasurer received expenses in 1313, covering 17 August to 6 September, 'for travelling at the king's command from London to Lincoln to be present at an assembly of sundry earls, barons, knights and others in order to discuss there in the king's presence the state of his kingdom and other business'.[77] A privy seal letter in French, dated 1 January 1330, summoned the abbot of Peterborough to a council at Westminster on 18 January: the abbot replied in Latin on 16 January to excuse himself and to appoint two proctors in his place at the conference (*tractatum*).[78] The expenses of the prior of Christ Church, Canterbury, in attending the king's council at Northampton early in January 1334 came to £8.7s.10½d but we do not know why he went there or what he did.[79] The king informed the sheriff of Lincoln 'that we have decided to hold a council at London on the Morrow of the Epiphany (7 January 1337) with the prelates, earls and other magnates of our realm to deal with some important and urgent business touching ourselves and the state of our realm'.[80] Though great councils often left no record behind them, though they had no regular or recognised constitution, they seem to have been summoned more frequently under Edward III than parliaments, and our assessment of their relative contribution to the governance of England will have to be correspondingly altered. Matters of public policy came before 'parliaments and councils' almost indifferently: war with France and taxation to pay for it;[81] the public welfare;[82] statutes and ordinances prejudicial to Rome;[83] the affairs of Gascony.[84] All such matters were common ground to them both. And great

[76] Published in 1839.

[77] E. 101/376/7 (Wardrobe Account, 9 Edward II), fo. 11. Cf. *Register of Walter Stapleton*, p. 431f. and Parry, *Parliaments and Councils*, 79, for the presence also of prelates.

[78] B.L., Cotton MS., Vesp. E. xxi (Register of Adam Boothby, abbot of Peterborough), f. 65.

[79] Lambeth MS. 243, fo. 52*b*. This is one of many councils not mentioned by Parry.

[80] Ancient Correspondence, LXI. 54. Cf. Parry, *op. cit.*, p. 103.

[81] *The County Palatine of Durham*, iii. 252–258 (1338).

[82] *Register of Ralph of Shrewsbury*, p. 357.

[83] Ancient Correspondence, XXXV. 33.

[84] *Ibid.*, XLIX, 104: below, p. 307.

councils continued the discussion of business that had begun in parliament,[85] and they adjourned business from themselves to parliament:[86] indeed, they could be regarded as an alternative to parliament. The king's bench might send a difficult case to parliament or great council equally well,[87] though it was parliament that was usually consulted. The border-line between the functions of parliament and council was always indistinct: is it perfectly clear today? Great councils could be summoned in a less formal way, at shorter notice, and with more variable composition than parliaments, and they were never given any technical definition. It must often have been a point of debate which kind of council should be convoked: in 1339 the chancellor and the treasurer were ordered to convene either a parliament or, if the earls who were members of the privy council agreed, 'a council of magnates and those of the community'.[88]

This phrase refers to a short-lived experiment under Edward III to summon popular representatives to some of the great councils.[89] The purpose may have been especially to hasten discussions on taxation and on related matters like the staple regulations for customs on wool, the Gascon trade and the alnage of cloth, but in fact the business transacted was as broadly based as in other great councils: foreign policy, the defence of the realm, sumptuary legislation, taxation, petitions.[90] Whereas by this time parliament after 1327 always required the attendance of two knights of the shire

---

[85] As in 1328: from a parliament at Northampton in April to the council at York in July (Parry, *op. cit.*, p. 93); and in 1331-1332: from the Michaelmas parliament of 1331 to the council in January 1332 (*Rot. Parl.*, ii. 146) and in 1340: from the July parliament to the October council (*ibid.*, ii. 117f.).

[86] As in 1330: from the council at Eltham to the parliament at Winchester in March (*Foedera*, II. ii. 783; *Cal. Close Rolls, 1330-1333*, p. 130), and in 1335: from the council at Nottingham in March to the parliament at York in May (Murimuth, *Chronicon*, p. 75, and Parry, *op. cit.*, p. 101).

[87] King's Bench Roll, no. 271 (Hilary 1328), ms. 102A - 102D.

[88] Chancery Parl. and Council Procs., 7/10.

[89] The councils may be briefly listed: at Lincoln on 15 September 1327; at York on 31 July 1328; at Nottingham on 23 September 1336; at Westminster on 26 September 1337; at Northampton on 26 July 1338; at Westminster on 23 September 1342; at Westminster on 16 August 1352; at Westminster on 23 September 1353. The Great Council at Winchester on 8 June 1371, like the Great Council in 1328, was summoned as a continuation of parliament for the simple purpose of completing the unfinished business of the preceding parliament, with as little inconvenience as possible, by summoning only a few lords and one half of the commons representatives who had attended the parliament.

[90] For further details see Sayles, *The King's Parliament of England*, pp. 131-132, and Richardson and Sayles, *The English Parliament in the Middle Ages*, XXI. 65-77.

and two burgesses, these councils paid no attention to such a requirement: they might be attended by only the commons south of the river Trent, as in 1342, or by only one knight and one burgess, as in 1352 in order to avoid interference with the harvesting, or by one knight and two burgesses, as in 1353, or by only half the knights and burgesses who had attended the previous parliament, as in 1371. Only the clergy of the province of Canterbury might be summoned, as in 1342, or none of the lower clergy at all, as in 1352 and 1353. The writs of summons allowed a reasonable time, often forty days or nearly,[91] though the writs for the first of these councils, that of 15 September 1327, seem to have been treated in a cavalier and offhand way.[92] The councils were of short duration[93] in comparison with the sessions of some parliaments.[94] Undoubtedly the similarities with the work performed by parliament caused some confusion,[95] yet it did not matter to a sheriff from a practical point of view whether he levied expenses for a parliament or a council. But those who had to differentiate between them in the pursuance of their duties found no difficulty in doing so.[96] Nor would modern historians have been confused but for their belief that the presence of the commons was

[91] I. e. 38 days in 1327; 41 in 1328; 30 in 1336; 38 in 1337; 40 in 1338; 34 in 1342; 27 in 1352; 40 in 1353.

[92] Writs and Returns of Members of Parliament, 5/1. The sheriff of Northumberland returned that the county was too devastated by the Scots to have the means to send knights, and the sheriff of Surrey and Sussex took no action because the writ, dated 7 August 1327, did not reach him until 7 September and no county court would be meeting until 15 September to elect knights and therefore there seemed no point in forwarding instructions to cities and boroughs.

[93] I. e. 8 days in 1327; 7 in 1328; 5 in 1337; 9 in 1352, 19 in 1353. No writs of expenses have survived for 1342.

[94] For example, eight weeks in 1313; seven weeks in 1311; nearly five weeks in 1315 (Lambeth MS. 242, fo. 285, 306*b*).

[95] Only the returns of Ipswich and Northampton in 1327, Shropshire and Kent in 1328, Scarborough in 1337, Norfolk and Suffolk in 1338, Wiltshire in 1352 and Lincoln in 1353 speak of 'parliament'; the many others use the correct nomenclature (Writs and Returns of Members of Parliament, 5/1; 6/13A; 6/5, 7; 7/5, 6). Cf. *Cal. Close Rolls, 1341-1343*, p. 109: a complaint that excessive sums were being levied for the expenses of knights and burgesses to 'various parliaments, councils and conferences'. The Lanercost chronicler (*Chronicon*, p. 287) twice refers to the meeting at Nottingham in 1336 as 'parliament or council', as did the bishop of Ely's summons to the clergy for the meeting in September 1353 (*Ely Episcopal Records*, p. 488).

[96] Richardson and Sayles, *op cit.*, XXI. 67, XXVI. 3 ff. And note Ancient Petition, no. 2262: a petition from the abbot of St. Mary's, York, which refers to his petition in the parliament of York in February 1328 and the grant of a charter to him 'au tretice' at York on 31 July 1328.

the criterion of a parliament.[97] The practice of summoning the commons in some form or other to great councils was allowed to lapse when the commons requested that legislation passed in the council of 1353 should be reconsidered at the next parliament and entered on the parliament roll 'in order that ordinances and agreements reached in councils should not be placed on record as though they had been made by a general parliament'.[98] The king agreed that greater assurance would be given thereby. However, if the work was to be done twice over, there was no point in convening great councils that included popular representatives, and such were therefore abandoned.[99] Thereafter, and throughout the fifteenth century, no burgesses were summoned to great councils and, though knights attended them, they came in answer to personal writs of summons and not, as they did in parliament, as representatives.

Whether in parliaments or councils the essential requirement in public affairs was the advice of the nobles and it is their presence or absence that matters. Indeed, parliament continued to function after the commons had been dismissed.[100] Looking at parliament as it were from the outside, the doge of Venice besought the settlement of current disputes 'in parliamento generali domini regis Anglie, archiepiscoporum, episcoporum, comitum et baronum Anglie',[101] and cardinal priests from Rome submitted their petition to the 'serenissimo principi domino Edwardo Dei gracia Anglie regi illustri ac prelatis et baronibus regni Anglie regium parliamentum tenentibus'.[102] This was under Edward II, but more than a century later Francesco dei Coppini, a papal legate, described the English parliament to the pope in 1460 as an assembly of prelates and nobles.[103] Edward III expressed it all in a phrase: 'Because of some

---

[97] This was the belief of T. F. T. Plucknett. It was also the belief of T. F. Tout. It led him to produce statistics to prove that London was not the place where parliament usually met before the Hundred Years' War. Under Edward I he found eight parliaments meeting at Westminster and one in London and seven elsewhere and thought that, though other calculations might produce slight variations, 'the net result would be the same' (*Chapters in the Administrative History of Medieval England*, iii. 61; *Collected Papers*, ii. 173-190). His figures have to be drastically altered to over thirty at Westminster and four in London and eleven elsewhere.

[98] *Rot. Parl.*, ii. 253, 257.

[99] For the Great Council of 1371 see n. 89 above.

[100] *Memoranda de Parliamento*, p.xxxvi; *Rot. Parl.*, ii. 65b (1332), 68 (1333).

[101] Chancery Miscellanea, 27/12 (26).

[102] Ancient Correspondence, XXXIII. 93.

[103] *Commentaries of Pius II*, Book III (translated in *Smith College Studies in History*, xxv (1939-1940), p. 270).

important and urgent business which concerns us and the state of our realm we have decided to hold a council at London with the prelates, earls and other magnates of our realm'.[104] In 1330 a proclamation was made that such business was to be dealt with henceforward by consultation with 'the great men of the realm and in no other way'.[105] The community is still being identified, as in earlier years, with the magnates. There is no mention that the commons must be in attendance: it was not a *sine qua non*. What was indispensable was that the king's policy should be shaped after discussion with the nobles, and this could doubtless take place in a council with more expedition and more convenience. But their absence from a council, as also from a parliament, was fatal to the successful prosecution of affairs. Military matters might require the nobles to be elsewhere,[106] and old age might be pleaded as an excuse, though on at least one occasion in 1329 the son was ordered to act for his father.[107]

Before the end of Edward II's reign the greater among the prelates and nobles, men who have no official status but who have received a personal summons to parliament, will come to be called 'peers of the land' or 'peers of the realm'.[108] It is far from certain that all those summoned by personal writ will be recognised as peers. The word is not yet a term of art and there will be no exclusive peerage, that is,

---

[104] Ancient Correspondence, LXI. 54: a privy seal writ to the sheriff of Lincoln, convening a council on 7 January 1337. The imperative need for consultation with prelates and barons is constantly stated: e.g. *Foedera*, II. i. 25 (1307), 152 (1311), *Rot. Parl.*, i. 305b (1314–1315), *Cal. Close Rolls, 1318–1323*, p. 713f. (1323), *1346–1349*, p. 523 (1348).

[105] *Foedera*, II. ii. 709.

[106] Ancient Correspondence, XXXIV. 57, 143. The nobles much preferred tournaments, the sports meetings of the day, to assemblies for the discussion of the king's affairs. It may be noted that in the 'full' parliament of September 1348 an aid was granted for the marriage of the king's daughter, and those nobles who were abroad with the king signified their assent by a letter read in parliament. Those present in parliament approved by word of mouth on behalf of themselves and 'the whole community of the realm' (K.R.Memoranda Roll, 22 Edward III, Trinity Recorda, m. 124).

[107] John de Mohun (Chancery Warrants 161/2574) see p. 394. Very few parliamentary proxies for temporal lords have survived but they show that Robert de Vere sent his son Thomas, and Robert fitz Walter his son Robert, to represent them in the Easter parliament of 1322. Henry earl of Lancaster sent his son Henry as his proxy to the parliament of York in 1334 and again to the parliament at Westminster in 1339. Such a practice must have done much to assist the conception of hereditary peerage.

[108] Sayles, *The King's Parliament of England*, p. 100f.

nobles succeeding by hereditary right, for a great many years.[109] There is no restriction on the king's right to summon whomsoever he will to counsel him, and in practice he may summon men whom it would hardly be accurate to call 'lords'. Nevertheless, the 'peers of the realm' were on their way to being an exclusive group with a recognisable membership, from which they could exclude others who sought entrance: they were 'juges de parlement' who could themselves be judged only by their fellow-peers on criminal charges.[110] There is a distinction by 1327 between the 'peers' on the one hand and the 'community of the realm' – all the rest – on the other.[111] The spiritual peers, including all the English bishops and a rapidly diminishing number of abbots and priors, were relatively insignificant when compared with the lay peers and many were willing to perform their duties by proxy, frequently appointing royal clerks of chancery and other departments as well as of courts of law to act for them.[112]

So the counsel of the lords was a necessary element, not only in the form but in the reality of government, a fundamental principle by which the English state was ruled. Judgement in parliament belonged solely to the king and the lords. Kingship came to be inseparably combined with peerage: 'the barons are a principal constituent of monarchy and the king cannot attempt or accomplish anything of importance without them' was the blunt statement of

[109] Cf. *Supplementary Stonor Letters*, sub anno 1378: les evesqes, ducs et countes qe sont les principales pieres du roialme.

[110] *Rot. Parl.*, ii. 53 (1330); *Register of Ralph of Shrewsbury*, pp. 398-399 (1341).

[111] *Annales Paulini*, p. 323 (1327); Murimuth, *Continuatio Chronicarum*, p. 119f.: praelati, comites et majores, scilicet pares et communitas regni, concorditer multas bonas petitiones pro communitate regni fecerunt (1340).

[112] Parl. Proxies. More then two thousand of these have been read, not to discover the absentees (for whom see J. S. Roskell in *Bull. Inst. Hist. Research*, xxix. 173-175) but the names of those who were active in parliament as their representatives. These royal clerks were prominent as proctors in the affairs of parliament: master John Bush, Adam of Osgodby, William Airmyn, Henry of Edwinstowe and Thomas Brayton, clerks of the parliaments; Robert Barlby, William Harlaston, Henry Cliff, Thomas of Cottingham and William Power, receivers of petitions; David Wooler, Michael Wath, John Waltham, John Burton, John Scarle, keepers of the rolls of chancery; John Fordham and John Prophet, keepers of the privy seal. The notorious Thomas Haxey was proctor for the abbot of Selby in 1385, 1391, 1393 (when he acted also for the bishop of Lincoln), 1394, 1395. Tout errs in his statement (*Chapters in the Administrative History of Medieval England*, iv. 18) that Haxey was not a proctor in the January parliament of 1397 where he was charged with treason: he was then still acting as before for the abbot of Selby (Parl. Proxies, 40/1964).

the contemporary chronicler of Edward II's reign.[113] No one challenged the principle and practice of monarchy. For it was the conception of men who did not think that the king and the nobles had a different or a divergent end in view: they had a common purpose in the right governance of the realm. As a natural corollary this meant that, when the king was a minor, the responsibility for government rested entirely with the lords.[114] The commons did not think otherwise. For in the thinking of medieval men God had made men high and lowly and ordered their estate, and they conceived of authority as divided into 'estates' and of parliament as composed of Lords Spiritual, Lords Temporal and Commons. In whatever kind of assembly it was, the elite groups are in control: prelates in convocation, prelates, nobles and gentry in local courts, commercial magnates in merchant bodies, magnates in parliaments and councils. Whenever a representative element is present, it always has a passive role to play. So the commons took for granted their subordinate place in parliament, standing in the parliament chamber when the lords sat,[114a] as they still do today at the opening of parliament.

It follows from what has been said that the discussion of public affairs, the *grosses busoignes* of the realm, was in no way peculiar to parliament and could and did take place out of parliament altogether. In the fifteenth century parliaments and great councils alternate, the same magnates may attend them, and they become grouped together in the same series, which is what we would expect when parliament was equally a vehicle to be used by the controlling nobility. To study parliament *tout seul* without an equally detailed study in parallel of great councils completely unbalances the picture and, despite disclaimers, perpetuates the 'Whig' view of developments that has so distorted the history of parliament.

We turn now to discuss parliament *per se*. The idea that parliament is exclusively competent to perform functions like legislating and taxing is of very slow growth. So much power lay in the discretion of the king and there was little that could be done in law to restrain him.[115] But he was fettered by custom and there were always limits beyond it was not wise to go: some matters would not normally be dealt with unless all whose co-operation was essential had been

---

[113] *Vita Edwardi Secundi*, p. 28. Cf. *Register of John de Grandisson*, ii. 840.

[114] *Ordinances of the Privy Council*, iii. 233: cf. *ibid.*, p. 238.

[114a] Modus Tenendi Parliamentum (Sayles, *Scripta Diversa*, p. 356).

[115] Richardson and Sayles, *The English Parliament in the Middle Ages*, XXIV. 22, n. 2.

consulted. For this purpose parliament stood over and above all other councils and was unquestionably accorded the highest status. For example, by 1300 it was thought that certain decisions must be left to parliament,[116] that what is done in parliament cannot be undone outside parliament,[117] that some questions demanded the advice of the peers in parliament.[118] As the earl of Lancaster expressed it when he was ordered to appear at Nottingham on 21 July 1317 to discuss with the king and some prelates and nobles and other councillors an invasion by the Scots:

> Sire, you should not be surprised because we are not coming on that day, for the business on which you wish to have our counsel, advice and assent, according to what you have told us, ought to be discussed in full parliament and in the presence of the peers of the land. We are, sire, sworn to do this. So, sire, you ought not to wish us to come in any way to discuss out of parliament the things which ought to be discussed in parliament.[119]

In 1322 it was argued that the decision to exile the Despensers, having been made in parliament, could only be rescinded in parliament.[120] The chancellor in 1338 refused to tolerate an action which was in his opinion contrary to a statute made in parliament and with the will of parliament.[121] In 1344 it was agreed by the magnates attending a council on 18 April that parliament ought to be summoned 'for various urgent matters touching the government and the safeguarding of the realm of England, which could not be expedited without parliament'.[122] The superiority of parliament was plainly expressed when in 1353 it was contended that statutes could be repealed or changed only in parliament[122a] and it was agreed that legislation in a great council was not of equal force with legislation in parliament.[123] And because it was a court of law, the highest in

---

[116] L.T.R. Memoranda Roll, no. 72 (28 Edward I), Trinity Communia, m. 45.

[117] *Rot. Parl.*, ii. 388 (1316); Historia Roffensis, fo. 36b (1321); *Cal. Close Rolls, 1327-1330*, p. 150f.; Sayles, *King's Bench*, v. p. 8 (1327).

[118] *Rot. Parl.*, ii. 7.

[119] B.L., Cotton MS., Claud. E. viii, fo. 256–256b: below, pp. 335–37.

[120] Historia Roffensis, fos. 37, 37b; *Register of Walter Stapleton*, p. 442; *Register of Thomas Cobham*, p. 118f.

[121] Ancient Petition, no. 12124B (Sayles, *King's Bench*, iii. p.cxxvii).

[122] *Rot. Parl.*, ii. 146a.

[122a] Chancery Parliament and Council Proceedings, 67/5. See also Ancient Petition, no. 2148, for a similar argument.

[123] Above, p. 34.

the land, a special peace was attached to parliament, and trespasses committed during its sessions were regarded as particularly heinous. All those who attended its meetings were not to be harassed by civil litigation against them while they were away from home, and in their own person they were free from distraint and arrest.[124] During their absence their houses, servants and tenants were to remain in safety. Even an innkeeper in Bristol came to be charged in 1378 for negligence in the accommodation he provided for a member of parliament.[125] Privilege came to be pushed too far, and in 1472-1473, after much deliberation, it was decided that, though magnates, knights and burgesses who came to parliament and their servants were not to be impleaded, arrested and imprisoned for trespass, debt, account, covenant or any other contract while attending parliament, this privilege did not stop legal proceedings already on foot.[126]

The discussion of affairs of state did not, however, form in practice the essence of parliamentary functions, for it could be done and was done elsewhere. But the dispensation of justice was indissolubly connected with parliament throughout the later Middle Ages. Even when the writ system had been developed to cover a vast area of litigation, there was always room for plaints about the failure or the lack of justice. As we have said, under Henry III when an aggrieved person of some standing could not for some reason or other obtain redress because a writ did not suit his case or proved ineffective, he might approach the king in parliament by favour of royal ministers or judges. And then, very early under Edward I, petitions from the people in general were allowed to be addressed direct to the king and council in parliament. We know that many of them asked for favours, but the government assumed that the petitions would deal largely with matters that were justiciable, with grievances which the petitioners looked expectantly to the king's power to remedy. The organised channelling of these petitions to receivers and auditors is a historical fact that admits of no denial and

---

[124] In 1340 John of Godsfield was released from imprisonment in the Fleet because at the time of his arrest he represented Bedford in parliament (K.R. Memoranda Roll, no. 116, Michaelmas Recorda: below, p. 430).

[125] King's Bench Roll, no. 471 (Michaelmas 1378), m. 54 (Sayles, *King's Bench*, vii. 11f.). See also Ancient Petition, no. 3308 and King's Bench Roll, no. 573 (Trinity 1404), m. 42 (Sayles, *op. cit.*, vii. 144ff.).

[126] Exchequer Plea Roll, 12 Edward IV, m. 57b. See also m. 70.

it is to be found in parliament and nowhere else:[127] not only are there the ordinances of 1280 and 1293 to witness it but also the mass of thousands of petitions that still survive and the formidable remains of a series of rolls of petitions.[128] The purpose of these ordinances was to make sure that the king and his council would be troubled with only important petitions.[129]

There is no indication that other business that came before the council in parliament was regimented in this way, nor did any other business come there in anything like the same volume or the same regularity. In comparison the discussion of legislation or taxation was absent or intermittent. Abstract the multitude of petitions and how much is left that could not have been equally well done at some other meeting of the council, suitably afforced to provide counsel and assent? What need otherwise could there possibly be for regular sessions of parliament to be arranged? The dispensation of justice was the essential, though not exclusive, parliamentary function under Edward I[130] and his successors, a time when petitions were invited and not merely tolerated. This contention can be supported by pointing to contemporary parliaments in other lands. The parliament of the French king, the parliament of the Scottish king, the parliament at Poitiers and the parliament at Dublin: all have this common characteristic. They have as well their own idiosyncracies and they will evolve in different ways. Whereas the parliament of Paris became more exclusively judicial, the English parliament saw

---

[127] The petition of the abbot of Stanley in 1333 shows quite clearly that parliament stood out quite distinctly from other meetings of the council so far as the cognisance of petitions was concerned (Richardson and Sayles, *The English Parliament in the Middle Ages*, XXVI. p. 4f.).

[128] *Ibid.*, XIX. 153, for a discussion of parliament rolls no longer extant. It should perhaps be remarked here that petitions to the king and council are not necessarily presented in time of parliament; nothing prevented them from being brought and heard at any other time if it so pleased the king. For example, a petition from John of Southwell was granted at St. Albans on 1 April 1314 when parliament was not in session (Ancient Petition, no. 11632: *Cal. Close Rolls, 1313-1318*, p. 97) And a petition from those investigating the affairs of the Templars *c.* 1309 was endorsed: 'concessa est per regem in ultimo concilio apud Westmonasterium' (Ancient Petition, no. 13806). We may mention a fake petition, made in jest (no. 9528): addressed to King Edward from his son Edmund (1301-1330), it made a request for 'a seal, as he dare not use his father's, and his mother's was too small. In any case, he had no wax'. The letter is dated 'the seventeenth day of my birth'.

[129] The petitions from Gascony in particular raised wide issues of foreign policy.

[130] Note that in 1285 the chancery clerks were instructed to submit problems and difficulties to parliament (*Stat. Realm*, i. 83f.).

private petitions dwindle in their number.[131] In Ireland, where the chancellor did not develop an equitable jurisdiction, the medieval parliament had to continue to hear petitions seeking equitable remedies. In Scotland justice is still today dispensed in the Parliament House,[132] as it is in the English house of lords. All these parliaments are rooted in the thirteenth-century conception of parliament as a time when the king will remedy defaults of justice.[133] Certainly the king could hardly have been presented at frequent intervals with a better picture of the way in which his government was working than through the plaints of his subjects from every corner of his dominions.

The notion of universal justice as the peculiar function of parliament endured. Bishop Adam of Orleton, referring to the first parliament of Edward III in 1327, speaks of parliament as established 'in order to provide justice to all'.[134] The very writ of 13 November 1347, summoning a parliament in the following January, explains that it was not summoned to obtain subsidies or impose other burdens upon the people: it was convoked 'in order to do justice to our people for the injuries and grievances done to them'.[135] The reason given by the commons in 1362 for requesting annual parliaments is so clear in its details that it is worth repeating: 'Inasmuch as this parliament was summoned to redress various mischiefs and harassments done to the commons and in order that everyone who feels himself aggrieved may put forward his petition, and lords and others would be appointed to hear them, and the lords thus appointed have endorsed petitions by 'before the king' (*coram rege*) if anything relates to the king and in consequence nothing is done and the mischiefs and harassments are not redressed, may it

---

[131] See below, p. 50.

[132] In 1389 reference was made to the parliament of the king 'at which and in which justice ought to be done to any party with a complaint', and in 1399 it was stipulated that 'ilke yher the kyng sal halde a parlement swa that his subiectis be servit of the law' (*Acts of the Parliament of Scotland*, cited by A. A. M. Duncan in *Introduction to Scottish Legal History*, p. 327).

[133] Ancient Petition, no. 12274: a petition requesting the king 'faire venir les ditz recordz et proces devant les triours assignez en parlement depuis qe aillours qe en parlement redressement ne se poet farie duement des dites choses' (Sayles, *King's Bench*, II. p. cxxviii); no. E. 187: endorsed (i) 'Adeat scaccarium et ostendat ibi warrantum suum si quod habeat de Rogero vel alio etc. (ii) Responsum iste est insuffiens, ideo sequatur novam peticionem ad proximum parliamentum. Et concessum est per thesaurarium et barones quod interim habeat respectum'.

[134] *Register of John Grandisson*, iii. p. 1544.

[135] *Lords Reports*, iv. 573.

please the king of his good grace to ordain that these petitions may be examined before the lords and answered in accordance with the advice of the chancellor, the treasurer and others of the king's council and endorsed as law and equity require, for God's sake and in aid of charity. And this should be done before the departure of parliament'.[136] To this the king gave his assent. In 1376 annual parliaments were again demanded so that error and wrongdoing in the kingdom could be put right.[137] Under Richard II the commons in 1377 found no anachronism in repeating the Ordinances of 1311 as indicating the business of parliament:[138] to settle litigation delayed in the courts because the king's interests had been alleged, to decide questions on which the justices were divided in their opinions,[139] to give protection from the unjust acts of the king's ministers, to hear and determine petitions. Such a statement could, indeed, have been made from the beginning of the king's grandfather's grandfather's reign.

In 1327 a feudal court, which the nobles dominated, became permanently a representative assembly, which the nobles continued to dominate. The knights of the shire and the burgesses of cities and boroughs are henceforward an indispensable element in the functioning of parliament, but this was not of their doing: it was an accidental consequence of a political upheaval in 1310-1311, in which they had no part. Popular representation must not, of course, be regarded as primarily parliamentary, for both principle and practice go back into unrecorded time and they had long been active in local government in county courts, hundred courts and borough courts. The sheriffs had sometimes been ordered to send local representatives to parliament, but the occasions were seldom in the thirteenth century and the fleeting appearance of the commons in

---

[136] *Rot. Parl.*, ii. 271f. Cf. *ibid.*, 275 (1363), 283 (1365), 289 (1366), 294 (1368), 309 (1372).

[137] *Ibid.*, ii. 355. In 1371 the commons had stated their belief that justice would be done them better in parliament than anywhere else (*ibid.*, ii. 304).

[138] *Ibid.*, iii. 23. And cf. *ibid.*, iii. 203: 'quodque dominus rex animum semper promptum et paratum . . . iusticiam cuilibet ligeo suo sibi per peticiones suas in presenti parliamento conqueri volenti facere ut tenetur. Ad quas quidem peticiones de conquerentibus recipiendas certi clerici de cancellaria per clericum parliamenti distincte et aperte sunt nominandi'.

[139] *Ibid.*, ii. 123a: the justices cannot agree and a decision is made in parliament in 1340; King's Bench Roll, no. 533 (Trinity 1394), m. 40a: a petition in parliament, complaining of obdurate delays in reaching judgement by the king's bench, and the consequent appointment of a commission in accordance with the statute of 1340 (*Stat. Realm*, i. 282f.).

parliament was above all a matter of administrative convenience and they could equally well be commanded to attend assemblies that were not parliaments. And when they attended parliaments, they were so insignificant beside the mighty lords that their presence went unnoticed. All the major chronicles ignored their attendance at Simon de Montfort's parliament of 1265, completely failing to recognise any importance in the event. Just as the doge of Venice and the cardinals of Rome had been oblivious of their existence,[140] so later on the fact of their presence was frequently passed over. The bishop of Worcester saw prelates, earls, barons and nobles at the parliament of 1320 but did not mention the commons.[141] The archbishop of York spoke only of 'the prelates, magnates and nobles' in 1327.[142] To all seeming 'the prelates, earls, barons and chief men of the realm and others of the council' met alone in 1336[143] when arrangements were made for the accommodation of 'prelates, earls, barons and other magnates and nobles'.[144] To the chronicler Murimuth 'the duke of Cornwall as keeper of the realm and many prelates and nobles' were alone worthy of attention in 1338.[145]

The prelates and abbots, the earls and barons, had long regarded themselves as representing the 'community of England',[145a] all the people in the land, and in that capacity they had been responsible for the Great Charter of 1215, the Provisions of Oxford of 1258, and the Ordinances of 1311.[146] By those Ordinances, as we have seen,[147] the nobles had secured control of the king's council in parliament. They sat there as the 'great council' to adjudicate upon petitions. But their political victory posed a problem for them. They could no longer be regarded as the mouthpiece of the community, presenting petitions in its name, for they now heard such petitions in their new role as

---

[140] Above, p. 34.
[141] *Register of Thomas Cobham*, p. 97f.
[142] *Letters from Northern Registers*, p. 344f.
[143] *Cal. Close Rolls, 1333-1337*, p. 725.
[144] *Cal. Patent Rolls, 1334-1338*, p. 362.
[145] *Chronicon*, p. 85.
[145a] Ancient Correspondence, XIII. 128: in a letter to prince Llewellyn of Wales Edward I uses the phrase 'cum comitibus, baronibus et communitate procerum regni nostri'.
[146] In 1297 the barons spoke on behalf of 'the whole community of the realm, clerks as well as laymen, who feel, both themselves and the aforesaid community, aggrieved' (L.T.R. Memoranda Roll, no. 68, m. 58d: *Trans. Royal Hist. Society*, New Series, iii (1886), 281-91. In such terms in 1301 they repudiated papal control of the king (*Parl. Writs*, i. 102f).
[147] Above, p. 28.

judges. The problem proved not hard to resolve, for knights and burgesses were accustomed to voice complaints from their constituents. They could be called upon to represent the 'community' and petition on its behalf. This is not the 'community' of knights and burgesses but the old 'community of the realm' which included also the prelates and nobles. But later on differentiations began to be made: 'the nobles and the community of the realm of England',[147a] 'the community of the land' paying a fifteenth and 'the cities and boroughs' paying a tenth.[147b] The old and the new concepts came awkwardly together as late as 1351; 'after long deliberation and discussion by the commons (*communes*) and the community (*communalte*) and the advice of some of the nobles sent to them'.[147c] But it came to be understood that 'the commonalty (*communalte*) of parliament was of three degrees', that is the proctors of the clergy, the knights of the shires and the burgesses 'who represent all the commonalty of England and not the magnates, for each of them represents only his own person in parliament and not anyone else'.[147d] To perform that duty it was necessary for them to attend every parliament, and this they did from 1327 onwards. This proved to be a momentous decision, a uniquely English development: the emergence of the nobles as judges had entailed the emergence of the commoners as petitioners and produced a bicameral institution with an hereditary house of lords and a representative house of commons.

We have said that the decision was momentous, but it was one of those events that are unremarked at the time as though nothing out of the way had occurred. We think that previous developments had quietly prepared for the change in procedure. The emergence of what we shall eventually call the 'commons' is hard to perceive through the medieval phraseology. *Communitas*, like *universitas*, was a very hard-worked word in the Middle Ages and may have many shades of meaning. No one English word will render all the senses in which *communitas* is used, and to simply translate *communitas* as 'commons' is as hazardous as to translate *universitas* as 'university'. From the beginning of Edward I's reign many petitions were said to issue from

---

[147a] Avesbury, *De gestis Edwardi Tertii,* p. 352f. (1343).
[147b] *Chronicon de Lanercost*, p. 287 (1336).
[147c] *Rot. Parl.*, ii. 237.
[147d] *Archaeological Journal*, xix. 173.

what describes itself as a 'community', a word used to denote some kind of grouping: the Jews,[148] the barony of Lewes in Sussex in 1278,[149] the 'seven places round the town of Winchester' in *c*. 1302,[150] the 'seven hundreds of Windsor',[151] the 'clergy of the province of Canterbury',[152] or the body of bishops as a whole.[153] But the local petitions – if we may so describe them – in which we are particularly interested are those coming from the 'communities' of Hampshire as early as 1278 or thereabouts,[154] of Nottingham in 1301 to which a favourable consideration was given,[155] of Dorset in 1305,[156] of North Wales in the same year, whose 'common petitions' apparently included within themselves the petitions of the poor villeins of Penros in Anglesey,[157] and of Chester.[158] Petitioners often claimed that, when they sought redress for their own grievances, they were acting on behalf of everyone else: 'community' means no more than 'all others'.[159] One petition exhibited on behalf of the people in 1302 complained solely of the wrongdoings of sheriffs in Shropshire,[160] and another petition, entered on the parliament roll with the rubric 'The Community of Devon', is identifiable with the original petition which simply reads 'To our lord the king and his council show the sheriffs, past and present, of Devon'.[161] There is no special category of 'common petitions' among the five different categories mentioned

---

[148] Ancient Petition, no. 2655 (Sayles, *King's Bench*, iii. p. cxiv).

[149] Ancient Petition, no. 13780 (cf. *Rot. Parl.*, i. 6).

[150] Ancient Petition, no. 13899 (cf. *Rot. Parl.*, i. 150-152): this is later equated with 'the abbots, priors, knights, serjeants and other poor men of the people'.

[151] Ancient Petition, no. 10865 (*temp.* Edward II).

[152] Ancient Petition, no. 1985 (1316).

[153] Chancery Parl. and Council Procs., 4/21; Ancient Petition, no. 1986: one of their requests in 1318 deplored that fact that the bishops who had not yet received their temporalities could not 'come to a council with their brethren in parliament, as appertained to their estate'.

[154] Chancery Parl. and Council Procs., 66/30 (cf. *Cal. Patent Rolls, 1272-1281*, pp. 192, 237).

[155] *Cal. Patent Rolls, 1301-1307*, fo. 47.

[156] Ancient Petition, no. 13547: La peticion la gent del conte de Dors': (*Cal. Patent Rolls, 1301-1307*, p. 317).

[157] *Record of Carnarvon*, p. 212: below, n. 162; cf. *Rot. Parl.*, I. 308a-309b.

[158] Ancient Petition, no. 13423 (Sayles, *King's Bench*, ii. p. cxlv).

[159] Ancient Petition, no. 10873 (*c*. 1317-19): Sayles, *Documents on the Affairs of Ireland*, p. 101: The earl of Kildare and John of Bermingham petition the king 'for the community of the land of Ireland and for themselves'.

[160] Ancient Petition, no. E. 216.

[161] Ancient Petition, no. 174: cf. *Rot. Parl.*, i. 381, no. 94. This was in 1320.

in 1318,[162] and the petition of the 'community of Kent' in 1320[163] is in the original addressed direct 'To the lords of the king's council'.[164] What the 'community of the realm' meant under Edward I has been carefully examined and it has been shown that, on the few occasions when elected representatives were summoned to attend parliament between 1290 and 1307, there is no evidence that they petitioned on behalf of their constituencies, whether shire or borough, and that the few petitions, ostensibly on behalf of the people of England, originated with the nobles.[165] In 1309 the knights and burgesses were said to have petitions to put in which could not be answered without special warrant, but these were to be presented individually and not in common.[166] Nevertheless, after 1311 we seem to perceive the growth of greater cohesion and an ability to act together in presenting petitions. The signs are few and hard to interpret but they are there. Thus a little light is thrown upon procedure in 1315 when it was argued 'that it was not in the power of those who answered petitions to authorise an unusual writ in prejudice of the Church without consulting the king or the great council'.[167] This is a direct criticism of the auditors of petitions and reminds them of the hierarchy of authority in parliament: the auditors, the great council, the king and

---

[162] Exchequer Parl. and Council Procs., 1/22, ms. 2-3 *Rot. Parl. Inediti*, pp. 70-80). The earliest use of the phrase 'common petitions' seems to be on the dorse of a petition presented in 1301 to the king and council (Ancient Petition, no. E.727). It is to all appearance an individual or, if we use the contemporary word, a 'singular' petition. John of Dovedale had married one of the two daughters of Sir Peter de Chauvent, a one-time steward of the king's household, and by her he had a son who was heir to half of Sir Peter's property and, as a ward of the king, he was entrusted to the keeping of Lady Alice, the widow of Sir Peter, who had lost her memory. The other daughter had married Gilbert de Briggeshale and she was, of course, the aunt of the boy, who was only six. John of Dovedale's request that he should be allowed the boy's ward and marriage was granted by the council on 12 February 1301 (*Cal. Fine Rolls* (1272-1307), p. 373). The petition was noted as having been enrolled but it is puzzling that it should also carry the endorsement 'Common Petitions'. But cf. n. 157, for the 'common petitions' in 1305 of those in North Wales.

[163] *Rot. Parl*, i. 377b, no. 58.

[164] Ancient Petition, no. 147.

[165] G. L. Haskins in *Eng. Hist. Review*, liii (1938), 1-20 and *Speculum*, xii (1937), 314-318. See also *Annales Paulini*, p. 267: propositi fuerant ex parte comitum et baronum quidam articuli pro proficuo terrae Angliae (in 1309).

[166] *Rot. Parl.*, i. 443 ff. The 'community of the realm' when petitioning was defined at Michaelmas 1318 as comprising 'the prelates, earls and barons and all others staying at parliament in the city (of York)' (Cole, *Documents*, p. 15)

[167] Exch. Parl. and Council Procs., 2/4 (below, p. 319).

great council.[168] Furthermore, the petition heard by the auditors alleged that it had been made 'at the request of the community of Devon'. But it was contended that 'this was not true, as can be ascertained from the knights sent to parliament for that county, one of whom was in town. For the petition had been brought in the name of the community by some individuals who were seeking to injure the bishop and clergy of Exeter by it'. When the petition came to be heard and adjudged, it was alleged 'that it does not belong to those who answer common petitions in parliament to appoint specifically named justices of oyer and terminer without obtaining greater counsel or a special mandate from the king'.[169] It may be deduced that the knights of Devon were known to present petitions on behalf of their county and could disavow any that had not proceeded from them, and that the auditors heard 'common petitions' on behalf of the groups and that there was still no access to the council except through the auditors.[170] It would certainly be surprising if the people of shires and boroughs, who had to pay the no light expenses of their representatives in parliament, did not demand that they should in some measure be repaid by services rendered: already by 1318-1319 Lincoln had made a bargain with its representatives even before they left the city.[171] And later on all the elected representatives seem to be speaking for the people at large. We may perhaps pick out petitions that came from them by the opening words: 'To our lord the king and his council be it shown'.[172] One such petition in 1320 is enrolled on the parliament roll as from 'the community of the realm'.[173] In 1321 'the knights, citizens and burgesses on behalf of the shires, cities and

---

[168] See generally *Rot. Parl.*, i. 288-333, and cf. Exch. Parl. and Council Procs., 2/ 5: 'It seemed to many of the council that such grievances ought to be dealt with in parliament and before the great council and by the greatest and wisest people'.

[169] For this see below, p. 319

[170] Chancery Parl. and Council Procs., 66/16: 'before the council, that is the chancellor, the treasurer, the justices, some clerks of chancery, the barons of the exchequer, and others of the king's council'; 7/21: the treasurer, the chancellor, eight justices, and two of the king's serjeants (5 November 1346). Cf. Ancient Petition, no. 2100: endorsed 'coram rege et parvo consilio. Coram rege et magno consilio'.

[171] King's Bench Roll, no. 240 (Easter 1320), m. 88 (Sayles, *King's Bench*, iv. 94. In 1384 one of the members returned to parliament by the burgesses of Shaftesbury had received his expenses 'as fully appears by a letter acknowledging it, sealed under their common seal' (Writs and Returns, 8/13).

[172] Ancient Petition, no. E. 744: this is in 1316.

[173] Ancient Petition, no. 129 (*Rot. Parl.*, i. 372b, no. 13).

boroughs of the realm' submitted a petition;[174] in 1322 a petition came from 'the knights of the shires and all the community of the realm';[175] in 1324 'the people of England' put in requests which were sent on to 'the prelates and nobles' or 'the prelates associating the magnates and justices with them';[176] in 1325 the 'petition for the whole community of the whole realm' contains five clauses with the answers written, as was usual later, beneath each of them.[177] It would seem natural that knights and burgesses should be asked in 1327 to do what they had already been doing.

The Work of the Commons in Parliament

When in 1327 the 'commons', as we may now safely term them, were required to submit 'common petitions', they accepted the duty placed upon them with enthusiasm. Their petitions were expected to be for the general welfare, seeking redress for mischiefs done to the people as a whole and requesting amendments in the law.[178] When they were summoned in September 1327 to a council meeting at Lincoln they sought to extend the practice and submitted a petition to the king and council 'on behalf of themselves and the whole community of the realm', but their efforts to proceed thus elsewhere than in parliament were unsuccessful.[179]

The commons had long discussions in deciding what ought to be included within their common petitions, as is shown by the preliminary drafts.[180] Some of those who thought that their own grievances and those of their constituents were worthy of a united backing but were apparently unsuccessful in making their point were not daunted but sent forward their petitions individually and asserted that they were speaking for the community. There was so much confusion at first in 1327 that the commons presented their own requests in the form of an indenture which could be checked and authenticated, and they repudiated all other petitions that pretended

---

[174] *Rot. Parl.*, i. 371.
[175] Ancient Petition, no. 3955.
[176] Chancery Parl. and Council Procs., 5/25.
[177] Ancient Petition, no. 392 (*Rot. Parl.*, i. 430).
[178] *Rot. Parl.*, ii. 160a (1346), 237b (1352).
[179] Ancient Petitions, nos. 13017, 13018 (no. 3935 is to the same effect): the treasurer was ordered on 24 September to have the matters settled at York.
[180] Richardson and Sayles, *Rot. Parl. Inediti*, p. 101.

to come from them.[181] The commons were feeling their way and they found that sending their petitions *en bloc* was a hindrance, causing too much delay in their final formulation and leaving too little time for any considered answers to be given them. Instead they forwarded the results of their deliberations as they reached them in single bills,[182] and some of them still survive. For example, two single petitions, one relating to writs brought by bondmen and the other relating to the staple at Calais and Scottish money,[183] came from the 'community' and are found incorporated in the list of common petitions enrolled on the parliament roll.[184] Other single common petitions are scattered about in various groups of documents in the public archives: for reform in procedure to compel prosecutors to answer to pleas of debt;[185] for an interpretation of statutory legislation[186] in regard to conditional gifts;[187] for a statute against false vouchers to warranty;[188] for an extension in the authority of puisne justices of the king's bench;[189] for redress against false acquittances, put forward to delay proceedings;[190] for the regulation of escheators;[191] for the exclusion of sheriffs from holding inquests or acting as justices of the peace within their own counties;[192] for a limitation to the jurisdiction of the Constable and the Marshal;[193] for the abandonment of exaction against ordinaries in probate of wills;[194] for writs of accounts against

---

[181] *Rot. Parl.*, ii. 10–12; cf. p. 203b. See above, p. 46f., for similar deceitful or at least improper practice in parliament in 1315.

[182] The entries concerning the action taken on two common petitions in March 1348 were each warranted 'by common petition of parliament' (*Cal. Patent Rolls, 1348–1350*, pp. 76–77).

[183] Chancery Parl. and Council Procs., 67/4, 6.

[184] *Rot. Parl.*, ii. 180 (the decision of the council is endorsed on it), 318.

[185] Chancery Warrants, I. 199/6342 (20 April 1333): (Sayles, *op. cit.*, iii. p. cxix) there is no endorsement.

[186] Westminster II, c. 1 (*Stat. Realm*, i. 72).

[187] Ancient Petition, no. E. 496 (*c.* 1341–1344): Sayles, *op. cit.*, iii. p. cxx). It is endorsed: coram magno consilio in xv. Pasche. Peticio fundata est super falsa causa. Ideo nichil.

[188] Ancient Petition, no. E. 15823 (*temp.* Edward III): Sayles, *op. cit.*, iii. p. cxxi. This petition was addressed to the chancellor. There is no endorsement.

[189] Ancient Petition, no. 3921 (*temp.* Edward III): Sayles, *op. cit.*, v. p. cxviii. It was endorsed: nichil potest fieri.

[190] Ancient Petition, no. 3943. It is endorsed: Ponatur consimilis peticio inter communes peticiones in proximo parliamento.

[191] Chancery Parl. and Council Procs., 7/11: endorsed 'coram rege'.

[192] *Ibid.*, 8/15: no endorsement.

[193] *Ibid.*, 8/19: endorsed 'devant tous les seigneurs de parlement'.

[194] *Ibid.*, 8/20, 21: no endorsement.

the executors of deceased bailiffs;[195] for more frequent gaol deliveries, the prevention of false returns by sheriffs as well as of abuse in the procedure of private courts.[196] These common bills, notably concerned with the administration of justice, passed direct to the clerk of the parliaments and he presumably exercised some discretion about what should be sent forward from him to the council.[197] He kept a file of common petitions and at the end of the parliamentary session a comprehensive document was drawn up containing what had survived the council's scrutiny and it was exhibited to the lords and the commons for their information.[198] If time were too short to answer all common petitions, those unanswered might be referred to a committee for consideration later.[199] The document containing the common petitions and the council replies should have been added to the parliament roll but this was not done before 1343 and even afterwards there was no uniform practice. One roll gives the common petitions in neat and careful writing and leaves space between them for the answers, and these have been inserted, jammed in in a rough and untidy handwriting.[200] Another roll has both common petitions and the answers to them written out in a single hand.[201]

Private petitions, 'singular' or 'particular' (i.e. ex parte) petitions, continued to be presented but in greatly decreasing numbers. Petitions or bills, as they were indifferently called, were now being brought with great frequency to central courts, local courts and private courts of law,[202] and there was therefore much less need to clutter parliament with them. The comprehensive dispensation of justice at the instance of private petitioners could only be sustained as long as parliament met frequently and regularly as it had done in the early years of Edward I's reign. When parliaments were summoned infrequently and irregularly, private petitions sought more accessible tribunals. Indeed, private petitions ceased to be written on separate rolls after 1332 and thereafter were simply filed, and furthermore they were brought by people of substance rather than those of humble

---

[195] *Ibid.*, 8/22: endorsed 'coram magno consilio. Non est adhuc lex ordinata in hoc casu'.

[196] *Ibid.*, 8/23 (Sayles, *op. cit.*, v. p. cxliii): no endorsement.

[197] They were answered by the king, prelates, earls and barons (*Cal. Close Rolls, 1374-1377*, p. 380f.).

[198] *Rot. Parl.*, ii. 165b; cf. p. 364b, where the answers were read before the king.

[199] *Ibid.*, ii. 334.

[200] Chancery Parliament Rolls, nos. 28, 29 (*Rot. Parl.*, ii. 309-320).

[201] Chancery Parliament Rolls, no. 31 (*Rot. Parl.*, ii. 361-375).

[202] Sayles, *King's Bench*, iv. pp. lxvii-lxxxvi.

status. They proceeded by the well-worn and traditional route, being first examined by the triers,[203] then answered by the auditors and, if necessary, forwarded from them to the council.[204]

But a private petition might reach the council by a different, a quicker and more official route if it could find its way into a petition presented in the name of the community of England, a phrase that indicates unanimity, a formal unanimity, it is true, just as the preamble to a modern statute ignores the dissent of a minority. As soon as the commons presented general grievances in 1327, their 'common petition' included a request from 'the people beyond the river Trent'.[205] It seems as though a group had at once exerted sufficient influence to get its sectional interests backed by the commons as a whole. The practice, however, whereby the commons, the petitioners, became also the petitioned, did not arrive in parliament full-born: it had been some time on the way. At the Michaelmas parliament of 1320 the bishop of London and the dean and chapter of St. Paul's prayed that the exchequer would bear in mind their privileges when dealing with the property of felons and fugitives. According to the endorsement on that petition they were told, perhaps by the auditors, that the exchequer had been instructed to take those privileges into consideration in accordance with the previous practice,[206] and this is the reply entered on the parliament roll.[207] But a duplicate of this petition, with a few insignificant variations in spelling, was endorsed: 'There is another general petition in common on behalf of the community of the realm'.[208] What this seems to indicate is shown by yet another petition on the same subject, but this comes from 'the archbishops, bishops, abbots, priors, earls, barons and all others' holding such privileges, and it is

---

[203] For example, the petition of the sheriff of Nottingham, accompanied by a petition from the community of Nottinghamshire and Derbyshire, was sent in 1351 before the triers of petitions, who sent all the documents to the exchequer (Exchequer K.R. Memoranda Roll, no. 127, Easter Recorda).

[204] When they did so the council might give a different answer from that the auditors had proposed (*Rot. Parl.*, ii. 438-439). In Richard II's time the practice has become common for parliament to give special authority to the chancellor so that he could redress injustice in cases where the alleged wrongdoer was the king (Ancient Petition, no. 11598) or a royal justice (no. 11074) or an over-powerful local magnate (no. 11531). Thus parliament handed equitable jurisdiction over to the court of chancery. See also nos. 9879, 11046-7, 11600.

[205] *Rot. Parl.*, ii. 10, no. 38 and 12, no. 40.

[206] Ancient Petition, no. 4273.

[207] *Rot. Parl.*, i. 380, no. 86.

[208] Ancient Petition, no. 169.

endorsed: 'Answer has been made in common in a petition presented before the king and council, which contains the substance of this petition and several other petitions concerning the community of the realm. And this petition remains in the custody of William of Harlaston'.[209] We conclude that there was in 1320 a 'common petition' resembling that presented in 1309,[210] that a senior chancery clerk who was one of the receivers of petitions in 1320 had it in his possession,[211] and that private petitions could be subsumed in a 'common petition'. After 1327 it is occasionally possible to see private petitions being incorporated in a 'common petition': in 1334 a petition from merchants,[212] in 1339 a petition from John Maltravers,[213] in 1376 a petition from the men of Devon against illegal purveyance carried out by military forces passing through the countryside on their way to Brittany: this was endorsed: 'It is answered among the common bills'[214] and appears on the parliament roll with its scope enlarged by a promise that an ordinance would be made by the king and his great council to provide redress in future.[215]

The commons could not allow a 'common petition' to contain so many private petitions that it went beyond reasonable limits and became meaningless. But there were many petitions towards which it turned a sympathetic eye and it was ready, if not to adopt them for inclusion in its own petition, at least to sponsor them and thereby inform the council that they were thought suitable for its attention. Instead, therefore, of using the old channel to the council by way of receivers and auditors, private petitioners found it preferable to use the newer channel by way of the commons, straight to the clerk of the parliaments for transmission to the council.[216] Of course, the

---

[209] Ancient Petition, no. 3296. This general petition has not come to light.

[210] Above, p. 46.

[211] He may not have been clerk of the parliaments, an office apparently still held by William Airmyn (Richardson and Sayles, *The English Parliament in the Middle Ages*, XLVII. 195). Cf. Ancient Petition, no. 4106, presented in 1318 and minuted: 'Dominus Willelmus de Herlaston' vidit alias peticiones prius responsas et responsum in eisdem indorsatum de manu Roberti de Askeby predicto modo'.

[212] *Rot. Parl.*, ii. 87b.

[213] Richardson and Sayles, *Rot. Parl. Inediti*, pp. 270, 285f.

[214] Ancient Petition, no. 655.

[215] *Rot. Parl.*, ii. 354a.

[216] *Ibid.*, ii. 304: 'Item prient les communes qe toutes leurs billes yci comprises et toutes autres mises devant nostre seigneur le roi, si bien celes qe sont pur severalles persones, villes ou contees come celles qe sont sur les communes suisdites de lour grevances en cest present parlement, soient baillez as aucuns seigneurs en mesme le parlement de les oier et mettre en due execucion, desicome en leur cas lour semble, q'en parlement mieltz qe aillours droit leur purra estre faite'. See Lansdowne MS.

acceptance of a private petition, either for inclusion within a common petition or for sponsorship, required influence and intelligent persuasion and it was natural for the petitioners to place their cause in the hands of an attorney or, better still, of a member of the commons who happened to be a lawyer. To build up a parliamentary practice in this way must have been very lucrative, but it proved too much for the tolerance of the rest of the commons, and in 1372 it was decided that lawyers should no longer be allowed to be elected as members of the commons.[217] The disqualification did not long prove effective, if at all. Presumably government clerks were appointed to assist the commons in the heavy clerical work involved in their labours[218] before the official appointment from the king's chancery of a separate clerk of the commons in 1363.[219] So from the closing years of Edward III and in Richard II's reign petitions were being addressed, not only 'To our most reverend lord the king and the most wise lords, the peers of parliament'[220] but also 'To the most reverend and most wise lords and commons of our lord the king's parliament',[221] 'To our lord the king, his most wise council and the knights of the shire for the commons of England',[222] and 'To the most honourable and wise knights of the shire and to the citizens and burgesses, being for the commons at this present parliament'.[223]

It may be thought that we have unduly neglected the part played by the commons in legislation, taxation and other public affairs. Our answer must be that we have arranged our priorities, not in accordance with modern assumptions and pre-conceptions but with the medieval ordering of business. When the duties of the commons were being revised in 1399, it was stated that 'the said commoners are petitioners and demandants, and the king and the lords have had from

---

482, fos. 23-30, for the transcript of a bundle of ten private petitions of 17 Richard II (1393-94), sent to the king from the commons. The transcript was authenticated by the Deputy keeper of the Tower Records in 1676. Later the bundle became mutilated and is printed in *Rot. Parl.*, iii. 447 and mistakenly attributed to 1 Henry IV (1399-1400). Three of the petitions, either indecipherable or lost, are preserved in the transcript.

[217] *Rot. Parl.*, ii. 310b.

[218] See, for example, *Rot Parl.*, ii. 104-106 (Michaelmas 1339), 226a (February 1351).

[219] *Cal. Patent Rolls, 1381-1385*, p. 535.

[220] Ancient Petition, no. 905.

[221] *Ibid.*, no. 11182: concerning Drayton manor in Berkshire in 1380 (cf. *Cal. Patent Rolls, 1377-1381*, p. 468).

[222] *Ibid.*, no. 6870.

[223] *Ibid.*, no. 5374.

the beginning and shall have of right the making of judgements in parliament in accordance with what the commons have shown; nevertheless the king may wish particularly to have their advice and assent in making statutes or grants or subsidies or the like for the common welfare of the realm'.[224] In the same parliament the knights were told that their functions lay 'in attending parliament and revealing the grievances of the people in every county and suing for redress therein as it seems best to them'.[225]

The work of the commons in politics could be regarded as secondary.[226] In the field of legislation the commons constantly complained that, though the lords had approved and the king had assented, their requests often failed to become enacted law. Towards the end of Edward III's reign they stated that none of their common petitions since 1362 had been published as a statute and enforced.[227] This petition has been looked at askance as misrepresenting the position but we can cite the commons themselves in more explicit form. They had presented one common petition in the parliament at Westminster in October 1383 and another common petition in the parliament at Salisbury in April 1384, but four years or so later they declared that, despite all promises, nothing had been done. They made a copy of the two petitions exactly as we find them on the parliament rolls[228] and handed it in at the parliament at Westminster in February 1388.[229] We imagine that no one would have been more surprised than they to learn that at this very time they are said to have 'held the political initiative'[230] and constituted 'the foremost of the three estates'.[231] Nevertheless, though not all legislation originated with the commons,[232] it became normal practice to found much of it on clauses of the common petitions which survived the scrutiny of the lords and the king. Yet in reality this meant little: though the bulk of the legislation is impressive, it is based on comparatively trivial

---

[224] *Rot. Parl.*, iii. 427, no. 79.

[225] *Ibid.*, iii. 420, no. 36.

[226] The proctor sent by the abbot of Reading to parliament in 1297 was required first to prosecute the abbot's business in the king's court and then grant taxes on the abbot's property (Parliamentary Proxies, 1/11).

[227] Ancient Petition, no. 3947.

[228] Exchequer, K.R. Brevia Baronibus, file for 11 Richard II: the mass of writs is as yet unsorted and unlisted.

[229] *Rot. Parl.*, iii. 161, 173f.

[230] B. Wilkinson in *Speculum*, xxxi (1956), 402.

[231] Stubbs, *Constitutional History*, ii. 320.

[232] Sayles, *Scripta Diversa*, p. 286.

matters and designed to solve an immediate problem, not to inaugurate a new policy. It is sufficient to say that the Inns of Court ignored it entirely when they began to give their regular courses of 'readings' on the statutes and thought nothing to be worth their attention that was enacted after 1327.

When we consider taxation we must remember that the question of consent to it had been raised and the battle won by the magnates long before parliament had taken shape.[233] The essential was indeed consent and not the institution in which it was given, and for long it was granted in councils, in non-parliamentary assemblies.[234] Only slowly was it established that the occasional grants of taxation should be negotiated solely in parliament. For previously it had been a matter of bargaining between the king and various groups of his subjects: with the Jews, with the merchants,[235] with counties,[236] with boroughs,[237] with the Church. There was always expostulation, resentment and opposition, and we should not really be surprised that the commons in parliament always looked for a *quid pro quo*. But they were never in a strong position, not even as strong as has been supposed. For many of the returns to writs of summons were not endorsed by any *plena potestas* or the equivalent *sufficiens potestas* which was reputed to give the representatives 'full authority' to act on behalf of their constituents,[238] nor was any government official apparently perturbed by such omissions. This presumably explains why the commons did not always possess power to bind their constituents to pay taxes and found it advisable, as in 1330 and 1339, to ask permission to go back to those who had elected them in order to consult them about a subsidy.[239] The king's demand for money was

---

[233] In 1405 a litigant, the prior of Effingham, stated that 24 March 1244 saw 'the first grant of a fifteenth in the realm of England placed on record' (Sayles, *King's Bench*, vi. p. 158).

[234] Above, p. 32, Note also *Rot. Parl.*, ii. 200, for a reference in 1348 to impositions 'by the privy council without their grant and assent in parliament'.

[235] As late as 1371 a subsidy was granted 'in our great council by prelates, magnates and the merchants of England' (Exchequer Plea Roll, 45 Edward III, m. 33).

[236] Hampshire was approached in 1319 for a voluntary subsidy and refused it because a common 'tallage' had already been imposed in parliament (Ancient Correspondence, LV. 46: below, p. 351). For separate discussions with counties in 1360 see *Cal. Patent Rolls, 1358-1361*, p. 404.

[237] *Cal. Close Rolls, 1333-1337*, pp. 484, 525, 628 for separate bargains with London, Northampton and Newcastle on Tyne.

[238] Writs and Returns, file 10.

[239] *Annales Londonienses*, p. 247 (1330), *Rot. Parl.*, ii. 103 (1349).

irresistible if he was to govern his kingdom and protect it against its enemies without and within. The issue was not one of conflict but of finding, in consultation with the lords, a compromise upon the amount to be raised and the conditions to be placed upon its spending, though not upon its purpose.[240] But when a parliament came to an end and the commons had gone home, they had no further means of audit and control, and another parliament could not meet except at the pleasure of the king, who found, as the fifteenth-century went on, that he could exploit other sources of revenue more profitably than parliamentary subsidies.

If taxation had lain at the heart of the medieval parliament, it is most unlikely that it would have taken a bi-cameral form. That form reflects its main occupation: the petitions of the commons and the adjudication of the lords. On that simple base was built a much more sophisticated system. For the government of the day, seeking assent for its policy, arranged for its measures to be included in the common petition, debated in the commons, and passed thence to the lords for their consideration. It is rash to assume that what is in the common petition always represents the views of the commons: the political machinations under Richard II warn us that we must often look for the cause behind the cause. The usual formula ran something like this: 'May it please the most wise commons of this present parliament to beseech the lords spiritual and temporal assembled in this said parliament to grant . . .'.[241] A writ neatly summarises the whole process as regards individual petitioners: 'To the chancellor, greeting. We wol and charge you that a comen petition made unto us in this oure parliament by the comens of this oure reaulme for our trusty and well beloved Richard Darcy and Henry Filongley, whiche is passed by the lordis spirituelle and temporelle of this oure said parliament, whereto also we have geve oure roial assent, ye do it to be exemplified by oure lettres patentz to be made undre oure greet seal in due fourme after the tenour of it and this oure assent and the assent of the said lordis'.[242]

Parliament, as we have earlier stressed, was only one form of the

---

[240] *Rot. Parl.*, ii. 103f (Michaelmas 1339): 'the commons pray that they be not charged to give advice in matters of which they are ignorant'; *ibid.*, ii. 105a: as regards sea defences, the commons again ask to be excused from advising in matters of which they have no knowledge; *ibid.*, iii. 145-148: similarly with regard to the expedition to Flanders in 1383.

[241] Ancient Petition, no. 4224.

[242] Exchequer, Treasury of Receipt, Council and Privy Seal, 1/75 (15 March 1445).

king's council, albeit by long tradition the highest in a variety of councils, and the commons did not call the tune. This is not to deny that the singularity of the English parliament was the presence of the commons within it. They were eager to fulfil the tasks assigned them, and the sessions of parliament, sometimes very long sessions, were not occupied all the time with legislation or taxation but with justice. Their main service was to petition the crown and secure answers to their requests on behalf of the community of the realm. From the constant discussion and debate there emerged the parliamentary procedure which was in its essentials to last until the present day: the several readings of common bills, the public acts of parliament based on those common bills, the private acts of parliament based on the private bills they sponsored. But it could not be taken for granted that parliaments would be summoned. Henry VII summoned only seven parliaments in the whole of his reign from 1485 to 1509, and in his last twelve years only one. No law of necessity compelled the use of parliament and linked it inexorably with the changes that would produce our modern form of government. Parliament had been a device of royal administration, liable, like all other such devices, to be outmoded and superseded or, as circumstances and convenience determined, resurrected and given a fresh vitality. It was Henry VIII and his ministers who found parliament in and after 1529 to their liking and adopted and used the procedures it had evolved to bring about revolutionary changes in Church and State.[243] In doing so they made it first and foremost a legislative assembly, the Legislative Assembly that seventeenth-century lawyers and antiquarians had seen in existence since, and even before, the Norman Conquest. Of them we may say: 'Il est des morts qu'il faut qu'on tue'.

Envoi

We must often invoke chance and happy accident to account for the evolution of the English parliament from a feudal court into a representative institution. Its functions were constantly altering and developing to accord with political and social changes and it is this dynamism and the consequent inter-relationships that are so difficult to grasp. The only sure guide is contemporary practice, but it does not disclose the whole story. For example, we can mark most of the

---

[243] B.L., Add. MS. 4491, fo. 126. The final conclusion of Thomas Madox was that 'the king would as easily have made himself arbitrary with a parliament as without one'.

stages in the evolution of peerage but we cannot point to any enactment, any contemporary definition, that will tell us what constitutes a peer and whence his powers are derived. Hereditary peerage is the result of the same silent forces as produced the hereditary fief of an earlier age. There was no splendid vision of the future granted to the unknown architects of parliament. Their conceptions, indeed, like bringing the lower clergy into parliament, were falsified time after time. Men planned for their own day and not for posterity and they made many blunders. It may be that the English people have a genius for getting obsolete and defective machinery to work. Certainly, in one way or another, parliament adjusted itself to the needs of the people, but the people, on the other hand, needed and still need to develop a long-suffering tolerance of the shortcomings of parliament. Centuries have gone to produce this result, centuries during which the English people have been sheltered from invasion and, very largely as a result, have been protected from tyranny. Wont and use, the absence of all need to make violent changes, these have contributed largely to give us the parliament we know. That other nations should come to look at English parliamentarianism as an ideal has a touch of absurdity in it. The English parliament required its English environment if it was to work with even partial efficiency. When the environment differed, as it does so clearly, for example, in the states of Africa, English parliamentary institutions transplanted abroad are not likely to function without such a measure of re-adaptation and adjustment as must, in effect, alter their character.

ILLUSTRATIVE DOCUMENTS

PARLIAMENT AT WESTMINSTER: Sunday before Mid-Lent, 1258

B.L., Cotton MS: Nero D.1, fo.78b
[Matthew Paris, *Chronica Majora*, vi (Additamenta), 392]

Henry, by the grace of God etc. to his beloved in Christ, the abbot of St. Albans, greeting. Since we have some important and pressing business to attend to concerning ourselves and our realm, and it needs the presence of you and our other prelates and magnates, we command and require you, in the fealty and love which bind you to us, to set aside all other business and be with us at Westminster on Sunday before Mid-Lent,[1] to discuss this business with us and with our other prelates and magnates whom we have caused to be summoned there on that day. And you shall in no way fail to do this as you love us and our honour and that of our realm. Witness myself at Windsor the twenty-fourth day of January in the forty-second year of our reign.[2]

Margin: When the magnates were summoned to parliament. But the instructions were suddenly changed.[3]

---

[1] 24 February 1258.
[2] 24 January 1258.
[3] The Parliament was apparently postponed until 7 April 1258: see the next documents.

PARLIAMENT AT LONDON: Easter 1258

i

Close Roll, no.73, m.10d
[*Close Rolls, 1256-1259*, p.302]

On behalf of John de Warenne

Note that the king, on account of the parliament (*colloquium*) he is at present holding in London, adjourned until the Morrow of Ascension next[1] the plea in the king's bench between the king himself, demandant, and John de Warenne, tenant, with regard to twenty-five acres of marsh-land and sixty-eight shillings' worth of rent in Seaford.[2]

ii

Patent Roll, no.72, m.10
[*Foedera*, I. i. 370; *Cal. Patent Rolls, 1247-1258*, p.626]

The king to all men etc. Whereas we had caused the nobles and loyal subjects of our realm to be summoned to us at London a Fortnight after Easter last[3] on account of pressing business concerning us and our realm, and we had carefully discussed with them this business, especially the furtherance of the Sicilian affair, and they said in answer to us that, if we would consider reforming the state of our realm with the advice of our loyal subjects and if the pope would better the conditions laid down with regard to the Sicilian enterprise so that we could further that business effectively, they themselves would loyally exert their influence upon the community of our realm so that a general aid for this purpose would be paid us, we have conceded to them that we will put the state of our realm in order by next Christmas with the counsel of the good and faithful subjects of our realm of England, together with the advice of the papal legate, should he come to England in the meantime, and we will firmly observe what is arranged. And to guarantee our faithful observance thereof, we are submitting ourselves to the coercion of the pope so that he can bind us to it by ecclesiastical censure as he thinks fit. We also affirm

---

[1] 3 May 1258.

[2] The next entry is dated 12 April 1258. This action was tried at Oxford at Midsummer 1258 (Curia Regis Roll, no.158, m.12d) where John argued that it should not be heard in the peripatetic king's bench because it was a common plea that ought to be pleaded in a stationary court in accordance with the terms of the Great Charter.

[3] 7 April 1258.

that Edward, our eldest son, has taken a corporal oath and granted by his letters that he will faithfully and inviolably observe all the things set out above, so far as in him lies, and that he will see to it that they are observed for ever. In witness whereof etc. In the presence of these witnesses: Edward, our eldest son; Geoffrey de Lusignan, William de Valence, our brothers; Peter of Savoy; John du Plessis, earl of Warwick; John Mansel, treasurer of York; Henry of Wingham, dean of St. Martin's, London; Peter des Rivaux; Guy de Rocheford; Robert Walerand and many other earls and barons of our realm. Given at Westminster the second day of May.[4]

[4] 2 May 1258.

PARLIAMENT OF OXFORD: June 1258

i
Close Roll, no.73, m.7
[*Close Rolls, 1256-1259*, p.223-4]

When these arrangements are described as 'the convenient occasion for a muster' before a campaign in Wales (R. F. Treharne in *E.H.R.*, lxxiv, 596) it is evident that the ominous implications behind the king's action have not been appreciated. The barons themselves were under no such misapprehensions about the possibility of a *coup d'état* and the dire consequences to their lives and property.

On behalf of the knights of Burgundy

Philip Lovel, the treasurer, is ordered to allow Henry de Peiny [and ten others], who have just come at our command to England to take part in our campaign in Wales, to have without delay at our exchequer the fee we owe them, or at least half of it, and to arrange for payment to be made to each of them by all possible means for their expenses in getting themselves ready to come to the king at the approaching parliament of Oxford as the king has commanded them and to proceed thence with the king on his campaign in Wales. And, as soon as the king learns how much he has paid them, he will let them have a writ authorising payment, should he not already have received one. Witness the king at Clarendon on the twenty-fifth day of May.[1]

ii
Gonville and Caius College, Cambridge, MS. 205, p.304

Aymer, by Divine permission the bishop-elect of Winchester, to William de Lisle, knight, greeting with sincere affection. We have received the king's order to come to the approaching parliament of Oxford with knights and arms. Wherefore, since we place special trust in your fealty and goodwill, we require you to come to us at Oxford with arms and horses on the Day of St. Barnabas the Apostle next.[2] And you are to inform us by the bearer of this letter what it has pleased you to do thereon. Given on such-and-such a day.

---

[1] 25 May 1258

[2] 11 June 1258. Aymer was Henry III's half-brother. Similarly, his nephew, Henry of Almain, was to appear with a body of young men, whose expenses the king would defray.

iii
Close Roll, no.73, m.7
[*Close Rolls, 1256-1259*, p.229]

Concerning the creation of a new knight

Richard of Ewell and Hugh of the Tower (or either one of them) are ordered to allow Guy de Chaunteny, the king's yeoman, whom the king will adorn with the belt of knighthood in the approaching parliament at Oxford, to have without delay the things which belong to his knighthood, such as the king is wont to find for his other new knights. Witness the king at Marlborough the sixth day of June.[3]

iv
The Provisions of Oxford
[B.L., Cotton MS., Vespasian E.iii, fos.83–85 ('Annals of Burton', printed in *Annales Monastici*, i. 446–53), collated with B.L., Cotton MS., Tiberius B.iv, fos.213–214]

There is no public document called the 'Provisions of Oxford', drawn up in authoritative form with preamble and attestation. The Lichfield Chronicle (B.L., Cotton MS., Cleopatra D. ix, fo.53b) noted that 'as regards the ordinances and provisions made by common counsel of the king and the community, the king's charters were written in Latin, French and English and sent to every county throughout the English kingdom'. But neither the chancery rolls nor the exchequer rolls bear any entry which embraces all that was done at Oxford in the summer of 1258. The decisions taken were promulgated as and when they were made and we can readily understand that the barons, in the dangerous conditions in which they were working, wished to have their proposals accepted and published at once and not kept for ratification as a whole at some doubtful time in the future. Nevertheless three documents have survived as memoranda of the activities in the Oxford parliament, presumably prepared for the information of some member or members of the council and corrected here and there in order to keep the information up-to-date. One is to be found in the 'Annals of Burton', another in a slightly variant form in Tiberius B.iv, the third in the Coke Roll (below p.74). The texts as we have them are in evident disorder and exhibit varying clerical methods. The writer of the Burton-Tiberius text, though writing in French, gave the names of appointees to various committees in Latin in the form in which they presumably came to him. The writer of the Coke text gives them in

---

[3] 6 June 1258.

French. Both writers provided some documents in the original Latin. We frankly admit that it is temerarious to alter the sequence of clauses without more evidence than we have and there is no sign that such is now likely to come to light. Nevertheless, we have assumed from normal medieval practice that the clause relating to the Church should not be placed half-way down but should come first, and we have placed the last thirteen clauses, headed by that on the Church, before the eleven clauses with which the Burton-Tiberius text begins. This very simple re-arrangement is suggested by the order of clauses as given on the Coke Roll as well as by protocol, and maybe the clerk who wrote the Burton-Tiberius text, copied his document back to front, not noticing a mechanical accident. If this reconstruction is considered dubious, it is easy to return to the original order by placing clauses 1-13 after clauses 14-24.

The 'Provisions of Oxford' provide the first written constitution of England and we have thought it proper to give the whole text of the reforms which included, as an integral and essential part of them, the arrangements for summoning three deliberately organised parliaments a year.

A word about the translation which is based upon the Burton-Tiberius text and is intended to give the meaning of the Old French as closely as it is possible to do in modern English. Sometimes the clerk has made a mistake and, for example, written 'et sun fez ensement', which has been recently translated as 'and in accordance with his fealty' (Treharne and Sanders, Documents, p.103): he should have written 'et sun fiz ensement', that is 'and his son also', indicating that the Lord Edward as well as the king would take a separate oath (as he did: above, p.63) to abide by the changes in the structure of government. Such corrections of the text are easy: what is not so simple is to understand what exactly is meant by even common expressions like 'prodes hommes': who are the people so described and what is the English equivalent? Some translate 'good', others say 'sound', but the medieval clerk had presumably something rather more precise in mind. The phrase 'de cours' (in Latin de cursu) has been translated differently in clauses 4 and 20: in both places what was chiefly in mind was the issue of writs 'of course', that is writs in set form which any litigant could obtain without question. Obviously there was no desire to obstruct the normal channels of justice. The term 'brief de cours' is found only in clause 20, but the whole context implies that the chancellor was free to deal with other routine matters on his own authority. And elsewhere some freedom in rendering informal and elliptical minutes is necessary to make the translation easily comprehensible: when it is said that on conviction an offender is to be put to ransom, the meaning is that he shall pay a heavy sum of money by way of fine or amercement and to translate simply as 'punish' (Treharne and Sanders, op.cit., p.108f.) does not indicate the nature of the punishment. Still, the passages where the meaning is not reasonably certain are very few and there is no excuse for the wooden translation given in Stubbs's

Select Charters. *A summary of the problems faced by the barons and the answers they found for them can be found in Sayles,* The King's Parliament of England, *chapter IV.*

The Provisions of Oxford

Of the State of Holy Church

[1]   Let it be noted that the state of Holy Church is to be amended by the Twenty-four chosen to reform the state of the realm of England, when they shall find a suitable opportunity, as they have been empowered to do under the letter from the king of England.[4]

Of the Chief Justiciar

[2]   Further, let a justiciar be appointed – or perhaps two – and what power he is to have, and let him be appointed for one year only, so that at the end of the year he may answer for his period of office before the king and his council and in the presence of his successor in office.

Of the Treasurer and the Exchequer

[3]   Similarly with regard to the treasurer: he too shall render an account at the end of the year. And other good men are to be appointed to the exchequer, as the aforesaid Twenty-four shall provide. And all the revenues of the land are to be paid in there and nowhere else. And let anything that appears to require amendment be amended.

Of the Chancellor

[4]   Similarly with regard to the chancellor so that he too is to answer for his period of office at the end of the year. And he is not to seal anything that is not a matter of routine at the simple pleasure of the king: but he is to do this by direction of the council in attendance on the king.

---

[4] For this letter of 2 May 1258, see above p.62.

Of the powers of the Justiciar and of Bailiffs

[5]   The chief justiciar shall have power to amend all the wrongs committed by all other justices and by bailiffs, including those of earls and of barons, and of all other men according to the principles of justice and the law of the land. And writs shall be pleaded according to the law of the land and in the proper places. And let the justiciar take nothing except gifts of bread and wine and such like things, that is to say, meat and drink such as it is customary to provide for the table of important men for a day. And the same rule is intended to apply to all of the king's counsellors and to all his bailiffs. And let no bailiff, by reason of a plea or of his office, take any reward, either by his own hand or that of any other man in any fashion: and if he should be convicted thereof, let him pay a heavy fine, together with him who made the gift. And if the king is agreeable, let him make gifts to his bailiffs or his justices and his servants, so that they shall have no need to take anything from anyone else.

Of Sheriffs

[6]   Let there be appointed good and loyal men and men of standing and landholders, so that in every county there shall be as sheriff a vavassor[5] of the same county who will deal with the people of the county well and loyally and justly. And let him take no reward. And he shall be able to serve as sheriff for only one year at a time and he shall render his accounts to the exchequer during that year and answer for his period of office. And let the king make him an allowance according to the amount of his receipts, so that he may keep the county justly. And let him take no [illicit] reward, neither himself nor his bailiffs. And if they shall be convicted thereof let them pay a heavy fine.

Of the Jewry

[7]   Let it be noted to make such amendment in the Jewry and regarding the keepers of the Jewry that the oath [of the Twenty-four] shall be kept.

---

[5]   A well-to-do property-owner.

Of Escheators

[8]   Let good escheators be appointed and let them not take anything of the goods of dead men whose lands should fall into the king's hand; but let the executors have free administration of the dead man's goods when they have satisfied the king, if a debt is due to him, and this shall be done according to the terms of the Charter of Liberties. And enquiry is to be made of wrong committed by escheators in times past, and let such be amended. And let [the escheator] take no tallage or anything else, except such as shall be due according to the Charter of Liberties.

Of the Charters of Liberties

[9]   Let the Charters of Liberties be strictly observed.

Of the Exchange of London

[10] Let it be noted to amend the exchange of London and the state of the city of London and of all the king's other cities, which have been brought to shame and ruin by tallages and other oppressions.

Of the King's and Queen's Household

[11] Let it be noted to reform the king's and queen's household.

Of Parliaments

How often in the year are they to be held and in what manner

[12] Let it be noted that the Twenty-four have ordained that there are to be three parliaments a year, the first at the Octave of Michaelmas, the second on the Morrow of Candlemas and the third on the first day of June, that is to say, three weeks before the feast of St. John. And to these three parliaments the elected counsellors of the king are to come, even though they have not been summoned, to survey the state of the realm and to discuss the public affairs both of the kingdom and of the king. And they shall meet at other times by command of the king when it is necessary.

Let it be noted that the *commune*[6] is to elect twelve men of standing who shall come to the parliaments, and on other occasions when it shall be necessary at the summons of the king and his council, to discuss the affairs of the king and the realm. And the *commune* shall accept as settled whatever these twelve shall do. And this arrangement is to be made to save the *commune* expense.

Fifteen shall be nominated by these four, namely the Earl Marshal, the earl of Warwick, Hugh Bigod and John Mansel, who have been chosen by the Twenty-four, to nominate the aforesaid Fifteen who are to be members of the king's council. When nominated they are to be confirmed by the Twenty-four or a majority of them. And the Fifteen shall be empowered to advise the king faithfully concerning the governance of the realm and all matters appertaining to the king and the realm for the purpose of amending and redressing everything they wish to have amended and redressed, and [they shall have authority] over the chief justiciar and all other men. And if the Fifteen cannot all be present, what the majority decide shall stand firm and good.

These are the names of the king's chief castles and of those who have them in their keeping[7]

[13] Bamborough, Newcastle upon Tyne .... Robert Neville
Tower of London .... Hugh Bigod
Winchester .... William de Clare
Corfe .... Stephen Longespée
Hadleigh .... Richard de la Rochelle
Hereford .... John de Grey
Oxford .... John fitz Bernard
Nottingham .... William Bardolf
Dover .... Richard de Grey
Portchester .... Richard of Samford
Glouchester .... Matthew de Besill
Salisbury .... Robert Walerand
Harstan[8] .... Hugh Despenser
Rochester, Canterbury .... Nicholas de Moules
Exeter .... Henry de Tracy
Bridgwater .... Peter de Montfort
Devizes .... Earl of Warwick

---

[6] I.e. the group of conspiratorial prelates, earls and barons who regarded themselves as representing the 'community' of England.

[7] There are differences in the lists in the Burton and Vespasian texts.

[8] Before the end of the fourteenth century this was becoming known as Horsley Castle, co. Derbys.

[14] It is provided that four reputable and law-worthy knights are to be chosen from each county, and they shall meet on whatever day the county court is held to hear all plaints of any trespasses and wrongs committed to any persons by sheriffs, bailiffs or any others and to make the attachments pertaining to these plaints until the chief justiciar shall first arrive in those parts in such wise that they take sufficient sureties from the complainant that he will prosecute and also from the defendant that he will come and stand trial before the justiciar as soon as he arrives. And the four knights are to arrange for the enrolment of all the aforesaid plaints with their attachments in orderly sequence, that is to say, for each hundred on its own and by itself, so that the justiciar as soon as he arrives can hear and determine the aforesaid plaints from each hundred separately. And they are to let the sheriff know that he is to make all the hundredmen and their bailiffs come before the justiciar at his next arrival on the days and at the places of which he informs them so that each hundredman shall cause all the complainants and defendants of his bailiwick to come one after another in accordance with the manner in which the justiciar shall decide to hear the pleas of the hundred, and he is to summon such-and-such a number of knights of such-and-such a kind as well as other free and law-worthy men of his bailiwick, by whom the truth of the matter can best be found, provided that they are not all inconvenienced at one and the same time, for only so many are to come as can plead and receive judgement in one day.

Likewise it is provided that no knight of the aforesaid counties is to be excused by virtue of a royal charter which exempts him from being put on juries or assizes, or given any acquittance so far as this ordinance, thus made for the common welfare of the whole kingdom, is concerned.

These are those chosen on behalf of the king

[15] The bishop of London; the bishop-elect of Winchester; Henry, son of the king of Germany; John earl Warenne; Guy de Lusignan; William de Valence; John earl of Warwick; John Mansel; Henry of Wingham; Brother John of Darlington; the abbot of Westminster.[9]

---

[9] For a comparison of the divergent lists given by the documents, see Richardson and Sayles, 'The Provisions of Oxford' in *The English Parliament in the Middle Ages*, III.

These are those chosen on behalf of the earls and barons

[16] The bishop of Worcester; Simon earl of Leicester; Richard earl of Gloucester; Humphrey earl of Hereford; Roger the marshal; Roger Mortimer; John fitz Geoffrey; Hugh Bigod; Richard Grey; William Bardolf; Peter de Montfort; Hugh Despenser.

And if any one of these happens of necessity not to be able to be present, the rest of them can choose whom they wish, that is to say, someone who is needed to take the place of the absent man in order to further the business.

The commune of England swore thus at Oxford

[17] We make known all together to all men that we have sworn on the Holy Gospels and are mutually bound by this oath and promise faithfully that we, one and all, will aid one another, we and our men, against all men, and will act justly and take nothing that we cannot take without wrongdoing, saving our fealty to the king and the crown. And we promise, by the same oath, that none of us will ever take any land or chattel whereby this oath can be impaired or in any way blemished. And if anyone should act contrary to this oath we will hold him as a mortal enemy.

This is the oath of the Twenty-four

[18] Each swore on the Holy Gospels that, in honour of God and fealty to the king and for the well-being of the realm, he will discuss and ordain with the aforesaid sworn members of the *commune* the proposals for the reform and amendment of the state of the realm, and that neither for gift nor promise, for love nor hate nor fear of any man, for gain nor loss, would he fail loyally to act according to the terms of the letter which the king and likewise his son have given thereon.[10]

The Chief Justiciar of England swore thus

[19] He swore that to the utmost of his power, he will well and loyally do what is required to render justice to all men, to the profit of the king and the realm, according to the provisions made and to be made by the Twenty-four and by the king's council and the great men of the land, who have sworn to aid and support him in these matters.

[10] See above p.62f.

The Chancellor of England swore thus

[20] That he will not seal any writ, except writs of course, without orders from the king and those of his council who are in attendance, nor will he seal the grant of a large wardship or of large sums of money or of large escheats without the assent of the great council or of the majority thereof, nor will he seal anything that is contrary to the instructions given or to be given by the Twenty-four or by a majority of them nor will he take any reward other than what has been assigned to others.

And[11] he is to be given a colleague in such form as the council shall provide.

This is the oath taken by the keepers of the king's castles

[21] They swear that they will keep the king's castles loyally and faithfully on behalf of the king and his heirs and that they will surrender them to the king and his heirs and to no one else and by [the order of] his council and in no other manner, that is to say by [order of] the reputable men of the land elected to his council or the majority of them. And this form is to be put into writing and is to last for twelve years. And from that time onwards they shall not be prevented by this ordinance and this oath from being able to surrender the castles freely to the king and his heirs.[12]

These are they who are sworn of the king's council

[22] The archbishop of Canterbury, the bishop of Worcester, the earl of Leicester, the earl of Gloucester, the earl Marshal, Peter of Savoy, the earl of Aumale, the earl of Warwick, the earl of Hereford, John Mansel, John fitz Geoffrey, Peter de Montfort, Richard Grey, Roger Mortimer, James Audley.

The twelve representing the king have chosen from the twelve representing the *commune*, Earl Roger the Marshal, Hugh Bigod.

The other side representing the *commune* have chosen from the twelve representing the king, the earl of Warwick, John Mansel.

And these four are empowered to choose the king's council. And when they have made their choice they are to present them to the Twenty-four, and the decision of the majority of them shall be binding.

[11] This, of course, is not part of the oath.
[12] The form of the oath is entered on the patent roll (C.66, no.72, m.6: *Cal. Patent Rolls, 1247-58*, p.637).

*These are the Twelve who are chosen by the barons to represent the whole
community of the land at the three annual parliaments
to discuss public affairs with the king's council*

[23] The bishop of London; the earl of Winchester; the earl of Hereford;
John Balliol; John de Verdun; John de Grey; Roger de Sumery; Roger de
Montalt; Hugh Despenser; Thomas de Greilly; Giles de Argentein;
Philip Basset.

*These are the Twenty-four appointed by the community to discuss
the aid for the king*

[24] The bishop of Worcester; the bishop of London; the bishop of
Salisbury; the earl of Leicester; the earl of Gloucester; the Earl Marshal;
Peter of Savoy; the earl of Hereford; the earl of Aumale; the earl of
Winchester; the earl of Oxford, John fitz Geoffrey; John Balliol; Roger
Mortimer; Roger de Montalt; Roger de Sumery; Peter de Montfort;
Thomas de Greilly; Fulk of Kerdistone; Giles de Argentein; Giles of
Erdinton; John de Crioil; Philip Basset, master William Powick; John of
Oare.[13]
　　And if any of these are unable or unwilling to serve, those who shall be
present are empowered to choose others in their place.

v
Inner Temple, London: Petyt MS. 553/6, fos.53-56
This is from a seventeenth-century abstract of the 'Provisions of Oxford',
made from a text once in the possession of Sir Edward Coke and now lost.
For a full copy, see Richardson and Sayles, 'The Provisions of Oxford:
a forgotten document' in *The English Parliament in the Middle Ages*, III.

The justices and other wise men are summoned that between that and the
next parliament they should consider of what ill laws and need of
reformation there were, and that they meet eight days before the
parliament begin again, at the place where it shall be appointed to treat etc.

[13] Twenty-five names are given in the Tiberius text: on this discrepancy see
Richardson and Sayles, *op.cit.*, III, pp.14ff. This list omits John de Grey. He is put at the
end of the names on the Coke roll, making twenty-six in all.

vi

Liberate Roll, no.35, m.5

[*Cal. Liberate Rolls, 1251-60*, p.455]

On behalf of William of Gloucester

The king to his barons of the exchequer, greeting. Allow William of Gloucester, keeper of our exchange, in the outgoings of the exchange, fifty marks which he delivered on our instructions to our beloved nephew Henry, son of the king of Germany, our brother, for his expenses in staying with his colleagues, who have taken an oath to reform the state of our realm in the parliament we held with our magnates at Oxford last summer. Witness the king at Westminster the twenty-sixth day of March.[14]

vii

B.L., Cotton MS., Vespasian E., f.83b

['Annals of Burton' in *Annales Monastici*, i. 4565-7; *Foedera*, I. i. 375]

Henry by the grace of God etc. to his beloved and faithful so-and-so, sheriff etc. Whereas recently in our parliament at Oxford it has been unanimously ordained that all serious offences, trespasses and wrongs, committed within our realm, are to be inquired into by four knights of every county so that, when the truth thereof has become known, they may the more readily be redressed, and these four knights have taken a corporal oath that they will faithfully make the inquiry in full county court or, if the county court is not to be held soon, before sheriffs and coroners in accordance with our instructions to each of our sheriffs: we command you, in the faith which binds you to us, that, having taken the oath as aforesaid, you are to make careful inquiries throughout the aforesaid county, by the oath of upright and law-worthy men of the county by whom the truth of the matter can best be known, concerning all kinds of serious offences, trespasses and wrongs committed in the county in times past by any persons whatsoever to any others, and this applies to justices and sheriffs as well as our other bailiffs and all other persons whatsoever. And you are to bring the inquisition made thereon to Westminster a week after Michaelmas under your seals and the seals of those by whom it was made and deliver it in your own person to our council there . . .

In witness thereof we send you these our letters patent. Witness myself

---

[14] 26 March 1259.

at Westminster the twenty-eighth day of July in the forty-second year of our reign.[15]

viii
Curia Regis Roll, no.158 (Trinity 1258), m.12
[*Cal. Documents Ireland, 1252-1284,* p.95, no.582]

The Month after Trinity at Oxford: continued.

Ireland

Instructions were sent on behalf of Edward, the king's son etc., to Alan la Zuche, his justiciar of Ireland, to this effect: whereas he had heard that in the plea before his justices at Dublin by the king's writ of right between John de Verdun, demandant and the abbot of Mellifont, tenant, with respect to eight carucates of land with appurtenances in Mulygadaveran and Tullyallen and five carucates of land with appurtenances save three acres of land for producing salt, reply has been made on the abbot's behalf that he cannot answer thereon without the king, and for that reason the justices are ceasing to proceed further in that plea, Alan was to let the abbot know that, on account of the danger of disherison which might befall John, he was to come without delay to England, should he think it advisable, to show if he had a document or anything else by virtue of which he could not and ought not to answer thereon without the king so that, after the king had been consulted and the assent of his council and of the justices of England had been obtained thereon, the said plea could be dealt with in accordance with the right procedure etc.

And the abbot came before the king at Oxford a Month after Trinity. And he put forward before the earls, barons and all the justices of England at the king's great parliament a charter of King Henry, grandfather of the present king in these words[16] . . . And William of Wilton comes on behalf of the Lord Edward, his master, and testifies that John de Verdun does not wish to sue against the abbot in the king's court here. And therefore the abbot is sent back to the parts of Ireland in the same condition he was in when he left home. And the Justiciar is ordered to have all the lands etc., which he had seized etc. in order to compel his appearance here before the king, to be handed over to the abbot.

---

[15] 28 July 1258.

[16] For Henry II's charter, granting lands for the purpose of founding Mellifont Abbey, and its confirmation by Henry III on 4 April 1253, see *Cal. Documents Ireland, 1171-1251,* p.9 and *ibid., 1252-1284,* p.26.

ix
Patent Roll, no.72, m.8
[*Foedera*, I. i. 372; *Cal. Patent Rolls, 1247-1258*, p.632]

The king to all bailiffs etc. Know that we have taken into our secure and safe conduct the envoys of Llewellyn son of Griffith, whom our beloved and faithful Peter of Montfort will bring with him to this, our parliament of Oxford, which will be a Month after next Whitsunday, in going to us, staying with us and returning home. And therefore we order you not to inflict or cause to be inflicted any loss, grievance or harassment upon the said envoys in coming to us, staying with us, and returning home. And if anything etc. In witness thereof etc. The safe conduct is to last until a Fortnight after St. John the Baptist's Day next.[17] Witness the king at Marlborough, the second day of June.[18]

---

[17] 8 July 1258.
[18] 2 June 1258. A truce, made in this parliament by counsel of the magnates, was to last until 1 August 1260 (*Cal. Patent Rolls, 1258-1266*, p.83).

PARLIAMENT AT WESTMINSTER: Michaelmas 1258

i

Close Roll, no.74, m.1*d*

[*Close Rolls, 1256-1259*, pp.332-3]

A curious story lies behind the enrolment of these writs. In the seventeenth century they were to be seen on the Close Roll and a precise reference to them was given (Brady, *Introduction to Old English History*, p.141; *Complete History of England*, Appendix, p.228). But in the twentieth century they had to all appearance disappeared from the membrane on which they had been written, though that membrane manifestly existed, and they defied the most painstaking efforts to find them (see the despairing note of R.G.D.Laffan in his translation of Pasquet, *Origins of the House of Commons*, p.231). In 1930 Mr. Hilary Jenkinson, then in charge of the Round Room in the Public Record Office, yielded with some reluctance to my importunities that we must reject the evidence of our eyes and have some repairing that had been done to the membrane expertly removed. The writs then came to light where they had always been and I left them to be printed officially in 1932 (as acknowledged in *Close Rolls, 1256-1259*, preface, p.v). Meanwhile the writs were printed, not quite accurately, by H.M.Cam in *Eng. Hist. Rev.* xlvi (1931), pp.630-632.

Because Robert of Cambo and his fellows of the county of Northumberland came, on the king's instructions, to the king at Westminster a Month after Michaelmas in the forty-second year of his reign for certain business concerning the community of the whole county, the sheriff of Northumberland is ordered to let the four knights of the county have their reasonable expenses in their going and returning. Witness the king at Westminster the fourth day of November in the forty-third year etc.[1]

Similar writs were sent to the sheriffs of eight other counties.

ii

The king to the sheriff of Huntingdon, greeting. Because our beloved and faithful W.le Moyne, W.of Washingley, Simon of Coppingford and Baldwin of Drayton have recently been occupied in making certain inquisitions concerning the general welfare of the county and afterwards

---

[1] 4 November 1258.

they waited before our council at Westminster in the parliament held there after Michaelmas last on account of that business, we order you to let the four knights have from the community of the shire the reasonable expenses they incurred in going and returning and waiting at that parliament by reason of that business. Witness etc.[2]

> Similar writs were sent on behalf of the knights from five other counties.

[2] The knights who were commissioned to inquire into wrongdoings within their shires had been ordered to bring their records to Hugh Bigod, the justiciar, at the Michaelmas parliament of 1258 (*Cal. Patent Rolls, 1247-58*, pp.645-9). They were not, of course, elected for the purpose of attending parliament.

PARLIAMENT AT WESTMINSTER: Candlemas 1259

i

Close Roll, no.74, m.14

[*Close Rolls, 1256-1259*, p.345]

The next two documents show that, though one clerk prefers to use the classical word *colloquium* and another clerk the vulgar *parliamentum*, they are both referring to precisely the same assembly.

Concerning Rutland Forest

Because the king has learned from Peter de Neville, keeper of Rutland Forest, that the forest is very greatly wasted and ruined by reason of the selling the king has authorised to be done there, Adam de Greinville is ordered to desist forthwith from such selling until the colloquy which the king is about to hold at the Feast of the Purification of the Blessed Mary next[1] so that he can then do thereon with the counsel of his magnates what ought to be done. Witness as above.[2]

By the justiciar.

ii

Ibid.

[*Close Rolls, 1256-1259*, p.350]

Concerning the custody of the castles of Bristol and Wales

Richard de la Rochelle is ordered to have Bristol Castle and the castles of Wales, which were in the custody of the lately deceased John fitz Geoffrey, safely and firmly guarded until the parliament which the king is about to hold at the next Feast of the Purification of the Blessed Mary so that then, by counsel of the king's magnates who are members of his council, these castles may be committed to him or someone else for safe custody. Witness as above.[3]

---

[1] 2 February: this is the same day as Candlemas.
[2] 24 November 1258.
[3] 5 December 1258.

iii

Assize Roll, no.873, m.6

[Richardson and Sayles, *Procedure without Writ under Henry III*, p.91]

Eudes of Timperley and other men of Witley, which was ancient demesne of the king and his predecessors, kings of England, complain against Peter of Savoy that, after the present king had given him this manor five years ago, he wrongfully increased their rent by £18. 7s. 6d. a year more than their predecessors were wont to pay during the time the manor was in the hands of the king and his predecessors, kings of England. And this is found to be so by jurors of the neighbourhood. And because Peter is not here present, therefore day is given them on the Morrow of the Purification of the Blessed Mary [4]at parliament[4]. And justice will then be done thereon etc.[5]

Margin: Let there be discussion.

iv

Ibid., m.7

Township of Kingston

Concerning plaints

Robert of Meleburn and Emma, his wife, complain of Guy de Lusignan that he had ejected them from their manor of Sheen at Martinmas in the forty-first year[6] and kept them out of that manor until the following Feast of the Purification of the Blessed Mary[7] and that Robert and Emma had made fine with Guy by twenty-seven pounds of silver before they could have entry into the manor. And in this respect he says that he has suffered damage and loss to the value of thirty pounds. And he produces suit thereof. And because no one comes to speak on Guy's behalf, therefore let a jury inquire into the truth.

The jurors say that it is true that a certain John, a convert, had at one time made Emma his wife, and in the process of time Emma claimed in court christian that the said Robert was her husband, alleging that a

---

[4-4] These two words are interlined.

[5] Another action, concerning the exactions from the men of Byfleet and Weybridge by Guy de Lusignan, recorded at the foot of the same membrane, is noted: 'let there be discussion at parliament'.

[6] 11 November 1256.

[7] 2 February 1257.

divorce had taken place between herself and John, with the result that she proved Robert to be her husband. And after the divorce between her and John, Robert came along with her to the manor of Sheen and they put themselves in possession of the manor, which is part of Emma's inheritance and which John had previously held with Emma. And afterwards John came to Guy and said that he had right in the manor and his talk so impressed Guy that he ejected Robert and Emma from the manor in John's name and kept them out of that manor until Robert and Emma made fine with Guy by the aforesaid twenty-seven pounds. And so Robert and Emma are told to be at the next parliament at Westminster, and in the meanwhile let there be discussion with the king.

Margin: Let there be discussion with the king.

v

Assize Roll, no. 362, m. 8d

[*Trans. Royal Hist. Society*, Fourth Series, v. 60 f.]

Pleas of plaints before Hugh Bigod, the justiciar of England, at Canterbury on Sunday before the Feast of St. Hilary in the forty-third year.[8]

Hundred of Larkfield

William son of Alexander of Preston complains against Henry Lovel that, whereas William had been amerced at one mark for a false appeal he made before Henry of Bath and his fellows and had paid that mark, Henry afterward distrained him for twenty shillings he did not owe.

And Henry comes and plainly acknowledges that he distrained him for twenty shillings, and this he did by summons of the exchequer, and in this regard he says that William impleaded him on another occasion before the barons of the exchequer on the ground that he unjustly distrained him for the aforesaid twenty shillings, and it was then proved before the barons that he distrained him justly. And as to this he puts himself on the rolls of the exchequer. Therefore a day is given at parliament. And let the rolls of the exchequer be then searched.

Margin: to parliament.

---

[8] 11 January 1259.

PARLIAMENT AT WESTMINSTER: Easter 1259

i

Liberate Roll, no.35, m.5
[*Cal. Liberate Rolls, 1251-1260*, p.457]

Because the fireplace in the king's chamber at Westminster is in poor condition, John de Crachal, the king's treasurer, is ordered to have it pulled down and a good strong fireplace built there immediately after the king's parliament which will be after the approaching Easter.[1] And when the king knows the cost he has incurred, he will have a writ of payment for it made out to him. Witness as above.[2]

Margin: cancelled.[3]

ii

And it is ordained that two or three of the members of the council who are of middle status[4] are to be constantly round the king from parliament to parliament. And at each parliament they are to be changed and others appointed. And what they have done is to be reviewed at each parliament and to be amended, should there be anything to amend, by those of the council. And if any weighty business arises between parliaments which cannot be settled by the aforesaid two or three councillors or which cannot be conveniently postponed until the next parliament, then all those of the council are to be summoned by writ to settle that business, and the writ shall indicate the reason for the summons unless it be a secret.

---

[1] Easter Day was 13 April.
[2] 7 April 1259.
[3] For the issue of fresh instructions see *Cal. Liberate Rolls, 1251-1260*, p.507. The reference (*Flores Historiarum*, ii. 428-9), given by R.F.Treharne, *Baronial Plan of Reform*, p.141, as evidence for a parliament at Midsummer 1259, speaks of the French, not of the English, parliament.
[4] This arrangement excused bishops and earls from routine business.

iii

B.L., Cotton MS., Nero D.I., f. 138b

[Jacob, *Studies in the Period of Reform and Rebellion*, p.373]

It is ordained that the chief justiciar, the chancellor and the treasurer are to remain in their offices until the next parliament.

Furthermore, good and wise men are to be chosen by the chief justiciar and the treasurer to decide, during this Advent and the Feast Days[5] in readiness for the next parliament, what will need to be amended at the Great Exchequer and the Exchequer of the Jews.

iv

Assize Roll, no.911, m.3d

[Jacob, *op. cit.*, pp.354–355]

William Marmiun complains against John de la Rede, the bailiff of Peter of Savoy, that, whereas it has been forbidden by the provision recently made in the king's general parliament by counsel of the nobles and magnates of the realm of England, that any money should be given for fair pleading[6] in the king's court or in any court whatsoever,[7] John in breach of that provision and after it had been made has now distrained William and his men of Berwick to give forty shillings for fair pleading in Peter's hundred court of Longbridge . . .

---

[5] By inadvertence Treharne and Sanders, *Documents*, p.155, reads 'first days'.
[6] No fines were to be imposed for permission to amend a defective plea.
[7] Provisions of Westminster, c.5 (*Statutes of the Realm*, i. 9).

PARLIAMENT AT WESTMINSTER: Michaelmas 1259

i
Close Roll, no.75, m.17d
[*Close Rolls, 1259-61*, pp.146-50]

Though parliament *eo nomine* is not mentioned, it was well known
that this legislation was enacted as the 'Provisions of Westminster' in
a 'general parliament' (see below, p.84).

In the year of the Incarnation of the Lord 1259 and in the forty-third year
of the reign of King Henry, son of King John, when the king and his
magnates met together at Westminster a Fortnight after Michaelmas,[1]
the following provisions were made by the king and the magnates, with
the mutual counsel and assent of the king and the magnates, and they
were published in this form.
[The Provisions of Westminster follow.]

ii
B.L., Cotton MS., Vespasian E. iii. f.89*b*-90
['Annals of Burton': *Annales Monastici*, i. 476]

It is also ordained that no one may come to parliament for the common
business of the land with horses and arms or armed, unless he has
received special instructions from the king or from his council or by
writ.[2]

---

[1] 13 October 1259.
[2] Cf. Charles Bémont, *Simon de Montfort*, p.350.

PARLIAMENT AT LONDON: Candlemas 1260

i
Close Roll, no.75, m.18
[*Close Rolls, 1259-61, p.15*]

On behalf of Maud de Kyme

Because Maud de Kyme has given the king security by Robert Aguillun and Geoffrey de Falencourt that she will hand over the four daughters and heiresses of William de Forz, her late husband, to the king or, if he is out the kingdom, to his council in the parliament which will be at the Feast of the Purification of the Blessed Mary next,[1] the sheriff of Somerset and Dorset is ordered to remove the distraint he imposed upon her at the king's command in order to get the heiresses delivered to the king and to restore to her her lands, should he on this account have taken any of them into the king's hand. Witness Hugh Bigod, the justiciar of England, at Westminster on the twenty-second day of November.[2]

A similar order was sent to the sheriff of Surrey. Witness as above.

ii
Close Roll, no.75, m.17
[*Close Rolls, 1259-61, p.17*]

On behalf of William de Bussey

William of Wendling, the king's escheator below the river Trent, is ordered to allow William de Bussey, who is in the king's Fleet prison for certain trespasses with which he is charged, to have a hundred shillings from the profits of his lands, which are in the king's hand and in your custody, in order to provide him with sustenance in that prison until the king's parliament at the Feast of the Purification of the Blessed Mary next so that other provision may then be made concerning his sustenance and his property rights. And when you have paid him this money, we will have it allowed to you in the profits of the said lands. Witness H. Bigod, the Justiciar of England, at Westminster on the twenty-eighth day of November.[3]

[1] 2 February 1260.
[2] 22 November 1259.
[3] 28 November 1259.

iii
Close Roll, no.76, m.3d
[*Close Rolls, 1259-61, pp.272-273*]

On behalf of the king

The king to the reverend fathers Boniface, archbishop of Canterbury and primate of all England, Walter bishop of Worcester, and to his beloved and faithful subjects, earl Simon de Montfort, Roger Bigod, earl of Norfolk and marshal of England, Humphrey de Bohun, earl of Hereford and Essex, Philip Basset, Richard de Grey, James de Audley and Peter de Montfort, greeting. Forasmuch as you have assured us of the peaceful state of our realm and that you are looking forward with all your hearts to our speedy return to England, as we have fully learned from your letters and from our beloved and faithful Philip Marmiun and Simon Passelewe, we, while obviously expecting therein the steadfast affection and loyalty you bear towards us, are most grateful to you because, whenever we are reliably informed of the prosperity of our realm, we are moved to no little joy. Indeed, we are ready to return to our kingdom, and we would have come a long time ago if we had not been too long detained in the kingdom of France for various reasons, some of which perhaps are no secret to you, and by other obstacles which we can more fully explain to you on our arrival. There is then one reason remaining, namely, the assessment of the sum required for maintaining five hundred knights for two years which the king of France is under obligation to pay us: the assessors, chosen on his side and on ours for this purpose, have been unable to reach an agreement about it, and we constantly begged that king that a fifth assessor should be appointed jointly by both sides who could put an end to the wrangling. And Peter Chamberlain was nominated for this purpose provided he would swear to undertake it and, because he was afraid to take this burden upon himself, the king of France wished to associate with him the bishop of Le Puy so that these two could act in place of a fifth assessor. And we, bearing in mind the difficulty of this business, have decided to postpone making our reply to the king until we have your counsel thereon. Wherefore we require you to consider how harmful a delay in this matter may be to us, and to take pains to inform us quickly, in the fealty which binds you to us, of your advice about what we ought to reply to the king thereon. And likewise you should advise us whether we should take the bishop of Le Puy, whom we believe to be a good and trustworthy man and whom the king of France has proposed to us, as a fifth assessor in assessing the value of the territory of the Agenais.[4] And whereas you have informed us about holding a parliament, we inform you that it is not our will that any parliament should be held in our realm while we are absent, since this is improper, and we do not believe it to be consonant with our honour. However, it is well pleasing to us that the highest justice should be shown to all and sundry in our realm by Hugh Bigod, the justiciar of England, to whom we have entrusted the custody of our realm in our absence, by means of your counsel, provided that no new change or ordinance be made in our kingdom unless we are there and give our assent. Witness as above.[5]

By the king, Richard earl of Gloucester, and John Mansel.

iv

Bibliothèque Nationale, ms. lat. 9016, no.5
[Bémont, *Simon de Montfort*, pp.350–351]

A memorandum of charges laid by Henry III in 1260 against Simon de Montfort, earl of Leicester, and the earl's replies to them when they submitted their differences to the arbitration of Louis, king of France. Five clauses are excerpted from amongst the thirty-nine clauses of the document.

The king says that at the Michaelmas parliament[6] it was provided that no one should come to the parliament with horses and arms.

The earl says that he was not there, but it was a good decision.

The king says that he instructed his justiciar in England that, while he was overseas, no parliament was to be held until his return.

The earl says that it could well be that he gave him these instructions.

The king says that the justiciar forbade the earl and others of the council who were then there to have discussions and hold a parliament until the king's arrival.

The earl says that it could well be that the justiciar forbade it.

The king says that the earl came to London at Candlemas and held a parliament.

The earl says that it is laid down in the provisions[7] made together by

---

[4] Gavrilovitch, *Étude sur le traité de Paris de 1259*, p.47f.

[5] At St. Omer on 19 February 1260. On 24 January the king at St. Denis had written that he did not wish any parliament to be held during his absence and he forbade the issue to any writs of summons (*Close Rolls, 1259–61*, pp.235, 268). Writs had presumably been sent out before the king's letter arrived.

[6] I.e. 1259 (above, p.85).

[7] The 'Provisions of Oxford': see above, p.69.

the king and by his council that three parliaments are to be held a year, one of which is to be at Candlemas. And to keep his oath the earl came there, just as the other good men of the council who were in England did. And there the justiciar came at once and said to them on the king's behalf that they should not have held a parliament until the king's arrival, and the king had informed him that he should arrive within three weeks. And for this reason the parliament was adjourned from day to day for three weeks.

The king says that the earl came there at that time with horses and arms.

The earl says that he did not come there with either horses or arms but only in the manner in which he was wont to travel around the country.

PARLIAMENT AT LONDON: Easter 1260

i
Close Roll, no.76, m.2
[*Close Rolls, 1259-61, p.251*]

The king to the sheriff of Kent, greeting. Because the king proposes, God willing, to come soon to England because he intends to be present at the parliament in London Three Weeks after Easter last,[1] the sheriff is ordered, in readiness for the king's arrival there, to provide him with wine, namely, four tuns at Dover, four tuns at Canterbury, two tuns at Faversham, four tuns at Rochester, one tun at Sutton and one tun at Lessness. And the cost he incurs therein will be credited to him at the exchequer. Witness etc.[2]

ii
Close Roll, no.76, m.2d
[*Close Rolls, 1259-61, p.282-3*]

On behalf of the king

Because the king wished to stamp out matters of discord and to suppress all disputes and causes of dissension in order to foster unity and peace in his city of London and elsewhere in his realm, and he has heard that his son, Edward, is making arrangements to lodge with horses and arms during this parliament in the house of the bishop of London within St. Paul's Close, and the citizens of London are greatly afraid that there is a threat of danger therein, especially since that parliament is held against the king's will,[3] Hugh Bigod, the justiciar of England, is ordered not to permit Edward or anyone else, against whom any evil suspicion may be entertained, to lodge or be put up within the city walls to the peril of the king and the city, and he is in no way to fail therein in the fealty which binds him to the king and as he desires to avoid the king's wrath. And he can inform John of Warenne that he may lodge at Clerkenwell or at the New Temple. Witness etc. at St. Omer on the tenth day of April in the forty-fourth year etc.[4] And similar instructions are sent to the mayor and community of London.

[1] 25 April 1260. The king returned from abroad and reached London on 30 April.
[2] 7 April 1260.
[3] Cf. *Close Rolls, 1259-61*, pp.253-4, for the king's abhorrence, expressed on 11 April when he was at St. Omer, of those who meant to hold a parliament in haste at London, 'for to those who had eyes to see, such an assembly would seem more like drawing a sword than sowing the seeds of peace', and he urged obedience to the justiciar until he arrived back in England.
[4] 10 April 1260.

iii
Close Roll, no.76, m.1d
[*Close Rolls, 1259-61*, p.286-7]

The sheriff of Kent is ordered to postpone until the parliament next held all the distraints he is making on the men of Faversham on account of certain disputes arising between the abbot of Faversham and these men, with regard to which the abbot has recently received a royal writ, appointing a day against them before Hugh Bigod, the justiciar of England, and he is to let the parties know that they are to be there before the justiciar to receive justice thereon. Witness as above.[5]

iv
Curia Regis Roll, no.167 (Easter 1260), m.10
[*Trans. Royal Hist. Society*, Fourth Series, v. p.62]

Pleas of the Fifth Week of Easter and the Morrow of the Ascension continued.

Kent

The abbot of Faversham came by his attorney on the fourth day against Richard le Jovene [and twenty-one others], men of the abbot of Faversham, on the plea that they should keep the fine made for him in the court of king's bench at Westminster, between the abbot, plaintiff, and his men, defendants, with regard to this, that his men were to do him the customs and services which they ought to do him for their free tenements which they hold of him in Faversham, and that these men of his have established many new privileges against the abbot by encroaching upon his franchises, whereof a chirograph etc. And they do not come etc. And they made many defaults so that the sheriff was ordered to distrain them by all their lands etc., and from the issues etc., and to have them in person at this day. And the sheriff makes a return that he has done nothing about it because the king had ordered him by his writ to postpone the distraint until the present parliament, namely until now,[6] because he wished to show both the abbot and his men full justice before himself in this matter etc. And therefore, as before, the sheriff is ordered to distrain them by all their lands etc. . . . and to have them in person Three Weeks after Midsummer.

[5] 23 April 1260. Cf. the next document.
[6] The case is continued on m.24 to Michaelmas term but no reference seems to be made to it on the Michaelmas roll (Curia Regis Roll, no.168). In view of all the evidence there seems no reason to query the use of the term 'parliament' for this assembly (*Handbook of British Chronology*, p.503).

PARLIAMENT AT LONDON: Midsummer 1260

i

Curia Regis Roll, no.167 (Easter 1260), m.26

[*Eng. Hist. Review*, xxxvii, pp.81-2, 320]

Let it be noted that, whereas some disputes had arisen between the king of England on the one hand and Simon de Montfort, earl of Leicester, on the other with respect to certain trespasses with which the king has charged the earl, as contained in some articles which the king caused to be delivered to the earl and similarly in some other articles which the king intends to put forward, should it seem to him expedient, at the parliament a Fortnight after Midsummer[1] in the forty-fourth year of the reign of King Henry son of King John, that is to say, on St. Margaret's Day,[2] the king for his part has, at the instance of his magnates, agreed and granted and likewise the earl for his part has agreed and at once besought that the reverend fathers Boniface, archbishop of Canterbury, Henry, bishop of London, Richard, bishop of Lincoln, Walter, bishop of Worcester, Simon, bishop of Norwich and Walter, bishop of Exeter, should make a careful inquiry into all those trespasses, by the oath of good and law-worthy men by whom the truth of the aforesaid matters can best be investigated in every possible way available to them, and when they have made sufficient inquiry therein, they shall report their findings to the king and his council so that the council can adjudge suitable compensation to the king for the trespasses, if such there be, committed against him by the earl, in accordance with the investigations, and in order to make that judgement there are to be added [to the council] enough magnates, that is, earls and barons, the peers of the earl. And this inquiry shall be completed within the Octave of the Feast of St. Margaret if it can be done adequately. Nevertheless the archbishop and bishops may make inquiries into the aforesaid trespasses beyond that term-date until an adequate inquiry therein has been made. But it is to be done as quickly as possible. And the king will cause those to come before the archbishop and bishops through whom it is known that they can best ascertain the truth of the matter, and they are to put them on oath before them as they see fit. And if it should happen that there are some articles about which inquiry cannot be made so quickly, let another suitable term-day be appointed for making the investigation adequately, provided nevertheless that judgement should be reached without delay in accordance with the principles of justice as

---

[1] 8 July 1260.
[2] 20 July 1260.

regards other articles about which sufficient inquiry has been made. And note that it is quite lawful for the king for his part, and similarly for the earl for his part, to speak and put forward before the aforesaid investigators what seems to them relevant, and likewise there is reserved to the king and to the earl when the point of making judgement has been reached, their reasonable challenges concerning the persons of those who shall be present at the judgement. And note that the archbishop and bishops shall swear upon the Gospels that they will make the inquiry faithfully and without deception. And if all of them, archbishop and bishops, cannot be present at the inquiry, four of those who are present may proceed to make the inquiry.

ii

Patent Roll, no.74, m.5

[*Foedera*, I. i. 398; *Cal. Patent Rolls, 1258-66*, p.85]

On behalf of Roger Mortimer

The king to all etc. Know that, whereas we commanded our beloved and faithful Roger Mortimer to be with us at London a Fortnight after Midsummer last[2] to discuss with us and with the magnates of our council important and urgent business concerning us and our realm, the said Roger came by our special command to our said parliament at London on Saturday before the Feast of St. Margaret the Virgin,[3] where it was announced to us and to him on Tuesday, the said Feast of St. Margaret,[4] that Builth Castle, which was delivered into his custody by our son, Edward, had been captured by our enemies, the Welsh, on the aforesaid Saturday.[5] We also declare that we and our aforesaid son, who was in our presence at Westminster, have absolved Roger from whatever may be alleged against him or required of him by reason of the capture of the castle. Witness the king at Westminster the thirtieth day of July.[6]

---

[2] 8 July 1260. On 3 July arrangements had been made for venison to be provided for consumption during the parliament (*Cal. Liberate Rolls, 1251-60*, p.513).

[3] 17 July 1260.

[4] 20 July 1260.

[5] The messengers sent by prince Llewellyn of Wales to this parliament were on 8 July given letters of protection which were to last until 15 August (*Cal. Patent Rolls, 1258-66*, p.81).

[6] 30 July 1260.

PARLIAMENT AT LONDON: Michaelmas 1260

Patent Roll, no.74, m.4
[*Cal. Patent Rolls, 1258-66*, p.89 f.]

On behalf of the moneyers and other servants of the Exchange at London and Canterbury

The king to all etc. Know that, whereas we have lately caused our cities of London and Canterbury to be tallaged and for that reason we asked a reasonable tallage from the moneyers and other servants of our Exchange of these cities with the result that they have stated that they have so far not been accustomed to contribute to the tallages of these cities along with the other citizens thereof, and the moneyers and servants have promised us two hundred marks as an aid on condition that we confirmed for them by our charter the franchises they were wont to have hitherto, so it is said, by reason of the said Exchange, we attest that we have received the two hundred marks from them on this condition, namely, that when the magnates who are members of our council meet in London a Fortnight after Michaelmas next, we will confirm for them, as properly as possible, the said franchises in accordance with the articles which they recently sought before us and our council in our parliament at London, if this can be done by our council and meets the wishes of our said magnates. Otherwise we will have the said money allowed to William of Gloucester, the keeper of our Exchange, in the issues of the Exchange, to be repaid to the moneyers and servants aforesaid. In witness whereof etc. Witness the king at Windsor on the sixteenth day of August.[1]

By the king and Philip Basset

---

[1] 16 August 1260. For an important case on 3 November 1260 before the justiciar of England, the magnates of the council, the justices of the bench specially appointed by the king, and the barons of the exchequer, which may well have been heard during this parliament, see Curia Regis Roll, no.168, m.8. It concerned to inheritance of Isabella de Forz (see above, p.86, below, pp.101, 109).

PARLIAMENT AT LONDON: Candlemas 1261

i

Close Roll, no.77, m.19d

[*Close Rolls, 1259-61*, p.457]

Concerning the knights coming to the king

The king to William de Kenes, greeting. Whereas we recently wrote to tell you that you were to come to us at once to talk with us, and we have just heard some reports which make it advisable for you to be summoned and come to our approaching parliament at London, we order and require you, in the faith and love whereby you are bound to us, that as soon as you have seen this letter you are to put aside everything else and come to us at London with horses and arms so as to be there at all costs in the aforesaid parliament. And you are in no way to fail to do this, as you love us and the safety of our realm. Witness myself at the Tower of London on the seventeenth day of February.[1]

> A similar letter was sent to twenty-six others, including the earl of Winchester and the earl of Warwick.

ii

Close Roll, no.77, m.17

[*Close Rolls, 1259-61*, p.343]

On behalf of Cok son of Aaron the Jew of London

Whereas the king at the instance of his son Edward has lately absolved John de Berners from the penalty of twenty pounds a year which he was bound to pay Cok son of Aaron the Jew of London because he did not keep the dates for the payment of debts he owed Cok, and the king has instructed the justices assigned for the custody of the Jews to restore to John his charter relating to that penalty which is in the chest of the king's Jews of London, and the king has now learned that this charter was made for a clear debt in accordance with the custom of the king's Jewry and not by way of a penalty, the king has given Cok, in return for a fine which he made with the king, a postponement in the restoration of the charter to John until the king's parliament Three Weeks after the Purification of the Blessed Mary[2] so that it can then be

---

[1] 17 February 1261.
[2] 23 February 1261.

discussed before the king's barons of the exchequer and before the justices whether the charter relates to a penalty or to a debt, as Cok states. And the justices are instructed to let Cok have a postponement in the restoration of the charter. Witness the king at Windsor on the third day of February.[3]

On behalf of John de Berners

Afterwards the justices were told that, notwithstanding the aforesaid instructions, they were to have the charter restored to John. Witness the king at Windsor on the sixth day of February.[4]

iii
Assize Roll, no.911, m.6
[*Trans. Royal Hist. Soc.*, Fourth Series, v. p.61]

Roger Bigod, the Marshal of England, comes by Walter of Bury St. Edmunds, his servant, and asks for custody of all prisoners who are adjudged to prison before the chief justiciar, together with the profits arising from such imprisonments, whether in the eyres of the chief justiciar throughout England or in the king's bench. And as regards these profits Walter says that the Marshal, his master, was in peaceful possession of them during the whole time of Hugh Bigod, formerly the chief justiciar,[5] in his various eyres throughout England. And because Hugh Despenser, the chief justiciar,[6] wishes that nothing prejudicial to the king shall be done in this matter and he does not know whether the custody and the profits belong to the king or to the Marshal, therefore Walter is told to have all the profits, arising out of such imprisonments in the eyre of that justiciar, before the next parliament, which will be a week after the Purification of the Blessed Mary,[7] readily available at that parliament so that they may be rendered to the king or to the marshal, his master, in accordance with what the magnates of the king's council shall decide. And the aforesaid custody is also to be discussed there.

---

[3] 3 February 1261.
[4] 6 February 1261.
[5] June 1258–October 1260.
[6] October 1260–June 1261.
[7] 9 February 1261.

PARLIAMENT AT WINDSOR: 21 September 1261

i
Close Roll, no.77, m.6*d*
[*Close Rolls, 1259-61*, p.490]

The barons' plans for reform had given parliament a prominent place
in the governance of the country. Had they authority to summon
parliament if the king failed to do so? This lay at the heart of the
contest between them, and to it the nature of the business before
parliament was irrelevant and indeed meaningless.

The king to the sheriff of Norfolk and Suffolk, greeting. Whereas on
the initiative of the bishop of Worcester, the earls of Leicester and
Gloucester and some other nobles of our realm three knights have been
summoned from each of our counties to be before them at St. Albans at
the approaching Feast of St. Matthew the Apostle,[1] to discuss with
them the general business of our kingdom, and we and our aforesaid
nobles are to meet at Windsor on the same day to confer about peace
between us and them, we command you to give firm instructions on
our behalf to those knights of your bailiwick who have been
summoned before them on the aforesaid day that they are to set aside all
obstacles and come to us at the aforesaid day at Windsor, and you are
also to forbid them strictly not to go on the said day anywhere else than
to us, but you are to have them come at all costs before us on the
aforesaid day to have discussion with us on the aforesaid matters so that
they can see and understand as a result of what is done that we are not
proposing to attempt anything save what we know befits the honour
and common welfare of our realm. Witness the king at Windsor on the
eleventh day of September.[2]

Similar instructions are sent to each of the sheriffs below the river
Trent.

ii
Ancient Correspondence, vii, no.33

Some historians have denied that any assembly met at Windsor,
others have been content to place a question mark against it, others
seem to have accepted it. It is perhaps impossible to be certain either
way, but this unique letter suggests that knights had indeed been

[1] 21 September 1261.
[2] 11 September 1261.

selected and were preparing to set off on their journey to St. Albans. It should be noticed that Philip Basset, the Justiciar, has no hesitation in terming the assembly the king's parliament.

To his most dear friend, Walter of Merton, the king's chancellor, Philip Basset, greeting and sincere affection. We beseech you to say to the king in the best way you can that he should dispatch his letters to Roger de Sumery [3-]at Bradfield[-3] to tell him to come to his parliament, just as he has instructed others to do. And this he should not fail to do, because we have learned from some people's information that he is proposing to go to St. Albans if he does not previously receive a letter of summons from the king.[4]

[3-3] Interlined in MS.

[4] Roger was lord of Dudley and one of those responsible for the Dictum of Kenilworth in 1266 (see below, p.112).

PARLIAMENT AT LONDON: Candlemas 1262

B.L., Cotton MS., Titus A 14
['Annals of Wykes' in *Annales Monastici*, iv. 130]

We have not been able to find an official document connected with this parliament. But it should be noted that on 11 December 1261 a writ was sent to the knights and free men of every county, informing them that, if they wished to have one of themselves appointed sheriff until Michaelmas 1262 by their own choice, then they were to elect four knights who were willing to assume that office and send them to Westminster at Hilary (altered to 26 February) so that the brother of the king, acting on his behalf, could make one of them sheriff, 'as arranged in the form of peace provided between us and our barons'. In the meanwhile they were to carry out the king's instructions, as sent to them by writ, in the sheriff's stead lest the absence of a sheriff should delay or prevent justice (Chancery Miscellanea, bundle 14, file 3, no.56). This interesting document seems to have escaped notice.

About the Feast of the Purification of the Blessed Mary[1] a parliament was held at London, and the king and the barons accepted the arbitration of the king of France and the king of Germany.[2]

[1] 2 February 1262.

[2] I.e. the king's brother, the earl of Cornwall.

PARLIAMENT AT LONDON: Michaelmas 1262

i

B.L., Cotton MS. Julius D.5, fo.35
[Gervase of Canterbury, *Historical Works*, ii. 217]

This information does not come from Gervase of Canterbury himself but is contained in an independent Canterbury chronicle in several recessions, one of which was made at Dover (Gervase, ii. p.xxii). Earl Simon landed at New Romney and must have passed through Canterbury. The king got wind of his intentions and wrote a letter of warning on 8 October (*Foedera*, I. i. 442) to Philip Basset and Walter of Merton, the chancellor. Then on 24 October he wrote to them again, as well as to the treasurer, ordering them to prevent any parliaments being held until his return to England (*Close Rolls, 1261-64*, p.162). A parliament had been held, however, and it remained in session until Earl Simon arrived. Quite clearly many of the barons regarded the Provisions of Oxford as still alive, no matter the papal bull the king had obtained for their annulment.

In this year the earl Simon of Leicester returned secretly to London, not yet having made his peace with the king of England, and he landed at New Romney on Thursday before the Feast of St. Luke,[1] that is, the Ides of October. And he came to London on the Feast of St. Edward[2] to the parliament held by Philip Basset, then the justiciar of England, and he brought with him a letter from the pope, ordering the Provisions made at Oxford to be held in all respects, for the pope said that he had been deceived, and his court had been deceived, when the king sued for a letter of absolution from the oath he had previously taken to observe the aforesaid Provisions. And after this letter from the pope had been exhibited to the barons of the land by Earl Simon although this was against the wishes of the justiciar, he went back overseas at once, crossing at Shoreham, and he left behind him in England many associates and supporters to further his proposals.

ii

Ancient Correspondence, vii, no.211

The top left-hand corner of this undated letter has been torn away so that the name of the writer is unfortunately missing but it was

---

[1] 12 October 1262.
[2] 13 October 1262.

probably Philip Basset, the justiciar,[3] who presided at a parliament in London at Candlemas in October 1262. It illustrates how parliament was being used at this time to settle private disputes likely to cause a serious breach of the peace.

[Philip Basset, justiciar] to his very dear Walter of Merton, the king's chancellor, greeting with sincere affection. Because in the uncertainty within the realm it is essential to protect as strongly as possible the franchises granted by kings and to defend them so that an occasion for offending may be removed from those who desire to promote dissension, we request you that, whereas a certain man called Hugh of Weston of the county of Shropshire has hunted in the warren of Henry of Pembridge, our kinsman, at Tong in the aforesaid county without Henry's permission in order thereby to create somehow a cause of dissension from which greater mischief may arise in consequence, you are for our sake to arrange for Henry to have such a writ as will compel Hugh to come before us in the next parliament to answer more fully upon the aforesaid trespass. Greeting.

Endorsed: To Walter of Merton, the king's chancellor.

---

[3] He held office from June 1261 to July 1263.

PARLIAMENT AT LONDON: 8 September 1263

Fine Roll, no.60, m.3
[*Excerpta e Rotulis Finium, 1226-1272*, ii. 402]

On behalf of Isabella de Forz, countess of Aumale, concerning her feudal relief

The king to William of Wayland, his escheator below the river Trent, greeting. Because John de Warenne, William de Valence, the king's brother, and Hugh Bigod have given a guarantee before us on behalf of Isabella de Forz, countess of Aumale, sister and heiress of Baldwin de l'Isle, late earl of Devon, that she will come in person to us in our next parliament, which will be at London on the Feast of the Nativity of the Blessed Mary next,[1] to do us homage for all the lands and tenements which belonged to Baldwin on the day he died and to pay us her feudal relief, we have committed the said lands and tenements to her. And therefore we order you to let Isabella have full seisin of all the lands and tenements of which Baldwin was seised in his demesne as of fee in your bailiwick on the day he died. Witness the king at Westminster on the seventeenth day of August.[2]

[1] 8 September 1263.
[2] 17 August 1263: see p.107f. below. The bishop of Bath and Wells, on account of illness, appointed the archdeacon of Wells as his proxy to this meeting: he gives simply the date and place and makes no reference to parliament (S.C.10, file 1, no.5).

PARLIAMENT AT LONDON: Michaelmas 1263

Patent Roll, no.79, m.2
[*Foedera*, I. i. 433; *Cal. Patent Rolls, 1258-1266*, p.280]

The envoys of Llewellyn ap Gruffydd, coming to the king at the parliament at Three Weeks after Michaelmas, have the king's letters of safe-conduct in going, staying and departing, to last until Martinmas next. Witness as above.[1]

[1] 18 September 1263.

PARLIAMENT AT LONDON: Midsummer 1264

i

Patent Roll, no.81, m.6*d*

[*Foedera*, I. i. 443; *Cal. Patent Rolls, 1258-1266*, p.365]

This is the form of peace approved by general agreement of the king and the lord Edward, his son, of all the prelates and nobles and the whole community of the realm of England,[1] namely, that a certain ordinance, made in the parliament held at London about the Feast of the Nativity of St. John the Baptist last,[2] for the preservation of the peace of the realm, is to stand firm, stable and unbroken until the previous peace between the king and the barons at Lewes[3] shall be completed in the terms of a certain agreement, to last throughout the life of the aforesaid king as well as the time of the lord Edward after he has become king until a date which hereafter has to be agreed.

The said ordinance is as follows.[4]

ii

Patent Roll, no.81, m.12*d*

[*Foedera*, I. i. 442; *Cal. Patent Rolls, 1258-1266*, p.360]

Keepers of the peace were appointed in each county and received instructions *inter alia* as follows:

And because it will needs behove us in our approaching parliament to discuss the business of us and our realm with the prelates and magnates and our other loyal subjects, we order you to send us on behalf of the whole shire four of the more law-worthy and distinguished knights of the shire, elected by assent of the shire for this purpose, so that they may be with us at London on the Octave of the approaching Feast of Holy Trinity[5] at the latest to discuss with us the aforesaid business. And you are to show yourself so loyal and diligent in executing all those matters

[1] In mid-August 1264.

[2] 24 June 1264.

[3] That is, the so-called Mise of Lewes in May 1264.

[4] There follows the 'Form to regulate the king and kingdom', as printed in *Foedera*, I. i. 443 and Stubbs, *Select Charters* (9th. ed.), pp.400-02. For a discussion of this and associated texts, see N.Denholm-Young, 'Documents of the Barons' War' in *Eng. Hist. Review*, xlviii, 558-575.

[5] 22 June 1264.

that we need not proceed against you and yours on account of your negligence. Witness the king at St. Paul's, London, on the fourth day of June.[6]

iii

Close Roll, no.81, m.4d (schedule)
[*Close Rolls, 1261-64, p.395*]

The king to the sheriff of Essex, greeting. Whereas it has not yet been decided by us, our prelates and barons, whether ecclesiastical persons ought to pay us a subsidy for the defence of our realm against invasion by foreigners, and whereas the men of Coggeshall, on the ground that we lately ordered you to arrange for four or six men from each township in your county, depending on the size of the township, to come to us at London, for whom expenses for forty days are to be provided at common charge, are demanding from the vicar of the church that he should, in discharge of the property of his vicarage, contribute to the expenses of the men of his township who are to be sent to us, we instruct you to have that demand postponed until our very next parliament so that provision may be made by counsel of our aforesaid barons concerning what should be done in the matter. And you are to have him released from distraint in the meantime, if any has been made upon him on this account. Witness the king at St. Paul's, London, on the twenty-eighth day of July.[7]

iv

Ancient Correspondence, ii. no.129

Greeting. Since the rebellion raised in our kingdom has recently by God's grace been suppressed, we have proclaimed that a parliament is to be held at London, and we have caused you, as well as other nobles of our realm, to be summoned by our special letters to discuss and ordain upon the state of the realm. Furthermore, we have ordered you and others that you are to take care to bring with you to the said parliament the prisoners whom you are keeping in your custody by authority of us or anyone else as well as in your own name. But whereas all others have done this with the promptitude arising from fealty and devotion, we marvel and at the

---

[6] 4 June 1264.

[7] 28 July 1264. An order was made on 7 August that ecclesiastics were not to be distrained for these expenses, 'especially since we intend by the counsel and assent of our prelates and nobles to have a suitable subsidy from them'. This was a tenth (*Close Rolls, 1261-64, pp.403-5*).

same time are perturbed that you and some others of our March of Wales have scorned our orders in this matter, you whom we believed we would have found readiest among all to obey them. And also – which we take most unkindly – you have added scorn upon scorn by presuming after our instructions to ransom for heavy sums some of the aforesaid prisoners whom you have in custody only by our authority. Therefore we order you and firmly enjoin you, in the fealty and homage whereby you are bound to us, that you are, as soon as you have seen our letter, to hasten to come to us wherever we may be in England with your aforesaid prisoners, as you hold dear your person and tenements and all the property you hold in our realm, to answer why you have not executed our orders in this matter. Otherwise, should we find you disobedient to our orders and contravening our peace, we will proceed with severity against your person, your tenements and all your property. And so that you can come to us in greater safety, we have decided to send you our letters of safe conduct. Witness.[8]

---

[8] This is a much corrected draft of the letter eventually sent to Roger de Clifford, Roger Mortimer, James Audley and Hugh Turberville on 3 July 1264 (*Cal. Patent Rolls, 1258-66*, p.362.

PARLIAMENT AT LONDON: Hilary 1265

Close Roll, no.82, m.11d (schedule)
[*Close Rolls, 1264-68*, pp.84-87]

Henry by the grace of God king of England, lord of Ireland and duke of Aquitaine, to the reverend father in Christ Robert, by the same grace bishop of Durham, greeting. Whereas after the grave peril lately arising out of the rebellion in our realm our dearly beloved son Edward, our first-born, has been delivered as a hostage in order to strengthen and confirm peace within our realm, and now, the aforesaid rebellion having, thank God, subsided, in order to provide for his safe release and to strengthen and bring fully to pass the complete assurance of tranquillity and peace to the honour of God and the welfare of our whole kingdom and in order to transact some other business of our realm, which we cannot expedite without your counsel and that of our other prelates and magnates with whom it is essential for us to have discussion, we order and require you, in the faith and love whereby you are bound to us, that you brush aside all hindrances and postpone all other business and be with us at London at the Octave of Hilary next[1] to discuss these matters with us and with our aforesaid prelates and magnates, whom we have caused to be summoned there, and to give us your counsel. And you shall in no way fail to do this, as you love us, and our honour and your own and the general tranquillity of our realm. Witness the king at Worcester the fourteenth day of December.[2]

> Similar writs were sent to other bishops, abbots and priors (120 prelates in all) and to twenty-three earls and magnates.

Likewise all sheriffs throughout England are ordered in the aforesaid manner to arrange for two knights from the most law-worthy, respected and distinguished knights of all the shires to come to the king at London at the said Octave.

Likewise the citizens of York, Lincoln and other boroughs of England are written to in the aforesaid manner to send two of the most distinguished, law-worthy and respected citizens as well as burgesses in the manner aforesaid.

[1] 20 January 1265.
[2] 14 December 1264.

Likewise the barons and respected men of the Cinque Ports received instructions in the aforesaid manner, as contained in the writ enrolled below.[3]

---

[3] A writ, dated 20 January 1265, ordering each of the Cinque Ports to send four men to parliament. Knights from Shropshire and Staffordshire failed to appear, and the sheriff received further instructions on 23 February to send them by 8 March (*Close Rolls, 1264-68*, p.98f.). It was noted on 15 February that the knights had had to stay at parliament longer than they had anticipated, and arrangements were to be made for them to receive their travel expenses both ways and the cost of subsistence while in London (*ibid.*, p.96). The parliament was still in session on 8 March (*Cal. Charter Rolls, 1259-1300*, p.54). The prior of Christ Church, Canterbury, received £14 for his expenses in going to London to the 'parliament after Christmas' (Lambeth MS. 242, fo.8b).

PARLIAMENT AT WESTMINSTER: 1 June 1265

Dangerous dissension forced Simon de Montfort to go to the west of England and this parliament did not meet, though even as late as 15 May it was still officially considered possible for it to assemble. The documents issued in anticipation of this parliament are too illuminating to be omitted on the ground that it did not meet.

i

Close Roll, no.82, m.7

[*Close Rolls, 1264-68*, p.36]

On behalf of Peter of Savoy, John de Warenne and others to be summoned

The king to the sheriff of Sussex, greeting. Summon by four law-worthy knights of your shire Peter of Savoy at Pevensey, John de Warenne at Lewes, and Hugh Bigod at Bosham to be before us and our council in our next parliament at London on the first day of June,[1] to do and receive justice. And you are to have it proclaimed in full county court that, if anyone in the service of Peter, John and Hugh wishes in the mean time to procure or ask for a safe-conduct in coming to us and staying to stand trial in our court, should anyone wish to complain against him, he may come with safety and we will have such a safe-conduct made for him. And you are to have there the names of the aforesaid four knights, and this writ. Witness the king at Westminster on the nineteenth day of March.[2]

By the whole council.

Similar instructions are given to the sheriff of Herefordshire for summoning William de Valence at Brickendon.

By the whole council.

ii

Close Roll, no.82, m.6*d*

[*Close Rolls, 1264-68*, p.118]

The king to the sheriff of Hampshire. Whereas John de Warenne, William de Valence and Hugh Bigod have lately guaranteed[3] on behalf of Isabella de Forz, countess of Aumale, sister and heiress of Baldwin de

---

[1] 1 June 1265.

[2] 19 March 1265.

[3] 17 August 1262 (see above, p.101).

l'Isle, late earl of Devon, that she would come in person to us at the Feast of the Nativity of the Blessed Mary in the forty-seventh year of our reign,[4] to do us her homage for all the lands and tenements which belonged to Baldwin on the day he died and to pay us her feudal relief at our exchequer, we therefore delivered the said lands and tenements to Isabella. And Isabella has not kept the said day. Therefore we have lately ordered you to take into our hands without delay the lands and tenements in your bailiwick which belonged to Baldwin and to keep them safely until we give you other instructions thereon. Wishing still to deal graciously with Isabella in this matter, we order you to permit the countess's bailiffs to have custody of the aforesaid lands and tenements in your bailiwick, without making any waste therein, until the next parliament which will be at London on the first day of June next. And if you have received anything from the profits of the aforesaid lands and tenements, you are to return it meanwhile to the said bailiffs without delay. Witness the king at Hereford on the twelfth day of May.[5]

By the Justiciar and Peter de Montfort.

iii
Close Roll, no.82, m.6d
[*Close Rolls, 1264-68*, p.117]

The king to the bishop of Bangor, greeting. It has been shown to us on behalf of Llewellyn ap Gruffydd that, whereas he has often offered you sufficient warranty for himself and his men that they would obey the lawful mandates of the Church, should they have offended in any way against you to the prejudice of the privileges of the Church, you have so far refused to accept such warranty and furthermore you have laid his chapel under an interdict for causes that do not pertain to ecclesiastical jurisdiction but solely to a lay court, for example, lay fees. And because we cannot tolerate this, as indeed we should not, especially since pleas concerning lay fees within our realm pertain to our crown and dignity, we order and require you to revoke the interdict without further delay or at least postpone it until our approaching parliament which we are about to hold at Westminster, where you will be present, together with other prelates of our realm, in accordance with our command, so that after discussion on the aforesaid matters there may be done therein to each party what of right ought to be done. Witness as above.[6]

---

[4] 8 September 1263.
[5] 12 May 1265.
[6] 15 May 1265.

iv

Close Roll, no.82, m.6d

[*Close Rolls, 1264-68*, p.116f]

The king to the dean and chapter of York, greeting. Whereas we have already caused the prelates and magnates of our realm to be summoned to be with us at Winchester[7] on the first of June next to discuss with us the business touching ourselves and our kingdom, and we cannot finally complete it unless they are present, we order you, in the faith and love whereby you are bound to us, firmly requiring you to send at all costs two of your wisest canons at the said day and place, and they are to have full power in your stead to discuss this business with us, together with the prelates and magnates, and to do in your name those things which you yourselves could do if you were there present. And you are in no wise to fail to do this, as you love us and the welfare of our kingdom. Witness the king at Gloucester the fifteenth day of May.[8]

v

Ancient Correspondence, iv. no.145

[Cf. Prynne, *Exact Chronological Vindication* (usually abbreviated as *Records*), iii. 122]

To his most serene prince and dearest lord Henry, by the grace of God the illustrious king of England, lord of Ireland and duke of Aquitaine, his ever most devoted in all things brother Hugh,[9] by Divine permission the humble minister of the church of Ramsey, wishing you the enjoyment of good health with devout and continual prayers of intercession. Since we are laid up in bed and labouring under a most serious illness and exceedingly weak we are not well enough to be at London on the Morrow of Trinity,[10] for which we are very sorry. Therefore we have appointed our beloved in Christ brother W.[illiam of Godmanchester], our sacristan, and William Chamberlain, our steward, to be, either one of them, our attorney to give assent in our place to the advice of the magnates then and there present and to do those things which touch your royal dignity and the welfare and peace of your realm, earnestly beseeching your royal majesty to admit our aforesaid attorneys in our place, bearing in mind the mercy of God and the frailty of man, and to hold our compulsory absence excused. May your royal lordship flourish evermore.

[7] A clerical error for 'Westminster'.

[8] 15 May 1265.

[9] Hugh of Sulgrave, abbot from 1254 to 1268. For his excuse, on the ground of illness, from attending the Hilary parliament of 1265 and appointing the same proxies, see S.C.10, file 1, no.6.

[10] 1 June 1265.

PARLIAMENT AT WINCHESTER: September 1265

i

King's Bench Plea Roll, no.37 (Easter 1278), m.32

An action between Richard of Culworth, plaintiff, and Adam of Montalt, Walter of Gayton and John of Montalt, defendants. In the course of the proceedings it was evident that an assize of novel disseisin, held during the Barons' Rebellion, had been so complicated that it baffled the justices appointed to take it. One of the defendants made this statement:

The war began to grow increasingly severe with the consequence that, if ever any judgement had been contrary to the findings of the assize jury, Richard procured that judgement to be made at that time, a time when, so it seems to him, judgements are binding upon no one, and particularly do not bind Adam and Walter in this case, for they faithfully adhered to the king's side at this time and they did not then dare to appear openly in order to claim their legal right therein. And afterwards, when the battle of Evesham was over, one Osbert Giffard came and occupied the tenement and held it thus occupied until after the parliament of Winchester when Adam and Walter recovered their right therein through the lord king Henry and his council to the effect, namely, that the freehold was to remain Walter's and the leasehold Adam's and Osbert was to have, in return for the seisin he had held, all the chattels found in the tenement at the time when the occupation was made. And John of Montalt says that after Adam's lease was up Walter enfeoffed the said John with the tenement. Wherefore he prays judgement whether an assize ought to proceed upon the aforesaid occupation made in time of war, an occupation which Richard plainly acknowledged had been made between the battle of Evesham and the parliament of Winchester, a time which was a time of war.

ii

Patent Roll, no.86, m.3

[*Cal. Patent Rolls, 1266-72*, p.265]

On behalf of William of Saham, clerk

The king to all etc., greeting. Know that, at the instance of our beloved and faithful Philip Basset and the lately deceased Hugh Bigod we remitted in our parliament at Winchester in the forty-ninth year of our reign all the resentment and rancour we conceived against William of

Saham, clerk, formerly in the household of Hugh Despenser, by reason of the trespasses alleged against him in the time of the recent rebellion in our realm, and we have pardoned him any trespasses and serious offences he may have committed at that time. And we will and command that, with respect to lands, tenements or any other goods of his, even though they have been seized into our hands on account of the said trespasses and offences, he shall henceforth be in no way molested or in any way harassed or aggrieved by us or ours. In witness whereof etc. Witness as above.[1]

[1] 20 October 1268. The property of rebels had, with the consent of the magnates in the parliament at Winchester, passed into the king's hands (*Cal. Patent Rolls, 1258-66*, p.490, *1266-72*, p.63).

PARLIAMENT AT NORTHAMPTON: 30 April 1266

Guildhall, London: Liber de Antiquis Legibus, fo.98
[*Liber de Antiquis Legibus*, pp.84–85]

Then, round about the Feast of the Apostles Philip and James[1] the king held a parliament at Northampton. To that parliament the city of London sent solemn envoys, petitioning the king that he would restore them to their former status and that they might elect sheriffs of their own who would answer to the king's exchequer for the ancient farm. Returning thence from the parliament they came to London on the Vigil of the Ascension[2] and brought close and patent letters from the king.[3]

[1] 1 May 1266.
[2] 5 May 1266.
[3] These letters granting the city's request are dated at Northampton on 30 April and 1 May.

PARLIAMENT AT KENILWORTH: 22 August 1266

Patent Roll, no.84, m.9d
[*Cal. Patent Rolls, 1258-66*, p.671 f.]

Whereas our lord Henry, by the grace of God king of England, at the Octave of the Assumption of our Lady in the fiftieth year of his coronation,[1] had summoned his parliament to Kenilworth at the request of the honourable father Ottobuono, legate of England, it was agreed and granted by common assent and by common counsel of the bishops, abbots, priors, earls, barons and all others that the six subscribed persons, namely, the bishop of Exeter, the bishop of Bath, the bishop-elect of Worcester, Sir Alan la Zuche, Sir Roger de Sumery and Sir Robert Walerand, by their oath which they there made, were to elect six others who should be under least suspicion and most knowledgeable and willing to follow their instructions, and one of these was to be a prelate and five to be knights. And these twelve were to swear on the Holy Gospels that they will rightly, loyally and carefully bring to pass what they understand to be best for the restoration and strengthening of the peace of the realm, that is to say, with respect to what pertains to the business and the estate of those disinherited by reason of the recent war in England, saving the estate and dignity of the king. And if it happens that the twelve cannot agree in something pertaining to this business, the aforesaid legate and Sir Henry of Almain shall be summoned to join the aforesaid twelve. And whatever is proposed by the party to which the legate and Sir Henry of Almain give their joint assent, is to stand firm and established. And if it should happen that all twelve are in agreement, they shall not say or do anything until they have reported to the king and the legate and Sir Henry of Almain, and to deal with this business the king shall summon whom he will. And whatever the king and the legate and Sir Henry shall agree or provide shall stand firm and established. And if the six disagree in electing the other six, that party shall prevail whom the legate and Sir Henry support. And if it happens that any of the twelve should die before this business is finished, those who are left shall have power to choose others in place of those who have died, provided that there are four prelates and eight knights. And it is to be noted that these twelve have power to make provisions and ordinances until the Feast of All Saints next. And if those who shall be summoned to accept the king's peace by such ordinance do not come to his peace within forty days after it has been published throughout all counties by the king and

[1] 22 August 1266.

by the legate, from that time forward they are not to be admitted to his peace by this ordinance. In witness and in establishment whereof the aforesaid lord the king and the lord legate and Sir Edward, the king's son, and the earl of Gloucester have put their seals to this writing. Given at Kenilworth the thirty-first day of August in the year of the Incarnation of our Lord 1266.[2]

[2] 31 August 1266. The committee's deliberations resulted in the Dictum of Kenilworth, published on 31 October 1266 (*Statutes of the Realm*, i. 12-17).

PARLIAMENT AT BURY ST. EDMUNDS: 7 February 1267

i

Patent Roll, no.85, m.23*d*

[*Cal. Patent Rolls, 1266-1272*, p.133]

The king to the legate, greeting. Having heard and understood what Master William de Clifford, our clerk, has expounded to us on your behalf, we wish you, father, to know that . . . as regards the legal rights and franchises of London, we will be at pains to decide in our present parliament at Bury St. Edmunds what will be most convenient for us and the aforesaid city to get done . . . Witness the king at Cambridge on the eighth day of March.[1]

ii

Close Roll, no.84, m.9*d*

[*Close Rolls, 1264-68*, p.364 f.]

Note that on the seventh day of February in the fifty-first year of the reign of King Henry, son of King John,[2] Geoffrey of Upton came to Bury St. Edmunds before the king and all his council in the king's chancery and of his own free and good will he gave, granted and quitclaimed on behalf of himself and his heirs to William Gifford and his heirs or assigns the said Geoffrey of Upton's manor with its member of Waldridge and everything else pertaining to that manor, and all his wood of Hampden with all its appurtenances save that croft in Hampden which Geoffrey had previously given to God and St. Mary Magdalen's church in Hampden in perpetual alms. And in order that the aforesaid gift, grant and quitclaim may achieve firm security, Geoffrey prayed that we would confirm it on behalf of the aforesaid William, his heirs and assigns, with respect to all the matters aforesaid.

---

[1] 8 March 1267. Parliament had been apparently in session at Bury St. Edmunds for a month or more: cf. the next document.

[2] 7 February 1267.

PARLIAMENT AT MARLBOROUGH: 18 November 1267

Red Book of the Exchequer, f. 243
[*Statutes of the Realm*, i. 19 ff.]

In the year of grace 1267 and the fifty-second year of the reign of King Henry, son of King John, at the octave of Martinmas[1] when the more distinguished men of the realm, both great and small, had been called together when the king provided for the betterment of his realm of England and the dispensation of justice as the service of his royal office demands, and it was provided, enacted and unanimously decreed that, whereas the kingdom of England, recently oppressed by many tribulations and the hardships of rebellion, needs her laws and customs to be reformed and thereby the peace and tranquillity of her inhabitants preserved, for which reason it was essential for the king and his loyal subjects to provide salutary redress, the subscribed provisions, ordinances and statutes are to be observed firmly and inviolably in future by all the inhabitants of the said kingdom, both great and small.[2]

[1] 18 November 1267.
[2] Then follows the Statute of Marlborough.

PARLIAMENT AT NORTHAMPTON: July 1268

B.L., Cotton MS., Domitian A. xiii, f. 59*b*
['Annals of Winton' in *Annales Monastici*, ii. 106–7]

The legate set out thence to Northampton where the king and other magnates of the realm held a great parliament at which the legate was present, and the legate begged leave to return home. And there the lord Edward and his brother Edmund and many other magnates of the realm were signed with the cross as crusaders by the said legate.[1]

[1] Cf. *Florence of Worcester, Continuation*, ii. 201: apud Norhamtoniam, rege ibidem cum proceribus parlamentum tenente.

PARLIAMENT AT LONDON: Michaelmas 1268

i

Close Rolls, no.85, m.4*d*

[*Close Rolls, 1264-1268*, p.552]

The king to the king of France, greeting and a happy issue to your desires. We admitted happily and joyously into our presence, as was proper, the distinguished Brother Roger, the prior of Valverde la Vega, sent as your messenger with full authority, and we offer praise to God because He has strengthened you in so solemn an undertaking, so pleasing unto Him. We are also grateful, indeed we give most fervent thanks unto the Lord, that you should deign to communicate it to us and to discuss with us in confidence how to accomplish it. And so, my lord, we would by all means come to you at Boulogne by the sea at the term appointed if the business of the crusade did not detain us. For we have convoked our general, full and solemn parliament at the approaching Fortnight after Michaelmas[1] at London so that we can discuss the business and provide in detail what can most safely be done and make more definite arrangements thereon with our nobles who are going on crusade. Wherefore we beseech your Highness with all possible affection that you should hold us excused at present and be good enough to provide and appoint another day for us after the approaching Christmas but please at the place mentioned so that we may direct our steps to you immediately after Epiphany. For we are hoping by God's grace to arrange what we do therein in such a way that, putting everything else aside, we may meet you in the aforesaid place, or in another as you shall decide to inform us, and the sooner the better for us, as you know. But, because messages have often been exchanged between us concerning the three bishoprics, namely Cahors, Limoges and Périgueux, and we ought at the approaching Martinmas to address ourselves specially to you on behalf of this business, and we are quite certain that it can be better discussed and even settled when we are present in person, we pray you to be so good as to postpone it until our arrival after Christmas, as we have suggested. But – and we add this most earnestly – we ask that the queen, our consort, may come then so that we can find comfort in seeing and conversing with her, as we are specially devoted to her. And in order that we can most usefully make our arrangements upon all the aforesaid matters, may it please you fully to announce your pleasure within a month after this approaching Michaelmas and we will take care to adapt ours to it as far as we can, God willing. Witness the king at York on the twentieth day of September.[2]

[1] 12 October 1268. Cf. Gervase of Canterbury, *Historical Works*, ii. 247.
[2] 20 September 1268.

ii
Assize Roll, no.618, m.17d

Walter Hyddeburn was attached by presentment of the jury of Fawsley to come here before the justices concerning a trespass committed by him in the time of the rebellion. And he came. And the justices charged him with being against the king and preaching on behalf of the earl, justifying the earl's side and criticising the king's side, wrongfully and against the peace etc. in the time of rebellion etc.

And Walter comes and denies force and whatever is in breach of the peace etc., and says that he never was against the king in deed or in preaching. And he asks for an inquiry to be made by the country.

And the twelve jurors of Fawsley, except William Evermond and Hugh le Botiler, together with the hundred of Cleyley and the hundred of Wymersley and Spelhoe, say on their oath as follows: Cleyley, Wymersley and Spelhoe do not agree with the hundred of Fawsley, but these three hundreds say on their oath that he never was against the king in deed or in preaching and he did not harbour any wrongdoers. When the jurors of the hundred of Fawsley were questioned, they say that, when William Marshal assembled the people of the county of Northampton at Cow Meadow near Northampton, Walter was William's assistant and, when William held his peace from preaching to the people on behalf of the earl of Leicester, Walter preached on the earl's behalf. And because the justices do not wish the jury of Fawsley to be discounted, they postpone the matter until parliament.

Margin: postponement until parliament.

iii
Curia Regis Roll, no.186, m.30

Hampshire

William of Ross sued for his land, which was taken into the king's hands, by replevin, and he has it until this present parliament in London, and he found these guarantors, namely, Gilbert of Cockerington and Thomas of Bentsham, Reginald fitz Peter and John fitz John de St. John, that he will come in his own person to the aforesaid parliament, to do and receive what his peers and the king's council decree should be done with regard to a certain plea between the king and himself.[3]

---

[3] The pleas on this membrane relate to Hampshire and m.31 records pleas held at Fordingbridge on 1 December 1268.

iv
Assize Roll, no.276, m.5

Gloucester

[The litigant] was to be here with the same rights as he had when he was given a day to be before the justices assigned to hear common pleas at Gloucester at a Month after Michaelmas. And the plea remained without day through the absence of the justices there, for they were then at London at the king's parliament.[4]

---

[4] Michaelmas 1268.

PARLIAMENT AT LONDON: Easter 1269

i

B.L., Cotton MS., Titus A. 14, f. 54
[*Annales Monastici*, iv. 221 f.]

1269. Having convoked at London a Fortnight after Easter[1] a great many of the magnates of England, the king held discussions with his nobles, as is his wont, for a long time but yet they came to nothing, for scarcely anything memorable came to pass save that, through the powerful influence of the king's firstborn, the lord Edward, and of Henry, king of Germany, it was by ordinance of his councillors enacted and publicly promulgated that the Jews, who have up till now intolerably oppressed the Christians by means of annual payments which the simple Christians, entangled very often by the wiles of the Jews, are bound by their charters to make to them at stated terms, should not henceforward have such payments and furthermore the deeds, which the Jews possess relating to such payments, are to be returned to the Christians without any gainsaying. And at this time, before the parliament was as yet dissolved, Edmund, the last son of the king of England, married the only daughter of the countess of Aumale and niece of the earl of Gloucester, at whose nuptials the king and the queen and nearly all the magnates of England were present.[2]

ii

Assize Roll, no.85, m.7*d*

This official document happily corroborates the evidence from a chronicle.

At a Fortnight after Hilary: continued.

The sheriff of Cambridge is ordered to arrange for Richard de Brus or the tenants of certain land in Stanton (which is worth twenty marks a year and which Simon de Montfort seized from Henry de Nafford by reason of the rebellion and died in possession thereof) to come[3] and show by what warrant Richard had made entry. On that day Roger

---

[1] 7 April 1269.
[2] 8 or 9 April 1269.
[3] *Margin*: Thursday.

Gernet of the county of Bedford and Matthew de Caumbrun de
Kertling of this county replevied the aforesaid land until the Fortnight
after Easter so that Richard will then be at the parliament at
Westminster to show his warrant for thus entering that land.[4]

---

[4] *Margin*: Westminster at the Fortnight after Easter. Cf. m.18*d* where it was stated
that Richard de Brus did not know by what warrant he held the land and it was
replevied until 'the parliament at London' (London and Westminster are often
alternative terms).

PARLIAMENT AT LONDON: Midsummer 1269

i
Patent Roll, no.87, m.14d
[*Cal. Patent Rolls 1266-72*, p.384]

The king to the archbishops etc. and all others about to come to the approaching parliament on the Feast of St. John the Baptist[1] in London, greeting. Because we cannot come as we wished to London on the aforesaid Feast according to our plans on account of a tertian fever by which we have been confined for some time and from which, by God's grace, we have now fully recovered, we, trusting very greatly in your love, affectionately request and pray you, out of reverence for us and our honour, to be so good as to stay there and wait a little while for our arrival. For on the Morrow of the said Feast we will, God willing, direct our steps thither and have treaty and colloquy with you as we formerly decreed. And to explain these matters more fully to you we are specially sending to you our beloved and faithful abbot of Westminster, Philip Basset and Stephen of Edworth, and we would have sent with them for this purpose the reverend father Nicholas, bishop of Winchester, had the renewed spirits which we wish to have from his presence all the time until our aforesaid arrival not prevented him from leaving our side. And so to the said messengers, when they come to you, kindly give full trust in these matters. In witness whereof etc. Witness the king at Winchester on the twenty-first day of June.[2]

ii
Assize Roll, no.42, m.8d

The abbot of Abingdon was attached and came. And the justices charged him with plotting against the king on behalf of the earl of Leicester and harbouring his enemies, especially John de Sancta Elena and others, and rendering aid to the earl by sending him money. Again, the abbot in the time of the king scarcely did his service to him in money, but in the time of the earl he compelled his knights by great distraint to go to the castle of Windsor and to hold it with John fitz John against the king, wrongfully and in breach of the peace and at a time of rebellion etc.

---

[1] 24 June 1269.
[2] 21 June 1269.

And the abbot comes and denies all enmity and whatever is against the peace etc. And he says that he never plotted against the king on behalf of the earl of Leicester, nor did he harbour John de Sancta Elena or other enemies of the king, nor did he give aid to the earl, but he acknowledged that by heavy distraint of the constable of Windsor Castle, who showed him a letter from the king and closed the doors of his granges and stores so that neither he nor his convent could have any victuals, he did his service to the castle by thirty knights' fees. And he asks for an inquiry to be made that in no other way nor by any enmity was he ever against the king.

Margin: Adjourned to parliament for discussion with the king.

iii
Ibid., m.8*d*

John of Benfield complains against Robert of Whitefield that Robert, together with others, pursued him from London Town and seized him and stole from him one belt, one crossbow, one gold ring and other goods of his, and brought him with him from London and had him imprisoned at Tonbridge Castle unlawfully and against the peace and in time of rebellion etc., to his loss of ten marks. And Robert comes and confesses that he seized and robbed him, but this was by order of the earl of Gloucester. And as to this he vouches the earl to warranty. And he has a day to produce his warranty at the Octave of St. John the Baptist[3] at parliament.

And Robert came then and produced the warranty he had from the earl, who warranted him with respect to the aforesaid deed. Therefore he is acquitted thereof.

Margin: At the Octave of St. John the Baptist at parliament.

iv
Ibid., m.10

The abbot of Reading was charged at the king's suit with many acts of enmity in time of war, and it is alleged against him that he harboured the king's enemies, sent his men to give assistance against his lord and gave aid out of his own money to the earl of Leicester and bound

---

[3] 1 July 1269.

himself by a deed of his to the earl of Leicester; and that, when Warin of Bassingbourn and other loyal subjects of the king came to release the Lord Edward at Wallingford, they came through the vill of Blewbury and there armed themselves, and in consequence one of the abbot's men immediately reported this to the abbot and the abbot reported it to the earl of Leicester, in great enmity to the king; and that he bought timber and had it transferred from the wood of Roger Mortimer at Stratfield by his own carts and household servants.

And the abbot comes and denies all enmity and whatever is against the king's peace. And he says that he never gave aid to the earl of Leicester or to any others against the king, neither in men nor in money. But he says that the king ordered his sheriffs to distrain archbishops, bishops, abbots, priors etc. to send their services to the king at Canterbury. The abbot, like his other peers of those parts, sent his services at the king's command. And because he says that he did it at the king's command, he has a day thereon before the king at the next parliament. And with regard to all the other articles he says that he is not guilty of anything alleged against him. And as to this he puts himself upon twelve sworn knights. And twelve sworn knights say on their oath that the abbot is not guilty of any charge alleged against him save only that the abbot entertained the earl of Leicester. But they say that this was a long time before the battle of Lewes.

Margin: To the next parliament.

v

Ibid., m.10

The prioress of Goring is indicted by the presentment of twelve jurors of Theale that in the time of rebellion she had by her men robbed Roger, the parson of Burghfield, of all his goods and unlawfully burned his houses etc. And she comes and denies whatever is in breach of the peace and says that she never procured any of the king's enemies to commit this robbery and arson and did not send any men there to do this evil thing. And she prays that inquiry may be made.

And the aforesaid twelve jurors, together with the hundred-jury of Reading, say on their oath that there was a dispute between the prioress, predecessor of this prioress, now deceased, and the rector over tithes, and the rector carried off the tithes with violence. And when the deceased prioress had shown the removal of the tithes to Richard of Havering, the constable of Wallingford Castle, who is the said prioress's patron, he came to Burghfield with many men, but not at the prioress's instigation, in order to recover the tithes. And because some of Richard's party were wounded there, he became thereby vexed and had three of the rector's houses burned down. But they say that the prioress did not procure the robbery or the arson. And the suit is postponed until the justices have consulted the king's council at the parliament at London.

Margin: At Wallingford or at Oxford.

PARLIAMENT AT LONDON: Michaelmas 1269

B.L., Cotton MS., Titus A. 14, fo.56
[*Annales Monastici*, iv. pp.227-28]

After the solemn rites attending so important a Translation[1] had been celebrated, the nobles began, as was their wont, to discuss the business of the king and of the kingdom by way of parliament. And in it through the craftiness of the king, indeed I truly say through the overriding force of extortionate greed which the magnates of the realm accepted or were afraid to oppose, it was agreed that a twentieth should be paid to him from all the movable property of lay men throughout the kingdom of England so that not only, as we have already said, were the purses of the clergy emptied by the four-yearly extortion of tenths but also the insatiable greed of the king has rummaged deep into the guts of the laity, and it is recognised that this has redressed the balance of justice so that the laity, who were wont to applaud the losses of the clergy with the greatest derision, at last mourn their own costs. And although certain persons were appointed by the king's counsellors to collect the said twentieth in all the counties of the realm, yet the money proceeding therefrom could not be quickly collected . . .

About the same time the earl of Gloucester, being unwell, as many have reported, and burdened in giving counsel, refused to attend the treaties or parliaments of the king and the nobles, with whom he was summoned and among whom he was considered first, inventing for himself reasons for being absent and frivolous excuses, such as that the lord Edward was secretly plotting to ambush him and to capture him treacherously as he came to court. Therefore limiting his activities and scorning parliaments, he betook himself to safer places.

[1] The translation of King Edward the Confessor's remains to a new shrine in Westminster Abbey.

PARLIAMENT AT WESTMINSTER: Easter 1270

i

Guildhall, London, Liber de Antiquis Legibus, fo.119b
[*Liber de Antiquis Legibus*, p.122]

Note that almost all the bishops, earls, barons, knights and freeholders of the whole realm of England assembled about Hockday[1] at London at the king's command, and a parliament then continued at Westminster to deal with several points concerning the customs of the kingdom of England and especially the quarrel between the Lord Edward and the earl of Gloucester. And the Lord Edward and the earl put themselves completely upon the arbitration of the king of Germany for the pacification of the quarrel.

ii

Chancery Miscellanea 14/3/59

Henry by the grace of God king of England, lord of Ireland and duke of Aquitaine, to his beloved and faithful,[2]   greeting. Whereas we and our sons, together with other crusaders of our realm, are about to set out on the Feast of St. John the Baptist next[3] in aid of the Holy Land and, since the date of our crossing over is such a short time away, it is essential for us to make provision with all haste and to arrange wisely with you and the other nobles and magnates of our realm concerning the state, peace, tranquillity and security of the realm after our departure, we command you, requiring and firmly enjoining you in the faith, homage and love whereby you are bound to us, that, putting all other things aside, you shall be with us at Westminster a Fortnight after Easter next[4] to speak with us and with the nobles and magnates whom we have likewise caused to be summoned for this purpose and to give us your advice. And as you desire to promote the business of the crusade and our honour and your own and the common welfare of the realm, you shall in no wise disregard this nor put forward any excuse therein because the shortness of time, together with the great speed required in the aforesaid matters, does not permit us very long to have discussion with you or to

---

[1] The second Tuesday after Easter Day, namely, 22 April 1270.
[2] As this is a draft the name has been left blank.
[3] 24 June 1270.
[4] 27 April 1270.

make arrangements therein. Witness myself at Westminster on the twenty-eighth day of March in the fifty-fourth year of our reign.[5]

iii
Ancient Correspondence, vol. ii, no.44
[Shirley, *Royal Letters of Henry III*, ii. 336 f.]

Henry by the grace of God king of England, lord of Ireland and duke of Aquitaine, to his beloved in Christ[6]   greeting. Whereas we and our sons, together with other crusaders of our realm, are about to set out overseas in aid of the Holy Land and we are to start our journey on the Morrow after Midsummer Day next;[7] and, since the date of our crossing over is such a short time away, it is essential for us to provide in all haste for the money and other necessities for it as well as for the peace and safety of our realm after our departure; wherefore we lately ordered you to be with us at a Fortnight after Easter last.[8] On that day the reverend father Walter, archbishop of York, and the bishops and prelates of our realm came at our command for the aforesaid business. And we then held a special conference upon the important matters touching us and our realm with the archbishop and bishops and other prelates and magnates of our realm. And we abstained at the time from conferring with you, and for that reason you departed from our court without having had any discussion with us. And afterwards, when this important business of ours had been completed, we asked the archbishop and bishops to grant us a twentieth part of the goods of themselves and their villeins in aid of the Holy Land, and they generously granted the twentieth to us of their grace. We, understanding that our aforesaid crossing could be easily held up if we were to have any discussion or conference with you about it, and expecting that, since the aforesaid bishops have given heed to the plea made to us by the Christian people inhabiting the Holy Land and have granted us this kind gift, as aforesaid, you would wish to grant us generously and courteously this twentieth in aid of the Holy Land, for you have until now kindly agreed to our royal entreaties, we affectionately request and pray you to grant us with equal courtesy the twentieth of the goods of you and your villeins and to permit our assessors

---

[5] 28 March 1270. It is worth noting that no writ of summons for this parliament was enrolled on the chancery roll, so casual was the procedure. There is another draft in Ancient Correspondence, vol. ii, no.126.

[6] A blank space has been left in this draft letter for an insertion of the name.

[7] 25 June 1270.

[8] 27 April 1270.

and collectors of the twentieth to assess the goods of you and your villeins and to collect that twentieth in the same way as the twentieth is assessed and collected elsewhere in our realm, so that we may at all costs have the twentieth touching you and your villeins, before the time of our crossing, to take it with us to the Holy Land. And you shall in no wise fail in this, as you love us and our honour and the business of the crusade and as we put our trust in you. For we have ordered our assessors and collectors to have the goods of you and your villeins assessed and the twentieth levied upon it according to the terms handed to them by us and enjoined upon them. Witness myself at Westminster on the twelfth day of May in the fifty-fourth year of our reign.[9]

[9] 12 May 1270. This letter, sent to the prior of Worcester, is entered on the register of Archbishop Walter Giffard, fo.74 (printed somewhat inaccurately in *Historical Papers and Letters from Northern Registers*, pp.24–5). What seems to be the record of the resolution of the assembled bishops is contained in Giffard's register, fo.105a (*ibid.*, p.23).

PARLIAMENT AT WINCHESTER: July 1270

i

Guildhall, London: Liber de Antiquis Legibus, fos.120*b*, 122
[*Liber de Antiquis Legibus*, pp.125, 129]

Note that in the parliament which was at Winchester in the month of July this year, with the assent of the bishops and magnates of the realm of England there present, the king entrusted the Cross which he had assumed to the Lord Edward, his son, so that he could set out, on behalf of himself and his father, to the Holy Land. And then the king granted to him all the money coming from the twentieth, collected throughout England from all the free men of the realm.

Note that last July the citizens of London forwarded a bond, sealed with the seal of the community, to the king in the parliament at Winchester, which states that John Adrian, the mayor of London, the barons, citizens and the whole community of that city have undertaken that they and their heirs and those who shall come after them will be ever and at all times loyal to the king and his heirs against all men. And if they or their heirs or those who shall come after them should depart as a community from allegiance to the king or his heirs and bear arms against him, then they grant by the aforesaid bond that they are to lose life and limb without any mercy and to be disinherited with their heirs for ever and to be excommunicated. And they are bound in several other ways in that bond. But yet, if any individual or individuals of the city should do anything contrary to their allegiance to the king or his heirs, they alone are to be punished and sentenced by the law of the land, without harm to other citizens.

ii

Curia Regis Roll, no.192 (Trinity 1270), m.15

Excuses for failure to come before the king's bench at the Octave of Trinity in the fifty-fourth year of the king's reign etc.[1]

Dorset

John of Beausale, the attorney of Gilbert de Clare, earl of Gloucester and Hertford, against the king with respect to a plea of land. [excuse] by Ralph of Tallington

---

[1] 15 June 1270.

John de Stanes, the other attorney against the king with respect to the same plea. [excuse] by Ralph de Stanes

On the Octave of St. John the Baptist's Day[2] on the security of William de Merlon, clerk.

The same day is given to Jordan of Daventry, who is suing in court on behalf of the king, by order of the king, because he wishes to take counsel with his magnates and the peers of the counties[3] then in parliament, and by reason of the journey to be undertaken by his son, Edward, to the Holy Land.

[2] 1 July 1270.

[3] For this phrase, used in 1284, see *English Hist. Rev.* xl. 233 and, used again in 1337, *ibid.*, lvii. 478, n.1.

PARLIAMENT AT WESTMINSTER: Michaelmas 1270

i

Register of Walter Giffard, fo.98*a*
[*Register of Walter Giffard*, p.211]

Walter by Divine permission etc. to Robert Burnell, archdeacon of York, greeting. You can well understand these days the perils that attend journeys and our preoccupation with many different matters, and therefore we confidently ask you to excuse us on the Feast of St. Edward[1] and in the succeeding parliament as best and conveniently as you can, because we will indeed make up for our present absence after Easter, God willing.[2]

ii

Close Roll, no.87, m.3*d*
[*Close Rolls, 1268-72*, pp.290-91]

The king to Llewellyn ap Gruffydd, prince of Wales, greeting and the affection of sincere love. Keeping in our heart the remembrance of how well and how great is our affection for you, we have recently informed you by our letters that we would send our beloved and faithful Robert Walerand and other loyal subjects of ours with full authority for the purpose of redressing the wrongs, done to you and yours by our men of Montgomery, so it is said, in accordance with the laws and customs of those parts at the Feast of the Nativity of the Blessed Virgin Mary.[3] Next we are forced to tell you by this present letter that, on account of the immediate start of the journey of our most dear son Edward, our first-born, to the Holy Land, who has remained with a host of crusaders a long time at Portsmouth awaiting a wind and keeping those who are members of our council and other magnates and loyal subjects of our realm with him, and, by reason of the contrary winds he has turned away from there to Dover, taking with him our said counsellors and all the others, to stay there in the hope of a better wind, we are hindered thereby from being able to send Robert and the others as we wished at the Feast of the Nativity of the Blessed Virgin Mary to the aforesaid parts for that business, and we find this very irksome and are greatly disturbed in mind. And because we repose special confidence in the constancy of your

[1] 13 October 1270.
[2] The date 'At Nottingham, 27 December', attributed to this letter in the printed version, does not seem to belong to it.
[3] 8 September 1270.

love, we affectionately request and pray that you will not take this badly but be kind enough to hold us excused in this respect and to defer for our sake the aforesaid business as patiently as before until the Feast of All Saints next[4] so that in the meanwhile we can arrange in our next Michaelmas parliament to send such men from our council to those parts who will have full authority in these matters, and thereby the said business should reach the desired, proper and fitting conclusion. Nor must you think or believe that we do these things in any way out of malice or to create delay but only for the aforesaid reasons, because at the aforesaid Feast of All Saints we will send there without fail and further delay those whom we shall appoint in this parliament for the purpose, and at that Feast you should likewise send some of your men there, to do and receive therein what ought to be done in accordance with the law and custom of those parts. And you should send us at Westminster at the aforesaid parliament at a Fortnight after Michaelmas[5] one of your men who can on our behalf inform you of the names of those whom we shall send for the said business to those parts and of everything else concerning that business. And you should also let us know in writing by the bearer of this letter what you mean to do in all these matters. Witness the king at Westminster on the twenty-fourth day of August.[6]

[4] 1 November 1270.
[5] 13 October 1270.
[6] 24 August 1270. See *Close Rolls, 1268-72*, pp.234-36, for the names of those appointed in parliament to go to Montgomery.

PARLIAMENT AT WESTMINSTER: Michaelmas 1271

Guildhall, London: Liber de Antiquis Legibus, fo.228*b*
[*Liber de Antiquis Legibus*, p.142]

In this year, in the parliament held at Westminster after the Feast of the Translation of St. Edward,[1] there came before the king's council those who had been sent on his orders throughout England to inquire about the goods and chattels of the Flemings and they said that the property found by them amounted in debts and chattels, together with debts to the king, to eight thousand pounds. Then it was decreed by the king's council that all the merchants of England, from whom the countess of Flanders had stolen anything, should come to Westminster at the next Feast of St. Hilary, to show and inform the king's council about what the countess had taken from them, each on behalf of himself in respect of the value of his property, and each man will then receive his share from the aforesaid property of the Flemings. And note that the chattels the countess took from the English amounted to seven thousand pounds sterling, leaving out of account the chattels of the merchants of Ireland, Scotland, Wales and the Lord Edward's tenants.

[1] 13 October 1271.

PARLIAMENT AT WESTMINSTER: Hilary 1272

Guildhall, London: Liber de Antiquis Legibus, fo.228*b*-229
[*Liber de Antiquis Legibus*, p.142]

Afterwards, in the parliament held a Fortnight after Hilary, some men whose property had been seized in Flanders, as noted above,[1] especially Londoners, hoping to get some money from the debts of the Flemings which had then been collected throughout England, certified each one on his oath with three supporting him to those who had been appointed for this purpose by the king and his council what goods the countess had taken from them and the value of them.

[1] As above.

PARLIAMENT AT WESTMINSTER: Michaelmas 1272

Close Roll, no.89, m.3
[*Close Rolls, 1268-72*, p.524]

The king to Ralph Hengham and his fellows, justices in eyre in the county of Shropshire, greeting. Whereas we have ordered our beloved and faithful Roger de Mortimer to be with us at our parliament, which we shall hold at Westminster immediately after the approaching Michaelmas, for which reason Roger cannot appear before you on the Morrow of Michaelmas[1] to sue and defend, as he finds it expedient, the pleas brought or to be brought for or against him, we wish to provide immunity in this matter, so far as it can be done with justice, for Roger and for our beloved and faithful Ralph de Mortimer, Hugh de Mortimer, Brian de Braunton and Walter of Pedwardine, who have lands and tenements in the aforesaid county and who are to come to us there with Roger for the aforesaid reason, and order you to adjourn before you for one month all pleas, brought or to be brought for or against them in the aforesaid eyre, provided that there is then done in the said matters what ought to be done of right and in accordance with the law and custom of our realm. Witness the king as above.[2]

---

[1]　30 September 1272.
[2]　17 September 1272.

EDWARD I

Edward I was in Sicily on his way home from his crusade in the East when he heard that his father had died on 16 November 1272. He did not hurry back: though he reached Paris in July 1273, he did not proceed to London but turned southwards into Gascony where he remained nearly a year. Not until after his arrival in England in August 1274 was his first parliament convened at Easter 1275: for that fact we have indisputable evidence, and assemblies before that date, whatever their purpose, were clearly not regarded by contemporaries as in the same category as parliaments. Nevertheless, the king's presence in his kingdom and the meeting of parliament were constantly expected long before he arrived.

i
Ancient Correspondence, vol. VII, no.82

The date of this letter lies between 13 October 1272, when Edmund was created earl of Cornwall, and 21 September 1274, when Walter Merton ceased to be chancellor. The Christmas Day mentioned must therefore have been in 1272 or 1273. This is the earliest reference, so far found, to parliament under Edward I. The letter takes it for granted that parliament will administer justice and it makes the supposition that a parliament might be held in the king's absence.

Edmund of Almain, earl of Cornwall, to the wise and distinguished Walter Merton, the chancellor of England, greeting. The wrong and the grave trespass, recently committed against W. Bolet, have not, we believe, escaped your notice, wherefore we send you word on behalf of the nobles staying with us at Wallingford this Christmas Day that you should give strict orders under the king's seal to the sheriff of those parts that, so far as the law allows, he is to attach all those guilty of the aforesaid trespass so that he may have them in person before the council of nobles[1] of England when they are in the next parliament at London. And this he should not neglect as he loves himself and his. Farewell.

[1] The clerk originally wrote 'before the nobles' (*coram nobilibus*). Then 'council' (*consilio*) was added above 'nobles' but without any consequent alterations. Cf. the phrase 'council of nobles of our realm in parliament', used in a royal letter below (p.141).

ii

Ancient Correspondence, vol. VIII, no.29

[Sayles, *King's Bench*, ii. pp.cxxx-cxxxi]

Edward by the grace of God king of England, lord of Ireland and duke of Aquitaine, to the reverend father in Christ Walter, by the same grace archbishop of York, primate of England, Roger de Mortimer and Robert Burnell, archdeacon,[2] greeting and love. When we directed our steps to the parts of Gascony, we believed that we would be coming to England in good time to be able, with you and our other loyal subjects, to make proper provision for the things that would be put forward at the approaching Council[3] on behalf of our realm and of ourselves. Since, however, other business has cropped up for us in Gascony, this makes it necessary for us to stay longer than we expected, and the time for which the Council has been summoned is near at hand. We instruct you to summon our faithful magnates and others whom you think it advisable to summon and to provide by their counsel for all the things which are to be put forward in the Council for the welfare and benefit of us and of our realm. Nevertheless, when you are also deciding upon competent and suitable messengers to expedite these matters, you are in no way to stress great wealth or rank in choosing them, provided they know how to carry out the things you enjoin upon them. Furthermore, you shall arrange that our envoy, whom we intend shortly to send to you with our authority and by whom we shall inform you of whatever decisions we ourselves have reached therein, shall find you assembled together. And you are to send to us the messengers you shall choose so that we can bestow authority upon them to prosecute the aforesaid matters. Given at Lectoure[4] on the eighteenth day of February in the second year of our reign.[5]

iii

Chancery Parliament and Council Proceedings, file 53, no.19

A draft summons. There is no corresponding enrolment on either the patent or the close rolls.

Edward, by the grace of God king of England, lord of Ireland and duke

---

[2] He was archdeacon of York (*Cal. Patent Rolls, 1268-72*, p.565). These three men were acting as regents during the king's absence.

[3] The Council of Lyons began its sessions on 7 May 1274.

[4] Agenais, France.

[5] 18 February 1274.

of Aquitaine, to his beloved and faithful,[6]   greeting. Because it is necessary with all possible speed, by the counsel of you and our other loyal subjects, to look after some important and pressing business concerning our realm and our crown and it specially requires your presence, we command and firmly enjoin you, in the faith and love whereby you are bound to us, that you are to set everything else aside and be with us or those holding our place at London on Wednesday[7] in Easter Week without further delay to hold a discussion upon the aforesaid matters and to give them efficient advice thereon. And you are in no wise to fail to do this. As for your own affairs and business you are so to arrange in this respect and provide in the meantime that, after you have had discussion at London with our loyal subjects who will assemble there with you at the aforesaid date, you can go thence to the Council, which the supreme pontiff has decided to hold at Lyons with other prelates, suitably instructed, as is fit and proper, about the matters which are to be done there on behalf of us and our kingdom and the preservation of our own rights and yours. And because in so great an emergency, which involves the fate of all, there is no place for excuses from those desiring and working for the honour and welfare of the people, let your fealty in no way neglect or leave undone what we have indicated to you by our present request. Given by the hand of Walter Merton, our chancellor, at St. Martins-le-Grand, London, on the thirteenth day of March in the second year of our reign.[8]

iv
Exchequer Miscellanea, Bundle 2, no.39

It was always essential for the council to have minutes made of business it transacted and the decisions it made. But after action had been taken, an action which is sometimes but by no means always revealed by entries on chancery or exchequer rolls, there was no need to retain the memoranda. We do not know for certain who was responsible for minuting the proceedings before 1290: in that year and for many years afterwards Gilbert Rothbury was 'clerk of the council' (*clericus consilii*), and he saw no reason to distinguish between what was done by the council when parliament was in

---

[6] A space has been left for the name.

[7] 4 April 1274. For the business done at this council, see the document printed by Henry Cole, *Documents Illustrative of English History*, pp.358-60. Proctors attended on behalf of the king as well as on behalf of earls and barons or, as they were described, messengers on behalf of the community of England – an excellent example of the identification of the magnates with the community of the realm.

[8] 13 March 1274.

session from what was done by the council when parliament was not in session. Some of his records, haphazard and jumbled, have come down to us, starting with what is generally regarded as our first 'roll of parliament' in 1290. It is therefore gratifying to find, many years before he assumed office, the minutes of a council meeting, perhaps extending over several days. It discloses the preparations being made in February 1275 for the meeting of the first parliament held by Edward I on 22 April. The document records many matters which had to be settled instantly and not deferred until parliament, particularly the affairs of the king's brother Edmund, and Edward's treatment of his brother is of great interest. However, only those entries which mention or indisputably refer to parliament are given here. What is important is this: three years have gone by since a parliament was last held in Henry III's reign but Edward I's ministers and judges in 1275 are the same as those of his father (a dozen of them are, indeed, named) and the parliament they have in mind is the parliament they have long known and served. To them it is not primarily a political assembly but a tribunal, established to deal on the highest level with the problems of administration and justice, with the maintenance of law and order, with the governance of the realm.

Day is given to the earl de Ferrers a Fortnight after Easter in parliament etc. concerning the demands upon his manor of Chartley.[9]

Of the form of writs concerning wool.

Of the form of writs concerning parliament.

Of the prisoners, taken within the Liberty of the abbot of Peterborough, who are to be handed over to the sheriff of Northampton etc. Otherwise let the abbot be given another day on the Morrow of the Close of Easter[10] to show his charters whereby he claims to have such prisoners in his custody.

Of the business of the Master of the Temple etc.: day is given him a Fortnight after Easter etc., and meanwhile let him have a respite from distraints etc.

Day is given to William Belet a Fortnight after Easter etc., and he shall show his charter concerning strengthening his house at Marham.

Let the record of the outlawry of Walter de Baskerville be sent before the king a Fortnight after Easter.

Of captives imprisoned in the time of King Henry: let the matter be postponed until a Fortnight after Easter etc.

---

[9] Cf. *Cal. Close Rolls, 1272-79*, p.546 (4 February 1274).

[10] I.e. 22 April, the day for which parliament was summoned (not 25 April, as in *Handbook of British Chronology*, p.507).

Let the park of Potterspury be restored to John fitz John until parliament etc. And the wood in Wiltshire.

Day is given to the attorney of Arnold du Bois with regard to the customs-dues of Haversham until parliament.

Let day be given to the abbot of Darnhall and the men of Memwich concerning the exaction of toll etc. a Fortnight after Easter, namely, in parliament.[11]

Let Roger of Clifford, justice of the forest, be written to so that he may inform the king in his parliament for what reason Thomas de Kenum was amerced before him etc. And meanwhile distraint is to cease etc.[12]

[11] The last three words seem to have been added in a different hand.

[12] The document ends with a writ, set down in full, to the treasurer and barons of the exchequer, dated at Windsor on 27 February.

PARLIAMENT AT LONDON: Easter 1275

i

Close Roll, no.92, m.21*d*

[*Parl. Writs*, i. 1; *Cal. Close Rolls, 1272-79*, p.229]

The king to the reverend father in Christ Robert, archbishop of Canterbury, primate of all England, greeting. Because we have for certain reasons adjourned until the Morrow of the Close of Easter next[1] our general parliament which we intended to hold with the prelates and magnates of our realm at London a Fortnight after the Purification of the Blessed Mary,[2] we order and require you to be present at the said parliament there on the Morrow of the Close of Easter to discuss and decide with the prelates and magnates of our realm upon the business of the realm. And you shall in no wise fail to do this. Witness the king at Woodstock on the twenty-seventh day of December.[3]

ii

Patent Roll, no.94, m.22d

[*Cal. Patent Rolls, 1272-81*, pp.119-20]

The king to his beloved and faithful Robert de Neville, Alexander of Kirketon, Ranulf Dacre, Guichard de Charron and William of Northburgh, greeting. Know that we have commissioned you as our justices to hear and determine all the disputes arising between our mayor, citizens and bailiffs of York and our beloved abbot of St. Mary's, York, in accordance with what was shown to us in our parliament at Westminster after the Close of Easter last on both sides, and to hear those disputes we appointed our beloved and faithful John fitz John and our beloved master Geoffrey Aspall as auditors in our said parliament. That is to say, you are to hear and determine those disputes in accordance with the arguments and allegations propounded and advanced before the aforesaid John and Geoffrey and recorded in a certain roll which we have arranged to send to you under John's seal, saving [the rights] etc. and

---

[1] 22 April 1275. The Close of Easter is the same as the Octave of Easter, i.e. a week after Easter Day.

[2] 16 February 1275.

[3] 27 December 1274. Shire representatives were summoned to this parliament, and over the next twenty years to the parliaments at Michaelmas 1275, Michaelmas 1283, Michaelmas 1290, Michaelmas 1294 and November 1295. Borough representatives were summoned to this parliament and to the parliaments at Michaelmas 1283 and November 1295. Their intermittent presence shows clearly that they did not form an essential element in the composition of parliament.

belonging to us therein. And therefore we command you to meet at a set day at York to hear and determine these disputes in the aforesaid form. For we have ordered our sheriff of York that at the set day etc. he should arrange for knights as well as others etc. to come etc., who are not under suspicion by either party, by whom etc. In witness whereof etc. Witness the king at Westminster on the twenty-sixth day of May.[4]

iii

Ancient Correspondence ,vol. XIII, no.191

[The draft of a letter enrolled on Close Roll no.92, m.9d (schedule):
Parl. Writs, i. 381; *Cal. Close Rolls, 1272-79*, pp.197-8]

To the most holy father and lord in Christ, Gregory, by divine providence the supreme pontiff of the Holy, Roman and Universal Church, Edward by the same grace king of England, lord of Ireland and duke of Aquitaine, greeting with reverence and honour, kissing the blessed feet. Your reverend Holiness formerly informed us by an apostolic letter, which we received with humble and devout mind, that we should arrange for the annual tribute, which you state we are under obligation to pay to the Holy Roman Church for the last eight years by reason of our kingdom of England, to be assigned freely and fully to the reverend Master Raymond de Nogeriis, your chaplain, in the name of the aforesaid Roman Church. But lately we have respectfully received another letter from you stating that – whereas we had thought to reserve an answer to the request for the payment of the said annual tribute, which your aforesaid chaplain has laid before us in your name and that of the Roman Church, until we had the careful deliberation of the council of nobles of our realm in parliament, which is usually held in England about the Octave of Easter, because at the time when your letter was received we had newly undertaken the governance of our kingdom – we should now cause full satisfaction to be given to the chaplain by paying the tribute without further delay. We do, indeed, acknowledge, most holy father and lord, that we did summon the prelates and nobles of our realm to our parliament at the Octave of Easter last and ordained many things there which with God's help will make for the bettering of the state of the English Church and the reform of the kingdom and produce an increase in the general welfare of the people. But before we were able to bring the said parliament to an end on account of the multitude of matters that stood in need of reform and while your chaplain was insisting that a proper answer should be given him at once, it pleased the Lord that a grave bodily illness should afflict us and prevent the completion of much

---

[4] 26 May 1275.

other business and the deliberation on the request for the annual tribute, and for this we are heartily sorry. And so, on account of such illness from which, by the grace of God who has the power of sickness and of health, we have begun to get better, the parliament was dissolved, and for that reason we have not been able to have deliberation on the request for the tribute with our aforesaid prelates and nobles, and without their imparted counsel we cannot answer your Holiness on the aforesaid matters, and we are bound by the oath we swore at our coronation to preserve the rights of our kingdom unimpaired and to refrain from doing anything touching the crown of this realm without seeking their advice. We humbly beseech your benign reverence and ask as a special favour that your Holiness will not be annoyed if for the present we cannot reply to you on these matters as we would wish and, indeed, that it may please you in your fatherly patience to have us graciously excused therein. And know for certain, holy father and lord, that in another of our parliaments which we intend to hold, God willing, after next Michaelmas, after we have consulted and conferred with our aforesaid prelates and nobles, we will give an answer thereon with their advice. May the Lord of his Holy Church keep you evermore. Witness myself at Westminster on the nineteenth day of June in the third year of our reign.[5]

iv

King's Bench Roll, no.16 (Easter 1275), m.55*d*
[Sayles, *King's Bench*, i. 13-14]

Kent

The men of Sandwich had resisted distraint for a trespass against the king and had refused for more than a month to allow his officials to enter the town.

Whereupon the constable of Dover came in person to Sandwich on Friday before the Feast of St. Gregory in the third year of the present king's reign[6] to redress this trespass. And after many delays in this business he reached the point where the whole community of Sandwich submitted completely to the king's will in order to redress the trespass, and it handed its letters patent thereon, sealed with the seal of the whole community of Sandwich, to the constable. And the constable delivered them to the king and his council and gave the community of Sandwich a

---

[5] 19 June 1275. It is to be noted that already on 16 May 1275 it was known for certain that the next parliament would be after Michaelmas (*Cal. Close Rolls, 1272-79*, p.167).
[6] 8 March 1275.

day before the king at the parliament at London, that is to say, a Month after Easter in the third year of King Edward's reign,[7] to hear the king's will thereon. On that day it was decided by the king and his council, in the presence of John Dennis, the then bailiff of Sandwich, and Henry Verreys, the then mayor, appearing on behalf of the whole community, that the mayoralty and liberty of Sandwich were to be taken into the king's hand on account of the trespass, and the custody of Sandwich is given to his constable of Dover to administer the town in accordance with the common law and custom of the realm, irrespective of any franchise. And the ditches, constructed there during the late rebellion in the kingdom, are to be filled in with earth and levelled at the community's expense. And the barbicans and the rest of the fortifications constructed there in opposition to the king are to be taken down at the community's expense and removed to Dover Castle. And certain of the community are to be arrested and kept safely in Dover prison until they are able to obtain the king's grace.

[7] 12 May 1275.

PARLIAMENT AT WESTMINSTER: Michaelmas 1275

i

Register of Walter Giffard, f. 133
[*Register of Walter Giffard*, p.305]

To his most excellent lord etc. For the business which your lordship has decreed must be dealt with and discussed with the prelates and nobles of your kingdom in the instant parliament, we have hereby appointed our beloved Master W., our official, the bearer of this letter, as our attorney or proxy, and those things which in our name he considers should be done therein we shall hold both right and approved. May the Lord keep you etc.[1]

ii

Ancient Correspondence, XX, no.180

To the most excellent lord, the Lord Edward, by the grace of God the illustrious king of England, lord of Ireland and duke of Aquitaine, Roger by the same permission the humble servant of the church of Norwich, greeting and reverence in due humility. Your lordship's orders, shown to us, contained among other things that we should appear in person before you at Westminster in your parliament after next Michaelmas[2] to discuss with you the settlement of the dispute between our church of Norwich and the citizens of the city of Norwich, the sentences of interdict and excommunication pronounced against the city and its citizens having in the meantime been remitted. Wishing to comply in every way with your requests and commands as far as our poor strength can go, we will be present, life and health being given us at your said parliament to do your pleasure as we ought. But since not only the canon law but legatine statutes expressly forbid all prelates of the Church from

---

[1] Written at Bolton in Craven on 7 October 1275. Cf. Gervase of Canterbury, *Historical Works*, ii. 281: 'in which parliament there were archbishops, bishops and almost all the magnates of the land. And in that parliament Master Roger Seaton, the king's justice [chief justice of the court of common pleas] spoke his discourse, relating and expounding the king's business, how he toiled from his youth in various lands and especially in the Holy Land and how he had expended his funds and the funds of his father. He asked them all for an aid. And on hearing his request, almost all advised that a fifteenth of all their goods should be given him. And it was so granted'.

[2] The writ, dated 16 May 1275, is to be found in Ancient Correspondence, vol. XIV, no.53.

remitting an interdict pronounced against cities and castles or other places unless satisfaction is first obtained, and the case relating to the aforesaid sentences of excommunication and interdict has been transferred by us to the Apostolic See in full and still pends there undecided, we cannot execute your orders as regards the remission of the sentences, for which we are sorry. May your lordship flourish and be a strength unto us evermore. Given at Broomhill on the third of the Nones of June in the year of our Lord 1275.[3]

[3] 3 June 1275.

PARLIAMENT AT WESTMINSTER: Easter 1276

i
Close Roll, no.93, m.14
[*Cal. Close Rolls, 1272-79, p.273-4*]

London

Concerning the Jews to be adjourned before the king

The king to his beloved and faithful Master Roger of Seaton and his fellows, the justices in eyre at the Tower of London, greeting. We have heard and fully understood the contents of your letter lately addressed to us about what has been done in connexion with the community of the Jews of London by reason of the death of a certain Christian boy, who was crucified by these Jews and blasphemously and wretchedly slain in insult to the name of Jesus Christ and in breach of the peace of the realm and who was cast ashore at Dowgate by the flood-water of the Thames, into which the Jews had secretly thrown him, and was there found. And we have taken advice and carefully pondered over what can be done most wisely, safely and salutarily in this matter. And, indeed, because we wish to have a special discussion with you and with our justices appointed for the custody of the Jews as well as with our councillors upon so loathsome a deed and how it should be punished in conformity with justice, and also because we wish to be more fully informed by you by word of mouth in these matters, and also because we purpose shortly to make an ordinance about some other things concerning the Jews and our Jewry, we order you to adjourn the said Jews before us in our parliament at London a Month after Easter so that they may then be there to do and receive what we cause to be provided by our council in these matters. And in the meantime you are to allow the Jews to have peace on these and other matters relating to them by reason of the Jewry. Witness the king at Liddington on the third day of March.[1]

ii
Close Roll, no.93, m.15
[*Cal. Close Rolls, 1272-79, p.272*]

The king to his beloved and faithful Master Roger of Seaton and his fellows, the justices in eyre at the Tower of London, greeting. At the

---

[1] 3 March 1276.

instance of our most dear mother Eleanor, queen of England, who has frequently and fervently made request in this matter, we order you to arrange for Robert of Montpellier, our citizen of London, arrested and imprisoned in our prison of Newgate for many trespasses whereof he is accused, to be delivered from the prison in which he is kept by adequate surety of respected and law-worthy men, provided that you are sure that he will stand trial before you in your eyre in connexion with all who wish to complain of him before you return from the Tower. And if he happens to have been arrested at our suit and not that of anyone else, and if he finds competent and reputable sureties who will undertake to have him before us in our parliament at a Fortnight after Easter next to stand trial as we think fit to ordain by your counsel and that of our other loyal subjects, then you are to deliver him in the meantime in bail to the sureties, as aforesaid, with his goods and chattels. And you are then to have before us the names of those sureties together with this writ. Witness the king at Rothwell on the twenty-eighth day of February.[2]

iii
Liberate Roll, no.52 (4 Edward I), m.1

Allowances to the Constable of Windsor Castle.

And £7.10s. which he spent at our command in providing ten thousand pieces of firewood and transporting them from our forest to Westminster in readiness for our parliament at a Fortnight after Easter last.[3]

[2] 28 February 1276.
[3] 19 April 1276. Note also the release of all his rights in the honour of Monmouth by Ralph Daubeny to the king, which was made on 7 May 1276 'at Westminster in the king's parliament' (Close Roll, no.93, m.13 d: *Cal. Close Rolls 1272-79*, p.338).

PARLIAMENT AT WESTMINSTER: Michaelmas 1276

i

King's Bench Roll, no.189 (Trinity 1307), m.54

[Sayles, *King's Bench*, iii. 191-92]

The petitions of Thomas Multon and Thomas Lucy in the parliament at Westminster in Lent 1305 and the parliament at Carlisle at Hilary 1307 concerning their claims in the inheritance of Aveline de Forz. Proceedings upon these petitions, dispatched from the king's council to the court, took place in the king's bench on 25 June 1307.

On that day the attorney on behalf of Thomas and Thomas comes and asks that he may show the right they had in the aforesaid manors, for which the king would wish to restore those manors to them as their inheritance in accordance with their petitions. And thereupon John of Chester, who sues for the king,[1] as well as the king's serjeants say on behalf of the king's right and estate therein that, at another time in his parliament before the king and his council at Westminster a Fortnight after Michaelmas in the fourth year of his reign,[2] a certain John of Eston asked the king to give him the tenements which Thomas and Thomas are now claiming, along with other lands and tenements with appurtenances, of which Aveline, daughter of William de Forz, died in possession etc. And this John afterwards granted and quitclaimed all these tenements to the king etc. in return for a hundred pounds' worth of land given to him by the king . . .

ii

B.L., Harl. MS. 395, fo.80

[*Statutes of the Realm*, i. 42-3]

In the presence of the reverend fathers Walter, bishop of Rochester, Robert, bishop of Bath and Wells, Walter, dean of Salisbury, Master Thomas of Wallenham, archdeacon of Dorset, Francis Accursius, doctor of laws, master Robert of Scarborough, archdeacon, Master Robert of Sutton, master Richard of Staines, Master Thomas de Hospital of Henningham, Walter of Boyton, John of Clare, archdeacon of Coventry,

---

[1] He was the king's attorney in the king's bench.

[2] Michaelmas 1276. The names of members of the king's council who were present at this time, when the king asserted his right to the castle and city of Bristol against the claims of the earl of Gloucester, are given in the record of the case on the King's Bench Roll, no.41 (Michaelmas 1276), m.26d (printed *Parl. Writs*, i. 6).

John of Cobham, master Ralph of Frenningham, Nicholas of Stapleton, William of Saham, Walter of Hopton, Walter of Wimborne, William of Northburgh, Solomon of Rochester, Geoffrey Newbald and master Thomas of Saddington, the constitutions written below were recited and recorded and afterwards heard and published in the presence of the king and his council. And all members of the council, justices as well as the others, agreed that they should be put in writing in perpetual memory and that they should be steadfastly observed.

[There follows the Statute of Bigamy]

iii
B. L., Harl. MS. 395, fo.73b
[*Statutes of the Realm*, i. 44]

Regarding those who shall be indicted of trespass where a heavy fine or imprisonment lies and appertains, let redress be immediately awarded to the plaintiff and execution thereof be made without delay. And let the transgressors be placed on good security to be before the king at the next following parliament, if they can find guarantors. And if they cannot, let them remain in prison. And let the justices inquire *ex officio* about the lands and chattels of those about whom men wish to complain and about the nature of the trespass, and let them inform the king at the said parliament so that he can then punish them according to their deserts.[3]

---

[3] This statute 'de justiciariis assignatis', popularly called 'rageman', was possibly made at the Michaelmas Parliament of 1276 and certainly before the autumn of 1278.

PARLIAMENT AT WESTMINSTER: Easter 1277

i
L.T.R. Memoranda Roll, no.50 (1276–77), Hilary Communia, m.3

To the barons on behalf of John de Vaux

Because the king of his special grace has given his beloved and faithful
John de Vaux, formerly sheriff of Norfolk and Suffolk, respite until his
next parliament for all the debts demanded from him by summons of the
exchequer in connexion with the issues from these counties etc., they are
ordered to let John have respite for these debts in the meantime, provided
he afterwards answers the king for the debts as by right he should etc.[1]

ii
Registrum Walteri de Bronescombe
[*Register of Walter Bronescombe*, p.89]

The dispute between the abbots of the Cistercian Order and the
bishop concerning the extent of his jurisdiction had caused the king
to appoint the dean of Salisbury and the archdeacon of Dorset, both
of them learned in civil and canon law, as mediators and they gave
the parties a day to appear in parliament.

And in that parliament, that is to say, on Saturday before the Feast of the
Invention of the Holy Cross in 1277[2] at Westminster the parties appeared
in person before these mediators and reached an agreement.[3]
[The terms follow].

---

[1] For preparations in readiness for this parliament see *Cal. Close Rolls, 1272-79*, p.372,
and cf. p.375.
[2] 1 May 1277.
[3] 5 May 1277.

PARLIAMENT AT WESTMINSTER: Easter 1278

i

Assize Roll, no.1238, m.4

An assize of novel disseisin of common pasture in Hayton in Yorkshire, in which the jury could not say whether the place had formed the subject of another action before justices in eyre and declared 'on their oath that this cannot be ascertained either by them or by any one of their neighbours'.

Afterwards, in the king's parliament after Easter at Westminster in the abovesaid year[1] the process and record of this assize was shown to the king and his council. And the king gave instructions that judgement should be proceeded with in accordance with the verdict of the jurors of the assize. And Thomas de Gunneys came by his attorney and prayed record and judgement for him with respect to the assize. And William Godard and the aforesaid others of Pocklington did not come, and they had a day at that parliament, and they are solemnly summoned and they do not come. Therefore let there be process of judgement by their default.

ii

King's Bench Roll, no.34 (Michaelmas 1277), m.5

Yorkshire

Day is given to the king, demandant, and to the mayor and bailiffs and citizens of York to hear their judgement in respect of the wapentake of Anesty at the next parliament after Easter wherever etc., that is to say, at Three Weeks after Easter etc., because judgement has not yet been made etc.

---

[1] I.e. 1278. It had been assumed in official circles that a parliament would meet as usual at Michaelmas 1277 and business was adjourned to it (*Cal. Close Rolls, 1272-79*, p.380; King's Bench Roll, no.34 (Michaelmas 1277), m.7d; L.T.R. Memoranda Roll, no.50 (1276-77), Easter Communia, m.5.), but Edward I was then on the borders of Wales and remained there almost to the end of the year.

A complaint by the prior and brethren of St. John's Hospital, Brackley, against a demand made on them by the justice of the forest and the exchequer. They went on to state:

This petition was delivered at another time to master Robert of Scarborough and master Nicholas of Stapleton, who were then appointed to receive petitions, and their answer was that he should go to the exchequer and there show the royal charters [put forward in evidence] and they would be allowed.

The prior's attorney therefore did so and the barons of the exchequer told him that no charter would be allowed without specific instructions from our lord the king. And therefore they pray for God's sake for some redress from the demand made on them by the sheriff.

Endorsed: Let the charter be examined in the chancery and let the court be informed of what the justice of the forest has done and enrolled and let justice be done.

PARLIAMENT AT GLOUCESTER: Midsummer 1278

i
Chancery Parliament and Council Proceedings, file 1, no.6

This is an extract apparently from council minutes. They were intelligible to the clerk who wrote them and they provide us with enough information for dating the document. But the meaning of many of the jottings, like the one reproduced, remains unknown.

Concerning the woman to be examined[1]

The women shall send someone to the parliament of Gloucester, and the king in the presence of his justices will there do what ought of right to be done.

Let him come to Gloucester etc.[2]

ii
Chancery Miscellanea, 3/21/3

Memorandum of the expenses, claimed and allowed to the bishop of St. David's,[3] incurred on the king's business during the whole of the time he was treasurer of the wardrobe.

He asks for £56 to be allowed him for his expenses in going on the king's orders on the Feast of St. Peter's Chains[4] to the parliament of Gloucester, and because of illness he could not arrive so soon, and he returned to the court at Rhuddlan after the Feast of the Exaltation of Holy Cross.[5]

---

[1] Written in the margin.
[2] The note of the action to be taken.
[3] Thomas Bek, keeper (or treasurer) of the wardrobe until 20 November 1280.
[4] 1 August 1278.
[5] 14 September 1278.

iii
King's Bench Roll, no.90 (Easter 1285), m.34*d*
[Sayles, *King's Bench*, i. 140-145]

The record of an assize of novel disseisin between Philip Daubeney and Robert Boyton, held before the justices in eyre in Somerset, was sent to the king's bench in 1285 on an allegation of error.

Afterwards, at a Fortnight after Hilary in the nineteenth year of the present king's reign,[6] Robert Boyton came, and so also did Philip Daubeney. And Philip says on behalf of himself that judgement cannot be made in this matter by the writ by which he was summoned to come to court. For he says that Mary, Robert's wife, is dead and therefore, should any judgement be based on this writ, it might happen that Robert and Mary would get recovery, because an error could be found in the record, and this must not occur. And if this is not sufficient, he will say something else etc. And Robert Boyton says that at another time in the king's court at Shrewsbury in the seventeenth year of the present king's reign[7] it was adjudged before the chancellor and the king's council that, notwithstanding that Mary was deceased, nevertheless an examination of the record can be proceeded with without offence to law. And as to this he vouches the record of the chancellor and council. Furthermore, he says that at another time in the king's court in his parliament at Gloucester in the sixth year of the present king's reign[8] Philip's seisin was annulled, and the error of Solomon of Rochester and Richard Boyland and their fellow justices can be clearly seen from that. And thereupon day is given them at Three Weeks after Easter wherever etc. And Robert is told to sue out a chancery writ in order to have the aforesaid record at the same term-day.

Robert says, moreover, that Philip was in litigation with him in the king's court after his wife's death, and he asks for this to be allowed. And if this is not sufficient, he will say something else. On that day the parties came. And Robert did not have the record of the chancellor and council, which he vouched to warranty, as he had vouched it. Therefore Philip goes for the present without day, saving Robert's right when he chooses to speak thereon. And Robert is to be amerced.

[6] 27 January 1291.
[7] 20 November 1288–20 November 1289.
[8] 1278.

PARLIAMENT AT WESTMINSTER: Michaelmas 1278

i

Patent Roll, no.97, m.4d
[*Cal. Patent Rolls. 1272-81*, p.293]

Concerning the hearing and determining of trespasses and appeals

The king to his beloved and faithful John de Luvetot and Geoffrey of Lewknor, greeting. Whereas we have lately appointed you to hear and determine certain trespasses recently committed in the priory of Newport Pagnell as well as certain appeals relating to that business and to deal full and speedy justice thereon in accordance with the law and custom of our realm, reserving to us the amercements and other things pertaining to us therein, and nothing has yet been done about this, so we have been informed, we wish the aforesaid business to be determined with as much speed as possible as well as various other trespasses, appeals and serious offences committed and done afterwards to our beloved in Christ Simon de Rede, prior of the said priory, by several men and even women, whereof some appeals and plaints are pending as well in the county court as elsewhere, and we wish all these things to be investigated and determined by you in the aforesaid form. We command you that, on the stated day and place you can arrange most quickly and conveniently for this purpose, you are to inquire into all the aforesaid matters by careful inquisition as well as by other means whereby the truth can be better and more carefully investigated and ascertained, and to hear and determine this business with everything connected with it in accordance with the contents of our aforesaid mandate so that in our next parliament after Michaelmas you can certify us upon that business. For we have instructed our sheriffs, in whose bailiwicks the trespasses and serious offences as well as the appeals have occurred, that on a stated day and place which shall be made known to them they are to arrange for such-and-such a number and such-and-such respected and law-worthy men of their bailiwicks, through whom the truth of the matter therein can best be known and investigated, to come before you. And they are also to arrange for the appeals in their present state to come before you. And as regards the trespassers and wrongdoers who may be convicted thereon before you, you are in this matter to cause to be done what you think for our part should be done to them. In witness whereof etc. Witness the king at Shotwick on the thirteenth day of September in the sixth year of the king's reign.[1]

---

[1] 13 September 1278.

ii
Patent Roll, no.98, m.24d
[*Foedera*, I. ii. 565; *Cal. Patent Rolls, 1272-81*, p.339]

Scotland

Concerning the hearing and determining of disputes

The king to William, bishop of Norwich, John de Vescy, master Robert of Scarborough and Thomas of Normanville, greeting. Whereas various disputes have arisen between Alexander, the illustrious king of Scotland, and the reverend father Robert, bishop of Durham, concerning certain rights and properties which the king says ought to belong to him as of his realm of Scotland and which the bishop claims to have as appurtenant to his church of Durham, we wish these disputes to be brought to a proper conclusion and to remain at rest, and we have appointed you to hear, redress and determine these disputes as in your discretion you shall think most fit. And therefore we instruct you that at the instant Sunday in Mid-Lent[2] you are to go to the parts of Northumbria and to the boundaries of the places wherein the king and the bishop in turn claim to have these rights and properties, and you are to hear, redress and determine these disputes in accordance with what was provided and ordained before the king himself and you in our last parliament[3] and afterwards before us and our council in the presence of that king's attorneys, whom he left behind on that account in our court after his departure from it, and according to what in your discretion seems most expedient. For we have ordered knights, free men and all others of those parts to be attendant upon you and to obey, advise and assist you in dealing with the aforesaid business according to what you tell them on our behalf, and we have ordered our sheriff of Northumberland that he is to arrange for such-and-such a number and such-and-such knights as well as freeholders etc. to come at the stated days and places about which you are to let him know, through whom the truth of the matter can best be known therein. In witness etc. Witness as above.[4]

[2] 5 March 1279.

[3] Alexander rendered homage to Edward I in the Michaelmas parliament of 1278 (*Cal. Close Rolls, 1272-79*, p.505).

[4] I.e. 4 February 1279 at Woodstock.

PARLIAMENT AT WESTMINSTER: Easter 1279

i

Chancery Parliament and Council Proceedings, file 1, no.13
[Richardson and Sayles, *Rot. Parl. Inediti*, 1–7]

Since this is the first direct record of decisions in parliament that has
come down to us, we translate it in full so that it may be clearly seen
what matters engaged the attention and occupied the time of
parliament.[1]

The parliament at Westminster after Easter in the seventh year of his
reign.

The king has of his special grace granted the men of Douai that they
may sell the cloths they have in England at the approaching fairs of St.
Ives and Boston without hindrance and take the cloths back home if it be
necessary and the cloths are henceforward to be the right measurement.

Again, it was unanimously agreed in the said parliament that all cloths
from overseas should be 26 ells long and 6 quarter-ells wide between the
edges in accordance with the old assize, so that after the next fair at
Boston all cloths found to be not of this measurement are to be forfeited
to the king.

Let an inquiry be made among the merchants of Germany and the
citizens of London whether those of Germany were accustomed to give
murage in the city of London and whether they ought to repair a certain
gate etc.

Let Hamon Hauteyn be associated with the justices of Kent.

The king has ordered that the justices in eyre are to receive their salary.

Let Nicholas fitz Martin have his scutage on the testimony of
Edmund, the king's brother.

The king adjourns four pleas concerning the master of the Temple,
which are before Ralph Hengham, until the Michaelmas parliament.

The king has pardoned the prior of Newport Pagnell his suit against
him, which pertains to him in preserving the peace, for the death of
Hugh the reeve, for which Isolde, his wife, has appealed[2] the prior.

The prior and convent of Carlisle were attached to answer the king on
this: whereas on the recent death of Robert, bishop of Carlisle, they had

---

[1] For a meeting of the council before this parliament and a list of acts, see Chancery
Parl. and Council Proceedings, 1/12.
[2] The process of personal accusation in cases of felony.

sought and obtained through some of their fellow canons a licence to elect, as is customary, and the said prior and convent, after an election had been solemnly proclaimed, had elected William, dean of York, who was well-known, and when the dean did not assent to the election, the prior and convent, without seeking or obtaining a licence, elected someone else as bishop, in prejudice and grievance of the king and his crown and to his damage of sixty thousand pounds; and whereas the prior and convent had been forbidden by John de Vaux and Thomas of Saddington, the king's justices, on the king's behalf to make another election without approaching the king again, they nevertheless made another election in contempt of the king, to the king's damage of forty thousand pounds, so it is said. And the prior comes and says that he and his convent did not understand that they had shown contempt or done prejudice to the king since they had first of all obtained a licence and, when the one they elected did not give his assent to the election, that restored matters as they had been, so they believe, but if there was contempt they submit themselves to the king's will etc.

The justices appointed for the custody of the Jews are ordered to hand over to Thomas of Wayland at a reasonable assessment the land of Kelling, which Abraham, the jew of Norwich, held on lease from James of Ilketshall.

There was disputation before the king's council concerning the record from John de Lisle. And because it was discussed at another time before the council and judicially decided and no error but correct process was found and proceedings were in order, therefore let the judgement stand etc.

Let inquiry be made into the losses the abbot of Quarr sustained from Adam of Stratton and let him be given damages.

The king pardoned Geoffrey Miller the suit against him which pertains to him in preserving the peace, for the death of John of Eastwood whom he killed for thieving, as found by John de Luvetot and his fellows. Let him have a charter if he wishes one.

The king granted to the abbot of Quarr that he would cause the record and process of the plea in the king's bench between him and Adam of Stratton, as well as a transcript of the countess of Aumale's charter which Adam tore up, to be sealed with his seal.

The king committed the business concerning Zeeland and some others of England to Roger Mortimer, John de Luvetot, Nicholas of Stapleton and Master Henry of Newark to hear and determine.

Let Ralph Hengham and his fellows hear the complaints against Ellis de Hauville and determine them.

Let the abbess of Fontevrault and those of the Carthusian Order have their fee every year at the exchequer and let it be written in the chancery roll that letters are to be made out to them each term of payment by order of the king.

Margin: The abbess of Fontevrault and those of the Carthusian Order.

Again, let the justices of the king's bench and the others of the common bench and the justices for the custody of the Jews have their salaries by the king's writs from the king's merchants, and let it also be enrolled in chancery.

Let the inquisitions arising from John of Kirkby's perambulation be handed in and action taken on them and redress made etc.

Margin: Perambulation.

Let the king's men of Bordeaux and La Réole have a period until the Michaelmas parliament to stay with their wines, notwithstanding the Londoners' petition that they should not stay beyond twelve weeks, because the king cannot disregard their petition about a charter made to them thereon.

Margin: Let a writ be made.

And let the murage the Londoners demand from them in respect of their wines etc. be suspended for two years.

Margin: Let a writ be made.

Let the justices of the bench hear and determine the presentments made in the eyre of Hertfordshire against William of Barrington and let his outlawry cease and let him be put on bail until the king's arrival. Let Thomas of Charlecote be released on bail until the Michaelmas parliament.

On Thursday after the Feast of St. Mark the Evangelist[3] Brother John of Darlington of the Order of Preachers, archbishop-elect of Dublin, in the presence of Master Ardicio, papal nuncio, rendered fealty to King Edward and his heirs, kings of England, for the temporalities of the archbishopric of Dublin in these words: I, Brother John of Darlington of the Order of Preachers, whom the pope has appointed by provision to the church of Dublin, swear on the book of the Holy Gospels that I will keep good faith with Edward, king of England, and his heirs, kings of

---

[3] 27 April 1279.

England, with life and limb and worldly honour against all men, and that I will faithfully perform the due and customary service for the temporalities of the archbishopric. And because he came in person and rendered fealty, as aforesaid, the king gave him the temporalities of the archbishopric, as is customary and normally done, and he ordered that he should have writs thereon.

The king pardoned the king of Scotland the hundred marks he was amerced by the justices in eyre last in the county of Middlesex on account of a man who was killed at Staines and buried without view of coroner.

Margin: Pardon

Let Ralph of Hengham and his fellows hear the record of the plea between John de Brus and Lettice of Theydon and dispense justice.

The dean and chapter of York and the abbot of York and the mayor and citizens of York have a day at a Fortnight after Michaelmas.

The king's council agreed, after the king's departure for the coast, that if the bishop of Durham who has a day at the next parliament, that is at Michaelmas, cannot come there, being prevented by important business, he may send faithful men of his to the king, and they are to be heard.

Agreement has been reached between the king of England and the count of Holland and his men until next Christmas, so that satisfaction is given every day on each side until the end of the Michaelmas parliament, and the count's envoys are to show adequate authority as proxies. And let all the merchants of England who have lost property be summoned to come and show in parliament what they have lost, and let satisfaction be then given, as mentioned on another membrane of the aforesaid parliament.

Margin: Zeeland

The sheriffs[4] throughout the whole kingdom are ordered to have it proclaimed in cities, boroughs, townships and throughout their shires that all those who have sustained losses from the men of the count of Holland are to come before the sheriffs, mayors, bailiffs and other reputable men of cities, boroughs and townships and there lawfully prove the losses they sustained from the aforesaid men. And the sheriffs are to send the rolls containing these losses under their seals and the seals of the mayors and the others to the king's council at Three Weeks after Michaelmas. And they are to let them know that they should then be

---

[4] This begins the second membrane, as mentioned, of the proceedings in the Easter parliament.

there to receive satisfaction, provided that, if they do not come then, they will not be heard thereafter. And let the said men state the names of those who did them wrong and let them be inserted in the rolls as well as the places where they were robbed, should they know them, and any other precise details. And let the proof be made in this form, namely, that a man who is robbed or has suffered loss shall swear upon holy relics what his losses are and shall prove them by two or three men at least.

Similar instructions are to be sent to those of the Cinque Ports. And likewise to the Justiciar of Ireland for him to have this business carried out throughout the land of Ireland in the form aforesaid and to send the rolls relating to it to the king at the aforesaid term,[5] and to let those who have sustained losses from the aforesaid men know that they are then to be there to recover their losses if they wish, and if they do not come then, they are not to be heard thereafter.

Thomas de Normanville is told that, whereas the king had lately taken into his secure and safe conduct all the merchants of the count of Holland when they come to England with their goods and merchandise, stay there and return thence, and had made out his letters patent for them in this matter to last until Michaelmas in the seventh year of his reign, and some men of the township of Lynn have seized some goods of the aforesaid men in contravention of the terms of the letters of safe conduct, he is to inquire if that seizure was made after the date of the safe-conduct and, if it should be found so, then if it was done by some individuals without the assent of the community, he was to have those persons then arrested and kept in safe custody until etc., and he is to have the said trespass redressed on behalf of the merchants.

Similarly let the contempt of the bailiffs of Lynn, who did not come on the king's orders, be punished.

A day is given to John Giffard and Maud, his wife, plaintiffs, and Rees Vaughan, tenant, at a Fortnight after Michaelmas with respect to the land of Llandovery because John and Maud vouch the king's record to warrant that Rees is in possession.

The said day is given to John, Maud and Rees with respect to the land of the commote of Perfedd.

William of Rainham has respite at the instance of the queen mother, from assuming knighthood for seven years.

The king will reply to the merchants of Douai about the payment by him of his father's debts in the Michaelmas parliament.

The same merchants have respite from murage until the aforesaid parliament and, if any has been taken, let it be returned.

The whole business between Isabella Mortimer and Llewellyn, prince

[5] That is, Three Weeks after Michaelmas.

of Wales, regarding trespass in Blancmuster wood is committed to Walter of Hopton.

ii

Fine Roll, no.77, m.1

[*Cal. Fine Rolls, 1272-1307*, p.120]

Whereas the king had lately sent for Nicholas of Weston in connexion with certain business on which the king wished to speak with him and he did not deign to come at the king's command but neglected it as though he were one who did not wish to make any answer to the king's writ addressed to him, and afterwards, when Nicholas was found in the king's court and was asked to account for the contempt done to the king, since he thought that he could not prove his innocence in the trespass he put himself therein on the king's will, therefore the king had fixed a day for him at his parliament a Fortnight after Easter next to hear the king's will. At that day he came. And the king on account of his other pressing business could not then manage to speak his will to him. Therefore he adjourned him from that parliament to the next parliament, namely, at Three Weeks after Michaelmas. And on that day he did not deign to come, committing one contempt of the king after another. The sheriff of Northampton is ordered to take without delay all Nicholas's lands and tenements within his bailiwick into the king's hands and to keep them safely until Nicholas comes to the king and makes satisfaction to him for these trespasses. Witness the king at Westminster on the fifteenth day of November.[6]

iii

Ancient Correspondence, vol. XVI, no.195

Eleanor, by the grace of God queen of England, to our most dear son, Edward, by the same grace king of England, greeting and our blessing. We have lately been in dispute and litigation with Lady Eleanor de Percy but, since we have now reached agreement, it is reasonable that we should speak on her behalf and for the business that concerns her. And because, dear son, we have learned that she has been summoned before your justices at York at a Fortnight after Easter to show by what warrant she claims to have free warren at her manor of Topcliffe, free snaring and impounding and other franchises she holds appurtenant to that manor,

---

[6] 15 November 1279.

and she will be unable to be there on that day because it is close at hand and, furthermore, because she cannot well go there without her mother who is not lightly to be taken across country, we beseech you that you may be pleased to put this matter before you at your parliament and to order your justices to send it before you. Dear sire, do this thing the more readily because she was the king your father's niece[7] and is your cousin. Greeting. To God we commend you.

[7] Sir Henry de Percy married in 1268 Eleanor, who was the daughter of John de Warenne, earl of Surrey, and Alice, uterine sister of Henry III, i.e. by the same mother but not the same father, for Alice was the daughter of Hugh de Lusignan, count de la Marche, and Isabella, widow of King John.

PARLIAMENT AT WESTMINSTER: Michaelmas 1279

i

King's Bench Roll, no.49 (Michaelmas 1279), m.23
[Sayles, *King's Bench*, i. 50-51]

Yorkshire

The king sent word to his justices on eyre at York that, because he wished for certain reasons to be informed about the record and process of a plea which is before them by the king's writ of right between the prior of Bridlington, demandant, and the abbot of Cîteaux, deforciant, with regard to the advowson of the church of St. Mary's, Scarborough, they should send the king plainly and openly under their seals without delay the record and process of that plea, along with the king's original writ and other writs of the king which they received thereon and with all other subsidiary documents concerning the plea, and with this writ, so as to have them Three Weeks after Michaelmas wherever the king should then be in England. And the justices did nothing about it but sent word that they could not send the record and process without William of Saham who then kept the principal roll or without their other colleagues who are at present in the king's parliament. Therefore William of Saham is told to have the record etc. in the king's bench a Fortnight after Hilary wherever etc. The same day is given to the parties etc.

ii

Welsh Roll, no.2, m.9
[*Cal. Various Chancery Rolls*, p.179]

Roger de Molis and Howel son of Meuric are appointed to hear and determine the plaints and the trespasses, committed by Canan son of Meriduc son of Owen and his tenants against the abbot and convent of Strata Florida, in accordance with right etc. And should there happen to be in this business any underlying cause or difficulty why they are unable to proceed with it, the parties are to be before the king in the king's next parliament to do and receive what is just in these matters. Witness as above.[1]

---

[1] I.e. 27 July 1279.

iii
Ancient Correspondence, vol. VIII, no.123

To his dearest lord in Christ, John Kirkby, archdeacon of Coventry, his Ralph of Hengham, greeting to himself and his. The diligence which the mayor of London, beloved of you and me, has given to repairing London Bridge is to be admired, and I marvel at his admirable expeditiousness because I myself came to London on Palm Sunday and crossed the bridge with my horses and my equipage, and I am quite certain that it will last for forty years if necessary. Therefore, so it seems to me, you and all the great and influential men of the Court ought to be all the more friendly and kindly disposed to him in all his affairs and particularly those which concern the community of the city. Whereas therefore he had lately received instructions from the king by writ that he was to have corn weighed before it was sent to the mill and likewise the flour when it came from the mill so that people in this way can prevent the wrongdoing of the millers, some of the city who have mills are relying on him so to oppose in this matter that he cannot fulfil the king's instructions. And when the mayor told me about it, my advice was that he should take into the king's hands all the mills, whosesoever they were, where he found the millers recalcitrant in the matter, until parliament, and that then the king with his council would decide about it as seemed best. Therefore, if perchance there are some who should propose complaining to the king thereon and in fact do so, interpose your counsel[2] and aid on behalf of the mayor and please show yourself well disposed to the bearer of this letter in those matters which concern the mayor and community of the city, for I have thought fit to request your special friendship on behalf of him to whom I am bound by particular affection. Farewell always in the Lord.

iv
Close Roll, no.96, m.1d
[Ryley, *Placita*, App. p.442; *Cal. Close Rolls 1272-79*, p.582]

Note that the reverend father John, archbishop of Canterbury, came before the king and his council in the king's parliament of Michaelmas at Westminster in the seventh year of the king's reign and, in respect of the statutes, provisions and their explanations which were promulgated by him at Reading in the month of August in this same year, he

---

[2] As clerk of the council Kirkby was in a position to exercise considerable influence.

acknowledged and agreed that, among some sentences of excommunication there pronounced by the archbishop, there shall first of all be deleted and regarded as not pronounced the clause in the first sentence of excommunication which mentions those who sue out royal letters to hinder process in actions which by the sacred canons etc., secondly, that the king's ministers shall not be excommunicated even though they do not obey the king's instructions by not arresting those excommunicated; thirdly, that as regards those who encroach upon the manors of clerks, the penalty imposed by the king shall be sufficient in this regard; fourthly, that he is not to place under interdict those selling victuals to the archbishop of York or anyone else coming to the king; fifthly, that the Great Charter is to be removed from church doors. He also acknowledged and agreed that nothing shall arise in future to the prejudice of the king or his heirs or his realm of England by reason of any other articles mentioned in the Council of Reading.

PARLIAMENT AT WESTMINSTER: Easter 1280

i

Patent Roll, no.98, m.5

[*Cal. Patent Rolls, 1272-81*, p.330]

On behalf of Pontius Elie and his fellows, merchants of Cahors

The king to all etc. greeting. Know that we have made a bond with our beloved Pontius Elie, Jake Johan and their fellows, merchants of Cahors, for £400 which they gave as a loan by the hands of our dear clerk, master Thomas Bek, keeper of our wardrobe, on Saturday, the Feast of the Apostles Simon and Jude in the seventh year of our reign,[1] and we promise in good faith to pay the merchants the £400 in our next Easter parliament, namely within a month from next Easter day etc.[2] Witness the king at Westminster on the twenty-ninth day of October.

ii

Ancient Correspondence, vol. XX, no.27

To the noble prince his lord, the reverend lord Edward, by the grace of God the illustrious king of England, lord of Ireland and duke of Aquitaine, John of Reigate and his fellows, his justices on eyre in the county of Dorset, greeting, unceasing service, reverence and honour. Whereas you had at another time informed us by your letter that, because Ellis de Rabayn remained constantly in the service of King Henry of celebrated memory, your father, as well as yourself and for that reason you understand that he may find many adversaries and accusers before us in our aforesaid eyre, we were to show him in the charges made against him before us all the grace and favour we can do him by way of justice without harming your crown and dignity, the said Ellis did afterwards appear before us at the end of our eyre before we departed. And in accordance with your orders, forwarded to us at another time by our beloved fellows Solomon of Rochester and William de Brayboeuf, we had careful investigations made not only into those things which concern your warren and castle of Corfe but also into other offences of his,

---

[1] 28 October 1279.

[2] It should be noted that a meeting of parliament was considered a precise date for the repayment of a loan and that the sequence of Easter and Michaelmas parliaments was taken for granted. Similarly, a plea conerning prince Llewellyn of Wales had been adjourned on 24 October 1279 to the Easter parliament of 1280 (Ancient Correspondence, vol.XIII, no.121).

prosecuted by any persons complaining against him. And from these inquiries we found that Ellis had committed a variety of offences, wrongs and extortions in his bailiwick. And so we have adjourned those matters which concern your warren and castle to your parliament after Easter next, and in the other matters we have proceeded as we ought to proceed in accordance with the custom of your realm. But Ellis at another time, after he had been sent to prison for some serious trespasses of which he had been convicted before us on your prosecution and that of certain others, later escaped from prison and fled to Dorchester and put himself inside the church of the Friars Minor and remained there for more than three weeks. And when he was asked by your sheriff and coroners to come to your peace, he scorned doing so. By reason of that flight and such withdrawal from justice we have adjudged that his chattels are to be forfeited and we have committed Ellis to your sheriff, to be kept in custody in your prison at Salisbury until you have considered what else should be done therein. May your excellency flourish evermore.[3]

iii

Chancery Warrants, file 1, no.35A
[*Cal. Chancery Warrants*, i. 591]

Edward by the grace of God king of England, lord of Ireland and duke of Aquitaine, to the reverend father in Christ, Robert by the same grace bishop of Bath and Wells, greeting. Whereas we have ordered Simon de Pierpont to desist at once from the wrongful oppression and exactions he is making on the men of Highweek lest an outcry should again come to us thereon, and Simon does not cease harassing these men still more in contempt of our order, as we have learned from the aforesaid men's complaint, we order you to have Simon summoned by our writ to be before us in this instant parliament of ours to answer to these men for the trespasses and to us for the contempt, in accordance with what in your discretion you think should be done. Farewell. Given under our privy seal at Stapleford on the first day of May in the eighth year of our reign.[4]

---

[3] Ellis had his property restored to him on 8 June 1280 (*Cal. Close Rolls, 1279-88*, p.23) and received a pardon for taking sanctuary in the church at Dorchester on the following 27 June (*Cal. Patent Rolls, 1272-81*, p.383).

[4] 1 May 1280.

iv

Ancient Correspondence, vol. X. no.36

Edward by the grace of God king of England, lord of Ireland and duke of Aquitaine, to his beloved and faithful John Kirkby, greeting. Because men of the Channel Isles have grievously complained to us that they have not been released according to our instructions to you, we command you that, if they be the men who had lately been brought into our presence at Westminster, you are to have them released without delay in accordance with what was provided by our council in the last parliament at Westminster. Given at Langley on the eleventh day of June, and because we do not have our own seal we have had the seal of our beloved Hugh fitz Otto affixed, in the eighth year of our reign.[5]

v

Ancient Correspondence, vol. XIII, no.124

The corrected draft of a letter.

Edward by the grace of God king of England, lord of Ireland and duke of Aquitaine to his beloved and faithful Llewellyn ap Gruffydd, prince of Wales, greeting. We desire, as we ought, that the truce, lately begun between us and you, should be firmly observed in every way in respect of all its articles, and we hope and believe that you for your part will readily act likewise. Nevertheless, because there are some things contained in that truce that have not yet been fully settled, we have lately had a long and careful discussion about them in our parliament with the prelates and magnates of our realm in the presence of your men, and it seemed to all of them and it was agreed with their assent that in such doubtful matters we could not do otherwise than was always wont to be done hitherto in the time of our predecessors, the kings of England. Nor ought you rightly to wonder that we make use of the advice of the prelates and magnates of our realm in these as in other matters. Nor is the said business so doubtful that we cannot always do, in accordance with the dictates of God and justice, those things which the prelates and magnates of our realm should think to advise us to do in these and other matters, especially since no one can be in doubt that men so wise and careful would not give us any advice that disagreed with the principles of justice and contradicted reason . . .[6] Witness me myself at Langley on the eighteenth day of July in the eighth year of our reign.[7]

[5] 11 June 1280.
[6] The king also informs Llewellyn about the steps he has taken to investigate alleged trespasses against his men and to release him from distraint by the justice of Chester.
[7] 18 July 1280.

PARLIAMENT AT WESTMINSTER: Michaelmas 1280

i
Patent Roll, no.99, m.13
[*Foedera*, II. ii. 582; *Cal. Patent Rolls, 1272-81*, pp.380-81]

Ireland

The king to the archbishops, bishops, abbots, priors, earls, barons, knights and all other English of the land of Ireland, greeting. A humble supplication has lately been made to us on behalf of the Irish of Ireland that we should of our grace deign to grant them that they may use and enjoy in common the same laws and customs in Ireland as the English use and enjoy there, and that they may be able to bring actions in future in accordance with these laws and customs. But because we do not wish such a concession to be made to them at present without your knowledge, we command you that you are to assemble at stated days which you shall arrange for this purpose, namely, before the Feast of the Nativity of the Blessed Virgin Mary,[1] in some appropriate places and there have earnest discussion among yourselves whether or not we can make this grant to them without prejudice to you or your liberties and customs or, indeed, your detriment and about all other circumstances relating to the grant. And you shall see to it that what you have done therein is made known to us plainly and openly before our next parliament, which will be at Westminster at a Month after Michaelmas, under the seal of our Justiciar of Ireland or his deputy and the seal of our beloved and faithful Robert Bagot,[2] together with your advice. And you shall in no wise fail to do this on account of the absence of some of your peers, who may not happen to be there, and of those who are under age and in wardship so that we, having immediately the fullest deliberation upon the matter, may cause to be provided thereon what seems to us and our council to be most expedient. In witness whereof etc. Witness as above.[3]

ii
Chancery Parliament and Council Proceedings, file 1, no.19
[A long document from which relevant extracts have been made]

These are the articles which are to be shown to our lord the king and his council by Boges de Knoville, his justice of West Wales.

---

[1] 8 September 1280.
[2] He was Chief Justice of the Common Bench in Ireland.
[3] At Westminster on 10 June 1280.

And let it be shown to our lord the king that at his county court of Carmarthen the English pleas are first of all pleaded and then the Welsh pleas and all in a single day, and thereby, sire, the bailiffs of Sir Edmund, your brother, who were in office before this time have sometimes had to hold their pleas up to midnight by candle-light. Therefore, sire, I have arranged for the English pleas to be heard on one day and the Welsh pleas on the following day. And the Welsh have told me that they would never do this and still do not do it. And therefore, sire, because grave peril can befall your bailiffs when they hold pleas by night in this country district, please send me your letter of warranty for holding the English pleas on one day and the Welsh pleas on another day.

To parliament and in the meantime let it be done as he provides.

And let it be shown to our lord the king that all the people of the county of Carmarthen who have pleaded have pleaded by the writ of Sir Edmund, your brother, who holds his chancery there for such pleadable writs of course, and from this he derives great profit because the people found it useful to have their writs so near at hand. Wherefore, sire, inform me whether it is your pleasure that the men of your county ought to plead by writ and obtain their writs as before.

To parliament

And know, sire, that Sir William de Valence made such a statute that, if any loyal man who was walking through or in any other way traversing the countryside was robbed by thieves or outlaws, then the lords and people in whose lands the robbery was committed should be answerable for the property taken by the thieves who did the robbery, and if it should so happen that the thieves by non-suit or negligence of the people of the countryside should escape after committing their robberies, then the people should answer to you, sire, first for the contempt of the non-suit and the escape and then they should render fully to those who have been robbed the value of their stolen goods[4] . . . And, sire, I have fully ordered that this statute should be held in order to destroy the thieves and to rid the country of them so that merchants and other loyal men can safely come and go. And the lords and people of the country were fully agreed to maintain the statute. Wherefore, sire, be pleased to send me your letter for pursuing this matter in the form you think best to be done in order, sire, to ensure that the lords and people of the countryside will be more eager and more painstaking in doing and achieving this when they see your letter.

Let the letter be made and the justice written to.

[4] This regulation in the Welsh marches anticipated the statute of Winchester, c.2, in 1285 (*Statutes of the Realm*, i.96).

iii

Close Roll, no.97, m.6*d* (schedule)

[Ehrlich, *Proceedings against Crown*, p.235; *Cal. Close Rolls, 1279-88*, pp.56-7]

Because men coming to the king's parliament are often subjected to delays and disturbance, to the great harassment of themselves and of the court, by the multitude of petitions brought before the king, most of which could be disposed of by the chancellor and by the justices, it is provided that all the petitions that involve the [great] seal are to come first of all to the chancery, and those that involve the exchequer are to come to the exchequer, and those that involve the justices and the law of the land are to come to the justices, and those that involve the Jewry are to come to the justices of the Jewry. And if the business is so important or a matter of grace so that the chancellor and the others cannot deal with it in the king's absence, then they shall bring it by their own hand before the king in order to learn his will thereon,[5-] and this means that no petition may come before the king and his council except by the hands of the chancellor and the other principal ministers,[-5] and thus the king and his council can attend to the great business of his kingdom and of his foreign lands without being burdened with other matters.

iv

Cotton MSS., Julius D 2, f.112

[*Parl. Writs*, i. 8]

The barons of Sandwich in the time of Abbot Nicholas of St. Augustine's of Canterbury complained to the abbot that his keeper of Minster had distrained on their stone at Minster by pickage[6] and building in prejudice of their franchises, and they asked for this distraint to be released and cease. And answer was made to them on the abbot's behalf that he does not believe that any wrong was done in the matter of this distraint and demand because he does not believe any franchise to be so extensive that it can steal another's land without leave, nor does he intend to release this distraint. Whereupon they brought him a writ of prohibition from the king to the effect that he was not to distrain them by any kind of customary right in prejudice of their franchise. And because the abbot does not mean any the less to stop distraining, they sued out another writ of the king, addressed to Sir Stephen of Penchester, keeper of the Cinque Ports, in the eighth year of the king's reign, stating that he was to have

---

[5-5] An insertion.
[6] 'Pickage' means to break ground in order to erect a stall.

their distraint released until the next parliament and to attach the abbot to be there to answer why he had distrained them. The abbot came to the parliament and appeared before the king's council. And the king sent Sir Stephen of Penchester, Master Henry of Brandiston, Sir Roger Loveday and Sir Ralph of Sandwich out of his chamber to hear the parties. And the men of Sandwich were summoned and came before them before the dais in the little room and said that they did not wish to plead or sue against the abbot, wherefore the abbot by judgement of the council was acquitted against them and went at this time without day and might resume his distraint. And thus the matter remains until now.

v

King's Bench Plea Roll, no.64 (Michaelmas 1281), m.31*d*
[Sayles, *King's Bench*, i. 91–93]

The record of a plea of 'quo warranto', heard in Yorkshire, was ordered on 12 July 1281 to be sent by the justices on eyre to the next parliament at Westminster.

And because by order of the king all original writs of 'quo warranto', both those begun and those finished, which the king brought in the county of Yorkshire, were sent to the Michaelmas parliament in the eighth year of his reign, and some of them remained there and some were sent back, and among those which remained was the original writ of this plea and it was not sent back, therefore it is not appended to this record nor transmitted with it etc.

vi

Harleian MS. no.667, f.3
[*Eng. Hist. Review*, XLIII, p.13, n.3]

Be it known to all men that, whereas some articles of ecclesiastical grievances had been shown on behalf of the archbishop of Canterbury and his suffragans to the lord Edward, by the grace of God, king of England, and they had reverently and humbly implored him to exercise his royal clemency, and, after obtaining the counsel of his nobles and having had numerous discussions with them on these matters in his winter parliament, held at London on the Morrow of All Souls in the year of the Lord 1280,[7] he answered in the form (as written below),

---

[7] 2 November 1280.

stating that he could not answer otherwise save by departing utterly from the counsel of his nobles, which would in no wise profit him or the Church or, indeed, the state of the realm of England. And because the king has postponed giving arbitration upon the grievances in writing because he wishes to reserve for investigation some things still requiring further delay and deliberation, we, having carefully committed to memory the answers to the articles in the king's presence and having had a very earnest conference with our fellow bishops and other wise men, have made a memorandum of them by their advice and agreement, setting down (as below) the answers to these articles in order by themselves.

PARLIAMENT AT WESTMINSTER: Easter 1281

i

Ancient Correspondence, vol. XXIV, no.74

[Sayles, *King's Bench*, i. pp.cxlii-cxliii]

To the reverend father in Christ and to his most dear lord, Robert, by the grace of God bishop of Bath and Wells, the king's chancellor, his devoted Solomon of Rochester and his fellows, the justices on eyre in the county of Devon, greeting with all reverence and honour. Because we do truly mean to finish our present eyre in Devon before Easter, we ask you to be so good as to tell us, as quickly as you can, to which county we ought to adjourn after Easter, and at which term, and whether we all ought to come to parliament, please remembering that, if we all were to come there, then the county court of Cornwall will not be able to be summoned conveniently before the Week or the Fortnight after Trinity by reason of the little time between the Week after Easter and parliament and of the long journey between Cornwall and London and of the long stay in parliament, as you know. And should you wish to prorogue the said eyre until after Michaelmas, you would confer a great benefit on the whole county and on us, because this year there is a lack of corn there and, if we come there this summer, we will bring back thin cheeks. Please signify your pleasure to us by the bearer of this letter. May your reverend lordship flourish evermore.[1]

ii

King's Bench Roll, no.60 (Easter 1281), m.19*d*

[Sayles, *King's Bench*, i. 78-79]

> The merchants of Flanders are impleading Millicent, sister and heiress of George de Cauntelo, in a plea of debt for four hundred marks owed by her brother.

The king gave the justices instructions at another time that they were to send him the record and process of that plea so that he could have them in his next Easter parliament, which will be at Westminster a Month after Easter etc.

    Afterwards Millicent comes here in the king's bench on this day and asks that the exceptions she has made should be allowed her, namely, that she should not be compelled to answer the executors [of George de Cauntelo] for the debt without John of Hastings, who is her coparcener

---

[1] For the date of this letter see *Cal. Patent Rolls, 1272-81* p.384

and under age in the king's wardship; for she is not alone in being George's heir nor, indeed, ought she to answer the executors for the debt, even if it were adjudged that she must answer them without John, inasmuch as George's executors have sufficient property of his for the payment of the four hundred marks to the merchants. And because it seems to the king and his council that Millicent is not bound to answer the merchants for the debt without John, her coparcener, it is adjudged that the plea is to stand over until John comes of age etc.

iii
Ancient Correspondence, vol. XIX, no.125

From the Easter parliament in the ninth year.

After an investigation had been made on the king's orders into the losses incurred by Pierre de Montravel, both in the demolition of his house at Cadillac and the theft of his goods therein committed by the sheriff of Fronsac, he received an answer from the king and council that, in addition to what the king has given him at another time in compensation for the aforesaid losses, he will still give him a hundred marks and, while he is prosecuting in his own person his business against the sheriff of Fronsac in the court of the king of France, he will give him fifty pounds Tournois[2] and furthermore he will arrange for Peter's case to be supported by his own advocates in that court, and if the king of England should happen to keep the fiefs, he will compensate Peter for the remainder of his losses so reasonably that Peter and his friends ought to be contented.[3]

---

[2] About a quarter of the value of pounds sterling.
[3] Cf. *Roles Gascons*, ii. 129a (dated 8 June 1281).

PARLIAMENT AT WESTMINSTER: Michaelmas 1281

i

King's Bench Plea Roll, no.64 (Michaelmas 1281), m.51

Kent

Henry son and heir of Ralph de la Woodgate who sues for the king came forward on the fourth day against William de Sulbesdon on this plea: when the king was lately at Canterbury, he had William de Sulbesdon come before him at Henry's suit to answer the king and Henry why, when it had been agreed a long time ago between Ralph on one side and William on the other that William should marry his daughter to Henry and give Ralph fifty three marks six shillings and eight pence for Henry's marriage-portion and Ralph should enfeoff William with all his land on condition that William re-enfeoffed Henry and his daughter with it conjointly, William refused to keep that covenant immediately after Ralph's death and sold all the land, of which Ralph had given William seisin according to the aforesaid covenant, to Jocelin de Badlesmere, to Henry's manifest disherison. And William, coming there before the king, acknowledged and agreed that he would keep the covenant. And a day was given to William to be before the king in the king's parliament after Michaelmas last to confirm the covenant, and a promise was then given by Stephen of Penchester and John of Ruxley that they would do all in their power to persuade Jocelin to restore the land to William. And Jocelin then agreed to this before the king, provided William restored to him the money he had received from Jocelin, as William then acknowledged he was willing to do. And he did not come. And the king, on the ground that William scorned to come to his parliament to confirm the covenant as aforesaid, ordered the sheriff to cause William to come here on this day to confirm his covenant and to do and receive further what justice advises.

ii

Ancient Correspondence, vol. XXIV, no.178

To the venerable father in Christ and his reverend lord, the bishop of Bath and Wells and the king's chancellor, if it please him his Alan of Walkingham, greeting with all reverence and honour and readiness to serve. Please bear it well in mind that on my departure from the last parliament at London[1] you said to me of your grace that, since I had no

---

[1] Michaelmas 1281.

special instructions to come to the king in the parts of Wales, I could well return home and take the assizes in various counties assigned to Geoffrey Aguillun and me. Wherefore we have already traversed those counties and taken the assizes which were ready and which we did not adjourn to come on stated days, as was wont to be done in accordance with the law and custom of the realm. And we instructed the sheriffs to cause all assizes, sued for in the mean time, to come summoned and ready, before us on appointed days. Therefore, as a result of this second appointment, we have a day at York on the Morrow of St. Peter's Chains to take many assizes, juries and attaints. Moreover, I have therefore not provided myself with suitable caparisoned horses, armour or adequate retinue to come to the parts of Wales. Now, however, I have received thereon the king's instructions at York a Week after Midsummer[2] that I should be at Rhuddlan on Sunday, the Morrow after St. Peter's Chains,[3] with horses and arms and with all the service I owe to the king, prepared to set out thence with the king on his campaign against the Welsh. And since I hold nothing in chief from the king save a mere five marks' worth of land by the enfeoffment made to me and my wife by the late Adam of Boltby from his barony of Langley in the county of Cumberland, and since Thomas de Lucy and his wife hold the rest of the barony and he has a writ from the king to come to the parts of Wales with his service, may it please your reverend lordship of your fatherly goodness to please let me indeed know with your accustomed kindness your good pleasure whether for so small an amount of land it is necessary for me to go in person with horses and arms to those parts or to send someone else, and to cease taking assizes or to do something else on behalf of that little bit of land, as you may see fit to decide, knowing moreover that after my illness I have not yet been able to attain full bodily health and have not yet stopped being troubled every day in some way by that illness. And although I do not hold more of the king than the five marks' worth of land, for various reasons and obstacles and difficulties I cannot worthily fulfil at the moment, as I would like, the king's instructions without much harassment. And I do not make excuses therein, save for some illness, loss or hardship, even though I should hold nothing in chief of the king, since my honour and advancement and what I am come from the king. And if you think it advisable, may it please your lordship to discuss this matter with the king and to please be so kind as to inform me truly of his wishes and your good pleasure by the bearer of this letter, either by a writ from the king or a letter from you, as you please.

May you, father, flourish evermore.

[2] 1 July 1282.
[3] 2 August 1282: for the date, see *Parl. Writs*, i. 7.

1282

It was assumed that parliaments would meet as usual at Easter and Michaelmas in 1282, 1283 and 1284, and constant adjournments of business and litigation were accordingly made by government departments and courts of law. But in the event war in Wales occupied the king's whole attention throughout this time and he could be persuaded only once, at Michaelmas 1283, to hold a parliament, and that on the borders of Wales, and only then at the insistence apparently of Robert Burnell, the chancellor. To give one illustration: the king apologised for not being able to attend to the business of the count of Flanders because of the Welsh war but when it was over 'and he will be in his parliament', able to have discussion with his council, he would then deal with it (Chancery Warrants, Series I, 1682/98).

PARLIAMENT AT ACTON BURNELL: Michaelmas 1283

i

Chancery Parliament and Council Proceedings, file 2, nos.2, 3
[Richardson and Sayles, *Rot. Parl. Inediti*, pp.12-16]

Replies to the Petitions at Acton Burnell in the Michaelmas Parliament in the
Eleventh Year of the Reign of King Edward, and some other
business concluded there, and Instructions

Order is made that someone should be appointed on behalf of the king
and someone on behalf of the executors of Patrick de Chaourches to
survey and assess Patrick's goods and chattels according to their true
value and to inquire in whose hands they were.

The escheator below the river Trent is ordered to restore to Aymer de
Peche the seisin of the manor of Steeple in Essex which Hugh fitz Otto
held of him.

Let Richard of Boyland be associated with John de Vaux in place of
Robert Baignard in taking the attaint which the prior of Bayham
arraigned against William of Pakenham.

Note the £331 of three terms, namely, Michaelmas term in the tenth
year of the king's reign and Easter term in the eleventh year and
Michaelmas in the eleventh year, for the fee of the constable of Dover and
the wages of the servants and chaplains etc.

Let it be ascertained from the king if he wishes Ralph of Hengham to
go to London with the king's pleas.

Let there be discussion with the king about the payment by
instalments of the debts of Philip of Stambourne and Hugh Bonting,
namely, of 200 marks.

Let a day be given to the bishop of Worcester and the abbot of
Westminster in the king's bench on the Feast of St. Andrew.[1]

Let the men of Stamford have a day, with respect to the assize of cloth,
at a Month after Michaelmas in the twelfth year of the king's reign,[2] and
in the meantime let them make their cloths according to their former
assize. And let them have a writ patent.

Concerning a certain burgage to be given to the prior and convent of
Bath.

Concerning the business of the abbot of St. Augustine's, Canterbury.

Concerning the petition of the bishop of Worcester for obtaining a
licence to enfeoff the chapter of York with the manor of Burley: it seems

---

[1] 30 November 1283.
[2] Michaelmas 1284.

to the justices that it is permissible if it please the king.

Let the lands of Isabella, who was Philip Burnell's wife, taken into the king's hands on account of her trespass, remain in the king's hands until the Easter parliament. And let her come then before the king and he will state his wishes etc.

Note the £20 of rent, granted to John of Brittany in the county of Lincoln at the king's will: let Nicholas of Stapleton come to Westminster and show the chancellor and council why the sheriff does not allow him to have the bailiwick from which the rent is levied, in accordance with the king's will. And the sheriff is ordered to come etc.

Concerning fixing terms for the payment of the debts of Hugh Lovel.

Concerning the debts of William Martin, namely, £100 – 50 marks a year.

Concerning the debts of John de Colombières, namely £80 – £20 a year.

Concerning the adjournment of the dispute between William de Valence and the earl of Hereford.

Concerning the attaint against John de Hastings on behalf of the earl of Cornwall.

Concerning the manor of Norton, to be delivered to the earl of Warwick. To the escheator that he make inquiry about the value and return the information.

Concerning the amercements pardoned the prior of Deerhurst at the instance of the abbot of St. Denis in France.

The business of the earl of Cornwall is committed to Walter of Amersham.

The business of Hugh de Plescy is committed to William of Hamilton.

Let the woman who is suing on behalf of the chaplain imprisoned at Nottingham go to Nicholas of Stapleton because he has been ordered to deliver him.[3]

Concerning sending Thomas of Tiltey to Chester and the search for charters.

Concerning the wives of Thomas of Withington and William Cook: let them make recognisances.

Concerning the brother of Robert Mortimer.

Concerning Roger of Butterleigh.

Concerning arrears in the salaries of those of the Court.

Concerning the business of Ralph of Hengham and the archbishop of York.

Concerning the business of the bishop of Norwich with respect to service due to the king.

---

[3] Nicholas was to try him on a commission of gaol-delivery.

Concerning the business of Solomon of Rochester.

The underwritten petitions are sent to Hugh of Kendale to be expedited

[there follow the names of twenty-two petitioners, and twelve of their petitions still survive[4] to show what action was taken upon them]

To Henry of Hamilton: the petitions of the woman of Ireland, master William of Farnham, Nicholas . . .

Let Hawis Tonere have a writ of entry.

John de Colombières: £20 a year.

Thomas of Thorney and someone else of Carlton, imprisoned at Aylesbury: let the justices take gaol-delivery of them.

Hawis Wake

Let the abbot of Haughmond have a licence to enclose four acres of meadow.

The township of Shrewsbury: let it have pavage for a term of three years.

The abbess of Lacock: that she can etc. the land.

ii

Ancient Correspondence, vol. XXV, no.153

To William of Hamilton, greeting. We send word that the demand which the sheriff of Buckingham is making upon Martin de Carron by an exchequer writ from the king is to be adjourned by the king's chancery writ until the next parliament in London. Farewell. Given at Acton Burnell the seventeenth day of September.

iii

Liberate Roll, no.61 (13 Edward I), m.5

Among allowances made to Reginald de Grey, justice of Chester:

For the expenses of six score footmen for two days, bringing David [5] from Chester to Shrewsbury in our Michaelmas parliament at Acton Burnell in the same year.

---

[4] *Rot. Parl. Inediti*, pp.17-25.
[5] David ap Gruffydd, brother of Llewellyn, prince of Wales.

PARLIAMENT AT WESTMINSTER: Easter 1285

i

Close Roll, no.102, m.5, schedule

[*Rot. Parl.*, i. 225; *Statutes of the Realm*, i. 104 f; Ryley, *Placita*, p.448;
Cal. Close Rolls, 1279-88, p.331 f]

Many of the king's realm, not only prelates, the religious and other
ecclesiastical persons but also earls, barons and other secular and lay
persons beseeched the king in his Easter parliament at Westminster in the
thirteenth year of his reign that he would of his grace confirm the charters
granted by his ancestors, the kings of England, or others to the
predecessors or ancestors of the said persons and to them. Wherefore the
king, having discussed the matter with his council, granted that
confirmations of the said charters should be made in the underwritten
forms.[1]

Of[2] exceptions that have been put forward and not enrolled.[3]

Of dykes knocked down at night.

Of women and children of either sex abducted.

We have also inspected another of our father's charters, made for our
said brother in these [words][4]

ii

Statute Roll, no.1, m.44

[*Statutes of the Realm*, i. 83 f]

And whenever in future it should happen in the chancery that a writ is
available in one case, and in a similar case, falling under the same
principles of justice, similar redress is lacking, let the clerks of chancery
agree either to make out a writ or to give those who ask for one a day in
the next parliament, and they are to write down the cases in which they
cannot agree and refer them to the next parliament, and a writ shall be

---

[1] The forms given established the standard formulas for the confirmation of charters.

[2] m.5d. The schedule, which represented memoranda of business done by council in
parliament, was not enrolled on the close roll but fortunately attached to it. These
jottings on its back were ignored by Ryley and the editors of the *Rot. Parl.* and *Statutes of
the Realm* but noted in the *Cal. Close Rolls.*

[3] The decision on this matter formed part of the Second Statute of Westminster
(1285), c.31. Arguments, rejected by the court and therfore not enrolled on the plea roll,
could be written down and the justices asked to authenticate the document with their
seals. It would then serve as a ground for an allegation of error, even though the court
record knew nothing of it. See Sayles, *Select Cases King's Bench*, ii. pp.c-ci.

[4] The document ends incompletely thus.

made with the consent of men learned in the law lest it happen in future that the court should too long fail in administering justice to those who seek it.[5]

iii

B.L., Harleian MS., no.645, ff.234b-225a

[*Eng. Hist. Review*, lii. 232-4; *Councils and Synods*, ii. 962 f]

> This seems to be the first clear example of committee procedure, though it must always have been common and will soon be a most marked feature of parliamentary practice.

These are the articles handed in at the Easter parliament in the year of our Lord 1285, to which no reply was then made by the king but by the chancellor only and those of the council who were then present.[6]

iv

King's Bench Plea Roll, no.95 (Michaelmas 1285), m.8

[Sayles, *King's Bench*, i. 157-8]

Chester

The citizens of the city of Chester came forward by their attorney on the fourth day against the community of the county of Cheshire on a plea of [distraint],[7] held before the king in his parliament at Westminster a Month after Easter, concerning this: that the citizens ought to have contributed with those of the community to the aid for constructing and repairing Chester Bridge. And at that parliament a day was given to the community of the county until this day etc. to show if they knew any reason why the citizens ought to have contributed with them to constructing and repairing the bridge. And they did not come. And the citizens came by their attorney. Therefore it is adjudged that the citizens are to go thereon without day and to have a writ to the justice of Chester to the effect that he is not to distrain them or molest them on this account or permit them henceforward to be molested etc.

[5] Statute of Westminster (1285), c.24.

[6] There follows an informal note of seventeen articles that were discussed and decided.

[7] The edge of the membrane is torn away.

v

B.L., Cotton MSS., Cleopatra C. VII, f.15b

Note that in the year of our Lord 1285 and the thirteenth year of the reign of King Edward son of King Henry, on the eve of Palm Sunday[8] which was then the sixteenth kalends of April, Thomas of Ringmer, who was then the prior of Christ Church, Canterbury, resigned the priory. And taking off the black habit, he put on the white habit of the Cistercians at Beaulieu in the diocese of Winchester. On hearing this, master Henry de Bray, then the king's escheator below the river Trent, took the entire priory into the king's hands, saying that the custody of the priory belonged to the king himself when the priory was void, a thing which he had never before seen with his eyes or heard with his ears. When they heard about this the sub-prior and chapter immediately sent two brethren to the king who was then in Norfolk in order to petition for redress.

And after the business had been expounded before the king, he delivered to them the whole priory with all the profits from it until his next parliament at London on the Feast of Pentecost following.[9] And the king instructed the treasurer and barons of the exchequer that in the meantime they were to inform him and his council at that parliament about what rights he might have in the aforesaid custody.

Thereafter at the Fortnight after Easter following,[10] Henry of Chester was created prior and he afterwards came to the said parliament on that business and appointed attorneys before the king to prosecute it. At last, at the end of parliament, the king had the attorneys summoned before him and he had the certification of the treasurer and barons of the exchequer read out in the following terms:

> Having scrutinised the exchequer rolls of the time of King John it is found in the rolls of the thirteenth and fourteenth years of the said king's reign[11] that, at the time when the archbishopric of Canterbury was in the king's custody, the priory of Canterbury was likewise in the king's custody. And having scrutinised other rolls of John's time as well as of the time of King Henry, his son, it was not found that the priory had been in his custody either before or after.

---

[8] 17 March 1285.
[9] 13 May 1285.
[10] 8 April.
[11] 1211-13.

And the aforesaid attorneys answered this certification in the following terms: O lord king, at the time mentioned in the certification the archbishop and the prior of Canterbury were in exile, and then your grandfather, King John, seized the entire archbishopric and priory, but not by right of custody because it was not legally void. But he was disturbed in mind and provoked to wrath against them, and this plainly appeared later on when the said king ordered everything taken from the archbishop and the prior to be fully restored.

And the king, after having had discussion with his council about this answer of the attorneys, finally replied with his own voice in these words: We restore to the convent the whole priory with all the profits therefrom, nor is it our wish that our escheator should henceforward meddle in any way during vacancies in the priory. And thereupon he ordered the following writ to be made.

Edward by the grace of God etc. to his beloved clerk, master Henry of Bray, his escheator below the river Trent, greeting. Because we understand for certain that the custody of the priory of Holy Trinity, Canterbury, was not wont to appertain to us or our predecessors, the kings of England, during vacancies, we instruct you to hand over to the prior and convent of the said place without delay all the profits you have taken to our use from the custody of the aforesaid priory during the late vacancy. And you are not to meddle henceforward with the priory on account of a vacancy within it. Witness myself at Westminster on the first day of June in the thirteenth year of our reign.[12]

By the king and his council

The aforesaid writ is registered in the rolls of the chancery registry among the close rolls of the thirteenth year of the reign of King Edward son of King Henry.[13]

vi

Registrum Johannis de Pontissara, fo.73a
[*Register of John de Pontissara*, i. 298 f]

*A letter from the bishop of Winchester to the bishop of Bath and Wells
on behalf of a priest who committed suicide*

To the reverend father in Christ Robert, by the grace of God the lord bishop of Bath and Wells, John by the same divine permission the bishop of Winchester, greeting and sincere and ever increasing love. The Most

---

[12] 1 June 1285.
[13] *Cal. Close Rolls, 1279-1288*, p.323.

High knows that we do not wish to damage in any way the rights and liberties of the church of Bath but to keep them unharmed to the best of our ability through respect for your lordship. Indeed, as regards the property of that wicked priest who committed suicide, about which you have recently taken trouble to have a discussion with us, various men skilled in the law and custom of England hold different opinions. Some state that such property ought to pertain to the Church or ecclesiastical court, and others say that it should belong to the temporal lord. Wherefore we most affectionately beseech your lordship that for love of us and for the zeal you constantly display for justice you should kindly supersede all process, held or to be held against any of our bailiffs for the aforesaid reason, until the next parliament, and there we shall be able to be more fully informed, God willing, about the said law and custom, knowing for certain that you will lose very little thereby, because we will take pains to look after this property in the meantime on behalf of you as well as on behalf of ourselves in good faith. May the Most High keep you in His sacred service for ever and ever. Given at Brightwell on the day of the Conversion of St. Paul the Apostle in the year of the Lord 1284.[14]

---

[14] 25 January 1285.

PARLIAMENT AT WINCHESTER: Michaelmas 1285

Statute Roll, no.1, m.41
[*Statutes of the Realm*, i. 98]

And in every hundred and liberty two constables are to be chosen to make the view of armour, and the constables are to show before the justices assigned, when they come into their district, the defects they have found with respect to armour and performance of watch-duties and highways, and they are also to present the people who lodge strangers, for whom they do not wish to be responsible, in villages in the uplands. And the justices assigned are to report to the king in every parliament, and thereupon the king will provide redress therein.[1]

---

[1] From the Statute of Winchester, published 8 October 1285 at Winchester: a police measure for the preservation of the peace.

PARLIAMENT AT WESTMINSTER: Easter 1286

i
King's Bench Roll, no.97 (Hilary 1286), m.1

Dorset, Devon

Richard du Bois, Ralph de Gorges of the county of Dorset, Gilbert of Brideshill of the county (*sic*), Peter of Grenham, knights, have undertaken to have Lawrence of Preston in person before the king at the next parliament at Westminster to do the king's will etc.

ii
King's Bench Roll, no.96 (Hilary 1286), m.2

Hampshire

The suit between the king, plaintiff, and Adam Gurdun, tenant, is adjourned until parliament.

By the king's instructions.

iii
Close Roll, no.105, m.4d
[*Parl. Writs*, i. 18: *Cal. Close Rolls, 1279-88*, p.547]

That no one shall take up arms in the realm whereby the peace can be disturbed

The king to his beloved and faithful Roger Bigod, earl of Norfolk and marshal of England, greeting. Whereas we gave instructions to you and the other magnates and nobles of our realm in our presence at Westminster before our recent departure therefrom[1] that our peace within the realm was to be inviolably preserved by you and them during our absence, we command you in the faith and love by which you are bound to us, firmly enjoining that, without orders in some emergency from us or our beloved cousin and loyal subject Edmund, earl of Cornwall, our deputy in England, you are in no way to make your way throughout the realm with horses and arms or in any other way with

---

[1] The king left England on 13 May 1286. According to the Annals of Osney, he had discussed his relations with France at a meeting after Easter (*Annales Monastici*, iv. 306). Edward I was at Westminster in the latter part of April (Gough, *Itinerary*, ii. 20).

armed force whereby the people can be terrified or our peace in any way disturbed. For if any dispute should arise among any of you, let him come before our cousin at a Fortnight after Michaelmas next at Westminster to show his arguments about the grievances done to him and further to receive the redress that our council will provide therein. And lest you attempt anything in breach of our peace, we sternly forbid you to do it on forfeiture of all that you hold of us. Witness the king's council at Westminster on the twenty-second day of August.[2]

---

[2] 22 August 1288.

1286-1289

Edward I went abroad on 13 May 1286 and did not return to England until 12 August 1289. He was French in speech, French in outlook, and the ruler of the French duchy of Aquitaine, and saw nothing strange in living so long out of England. Nevertheless, he was always expecting to be back long before he returned. Edmund of Cornwall, his cousin, who acted as regent, kept in constant touch with him and held sessions of the council at the four law-terms of Hilary, Easter, Trinity and Michaelmas to consider problems of law and administration, such as would normally have come before parliament.[1] He too did not think that the king would be absent for more than three years, and departments and courts continued to make adjournments to 'the next parliament' or 'to the next parliament after the king's arrival in England'.[2] It is clear that the king was unwilling that parliaments should be held save in his presence, but at Easter 1289 he apparently permitted a parliament to be assembled. We know very little about it and have only one document to indicate its existence (no.iii). We conjecture that on this exceptional occasion the king conceded that matters which concerned him in person need not be referred to him abroad or postponed until his return but be dealt with in London.

i

Ancient Petition, file 260, no.12998

To the earl and the council prays William de Munchensy of Edwardstone that, whereas he is in the peace and fealty of our lord the king and in his prison, he may have justices before whom he can clear himself by the common law as regard the wrongdoing which has been alleged against him, for he has none of his lands or of his chattels and has had none for a long time on which he can live, except for what his friends find for him. Wherefore he prays you to be so good as to have pity on him.[3]

Endorsed: The earl will inform the king about this business and other matters.

---

[1] *Bull. Inst. Hist. Research*, v. pp.141-3.

[2] King's Bench Roll, no.106 (Trinity 1287), m.24 (Sayles, *King's Bench*, i. 166-67); Exchequer, Treasury of Receipt, Forest Proceedings, 127 m.14 (Harcourt, *His Grace the Steward*, p.316).

[3] He had submitted himself to the king's will in February 1286 (*Cal. Close Rolls, 1279-88*, p.409) but was apparently still in prison in 1290 (*ibid., 1288-96*, p.68).

ii

Ancient Correspondence, vol. XII, no.147

Edward by the grace of God king of England, lord of Ireland and duke of Aquitaine, to his beloved kinsman and loyal subject Edmund, earl of Cornwall, his deputy in the realm, greeting. We have heard the grievous complaint of Walter de Reingny, clerk, as follows: whereas he had been for some time the keeper of the wardrobe of Boges de Clare, having charge and administration of money as well as jewels and other things pertaining to such an office, and afterwards he had presented Boges's accounts and been given his allowances and made his final reckoning, Boges, although he was indebted to Walter for a great sum of money at the end of the aforesaid accounting, nevertheless incessantly harassed Walter before the treasurer and barons of our exchequer, term after term and day after day, by reason of this accounting, nor does he cease to disturb him wrongfully, to his manifest loss. We therefore who are bound to give justice to all the inhabitants of our realm command you to call before you the treasurer and barons as well as our justices of both benches and the other loyal members of our council in England who may happen to be then and there present, and to summon the parties, and when you have heard the arguments concerning this business which the parties may wish to propound before you and which, so it is said, are in need of the fullest examination, you are to cause due and speedy justice to be done in full to Walter as well as to Boges on each and every one of the abovesaid matters without further delay, no favours preventing it, lest – which God forbid – with so many distinguished and wise men assembled together the parties should be seen to depart without sound redress. Witness myself at Bordeaux on the fifteenth day of February in the sixteenth year of our reign.[4]

iii

King's Bench Roll, no.121 (Michaelmas 1289), m.41

[Sayles, *King's Bench*, I. 179–81]

Dorset

Whereas in the parliament at Westminster after Easter in the seventeenth year of the present king's reign before the earl of Cornwall and the king's council various inquisitions made between Joan of Little Puddle, who is suing for the king, and the prior of Christ Church, Twyneham, had been read out with regard to a certain pasture alienated in mortmain, and on

---

[4] 15 February 1288.

this account the pasture ought to go to the king as forfeiture, and the inquisitions have for various reasons been challenged, it was provided that an inquisition should be made afresh before Ralph of Hengham in the presence of the parties when he came into those parts. And he came to Mere in Pentecost week in the aforesaid year of the present king's reign[5] and he caused the jurors to come into the presence of the parties. And the parties could not agree concerning the jurors. Therefore on that day the inquisition remained to be taken.

> The men of Joan of Little Puddle had complained that the prior's men had arrested and imprisoned them while they were tending their cattle on the pasture land. But the prior argued that they had been prosecuted as thieves caught red-handed in his hundred court of Puddletown and set free by judgement of that court, a statement that was disproved when a record of the court's proceedings was produced. The hundred was in consequence taken into the king's hands.

Afterwards the prior came to the king and asked for the hundred to be given back to him until the king's parliament after Christmas.[6] At that parliament the king of his special grace granted him the hundred. Therefore let it be restored to him etc.

iv
King's Bench Roll, no.120 (Trinity 1289), m.30

Edward, by the grace of God king of England etc., to his beloved and faithful Ralph of Hengham and his fellows, the justices assigned to hear and determine his pleas, greeting. Whereas Master John Fleming has impleaded Walter Bek and Joan, his wife, by our writ before our justices lately on eyre in Wiltshire with respect to one messuage and one carucate of land with appurtenances in Haxton near Fittleton, and the said justices have adjourned the plea before you on account of a certain allegation made on our behalf before them, we do not wish John to be harmed in any way, for he has stayed overseas in our service by our orders, and we instruct you that, although the plea concerns us, yet you are not to await our presence but to proceed to judgement in that suit without any hesitation so that John's right in these matters is not held up by reason of the said allegation. We are instructing our beloved and faithful cousin,

[5] 5 June 1289.
[6] This phrase is not uncommon to indicate the parliament at Hilary (below, p.195).

Edmund, earl of Cornwall, deputising for us in England, to have this done. Witness myself at Condom on the eighteenth day of April in the seventeenth year of our reign.[7]

> At a Month after Easter (8 May 1289), the day to which the justices in eyre had adjourned the parties to the king's bench, John recovered through default of the defendants.

---

[7] 18 April 1289.

PARLIAMENT AT WESTMINSTER: Hilary 1290

The celebrations at Christmas, when the king held high court, were often followed by a meeting of parliament some time after Hilary, and both were sometimes regarded as one occasion. Thus in 1265, when the prior of Christ Church, Canterbury, was paid his expenses for attending the parliament summoned for the Octave of Hilary, i.e. 20 January 1265, at London, it was described as 'the parliament after Christmas' (Lambeth MS., 242, fo.8b). Similarly, official documents could refer to the parliament 'after Christmas at Westminster' in 1289 (Rot. Parl., i. 32; King's Bench Roll, no.121 (Michaelmas 1289) m.11), and later speak of it as meeting at the Octave of Hilary 1290 and specifically state that this was the king's 'first parliament' after his return from abroad (King's Bench Roll, no.124 (Trinity 1290), m.39). Again, when a plea 'in the king's parliament after Christmas' was postponed for consideration 'at the next parliament', it was heard at Easter, not Hilary (Rot. Parl., i. 35, 37). And the proceedings in the parliament after Christmas 1289 (ibid., i. 84) and entered on its rolls are to be found on the roll of the Hilary parliament (ibid., i. 16-17). See below (p.199, n.1) for a reference to two successive parliaments, one after Christmas and the other after Easter. In September 1296 there is a reference to the king's 'next parliament at London after the Nativity' (Cal. Close Rolls, 1288-96, p.492). In brief, there were not two parliaments, one at Christmas and the other at Hilary, as stated in the Handbook of British Chronology, *p.509.*

i

Close Roll, no.106, m.2d

[*Foedera*, I. ii. 712; *Cal. Close Rolls, 1288-96*, p.55]

The king to the sheriff of Nottingham, greeting. Heartily desiring, as we ought to do, the peacefulness of our realm and our people, we have appointed the reverend fathers John, bishop of Winchester, and Robert, bishop of Bath and Wells, and our beloved and faithful Henry de Lacy, earl of Lincoln, John de St. John, William Latimer, master William Louth, keeper of our wardrobe, and master William March to hear such grievances and wrongs as have been done or committed by our servants to any persons of our realm whilst we were lately out of our kingdom, so that these our loyal subjects, having heard complaints upon such matters and the answers of the said servants, may report and give an account of them to us in our next parliament in order that they may be duly redressed. We therefore instruct and firmly enjoin you to inform clearly and openly all and sundry of your county that, if any feel themselves to have been aggrieved by our servants whilst we were out of our kingdom and wish to complain about it, they are to come to Westminster on the Morrow[1] of the approaching Martinmas to show and prosecute their grievances in good faith before our aforesaid loyal subjects. And you are to execute this our command, as you love yourself and yours, in such a way that you shall not be found so negligent and remiss in these matters that we must betake ourselves grievously against you as one who has scorned our orders. And you are to have there this writ. Witness the king at Westminster on the thirteenth day of October.[2]

An order is sent in similar terms to every sheriff in England. Witness as above.

ii
Chancery Miscellanea 4/5, fo.10d

This document shows the close connexion between the auditors of plaints, appointed in 1289, and the parliaments of 1290.

The clerks with the auditors of pleas

To Henry of Lichfield, clerk, and his two fellows, writing out the pleas of the king under the auditors of plaints at two parliaments at Westminster, namely, after Christmas and again after Easter, for their salaries and expenses for the whole of the time for which they thus served: to them on the king's behalf by Henry's hands . . . 60s.

To Nicholas of Tickhill, clerk, being in the same way with the said auditors to serve them similarly for the same time, for salary by his own hands . . . 20s.[3]

iii
L.T.R. Memoranda Roll, no.61 (18 Edward I), m.19 (Trinity Communia)

Concerning Roger Lestrange and his fellows, justices of the forest, accused before the king, and concerning the fine imposed on them

Roger Lestrange and John son of John fitz Neal and Peter Lench, then the justices for pleas of the king's forest below the river Trent, were accused before the king himself in his recent parliament after Hilary in the eighteenth year of the said king's reign by the servants of the bishop of Coventry and Lichfield on this ground: that the justices had received £50

---

[1] 12 November 1289.
[2] 13 October 1289.
[3] From a Wardrobe Book, 18 Edward I (1289–90).

sterling from the bishop at the hands of his servants so that he could have some complaints adjourned that had been alleged against him with regard to the forest. And this was to the king's scandal, who had forbidden his justices to do such things, and was a pernicious example to others and in grave prejudice of the bishop himself, who was brought to do it against his will by the wrongful harassment of the justices. And out of this sum Roger Lestrange received £30 and John £10 and Peter £10, as stated before the king. And after these matters had been heard and considered, the king ordered John, bishop of Ely, then his treasurer, and the barons of the exchequer to call the aforesaid justices before them and make inquiries and examine the parties and the persons by whom the truth in these matters can be made known and they can more fully be informed.

John fitz Neal and Peter Lench acknowledged their guilt and paid, the former £300 and the latter £200, to obtain the king's forgiveness. Roger Lestrange disputed the charge but, when it was proved after a lengthy investigation that money from the bishop had been used to pay off Roger's debts, he also submitted himself to the king's will.

iv
Exchequer Parliament Roll, no. 1, m. 4
[*Rot. Parl.*, i. 17]

The prior of Holy Trinity church, London, and Boges de Clare were attached to answer the king, Peter Chauvent, the king's steward, Walter de Fancurt, the king's marshal, Edmund earl of Cornwall, and the abbot of Westminster on this ground: whereas the earl had come on the king's orders to this, his parliament at London, and had gone through the Great Hall of Westminster towards the king's council where everyone within the king's realm and peace should be able lawfully and peacefully to come and pursue his business without accepting there any citations or summonses, the prior on Friday before the Purification of the Blessed Mary this year[4] in the aforesaid Hall, at Boges's instigation, cited the earl to appear before the archbishop of Canterbury at a certain day and place to answer allegations made against him, which was in open contempt of the king and his disparagement to the extent of ten thousand pounds and in breach of the franchise, granted by the Roman Curia and belonging to the abbot's church because the aforesaid place is altogether exempt from the jurisdiction of any archbishops or bishops by the franchises granted to the abbot and his church of Westminster, and to the abbot's damage of

---

[4] 27 January 1290.

a thousand pounds, and in manifest prejudice of the office of the steward and the marshal and to their no slight damage, since it belongs to their office and not to anyone else to make summonses and attachments within the king's palace, and also to the earl's damage of five thousand pounds. And they produce their suit thereon etc.

> The two defendents confessed their wrongdoing and were sentenced to imprisonment in the Tower of London, but they found guarantors that they would make a satisfactory settlement with the king before he departed from the parliament then being held at Westminster.[5]

v

Muniments of Dean and Chapter of Canterbury Cathedral:
Letters of Prior Henry Eastry
[*Historical MSS. Commission, Reports on Various Collections* (1901), i. 257]

To his reverend lord, [the writer] himself. May your lordship know that all those who were at Westminster for the plea of 'quo warranto'[6] on this Thursday, the Morrow of St. Edmund the Confessor,[7] were adjourned by the whole council of the king until a Fortnight after Easter because the justices refuse to proceed in this plea until it has been unanimously decided therein before the king and his whole council in the next parliament how and in what manner they ought to proceed therein. Furthermore, I have been led by many to understand that you will most certainly have a judicial eyre at a Fortnight after Easter: who the justices are to be I cannot yet find out. As regards suing out writs for you with regard to the warren and to Sandwich I can accomplish nothing. But William of Hamilton's advice[8] is that you should further your business about the warren through your petition before the king and his council in the next parliament, and there you will have redress thereon. The archbishop came to Lambeth this Friday before the Feast of St. Edmund king,[9] for the business of Thomas Wayland.[10]

---

[5] Entered also on King's Bench Rolls, nos. 124 (Trinity 1290), m.68d, 135 (Hilary 1293), m.17.

[6] An investigation into 'by what warrant' lands were claimed to be held.

[7] 17 November 1289.

[8] Hamilton was a senior chancery clerk.

[9] 18 November 1289.

[10] Wayland had been chief justice of the court of common pleas from 1278 until Michaelmas 1289 when he was dismissed and imprisoned by the king during the purge of the administration and judiciary after his own three years' absence from his kingdom.

PARLIAMENT AT WESTMINSTER: Easter 1290

i

Exchequer Parliament and Council Proceedings, roll 7, m.5

This so-called 'roll' is a file of documents relating to the law-suit of William of Valence by which he sought to prove that Denise de Munchensy was illegitimate and could not inherit her father's lands. This is an important case because it defined the attitude of the English courts to the papal curia in questions of bastardy. The documents include extracts from the parliament rolls of 1290, printed in *Rot. Parl*. i. 16b-17a, 39b. Gilbert Rothbury was the first to be given the title of 'clerk of the council', though he was not the first to carry out the duties of that office.

These things will be found in the council rolls of King Edward in regard to his parliament of the eighteenth year of his reign. And the rolls remain in the wardrobe,[1] and there is a transcript of them in the possession of Gilbert Rothbury, then clerk of his council.[2]

ii

Exchequer Parliament Roll, no.1, m.7
[*Rot. Parl*. i. 61*b*]

The Master of the Temple prays that he may distrain[3] the bishop of St. David's for thirty shillings' annual rent and ten years' arrears for a house in London, on which he cannot distrain except in time of parliament. He prays leave to distrain in time of parliament.

Answer: It does not seem proper that the king should allow those of his council to be distrained in time of parliament, but let him distrain at some other time by doors and windows, as is the custom.

---

[1] Cf. Parliament Roll, no.4, m.1*d* (Cole, *Documents*, p.82): 'Petitions of Ireland, delivered to the wardrobe by the hands of Peter Chauvent at the end of the king's parliament a Month after Easter in the eighteenth year of his reign, together with the Irish roll of the parliament last Christmas'.

[2] It should be noted that the expression used is not 'clericus de consilio' but 'clericus consilii'.

[3] *Rot. Parl*. reads 'dare' incorrectly for 'distringere'.

iii
King's Bench Roll, no.124 (Trinity 1290), m.54d
[Sayles, *King's Bench*, ii. 15]

London

An order was sent, as often, to the sheriffs of London that they should cause to be executed without delay the judgement lately given with respect to the suit which was before them by the king's writ in the king's court of London between Thomas of Somerton and Alice, his wife, and master William Corbridge and Thomas Corbridge concerning a debt of a hundred and five shillings which Thomas of Somerton and Alice are demanding from William and Thomas Corbridge, or that they should notify the king of the reason why they would not or could not execute it. And, scorning the king's orders, as the king learns, they took no pains to execute the judgement or at least to notify the king as yet of the reason why they would not or could not do it, to the no slight damage and grievance of Thomas of Somerton and Alice and the open contempt of the king's orders, at which the king marvels and is disturbed. Another order was sent to the sheriffs to have the judgement executed in accordance with the terms of the king's instructions previously addressed to them, or to be before the king etc. And the sheriffs sent word that they distrained master William Corbridge by certain goods and chattels of his, found in their bailiwick. And afterwards the distraint was released by order of the king's council because master William is a king's clerk in his parliament, and the council does not allow him to be distrained or attached during parliament.[4] As regards Thomas Corbridge, they say that he has no goods or chattels from which any money can be levied. And this is the reason etc. Therefore an order is sent, as often, to the sheriffs to have the judgement executed without delay in accordance with the terms of the king's instructions or to notify the reason to the king at a Month after Michaelmas wherever etc. And let the sheriffs be then etc.

iv
Chancery Warrants, file 1538, nos.3, 4
[Sayles, *King's Bench*, ii. p.lviiin]

When a plea of 'quo warranto' was brought in 1298 in the court of common pleas, reference was made to an ordinance made in 1290

---

[4] See *Rot. Parl.*, i. 48 (32) for a note of Corbridge's presence in the Michaelmas parliament of 1290.

which laid down the procedure to be followed in such pleas. The king wrote to Gilbert Rothbury, clerk of the council, on 31 December 1298, for information and was sent the relevant extract from the parliament roll of Easter 1290, together with the following comment.

This is the ordinance made. And in accordance with the said ordinance it seems to John Mettingham[5] and his fellows and to me that all pleas of 'quo warranto' ought to be pleaded and determined before justices in eyre during their eyres and not anywhere else. And it is good that the king should keep the grace conceded and the promise made to the people. This is our advice.[6]

v

L.T.R. Memoranda Roll, no.61 (18 Edward I), m.14 (Easter Communia)

Concerning the aid granted to the king for the marriage of his eldest daughter

Note that on Thursday, the first day of June in the eighteenth year of King Edward's reign,[7] when there was assembled before the king at Westminster the bishops of Winchester, Bath, Durham, Carlisle, and master William of Louth, the bishop-elect of Ely, Edmund the king's brother, William de Valence the king's uncle, Gilbert Clare earl of Gloucester, John Warenne earl of Surrey, Henry Lacy earl of Lincoln, Hugh Bohun earl of Hereford, and some other barons as well as magnates of England, it was agreed and unanimously granted that forty shillings should be given from every knight's fee as an aid for the marriage of the king's eldest daughter in such a way that the present grant should not yield to their prejudice in that an aid, granted in like case at another time, should be increased or reduced in accordance with what the magnates of England of that time thought to grant, and that this aid should be levied from the same fees on which the aid, granted on another occasion, was accustomed to be levied.[8]

---

[5] John Mettingham was the chief justice of the common bench.
[6] The advice was followed (*Cal. Close Rolls, 1296-1302*, p.247).
[7] 1 June 1290.
[8] Recorded also in *Rot. Parl.*, i. 25.

PARLIAMENT AT CLIPSTON: Michaelmas 1290

L.T.R. Memoranda Roll, no.62 (19 Edward I), m.7d
[Sayles, *King's Bench*, iii. p.cxxii]

Because the abbot of Ramsey claims by charters of the ancestors of the kings of England to have the amercements of his men in whatsoever royal courts they may have been amerced, and also, by some general words contained in the said charters, the chattels of fugitives and convicted felons, and he states that, after the charters were made, he had received these amercements and chattels by reason of these words, and he had frequently requested the king to be so good as to make these general words specific and to mention them in these charters as being a special grace from the king, the king instructs the barons of the exchequer that, with respect to the things that the abbot and his predecessors have for a long time used and enjoyed in the aforesaid matters – matters of which they cannot have cognisance without consultation with the king in accordance with the terms of the document delivered to them by the king and his council regarding the examination of such franchises – they are to inform the king thereof clearly and openly in the next parliament and in the meantime to let the abbot have peace from the demands made upon him thereon by the barons so that what the king with his council thinks it expedient to do thereon may then be done. Witness the king at Nottingham the twelfth day of September in the eighteenth year.[1]

---

[1] 12 September 1290. For other proceedings in this parliament see *Rot. Parl.*, i. 45–62; *Cal. Patent Rolls, 1281-92*, p.393.

PARLIAMENT AT ASHRIDGE: Epiphany 1291

L.T.R. Memoranda Roll, no.62 (19 Edward I), Michaelmas Communia, m.3

Concerning John Dagworth's heir, surrendered to the king by John Filiol

John Filiol was brought into the presence of the barons of the exchequer on Monday before the Feast of St. Margaret in the eighteenth year[1] etc. and was asked in open exchequer why he had withheld the marriage of John, son and heir of John Dagworth, from the king, for his marriage ought to pertain to the king by reason of the manor of Dagworth.

> Filiol in his defence argued that Dagworth's ancestors had held nothing from the king save by petty serjeanty, that is the rendering of three arrows a year. John surrendered the person of John Dagworth until the dispute had been settled.

And in order that John Filiol should answer thereon with wise deliberation and the fullest advice, a day was given him at a Fortnight after Martinmas to show precisely on his own behalf if there was any reason why the marriage and wardship ought not to pertain to the king. Afterwards he was adjourned before the king's council, and on Wednesday after Epiphany when the king and his council were then at Ashridge,[2] the whole business was recited before the council. And because John Filiol had by his own deed appropriated nothing to himself in the wardship and marriage but simply continued the possession which his ancestors had therein, as he said, the council agreed that John should not answer thereon without a writ and that the body of the heir as well as the manor of Doddinghurst in Essex and the manor of Dagworth in Suffolk, which belonged to John Dagworth and which were taken into the king's hands for the aforesaid reason, should be restored to John Filiol, provided he answered to the king for the wardship and marriage when he was summoned by the king's writ to do so and for the profits of the manors, should they belong to the king. And he was forbidden to have the heir married until it was discussed in the king's court whether the wardship ought to belong to the king or to John. Afterwards the

---

[1] 17 July 1290.

[2] 10 January 1291. The parliament, so described, is said to have been held 'after Christmas' (*State Trials*, p.36), with which cf. King's Bench Roll, no.125 (Michaelmas 1290), m.72 (Sayles, *King's Bench*, ii. 28–29) which speaks of a judgement given 'before the king and his council at Ashridge at Christmas 1290 in the presence of the reverend fathers Robert, bishop of Bath and Wells, and William, bishop of Ely, and the justices of both benches'.

sheriff of Essex was instructed to make John Filiol come before the barons of the exchequer on the Morrow of the Purification[3] to answer to the king for the wardship. He did not come on that day. Therefore the sheriff was instructed etc. at Three Weeks after the Purification.[4] On that day he came and answered etc., as set out in the memorandum of this year in Hilary term.[5]

[3] 3 February 1291.
[4] 23 February 1291.
[5] For further proceedings which noted, among other things, 'that the said John had not been fully repossessed of the wardship, as was adjudged before the king at Ashridge', see L.T.R. Memoranda Roll, no.62 (19 Edward I), Hilary Communia, m.11d.

PARLIAMENT AT NORHAM: May 1291

Liberate Roll, no.67, m.3

For the executors of the will of Richard of Williamscote

The king [to the treasurer and chamberlains], greeting. Allow to the executors of the will of Richard of Williamscote, our late sheriff of Oxford, in his account at the exchequer £2.6s.8d. which Richard delivered by our orders during his life-time to master Nicholas of Whitchurch and master William of Kilkenny, sent by the university of Oxford to us at Norham at our parliament, for the expenses of themselves and their groom and their seven horses and of taking those horses from Oxford to Norham, the details of which have been scrutinised in our wardrobe and remain there in the nineteenth year of our reign. Witness as above[1] by bill of the wardrobe.[2]

---

[1] 15 May 1291.

[2] This document, cited in Stones and Simpson, *Edward I and the Throne of Scotland*, ii. 5, seems to settle a vexed question about the nature of this assembly, for which see Richardson and Sayles, *The English Parliament in the Middle Ages*, XIII, 306, n.3. See also for other evidence King's Bench Roll, no.192 (Easter 1306), m.36 (Sayles, *King's Bench*, iv. pp.11,14): 'An ordinance and provision, enrolled in the rolls of the king's council, which are in the keeping of Gilbert of Rothbury, then clerk of the council' begins 'Note that on Saturday, the Feast of the Invention of Holy Cross in the twentieth year of the reign of king Edward (3 May 1292) it is thus agreed before the king's council with the king's consent' [for an extent of land to be made], and the provision is later described as 'made before the king and his council and agreed by the king . . . and enrolled in the council rolls' and 'made with such solemnity in the presence of the king himself', and *ibid.*, m.11d: '. . . by examination of the terms of a certain ordinance . . . it is manifestly clear to the king that it was agreed and ordained before the king and his council at Norham a Month after Easter in the nineteenth year of his reign in the presence of John, then archbishop of York, master Henry of Newark, then dean of York, and John le Spicer, executor of Gilbert of Louth's will . . .' See also *Year Book, 16 Edward III*, p.298.

PARLIAMENT AT WESTMINSTER: Epiphany 1292

At Easter 1291 it was thought that a parliament would be held somewhere at the following Martinmas, for a plea relating to the city of Canterbury was adjourned 'until a Fortnight after Martinmas wherever [the king might be] in parliament by a writ from the king's chancery, which is to be found among the precepts of Easter term 1291' (King's Bench Roll, no.129 (Michaelmas 1291), m.12d): for charges in full against the archbishop of Canterbury and his replies, see no.130 (Hilary 1292), ms.35-36b and no.131 (Easter 1292), m.11).

i

King's Bench Roll, no.133 (Trinity 1292), m.22
[Sayles, *King's Bench*, ii. 120-22]

Essex

An order attested by Gilbert Thornton[1] was sent to the sheriff, by authority of a petition sent from the king's council, which is to be found on the file of petitions for Hilary term last, to this effect: Richard of Spain, brother and heir of the late John of Spain, had come before the king and the king's council in his last parliament at Westminster and had shown the king that the lands and tenements belonging to John had come into the king's hands because John was an idiot, and he had stated that he was John's nearest heir and had prayed for justice therein to be shown him by the king . . .[2]

---

[1] He was chief justice of the king's bench.

[2] For business before the king's council in parliament which was transmitted to the king's bench for further action, see King's Bench Roll, no.130 (Hilary 1292), m.6: 'Petition sent from the council' (Sayles, *King's Bench*, ii. 67-68); ms.14-16: 'Record sent from the council' (*Rot. Parl.*, i. 70-77); m.31d: 'Petition of Philip Willoughby, king's clerk, sent from the king's council'; cf. no.131 (Easter 1292) m.42; m.44, 'Petition of Geoffrey Byssey, sent from the council', 'Petition of master Bonacius de Bolan, sent from the council'; m.44d, 'Petition of the prior and convent of Daventry, sent from the council' (*King's Bench*, ii. 79-80); m.55d, headed 'Pleas and petitions continued': 'Petition of William Turville, sheriff of Bedford and Buckingham, sent from the council etc.', 'Petition of John Padmere, sent from the council' (for both these cases see *King's Bench*, ii. 80-82); m.56: 'Petition of Robert the tanner of Retford, sent from the council' (*King's Bench*, ii. 82-84); King's Bench Roll, no.131 (Easter 1292), m.49: 'Petition sent from the council' (*Rot. Parl.* i. 82-83); m.50: 'Petition sent from the council on behalf of James Astley' (*King's Bench*, ii. 97-112: cf. *Rot. Parl.* i. 83).

ii
Exchequer Parliament Roll, no.5, m.4
[*Rot. Parl.*, i. 79; *Statutes of the Realm*, i. 109-110]

This case which established the so-called Statute of Waste is given in full because it provides an unusual insight into the discussions before the king's council in parliament.

That heirs should have an action by writ for the waste done in the
time of their ancestors

William Butler, who is under age in the king's wardship, has shown the king that Gawayn Butler, his brother, whose heir he is, had lately impleaded Walter Hopton by the king's writ for the waste and destruction Walter committed in some lands and tenements belonging to the inheritance of Gawayn, which Walter held for the term of his life in Wem and in Tirley. And before judgement was reached Gawayn had died. And after his death William impleaded Walter by a similar writ for the aforesaid waste and destruction, committed over a long time.

And Walter came before Gilbert Thornton and his fellows, assigned to hold the pleas of the king, and said that he ought not to answer William for waste and destruction committed in someone else's time and before the right of inheritance had descended to him. And he prayed judgement thereon.

And some justices did not agree in rendering judgement because it seemed to some that it would not be consonant with the principles of justice if by this writ, which is a writ for trespass done to a specific person, any person could sue for recompense or redress other than the person to whom and in whose time the trespass was committed. But other justices and the greater part of all the king's council were of the contrary opinion and stated by various arguments that William ought to be heard and to be answered thereon as well as any others in like cases, or else similar trespasses in like case would for ever remain without redress and the trespassers be unpunished: which would be a harsh thing and bear hard upon the heirs to whom such a trespass was done.

Whereupon the king, after having careful discussion in his full parliament on the Morrow of the Purification of the Blessed Mary in the twentieth year of his reign,[3] later decreed in common with his council and ordered it henceforth to be firmly observed that heirs, no matter in whose wardship they were and whether they were of full age or under age, are to have their recovery by a writ of waste in the aforesaid case, and

---

[3] 3 February 1292.

in others where the said writ is appropriate, for waste and destruction committed in the lands and tenements of their inheritance in the time of their ancestors as well as in the time from which the right and fee of the inheritance descended to them, and they are to be answered thereon, and they are to recover the tenements wasted and damages, as is ordained in the last statutes of Westminster concerning the recovery of damages by a writ of waste,[4] should the tenant be convicted of waste.

And the king ordered Gilbert Thornton and his fellows to proceed thus in future in this and similar pleas and to render judgement in accordance with what the findings might be.

And the justices of the common bench were likewise orderd in full parliament to see to it that this was firmly observed before them in future etc.

iii

Cambridge University Library, Dd.7.14
[*Year Book, 20 and 21 Edward I*, p.94]

The abbot of Reading was in litigation with the bailiffs of Hereford over rights of murage and pavage. The bailiff's counsel advanced the following argument.

As to the murage and pavage we answer thus: that it is only a special grant for three years, more or less, which the king sometimes makes to the good men of this town. And thereupon, Sir, we tell you that, at the time when the king granted the franchise of etc. to the good men of this town, the town was not very well walled. Wherefore our present lord and king seven years ago, at the entreaty of the good men of the town, granted them murage and pavage. And so, by virtue of the grant from our lord the king, we came and distrained the abbot and his men to give murage and pavage. Thereupon they came and brought the prohibition etc. Then we, by reason of the king's command, ceased [distraining] until the Feast of St. Hilary last year, when we went to our lord the king and his council when the parliament was at London to ascertain from the king from whom we were to take murage and pavage. Our lord the king sent us word by Sir Robert Malet[5] that we were to take murage etc. from all in the county except the master of the Hospital of C. And when we were thus informed by our lord and king, we took murage and pavage from the abbot etc. as well as from the other people of the county. And that our lord and king did thus command us, as we have said, we vouch the record of our lord the king.

---

[4] Second Statute of Westminster (1285), c.14.
[5] He was a justice of the king's bench.

PARLIAMENT AT WESTMINSTER: Easter 1293

For the intention, expressed in the Epiphany parliament of 1292, to hold a parliament at Easter 1292, see Rot. Parl., *i. 86, 89;* Cal. Fine Rolls, *i. 294, 295. And a writ, dated 12 August 1292, postponed a plea 'to our next parliament which will be after next Easter' (*King's Bench Roll, *no.134 (Michaelmas 1292), m.12). This in itself, apart from other reasons, eliminates the assembly at Berwick at Michaelmas 1292 (accepted as a parliament in* Handbook of British Chronology, *p.510). Cf. also the references on 9 July 1293 to 'our last parliament held at Westminster (below p.209f.).*

i

Close Roll, no.110, m.7 (schedule)
[Ryley, *Placita*, p.459; *Cal. Close Rolls, 1288-96*, p.289]

Concerning the ordinance about petitions of parliament

The king wills and ordains that all the petitions, which shall hereafter be delivered to parliaments and to those whom he shall appoint to receive them, shall at once, immediately after they have been received, be well examined; and that those which concern the chancery shall be put on a file by themselves, and others which concern the exchequer on another file, and those which concern the justices shall be dealt with in a similar way. And then those which are to be before the king and his council shall be put by themselves on another file. And also those, which should have been answered before, [are to be put] on a separate file. And so let these matters be thus reported before the king before a start is made in deciding them.[1]

ii

Chancery Parliament and Council Proceedings, file 44, no.12

Edward by the grace of God king of England, lord of Ireland and duke of Aquitaine, to his beloved and faithful clerk, John Langton, his chancellor, greeting. We command you to have before us on the Feast of the Assumption of the Blessed Mary next,[2] wherever we then may be, all the petitions concerning Eleanor, formerly queen of England, our consort, which remained in your keeping after our last parliament, held

---

[1] The ordinance is also enrolled on L.T.R. Memoranda Roll, no.64 (21 Edward I), m.26, Trinity Communia.

[2] 15 August 1293.

at Westminster, had ended. And you are to let this be quickly known with regard to similar petitions which at that time remained in the possession of our dear clerk, John of Caen. Given under our privy seal at Ospringe on the twenty-ninth day of July in the twenty-first year of our reign.[3]

iii

Ancient Petition, File 326 no. E.725

To our lord the king and his council prays Robert of Muncaster that, whereas he had pleaded before the barons of the exchequer at Easter term in the twentieth year[4] against Geoffrey de Mowbray and judgement thereon was adjourned until the present parliament, our lord the king may be so good as to command that the plea may be examined and expedited according to what is right.

Endorsed: The reason why the judgement was adjourned until parliament was so as to have better advice and counsel from the justices and learned men in rendering the judgement. And the treasurer and barons are now sufficiently advised for proceeding to judgement.

iv

L.T.R. Memoranda Roll, no.65 (22 Edward I), m.21 (24), Michaelmas Communia

Whereas Roger Bigod, earl of Norfolk and marshal of England had sought the king's grace in his parliament at Westminster a Month after Easter in the twenty-first year [of his reign][5] with regard to the net debts for which he must answer to the king at the exchequer . . . the king at the earl's request in this parliament gave instructions to his treasurer and barons of the exchequer, by information of Robert Tibetot and other loyal subjects of the king.

> They were to examine the evidence about all his debts and make him allowances in accordance with the custom of the exchequer and then report to the king. After much debate and argument the earl agreed that he owed £2802.7s.2d.

---

[3] 29 July 1293.
[4] Easter 1292.
[5] 26 April 1293.

v

L.T.R. Memoranda Roll, no.64 (21 Edward I), m.23d, Easter Communia

Hereford

Concerning men who have been adjourned

William Jocelyn, Hugh Preston, John son of Richard son of William Caperun, Walter Mareys, who were adjourned from John Berwick's eyre in Herefordshire to parliament after Easter, and from parliament to before the treasurer and barons of the exchequer, have a day a Fortnight after Trinity in the same status as at present.

vi

L.T.R. Memoranda Roll, no.63 (20 Edward I), m.10d, Hilary Communia

To the barons on behalf of John Giffard and Ralph Pipard

An attempt in the exchequer to settle a dispute over the view of frankpledge at Twyford had failed.

Afterwards, on Saturday before the Feast of the Apostles Peter and Paul in the twenty-first year of the reign,[6] the king in his parliament at Westminster, having regard to the dissension and discord between Ralph and John over the view of frankpledge and understanding the danger that could befall each of them by reason of this dispute and that disagreement thereon may in future arise between them, has taken the view of frankpledge into his own hands so that neither party may henceforth intermeddle with that view, and the sheriff of Bedford for the time being is instead to hold that view and to answer every year at the exchequer.

[6] 27 June 1293. The parliament was a long one, lasting from late April and continuing from Westminster at Canterbury until at least 24 July (Richardson and Sayles, *Rot. Parl. Inediti*, pp.26-29).

PARLIAMENT AT WESTMINSTER: Michaelmas 1293

i

L.T.R. Memoranda Roll, no.65 (22 Edward I), m.9, Michaelmas Communia

Concerning a certain petition of parliament, delivered to master Thomas Lugorre

Note that on the nineteenth day of November in the twenty-first year [of the reign][1] John Kirkby, remembrancer of the exchequer, handed over to master Thomas Lugorre, clerk, an inquisition, made by authority of the king's writ by Malcolm Harley, the king's escheator below the river Trent, with regard to a tenement held by Richard Halford by gift and grant of Robert le Waleys, as he says, as well as the said same writ etc.[2]

ii

Ancient Petition, no.1765
[Sayles, *King's Bench*, ii. p.cxli f.]

Because it was before this time ordained by our lord the king and by his council at his parliament at Westminster in the thirteenth year of his reign[3] that, in the case where there was no specific redress previously provided in the chancery, this case should be shown to the king and his council, and such redress should be provided thereon that no man would depart from the court without having a remedy, for this reason Gerard Braybrook prays the king and his council for grace and redress in this matter. The said Gerard was enfeoffed of Colmworth manor from John Braybrook and Joan, his wife, whose inheritance it was. And this enfeoffment contained an agreement between John and Joan and Gerard to the effect that Joan should have sustenance from the manor to the amount of forty pounds all her life. And should she survive her lord, it was for her to choose whether to take this sustenance from the manor or have the tenements for the term of her life. And she took the sustenance after her lord's death during her widowhood and was possessed of it. And afterwards she brought a writ of entry against master William Meynell by collusion between them, William being at that time the leasehold tenant of the manor which Gerard had leased to him for life to

---

[1] 19 November 1293.

[2] See also *ibid.*, Hilary Communia, m.25, concerning a case transmitted to parliament from the justices in eyre in Staffordshire: 'and let it be remembered that these two records returned with the writs will be found among the records and petitions returned from the parliament after Michaelmas 1293'.

[3] Easter 1285. The ordinance is the Statute of Westminster (1285), c.24.

find the sustenance, and for which William vouched Gerard to warranty. And inasmuch as it was discovered by an inquisition before Sir Roger Brabazon that Gerard's deeds had been stolen from him and inasmuch as Joan had taken her sustenance by virtue of the said agreement during her widowhood, William surrendered the tenements in fee to Joan, though he had no estate in them save for a life-term, and he agreed to waive his warranty. Therefore Gerard prays the discretion of the king and his council, since she could have claimed the manor in form of law and, by collusion between William and herself, she received it by his surrender [and not] in accordance with the agreement, whether by that surrender William can discharge the tenements of the forty pounds a year which Gerard holds in fee.

Endorsed: Let him go to the chancery. And let the clerks meet and reach agreement if they can. And if they cannot reach agreement, let him come back to the next parliament etc.

iii
King's Bench Roll, no.131 (Easter 1292), m.43
[Sayles, *King's Bench*, ii. 86–97]

In 1288 Martin fitz Osbert recovered land from the prior of Butley by an assize of novel disseisin, taken before John Luvetot. After auditors were appointed in 1289 to investigate charges of official misconduct, the prior complained to them that serious error had occurred in the proceedings before Luvetot and, on examination, the auditors at Michaelmas 1290 quashed his judgement in favour of Martin and restored the land to the prior. Thereupon Martin complained that the auditors themselves were in error, and they were ordered in August 1291 to send the record of what had taken place before them to the court of king's bench. Here eventually at Michaelmas 1293 the arguments of the parties were put forward in detail. Among other points the prior made the following submission to the court, though unfortunately no judgement on the case is entered on the plea roll.

And the said prior says that the judgements and records of the auditors rank higher than those of any other justice, wherefore it seems to him than no one else but the king in his parliament ought to have cognisance of the judgements of the auditors, and on this he prays judgement . . . Moreover, the prior says that the auditors had full authority, not only by the king's writ but by his specific command, to correct records of justices that are found to be mistaken and erroneous – and this is quite evident to the king and his council – and because the auditors found many errors in John Luvetot's record, they annulled it and adjudged it erroneous.[4]

---

[4] Tout was mistaken (*Chapters*, ii. 66n) in his belief that the auditors had authority only to hear evidence and not make judgements. He did not realise that the proceedings in 1289-93 followed a normal and well-known procedure and were not peculiar.

PARLIAMENT AT WESTMINSTER: Easter 1294

i

L.T.R. Memoranda Roll, no.66 (23 Edward I), m.12 (35), Hilary Communia

Concerning the lands which belonged to Geoffrey Rous and which were taken into the king's hands and later released

> A writ, dated 11 February 1294 and addressed to the king's escheator below the river Trent, ordered him to hold an inquisition into the lands belonging to the lately deceased Geoffrey Rous. The inquisition was taken at Stratford Bridge on 14 March 1294.

And this inquisition was returned into the chancery by the escheator. And it was afterwards recited before the king and his council at his parliament after Easter in the twenty-second year[1] and it was there endorsed thus: Let it be handed to the exchequer and let it be seen whether the king has custody arising out of such feudal tenure etc. And so it was returned to the exchequer. And this inquisition will be found among the inquisitions returned to the exchequer in the twenty-third year.[2] And because it was found by the inquisition that Geoffrey held nothing of the king by military service on the day he died, and nothing is found in the rolls of the exchequer, examined for this purpose, whereby custody of the lands and tenements, belonging to Geoffrey on that day, should pertain to the king at present, the escheator is ordered by the king's writ under the exchequer seal on the twenty-fourth day of February in the twenty-third year[3] not to intermeddle any more in the lands and tenements which he had taken into the king's hands on account of Geoffrey's death.

ii

L.T.R. Memoranda Roll, no.65 (22 Edward I), m.51, Easter Communia

Devon

Concerning the county surrendered into the king's hands

Note that the reverend father William, bishop of Bath and Wells, the treasurer, has recorded that in the king's parliament recently held here at

---

[1] I.e. 1294.
[2] 20 November 1294–19 November 1295.
[3] 24 February 1295.

Westminster Matthew fitz John, who had custody of the sheriffdom of
Devon, together with the castle of Exeter, for the term of his life by the
king's grant, has surrendered into the king's hands the aforesaid
bailiwick and whatever rights he had therein by the aforesaid grant. And
by virtue of that surrender the king has entrusted the county and castle to
Gilbert Knoville as his sheriff, to be held from the sixteenth day of
October in the twenty-second year [of the reign],[4] as mentioned in the
memoranda of the following year.

iii

Pipe Roll, no.139, m.5d

And to Alexander of London, clerk of the treasurer of Ireland, going to
England on three occasions and staying there at three parliaments in
order to prosecute and defend the king's business.[5]

---

[4] 16 October 1294.

[5] From the account of William of East Dean, treasurer of Ireland, covering the period
June 1292 to June 1294. The three parliaments must be those of Easter 1293, Michaelmas
1293 and Easter 1294. There is no place here for the fourth parliament after Christmas
1293, which has been accepted by the *Handbook of British Chronology*, p.510. Moreover,
when the king declared on 18 April 1294 his intention of holding a parliament after Easter
(*Cal. Close Rolls*, 1288–96, p.384–5), he referred to complaints from Ireland 'in his last
parliament at Westminster': this refers, not to Christmas 1293 but to Michaelmas 1293,
for a parliament roll of Michaelmas 1293 records the actual Irish petitions to which
allusion is made (Chancery Parliament Roll, no.8 m.2d: *Rot. Parl. Ined.*, pp.30–45,
especially p.43, no.16).

PARLIAMENT AT WESTMINSTER: Michaelmas 1294

i
Chancery Warrants, Series I, file 1, no.567
[*Cal. Chancery Warrants*, i. 42]

Edward by the grace of God king of England, lord of Ireland and duke of Aquitaine, to his dear clerk and loyal subject John Langton, his chancellor, greeting. Because we have heard that the Lady Joan la Forestière, who is in our wardship, was ready of late to prove that she had come of age, and Gilbert Thornton and his fellows, our justices assigned to hold our pleas, refused to take her proof of age on the ground that her husband was under age, we wish for certain reasons to do her a special favour in the matter and we order you to have a writ quickly made for assembling a jury and proving her age. And if her age can be proved in proper form, we wish her inheritance to he handed over to her husband and to herself, notwithstanding that her husband is under age, and you are to hand it over speedily when her age is proved. Nevertheless, before you do this, take such fealty as pertains to it and the homage may remain over until our arrival at this next parliament. And her husband alone is responsible for that homage, and they are to have seisin of that inheritance from the time that the Lady's age is proved in proper form and fealty taken. And know that the reason which moves us most in this business is because we have made a gift of the wardship of the Lady's lands and we would have it as a load upon our conscience if by reason of our gift the seisin of her lands should be withheld from her. And we will that everything pertaining to this matter, except the homage, shall be done before we come to our next parliament in accordance with the terms of our orders. Given under our privy seal at Wrotham on the sixth day of May in the twenty-second year of our reign.[1]

---

[1] 6 May 1294.

ii

King's Bench Roll, no.142 (Michaelmas 1294), m.3d

[Sayles, *King's Bench*, iii. 28]

Parliament

The king in his Michaelmas parliament at the end of the twenty-second year and the beginning of the twenty-third year [of his reign][2] granted out of favour to his people and on account of the present Gascon war that all his writs of 'quo warranto' as well as of pleas of land would remain without day for the moment until he or his heirs may desire to speak about them.

iii

King's Bench Roll, no.140 (Easter 1294), m.16

[Sayles, *King's Bench*, iii. 11-18]

A plea between one who claimed to be the rector of Thame church in Oxfordshire and Oliver Sutton, bishop of Lincoln, and his nephew, who were charged with forcibly blockading the church with the assistance of William of North Leigh and many others.

[3-]Afterwards, in the Octaves of Michaelmas in the twenty-second year of the present king's reign, the king in his parliament of the said term ordered that the aforesaid plaint should remain without day against them all, saving the king's right etc.[-3] Afterwards Gilbert Rothbury came into the court and said that the king gave remission in the following terms, and he made thereon a little note: Afterwards the king at his parliament after Michaelmas in the twenty-second year of his reign, of his special grace and also at the instance of the reverend father Oliver, by the grace of God bishop of Lincoln, forgave on behalf of himself and his heirs William of North Leigh and the others the suit which pertains to him for the maintenance of his peace by reason of the aforesaid trespasses, and he granted them his enduring peace therein, provided however that they stand trial in his court if anyone else should wish to speak against them.

---

[2] I.e., 1294. This well-authenticated parliament is termed a 'council' in *Handbook of British Chronology*, p.511. Since the parliament lasted until the beginning of the twenty-third year, i.e. 20 November 1294, the knights summoned on 8-9 October presumably attended this parliament where on 12 November the subsidy of a tenth was granted. Similarly, in 1290 knights were summoned to attend on 15 July a parliament which began on 22 April (Richardson and Sayles, *The English Parliament in the Middle Ages*, V, 144.

[3-3] This passage has been cancelled on the roll.

iv

L.T.R. Memoranda Roll, no.65 (22 Edward I), Michaelmas Communia,
m.16d (19d)

Of the judgement made for the king against William de Say with respect to the
wardship of the heir of Adam de Bavent

Immediately after the death of Adam de Bavent the king had taken
his lands into his hands, together with his heir, Roger, on the ground
that Adam was his tenant-in-chief. William de Say sought the
wardship because Adam held in chief from him by military service
and held nothing in chief of the king.

In consequence, he asked for the wardship to be restored to him as his
right and inheritance, immediately praying and beseeching that the
treasurer and barons should attempt nothing in this matter to his
prejudice or proceed thereon to judgement against him but that they
should rather adjourn the business as it was until the king's parliament
after Michaelmas in the said year so that then before the king and council,
after William's right therein had been fully investigated, he should have
done for him in the aforesaid business what of right ought to be done.
And a day was given to him at the aforesaid parliament in the aforesaid
form.

At this parliament, after the said business had been fully discussed at
William's suit and his right in this respect had been shown by him and
very fully examined there by the king and council, and after the treasurer
and barons of the exchequer had likewise been summoned and
questioned thereon on the king's behalf, because Adam held a knight's
fee in Hatcham of the king in chief as of the crown on the day he died, as
aforesaid, William was told by the king to go to the exchequer to receive
there what justice advised in this matter. And thereupon William's
petition, brought before the king and council in the said parliament, was
forwarded to the exchequer. And the treasurer and barons, associating
with themselves the justices of the bench and having William in person in
full exchequer and having listened to his arguments, ordered the rolls and
memoranda of the exchequer to be examined thereon. And because it is
discovered from these memoranda and rolls that Richard de Vabadun,
whose heir Adam de Bavent was, held the aforesaid knight's fee in
Hatcham in the county of Surrey of the king in chief as of the crown, as
aforesaid, and Adam died seised thereof, and the negligence of the king's
bailiffs and ministers whenever they held office is not and should not be
so prejudicial to the king that he ought not to have his right in those
things belonging to him at whatever time his right is discovered and

shown, notwithstanding anyone's unlawful seizure and continued seisin by the passage of time, especially as no time runs against the king, therefore it is awarded that the king is to have for ever the wardship of the land and heir of Adam de Bavent as his true tenant in chief of the crown, notwithstanding the seisin of William de Say or any of his ancestors whatsoever, and that William, his heirs and assigns, are henceforth to have nothing therein.[4]

v

L.T.R. Memoranda Roll, no.70 (27 Edward I), Hilary Communia, m.30 (32)

Shropshire

Concerning a fine for relief

Adam son and heir of William of Orleton gives the king 16s.8d. for his relief, namely, for the vill of Orleton in Shropshire, which William, his father, held of the king in chief by the service of the tenth part of one knight's fee and by the service of rendering to the exchequer half a mark every year at the Feast of Michaelmas, for which service William did his homage to the king in the king's parliament after Michaelmas in the twenty-second year.

---

[4] A head surmounted by a coif has been drawn in the margin.

PARLIAMENT AT WESTMINSTER: 1 August 1295

i

Chancery Warrants, file 10, no.932

[*Cal. Chancery Warrants*, i. 63]

Edward by the grace of God king of England, lord of Ireland and duke of Aquitaine, to his beloved and faithful clerk, John of Langton, his chancellor, greeting. If, before you receive this letter, you have not by letters under our great seal ordered the bishops of Winchester, Worcester and London as well as the archdeacon of Chester, the deans of York and Lichfield, and Master John de Lacy, and all our justices and others, as well prelates as others of our realm, especially the learned men who are members of our council, to be at our parliament at Westminster on the first day of August or within three days following, as we have recently commanded you by letter, then as soon as you see this letter you are to have this done and to write back by the next courier to tell us what you have arranged to do in this matter. Given under our privy seal at Aberconway on the third day of July in the twenty-third year of our reign.[1]

ii

L.T.R. Memoranda Roll, no.66 (23 Edward I), Easter Communia, m.32 (35) schedule

The citizens of Bristol had been required to show by what warrant they had elected a mayor and bailiffs.

Afterwards in the king's parliament at Westminster after St. Peter's Chains the burgesses of the city came and presented a petition to the king as follows:

The burgesses sought the restoration of their ancient liberty which had been taken away from them by the treasurer, who had deposed their duly elected mayor and bailiffs.

This petition was sent here to the exchequer by the king's council. And the petition will be found among the petitions returned to the exchequer

---

[1] 3 July 1295. It had been expected that a parliament would meet as usual at Easter (*Cal. Patent Rolls, 1292-1301*, p.108). Note also Exchequer T.R. Misc. Books, no.202 (23 Edward I), p.44, for payments to William of Gainsborough of the Franciscan Order in coming to London at the king's command to the parliament in August.

from the parliament, and the petition is endorsed by the king's council thus: The king grants that they may have a mayor as before, provided the mayor comes to the exchequer and there, like others, takes an oath, reserving always any action the king may have in future.

> An exchequer writ, attested by John Cobham on 19 August 1295, was issued accordingly.

iii

L.T.R. Memoranda Roll, no.69 (26 Edward I), Hilary Communia, m.50d

Concerning the statute of Acton Burnell granted to the citizens of Norwich

Note that Thomas Framingham, who now comes here on behalf of the citizens of Norwich, has shown the treasurer and barons that the king lately granted to the citizens in his parliament held at Westminster in the twenty-third year of his reign that they could enjoy in the aforesaid city the statute of Acton Burnell, issued on behalf of merchants for recognisances of debts, and a seal in accordance with the terms of that statute, such as the city of London possesses, and that by virtue of that grant the king's beloved and faithful Gilbert of Rothbury, the clerk appointed to receive petitions in the said parliament, then came here by the king's instructions and on the king's behalf informed the reverend father William, bishop of Bath and Wells, the then treasurer, of that grant and said that the treasurer was to have a seal made at the citizens' expense to allow recognisances of debts in the city according to the terms of the statute. And on that information the treasurer then had such a seal made, and it remains here in the exchequer in the custody of the remembrancer. And he asked on behalf of the citizens that the treasurer and barons should assign custody of the seals[2] to some specific persons of the city so that they could use them in this matter in accordance with the king's grant. At his request the rolls of the aforesaid year are examined to see if anything could be found to have been entered in them, and on examination nothing could be found. Therefore the treasurer and barons, whose duty it is not to meddle with such things without a special mandate addressed to them thereon from the king, told Thomas that they would not meddle in the business. Afterwards, on the next day Gilbert, now one of the justices of the king's bench,[3] was called before the treasurer and recorded that the king had granted that the citizens

---

[2] The cocket seal was in two parts, the smaller portion being in the custody of a clerk.
[3] For his appointment in 1295 see Liberate Roll, no.76, m.9.

should have the statute in the aforesaid terms and that seals should be authorised for this purpose and delivered by the treasurer and barons to specific persons, to be kept in accordance with the terms of the statute etc. By reason of that record the treasurer granted that the citizens should be ordered to choose some of their fellow citizens whom they considered suitable for the purpose and to have them sent here to receive the seals in the aforesaid way. On that day the citizens sent here William But, their fellow-citizen, chosen to keep the greater part of the seal and that part is delivered into his custody in the exchequer etc. And the other part of the seal is delivered to John de Kirkeby, fellow-citizen of the city, who is deputed to hold the place of the clerk in those matters which were attached to that office. And William and John immediately took an oath that they would behave themselves properly and faithfully in everything pertaining to this office. And the treasurer and barons sent John Langton, chancellor of England, a letter in these words: To the wise and distinguished John Langton, the chancellor of Edward, the illustrious king of England, his fellows and friends, the treasurer and barons of the king's exchequer, greeting. Whereas our lord the king has lately informed us by his beloved and faithful Gilbert of Rothbury that his special royal grace to his citizens.[4]

iv

Exchequer Parliament and Council Proceedings, roll 8
[Leadam and Baldwin, *Select Cases before the King's Council, 1243-1482*, 10 f.]

To our lord the king and to his council Peter Tadcaster shows that master William March, bishop of Bath and Wells, wrongfully had him imprisoned in irons in the Fleet prison for a year and a half by his clerks, Hugh Nottingham and John Kirkby, for some arrears in the accounts of master Robert Tadcaster, his deceased brother, to whom Peter was neither heir nor executor, yet they have possessed themselves of all his goods and chattels, and still possess them, for some arrears that they are wrongfully demanding from him. And at the last parliament a Month after Michaelmas[5] last he bought three writs of the king, addressed to the keeper of the Fleet and based upon the statute of account,[6] in order to obtain his deliverance, and he frequently offered sufficient bail. But the keeper dared do nothing in answer to the king's instructions but replied

---

[4] The entry ends abruptly at this point. In the margin the words 'up to here' have been written, and a space left for the completion of the entry.

[5] In 1294.

[6] Statute of Westminster (1285) c.23: *Statutes of the Realm*, i. 83.

that the bishop ordered that no deliverance of his body should be made unless he found a surety for £320, which was contrary to the contents of his writs and the terms of the statute. And now at this parliament[7] he purchased a new writ and found good bail. But the bishop would not suffer his deliverance so long as he remained treasurer.[8] Wherefore Peter now prays our lord the king for God's sake that right be done him in respect of this great hardship and heinous imprisonment and detention in defiance of his writs.

v

L.T.R. Memoranda Roll, no.67 (24 Edward I), Hilary Communia, m.17

The record sent to the king on behalf of Nicholas of Yokefleet

A writ of *certiorari*, dated 26 October 1294, was addressed to Hugh of Cressingham and his fellows, justices in eyre in Yorkshire, asking for information on why they had taken into the king's hands five marks' worth of land in Burton in Lonsdale in Yorkshire which had belonged to Nicholas of Yokefleet. The record of pleas at York in the Trinity term of 1293 showed that the land had been alienated to Nicholas by a tenant-in-chief without licence from the king.

Afterwards, when this record had been read before the king and council in full parliament, Nicholas of Yokefleet was told to go to the exchequer and make fine with the king for the trespass he had committed in entering the king's fee without the king's licence, as aforesaid. And Gilbert of Rothbury, the king's clerk, sent this record to the exchequer under his seal for the fine to be made etc. And thereupon Nicholas came before the treasurer and others of the king's council at St. Albans at the Feast of the Circumcision this year[9] and asked that he might make fine in the aforesaid form etc. And the treasurer said that, since the exchequer was open after the Feast of Hilary, he should go to the exchequer and make fine there before the deputy treasurer and the barons in the aforesaid terms.

---

[7] In August 1295.
[8] He was dismissed on 16 August 1295.
[9] 1 January 1296.

PARLIAMENT AT WESTMINSTER: 27 November 1295

i

Petyt MSS., Inner Temple, vol. 15, fos.101-2
[*Parl. Writs*, i. 37-38]

The writ of summons to the sheriff of Gloucester bears an endorsement, giving the names of two knights of the shire and two burgesses for Gloucester and two burgesses for Bristol and continuing thus.

There is no city in my bailiwick. The king's writ, previously addressed to me[1] to cause knights, citizens and burgesses of my bailiwick to come in accordance with the terms of that mandate, I have had delivered to Gilbert of Rothbury at London on Sunday after Martinmas.[2] And the king's writ, attached to this schedule,[3] was delivered to me at Gloucester on Saturday after Martinmas.[4]

ii

King's Bench Roll, no.146 (Michaelmas 1295), m.65d

Cumberland

The men of Carlisle who came to parliament put Alan de Gremisdale in their place to hear and do the king's will.[5]

---

[1] On 2 October 1295 for the meeting of parliament on Sunday after Martinmas.
[2] 13 November 1295.
[3] Dated 2 November 1295: the day when parliament had been prorogued to 27 November 1295.
[4] 12 November 1295.
[5] It will be observed that the parliament to which so much attention has been given as the so-called 'Model Parliament' has left little or no trace of what it did.

PARLIAMENT AT BURY ST. EDMUNDS: 3 November 1296

This parliament is particularly remarkable for the fact that Scottish magnates were required to attend it (Stevenson, Documents Illustrative of the History of Scotland, *ii. 31, 136-7), the first 'Union Parliament'.*

B.L., Additional MS. 7965, f. 14*b*

The carriage of oats by the sheriff of Norfolk

To William Kerdistone, sheriff of Norfolk and Suffolk, for money paid by him for the carriage of 358½ quarters of oats out of the 504½ quarters of oats, sent by him from various places of his bailiwick to Bury St. Edmunds, in readiness for the king's parliament there in the month of November at the close of the twenty-fourth year [of the reign], for fodder for the king's horses, as appears from the details thereof delivered by the sheriff into the wardrobe by the hands of Geoffrey Cawston, his clerk, at Walsingham on the third day of February[1] . . . £4.8s.1½d.[2]

---

[1] 3 February 1297.

[2] Wardrobe Account for 25 Edward I, covering 20 November 1296–19 November 1297. For a letter from the archbishop of Canterbury, referring to his departure from this parliament, see *Hist. MSS. Reports, Various Collections*, i. 263. It had been as usual assumed that there would be a parliament at Easter 1296 (*Cal. Close Rolls, 1288-96*, p.424; L.T.R. Memoranda Roll, no.65 (22 Edward I), m.34).

PARLIAMENT AT SALISBURY: 24 February 1297

B.L. Additional MS. 7965, fo.108[1]

Writs sent out for the parliament of Salisbury[2]

To Boves, the messenger bearing the king's letters under the great seal, in going to the sheriff of Norfolk in order to have them sent by the sheriff to those to whom they are addressed, namely:

The earl of Norfolk, the earl of Oxford, and eight others

and to the sheriff of London in order to have them sent likewise to, namely:

The earl of Cornwall and nine others, mainly judges

and to the sheriff of Kent in order to have them sent to, namely:

William de Braose and two others   for his expenses, 4 shillings.

To Nicholas Ramage, the messenger bearing similar letters to the sheriff of Cambridge to have them sent by him to:

Richard Basset, Roger Brabazon and four others

and to the sheriff of Oxford for sending them to:

Alan Plucknet and five others

and to the sheriff of Somerset and Dorset for sending them to:

Henry de Lorty and six others

and to the sheriff of Devon for sending them to:

Oliver Durant and two others   for his expenses, 7 shillings

---

[1] The wardrobe account, from which the previous extract has been taken.
[2] A writ, dated on 30 September 1296 at Morpeth in Northumberland, had expected a parliament to meet at London after Christmas (*Cal. Close Rolls, 1288-96*, p.492).

To William of Ledbury, the messenger, bearing similar letters to the sheriff of Shropshire and Stafford in order to have them sent to:

> the earl of Warwick, the earl of Arundel, and fourteen others

To Simon Lonwys, the messenger bearing similar letters to the sheriff of York for:

> the earl of Angus and twenty others   for his expenses, 5 shillings

On 28 January to Roger Hurlemontayne, the messenger bearing similar letters from the king to:

> John son of Reginald and John Tregoz   for his expenses in going
>   with haste, 5 shillings

PARLIAMENT AT WESTMINSTER: 8 July 1297

i

L.T.R. Memoranda Roll, no.68 (25 Edward I), Trinity Communia, m.51d

Note that on 22 July, when the king was busy at Westminster in his parliament, it was agreed by the king and his council that all who did their service in the Welsh campaigns in the fifth and tenth years[1] and whose names are included in the marshal's rolls of those campaigns, although scutage is being demanded from them for more fees than they did service for, shall nevertheless have a postponement as regards the demand for all the said scutage until the king has considered making another ordinance thereon. Because all who did service in the said campaigns claim to be discharged of all scutage demanded from them etc. by the service they did there etc.

ii

L.T.R. Memoranda Roll, no.69 (26 Edward I), Michaelmas Communia, m.14d

Berkshire

Petition of John Sparholt

Note that at the king's parliament, held at Westminster a Fortnight after the Nativity of St. John the Baptist in the twenty-fifth year of the reign,[2] a petition was sent by the king and his council to the barons here on behalf of John son of William Sparholt, and its tenor is as follows:

William Sparholt had leased the manor of Hagbourne in 1273 at a yearly rent of £10.8s.10d. until Richard of Windsor, then the king's ward, attained his majority. Richard proved that he had reached it in 1278 and was given possession of the manor. Nevertheless the treasurer and barons of the exchequer continued to charge William the rent.

Nothing about Richard's majority could be found on the chancery rolls but an inquisition at Michaelmas 1284 revealed that he had come of age about the Nativity of the Virgin Mary in 1278[3] and that he had proved it before John Kirkby and Nicholas of Stapleton and

---

[1] 1277 and 1282.
[2] 8 July 1297.
[3] 8 September 1278.

immediately afterwards obtained possession of the manor. John Sparholt was accordingly discharged from responsibility for the rent thereafter.

iii
Ancient Correspondence, vol. XLVII, no.92

Edward by the grace of God king of England, lord of Ireland and duke of Aquitaine, to his dear and faithful aunt, Joan de Valence, countess of Pembroke, greeting. Whereas you have heard that the wool and leather of the Welsh counties have been gathered together at the chief town of each county, such as Chepstow, Cardiff and Brecknock, and you would like the wool and leather of your county of Pembroke to be likewise brought and gathered together at Pembroke, we would have you know that we and those who are about us at the moment do not remember what was decided in this business. But you can send one of your men to our parliament, when we shall have come to London where we will have those who are appointed to deal with such matters, and we will then do what we can in good manner. And as for the demands made on you for the debts of your lord, for which Aymer, your son, has found security at our exchequer, as you have told us, we are sending you our letters addressed to those of the exchequer, by which we order them to leave you in peace as regards the said demands and not to cause you to be distrained in any way in contravention of the terms of the aforesaid security and, if they should have caused you to submit to a distraint on this account, they are to order what is distrained to be released without delay. And as for your franchise of Walwyns Castle, wherein our bailiffs of Haverford have given you some harsh treatment and damage, as you have told us by your letter, we wish you to send to our said parliament some of your men, if you think this should be done, and we will order our bailiffs, if you wish, to be there also, and, having thus heard your complaint and their reply, we will willingly do for you whatever we can reasonably do. Given under our privy seal at Ilsington the seventh day of April in the twenty-fifth year of our reign.[4]

---

[4] 7 April 1297.

PARLIAMENT AT LONDON: Michaelmas 1297

i

Close Roll, no.114, m.4

[*Cal. Close Rolls 1296-1302*, p.67]

*Concerning the arrangement provided between the men of Yarmouth
and the men of the Cinque Ports, to be sealed and sent to the king*

The king to the bailiffs, worthy men and community of both towns of
Yarmouth,[1] greeting. We have sent you, enclosed herein, the arrangement provided by our council in the parliament of Edward, our most
dear son, our deputy in England while we are busy outside the kingdom,
between you on the one side and the men of the Cinque Ports on the
other, which must be sealed by you and returned to our council within a
Month after Michaelmas last, as we have enjoined upon John Wyth and
his fellows, sent by you to our council. And therefore we order you to
send to our council the arrangement sealed for both your towns and their
members so that the council may have it under seal at the latest within the
said Sunday.[2] For we forbid you, under forfeiture of life and property
and all you can forfeit, to inflict in the meantime, yourselves or by any
others, any injury, harm or wrong by land or sea upon the men of the
Cinque Ports or any of them. Witness Edward, the king's son, at
Westminster on the twelfth day of October.[3]

ii

L.T.R. Memoranda Roll, no.69 (25 Edward I), Michaelmas Communia, m.20

London

The Petition of Cecily de la More

Note that a certain petition was sent here by the council of Edward, the
king's son, deputising for him at present in England, and its tenor is as
follows:

[1] I.e. Great Yarmouth and Little Yarmouth.
[2] 27 October 1297, which was a Month after Michaelmas and a Sunday. The
parliament was summoned to meet at London on 30 September 1297 (*Parl. Writs*, i. 56b,
57a).
[3] 12 October 1297.

To our lord the king and his council shows Cecily de la More of London that, whereas she had left in the hands of the customs-collectors of London up to ten sacks of wool in pledge for £30, being the customs on the wool she had caused to be transported a long time before Easter, and these same sacks of wool have been seized and sequestrated and sent away to be sold, and those who seized the wool at London caused the said sacks of wool to be valued at £53.18s.4d. And therefore she prays for God's sake that the £30 she owes for the customs may be allowed against the said sacks of wool and that the lord our king may make his grace to her for the remainder, for she has lost much on the sea on account of this war.

And the petition is endorsed thus:

Let her go to the exchequer and, if it be so, then allow her in the price of the said sacks of wool what she owed for the customs on her wool which at another time she caused to be transported.

PARLIAMENT AT LONDON: Easter 1298

Exchequer Parliament Roll, no.11, m.1
[*Rot. Parl.*, i. 143]

*Of the parliament at London at Easter in the twenty-sixth year
of the reign of King Edward*[1]

*Ordinance made by the king and his council for removing the exchequer
and the common bench from London to York*

It is ordained that the exchequer and the common bench are to be at York
after the Feast of Trinity: that is to say, the exchequer on the Morrow of
Trinity[2] and the common bench on the Octave of Trinity;[3] and that the
exchequer and the common bench are to be within the castle; and that, if
houses or other things are in disrepair, the sheriff is to be ordered to cause
to be done etc.

*Petition of the countess of Cornwall with respect to a settlement
arranged between the earl, her husband, and herself*

It seems to the council that, with respect to the lands which were assigned
to her by her lord for her sustenance, from which she complains she has
been ejected, the king's court cannot help her in regard to any settlement
arranged between the earl, her husband, and herself.

---

[1] Easter Day was 6 April.
[2] 2 June 1298.
[3] 8 June 1298.

PARLIAMENT AT WESTMINSTER: Lent 1299

i

Chancery Warrants, file 20, no.1911

[*Cal. Chancery Warrants*, i. 101]

Edward by the grace of God king of England, lord of Ireland and duke of Aquitaine, to his dear and faithful clerk, John Langton, his chancellor, greeting. We command you that, as hastily as possible, you are to have instructions given by letters of our great seal in suitable form to the archbishops, bishops, abbots, priors, earls and barons and to all those of our realm who hold by barony and to all those who are members of our council and to Sir Robert fitz Robert and to Sir John Segrave, because they are of our council, that they are all to be with us at London on the first Sunday of Lent[1] next to deal with our business overseas wherein we wish to have their counsel and their advice. And we will that you go with all the chancery to London to put your affairs in order for your journey to the court of Rome and that you remain in London until we arrive there and then make arrangements for the custody of our seal by your counsel and that of other worthy men of ours, as shall seem best to us. Given under our privy seal at Theel Bridge[2] the sixth day of February in the twenty-seventh year of our reign. [3]

ii

Guildhall, London, Letter Book C, f. 28

[*Parl. Writs*, i. 80]

Note that on Wednesday, the Feast of the Annunciation of the Blessed Mary in the twenty-seventh year of the reign of King Edward,[4] William of Leire, William of Bethune, Adam of Roxley, Walter of Finchingfield were chosen by the mayor and aldermen to prosecute the business of the city before the king and council in the parliament at Westminster, begun on the first Monday of Lent in the abovesaid year.[5]

---

[1] 8 March 1299.
[2] *Alias* Stanstead St. Margaret, co. Herts.
[3] 6 February 1299.
[4] 25 March 1299.
[5] 9 March 1299.

iii

L.T.R. Memoranda Roll, no.70 (27 Edward I), Easter Communia, m.37

The petition of the executors of the will of master William of Louth,
late bishop of Ely

The executors of the will of William, late bishop of Ely, deceased, of blessed memory, formerly keeper of the king's wardrobe, presented a petition to the king's council in the king's parliament at Westminster in Lent of this year in these words:

To our lord the king show the executors of the bishop of Ely, late keeper of his wardrobe, that, whereas the clergy of the province of Canterbury have granted to our lord the king a fifteenth of their goods in the tenth, eleventh and twelfth years,[6] and the clergy of the province of York have granted him a tenth of their goods in the tenth and eleventh years,[7] William of Beverley, clerk, was appointed collector of this tenth and sent money on several occasions to the wardrobe from that tenth. And the clerks who then were in the wardrobe under the keeper entered in their rolls 'fifteenth' for 'tenth' because they did not know the distinction whereby one province gave a fifteenth and the other a tenth. And by that error the said keeper was charged in rendering his accounts at the exchequer for a fifteenth received from William of Beverley, collector of the province of York, whereas he ought to have said 'collector of the tenth of the province of York'. Therefore the executors pray our lord the king that of his grace he may instruct the treasurer and barons of the exchequer to correct their rolls regarding this misunderstanding and to make full allowance to the executors for the money for which the deceased man is charged in his account.

And this petition was sent, together with other petitions, from the aforesaid parliament to the exchequer here for expedition, and they are in the custody of the treasurer's remembrancer.[8] And the petition is endorsed thus:

It is clear to the king and his council that in the tenth and eleventh years the clergy of the province of York granted the king a tenth only of their goods and in the same tenth and eleventh years and in the twelfth year the clergy of the province of Canterbury granted the king a fifteenth of their goods. Therefore the treasurer and barons of the exchequer are to have the error in speaking of the fifteenth of the province of York corrected,

[6] 1282-85.
[7] 1282-84.
[8] Cf. also *ibid.*, m.39d (petition of William de Derneford and Joan, his wife).

and in place of this fifteenth they should have 'tenth of the province of York' written in all the rolls concerned with the said tenth, as well in the rolls and counter-rolls of the king's wardrobe as in the rolls of the said William's account rendered at the exchequer.

And by reason of this petition the treasurer and barons caused to be examined the rolls and counter-rolls of the wardrobe and the rolls of accounts rendered by William at the exchequer for the king's wardrobe in the ninth, tenth, eleventh and twelfth years, and the great rolls of accounts of the twelfth and thirteenth years, in which the aforesaid account is written.

> It was found that the clerks of the wardrobe had, indeed, made a mistake and the treasurer and barons had the relevant records duly corrected and an allowance made to the late bishop of Ely's executors.

PARLIAMENT AT WESTMINSTER: Easter 1299

Coram Rege Roll, no. 163 (Hilary 1301), m. 9
[*Statutes of the Realm*, i. 131-3]

The king, giving heed recently to the state of his realm which has suffered grave damage and almost incalculable loss through forgers who bring false, forged and debased money into our kingdom from abroad, was then led to ordain among other things in his parliament at Stepney near London[1] by common counsel of his realm that all those who bring money in sterling from abroad into the realm or elsewhere within his jurisdiction are at once to present themselves before the keepers of the ports where they happen to land, to deliver and hand over to them the money they have brought so that they can send it to the nearest assayers of his money to inspect and test whether it is good and legal, in accordance with what is contained more fully in the ordinance sent to his sheriffs under his seal.

> This is the Statute of Money, which goes on to give a description in detail of how it is to be enforced.

[1] Parliament was summoned on 10 April 1299 to meet a Fortnight after Easter at Westminster (*Cal. Close Rolls, 1296-1302*, pp. 300, 390: *Parl. Writs*, i. 80f) and appears to have moved to Stepney. Cf. Assize Roll, no. 1014, m. 8: pleadings before the king at Stepney at Easter 1291; *Rot. Parl.*, i. 87: litigation at Easter 1294 before the king's council, 'then being at Stepney outside London'.

PARLIAMENT AT LONDON: Michaelmas 1299

Close Roll, no.54, m.6
[*Cal. Close Rolls, 1296-1302*, p.270 f.]

On behalf of Richard fitz Alan, earl of Arundel

The king to his beloved and faithful John of Havering, his justice of North Wales, greeting. Because we have of our special grace caused to be restored until our next parliament to our beloved and faithful Richard fitz Alan, earl of Arundel, his town and land of Oswestry which for certain reasons you have taken into our hand as well as Thomas of Winsbury, his bailiff there, whom you have, so it is said, also arrested for certain reasons, so that the earl and Thomas may be before us at our next parliament to do and receive what our court shall award in this respect, we order you to deliver the town and land as well as the bailiff to the earl in the meantime on the aforesaid terms, releasing meanwhile such distraint as you may have made upon the earl on this account. And you are to be at the parliament in your own person to inform us more fully about the aforesaid matters. And you are then to have there this writ. Witness the king at Canterbury on the sixteenth day of September.[1]

By the king himself.

[1] 16 September 1299. A few writs of summons are enrolled for a parliament, to be held at London on 18 October 1299 (*Parl. Writs*, i. 81; *Cal. Close Rolls, 1296-1302*, p.318).

PARLIAMENT AT WESTMINSTER: Lent 1300

i
Chancery Warrants, Series I, no.2013
[*Cal. Chancery Warrants*, i. 106]

Edward by the grace of God king of England, lord of Ireland and duke of Aquitaine, to our dear clerk and loyal subject, John of Langton, our chancellor, greeting. We command and firmly require you to have writs issued from our chancery without any kind of delay in order to summon our parliament as we have already instructed you, that is to say on the second Sunday of Lent.[1] And you are also to have letters of summons concerning our arrival at Carlisle at the Nativity of St. John the Baptist next,[2] which we intend to be both an order and a request. And you are also to summon the military services[3] according to our instructions to you by our letters and by our messenger. And we charge you to make these letters as speedily and as urgently as you can in accordance with the form that has been used in similar case before this time and according to the purport of the order we have given you thereon. And having made these letters, you are to have them sent out at once without any kind of delay. And these matters are not to be in any way left undone because of any instructions or anything else you may be given to understand. And be aware that we well know the day when our messenger will be able to reach you and we have calculated how long it will take for the letters to be made. Wherefore we let you know that, if all the letters are not sent out as we have instructed you, we shall not hold ourselves well pleased with you, so let this be done quickly and soon. Given under our privy seal at Bamborough on the first day of January in the twenty-eighth year of our reign.[4]

ii
L.T.R. Memoranda Roll, no.71 (28 Edward I), Hilary Communia, m.28

Note that on the Monday of St. Peter in Cathedra in the twenty-eighth year of the reign of King Edward[5] John de Lisle, baron of the exchequer, and Hugh of Nottingham, clerk of the exchequer, then present in the exchequer, delivered the under-written [documents] to Nicholas of

---

[1] 6 March 1300.
[2] 24 June 1300.
[3] *Cal. Close Rolls, 1298-1302*, pp.380–81 (14 January 1300).
[4] 1 January 1300.
[5] 22 February 1300.

Oakham, clerk of the king's Receipt, to be carried to the king at his parliament at Westminster on the second Sunday of Lent in the aforesaid year[6] by virtue of the king's writ of privy seal, addressed to the treasurer, barons, chamberlain, remembrancers of the exchequer and the aforesaid Hugh of Nottingham and to each of them or their deputies or deputy to whom the said writ shall come, the writ being enrolled in the memoranda of the exchequer in Hilary term of the said year: namely, in one bag the great rolls of the time of King Henry, son of King John, covering the second to the twelfth years of his reign, together with one roll in the same bag of transcripts of certain charters – the first year not counting at the exchequer because it was a time of war. They also handed over the red book of the exchequer. They also handed over various transcripts of various charters [of many named abbots and priors] and the two books which are called Domesday.

iii

King's Bench Roll, no. 189 (Trinity 1307), m. 41
[Sayles, *King's Bench*, iii. 180 f.]

Sussex

Gilbert, the present bishop of Chichester, delivered to the king in his parliament at Lincoln in the Octave of Hilary[7] a petition in these words:

To our lord the king and his council prays, if it please him, his chaplain Gilbert, the bishop of Chichester, thus: the bishop prayed our lord the king at a parliament at Westminster a long time ago that those who have by colour of our lord the king's gift entered some prebends of Hastings, which are parish churches with cure of souls, without being presented to him, that is to say, master Thomas de Logorre, Edmund of London, Walter of Amersham, Adam of Blyth and Andrew of Lincoln, should be presented to him, as the prebendaries of Hastings were wont to be presented to him and his predecessors all the time before the barony of Hastings with the castle and the advowsons of the prebends escheated into the king's hands by escheat of the Normans[8] and after that escheat, and the bishop has these presentations, made by letters under the seals of our present lord king and of his father, King Henry, ready to exhibit when it please our lord the king and his council. And at the said parliament our lord the king commanded that the rolls of chancery

[6] 6 March 1300.
[7] Hilary 1301.
[8] Those who rebelled against King John before the loss of Normandy in 1204.

should be searched upon this matter and an inquiry held, and this inquiry is held and is returned into the chancery, and the rolls were searched by Adam of Osgodby and are in his custody. Wherefore the said bishop prays that, inasmuch as he has sued a long time from parliament to parliament and was adjourned at the last parliament at Westminster, which was in Lent last,[9] to the parliament next following which is the present one (and Gilbert of Rothbury was ordered to have this adjournment enrolled on his roll), our lord the king and his council should be so good as to expedite his business in accordance with the inquiry held and with the record of the chancery rolls and with the evidence that the bishop wishes to show shortly and as they think reason and the principles of justice shall require, for in delay there is great peril of souls.

iv

B.L., Cotton MS., Vespasian E. XXII, fo. 46*b*

John Spigurnel

Note that on Saturday, the Feast of St. Gregory the pope in the twenty-eighth year of the king's reign[10] at the Temple, London, in full parliament John Spigurnel did homage and fealty to Godfrey, abbot of Peterborough, for the tenements he claims to hold of him and does hold in the vill of Woodford. In the presence of Master Geoffrey of Maxey, Robert of Thorp and John of Oundle and others.

v

L.T.R. Memoranda Roll, no. 71 (28 Edward I), Trinity Communia, m. 45
[Sayles, *King's Bench*, iii. p. cxxiv]

Cambridge

On behalf of the bishop of Ely

On Saturday, the Feast of St. Barnabas the Apostle,[11] Robert Hereward, the bishop of Ely's steward, came here and showed on the bishop's behalf to the treasurer and barons and others of the king's council who were present in the exchequer that the bishop had lately claimed this franchise in the king's bench when it was at Ely: namely, that neither the stewards

---

[9] Lent 1300.
[10] 12 March 1300.
[11] 11 June 1300.

nor the marshals of the king nor any other minister of his ought to perform or exercise any duties within the Isle of Ely except through the bishop's servants. And the king then adjourned the bishop so that he might now, on the arrival of the king here, prosecute his claim, either himself or by one of his servants, before the king's council and put forward and exhibit anything etc. on his own behalf. Wherefore Robert came forward in the name of the bishop before the said council to prosecute the said claim and to propound and show on the bishop's behalf how he claims to have the aforesaid franchise etc. And because it seemed to the treasurer and the others of the king's council here present that discussion on the said business ought to be made in the king's parliament before him and his council and nowhere else unless the king specially commands it, Robert is told that he or someone else in the bishop's place is to prosecute the aforesaid business at the next parliament etc. and there show and propound whatever he has etc.[12]

[12] Note also Dean and Chapter, Canterbury, MS. m.260: 'Articles presented to the lord king Edward on behalf of the prelates and clergy of England in his parliament at London at Lent 1300 in the time of Robert, archbishop of Canterbury. And the said articles were later presented to the king in the parliament at Lincoln in the Octave of Hilary in the presence of the prelates and nobles of the whole realm'. The articles follow (for which see Powicke and Cheney, *Councils and Synods*, ii. 1206ff).

PARLIAMENT AT LINCOLN: Hilary 1301

Writs were issued for a parliament to be held at Michaelmas 1300 (Cole, Documents, pp.333 ff.) but it was apparently adjourned until Hilary 1301, for the same persons were summoned again. Documents bearing upon the expenses incurred in holding parliament are numerous and stretch back to at least 1258. This one is given to bring out in the most striking manner the fact that the venue of parliament should normally be in or near the largest towns in England, where a large influx of visitors could be accommodated without too much difficulty. This is an aspect of the historical development of institutions which we should bear in mind.

Exchequer, King's Remembrancer's Accounts, 568/4, writ no.3

Edward, by the grace of God king of England, lord of Ireland and duke of Aquitaine, to the sheriff of Lincoln, greeting. Inasmuch as it is necessary for us to have a great store of all kinds of foodstuffs for our next parliament which we wish to hold at Lincoln, we command you on sight of these letters to let us be provided within your bailiwick with 400 quarters of wheat, 400 quarters of corn, 1000 quarters of hay and as much straw as is sufficient for 400 horses for a month, and 100 oxen and cows, 100 pigs and 300 sheep, and you are to have them well looked after and kept until you have further instructions from us. And you are to cause proper indentures, which shall contain what is purveyed and its cost, to be made between you and all those from whom these purveyances shall be taken so that we can duly meet their demands from our wardrobe when we come there to the said parliament. Given under our privy seal at Dumfries the twenty-eighth day of October in the twenty-eighth year of our reign.[1]

ii

Chancery Warrants, Series I, file 22, no.2207
[*Cal. Chancery Warrants*, i. 120]

Edward, by the grace of God king of England, lord of Ireland, and duke of Aquitaine, to our dear clerk and loyal subject, John Langton, our

---

[1]   28 October 1300. This is the original writ, still bearing the privy seal. A second writ, dated 9 November 1300 at Carlisle under the privy seal, gives further instructions. Then follows a long financial account from the sheriff of Lincoln in which he claims allowances for the costs of conveying grain and animals, dead or alive, by land or water, from every part of Lincolnshire. For further details, see *Birmingham Historical Journal*, iii (1951), 16-32.

chancellor, greeting. Whereas we have ordered and required you before this that you were to cause to be searched the rolls and all the memoranda relating to the perambulation[2] in our exchequer as well as in our chancery and anywhere else you think something thereon may be found, we order and require you again to have searched at our exchequer at York the Domesday, the Red Book, and all the other rolls of the exchequer as well as of the chancery so that nothing remains that has not been well and carefully searched before you go thence to London to search thereon the other rolls that are there. And you are also to cause to be searched all the memoranda relating to the business of Scotland so that we can have it at our next parliament. For we wish then to reply to the pope about other matters, of which he has informed us with regard to the said land of Scotland. And in these matters you are to trust our dear clerk John Bush regarding what he will tell you on our behalf. Given under our privy seal at Carlisle the thirteenth day of November in the twenty-eighth year of our reign.[3]

iii

Dean and Chapter, Canterbury, MS. G 9, fo.214*b*

[*Parl. Writs*, i. 104]

A bill delivered on the king's behalf to the prelates and nobles in his parliament at Lincoln in the Octave of Hilary 1301 in the twenty-ninth year of King Edward's reign

As regards the perambulation made, the king wills that this be shown to the good people who have come to this parliament. And when they have examined it – and clearly understood how and in what way and by what exercise of learning, memory and argument it was made in all its details and as a whole – together with the evidence that the king understands he has on his behalf, if they wish thereon to say by their homage and the fealty they owe him and the crown that the perambulation has been well and faithfully done and ridden[4] on behalf of the king and his crown and his people with adequate advice and trustworthy information and that he can confirm it without tarnishing his oath and without disinheriting his crown and that they agree to advise it, the king indeed wills that it be so. And if there was anything to correct or to change, then let it be corrected without delay in any suitable way they can decide by their deliberations on the said articles. And if this way is unacceptable, then let some middle

---

[2] This refers to an investigation into the extent of the forest lands.
[3] 13 November 1300.
[4] Cf. the phrase 'to ride the borders'.

way be found how the matter may be resolved in proper form in maintaining the estate of the crown lest it be diminished and thus the oath of the king and of themselves as regards the crown may be preserved.

A bill from the prelates and nobles of the realm delivered to the king on behalf of the whole community in the parliament of Lincoln in the aforesaid year

The people of the community of his land would have our lord the king know that, with respect to the two ways suggested to them by him,[5] they would commit no offence for which they might be challenged in any manner and would not dare to undertake to answer in the form these two ways provide on account of the perils that could ensue therefrom.

> Twelve articles were then submitted to the king, requesting the confirmation of the Great Charter and the Charter of the Forest, immediate disafforestation, the redress of abuses of purveyance and other grievances. Three of the articles are given below:

And that what has been wrongfully done by any minister may be redressed in accordance with its gravity by auditors appointed for this purpose, who are not under suspicion by the prelates, earls and barons of the land by reason of what they themselves have done before this time, and that this be now put in hand.

The king means to provide another remedy thereon but not by such auditors.

The people of the realm, in order that all the aforesaid things may be done and securely confirmed and completed, grant him a fifteenth in place of the twentieth granted before this time on condition that all the aforesaid things be done between now and next Michaelmas: otherwise nothing is to be levied.

It expressly pleases the king.

And on account of the abovesaid matters the prelates of Holy Church cannot and dare not agree that any contribution should be made from their property or the property of the clergy against the pope's prohibition.

It did not please the king: but the community of the nobles approved.

---

[5] As previously stated the bill put forward on the king's behalf could be accepted as it was or it could be amended.

iv(a)

L.T.R. Memoranda Roll, no.76 (34 Edward I), Trinity Communia, m.40 (47)
[Madox, *History of the Exchequer*, p.615, note p.]

To the treasurer on behalf of the king

Edward by the grace of God etc. to the reverend father in God Walter, by the same grace, bishop of Chester, our treasurer, greeting. We are sending you by the bearers of this letter Sir Henry Keighley who has been before us, and we have clearly discovered from his own confession that he is the one who brought us the bill on behalf of the archbishop of Canterbury and the others who harassed us outrageously at the parliament of Lincoln. And we have made a long search for him. And we order you to have Henry put in safe custody in the Tower of London to remain there until we can be satisfied that he is sorry for what he has done and until we decree otherwise thereon. And know that we wish Henry to be courteously and safely guarded in the Tower and unfettered but let this courtesy and guard be so arranged that he can think it comes from your courtesy and not from us. Given under our privy seal at Tindon End on the fifth day of June.[6]

iv(b)

L.T.R. Memoranda Roll, no.76 (34 Edward I), Trinity Communia, m.44d (51d)

Lancashire

Concerning Henry of Keighley, delivered to the Tower of London

Note that on Saturday following the Fortnight after Midsummer[7] Nicholas of Chilham and John Rastel, the king's yeomen, now came here before the treasurer, barons and some others of the king's council who were present, and they brought with them Henry Keighley, knight, of the county of Lancaster. And they handed to the treasurer a writ of privy seal whereby the king gave the treasurer instructions that the said Henry was to be delivered in person to the keeper of the Tower of London, to be kept safely there until the king gave further instructions thereon, on account of a petition which Henry presented to the king in his parliament at Lincoln in the twenty-ninth year on behalf of the archbishop of Canterbury and many others of the kingdom, who were for a little while opposing the king there at that time and praying by the aforesaid petition

---

[6] 5 June 1306.
[7] 9 July 1306.

for various things to be done against the king's estate etc. And so Henry is immediately committed to Ralph of Sandwich, the constable of the Tower, who is present in the Exchequer, to be led to the Tower etc. and there to be in custody until the king decrees otherwise thereon etc. Yet because the king's writ in the possession of the treasurer contains that Henry is to be kept courteously in the Tower and not in irons etc. and that the treasurer was to cause to be done therein what etc., the treasurer at once ordered the constable to keep Henry in custody in the aforesaid way.

Afterwards at the octave of Trinity in the thirty-fifth year[8] the king by his writ of privy seal given at Carlisle on the fifth day of April in the said thirty-fifth year[9] – a writ which is enrolled in the memoranda of this year in Trinity term and is among the 'communia'[10] of the said year – ordered his treasurer to summon Henry before him here and to take a corporal oath from him that he will behave himself properly and faithfully towards the king and his heirs and in everything pertaining to the crown of England and that he will in no way offend in future against the king, the king's heirs, or the crown of England, and he is to have Henry released from prison. And thereupon Henry, having been summoned here on Wednesday, the last day of May,[11] took an oath in the aforesaid terms and is released from prison etc.

v

Chancery Parliament and Council Proceedings, file 3, no.1

> This draft of the Statute of Escheators contains the names of the experts in administration and law who gave advice. They are omitted in the version of the statute on the rolls of the parliament (*Rot. Parl.*, i. 145) but are in the version on the statute roll (*Statutes of the Realm*, i. 142).

At the king's parliament at Lincoln in the Octave of Hilary in the twenty-ninth year of his reign, it is agreed by the king's council before the king, the king giving his consent and ordering it to be done and observed henceforward, by the counsel of the reverend father Walter Langton, bishop of Coventry and Lichfield, then the king's treasurer, John Langton, then chancellor, Roger Brabazon, John Mettingham, Ralph Hengham, William Bereford, Roger Hegham, Gilbert Rothbury, William Haward, William Carleton, William Inge, John Lythegreyns, Adam

---

[8] 28 May 1307.
[9] 5 April 1307.
[10] I.e. the day-to-day entries.
[11] 31 May 1307.

Crokedayk, William Brompton, John Droxford, John Benstead, William Mortimer and Walter Gloucester, then escheator below the river Trent [the statute then follows].

vi

B.L., Additional MS. 7966 A[12]

fo.1b

By the hand of Ferrand of Spain, who received money for his expenses while awaiting the expedition of his business at the next parliament: on the last day of November[13] 20s.

By the hand of John Russell for canvas, wax, some string and a hamper bought for packing the two Domesday books, the eyre rolls of justices of the forest, and other memoranda concerning forests and perambulations so that they could be brought to the king: the same day 6s.3d.

fo.30

The expenses of master Andrew Tange

To master Andrew Tange, notary public, going on the treasurer's instructions from York to London in order to make a record of proceedings relating to the acts of homage and fealty of the Scots: for his wages and expenses from 21 December to the last day of February,[14] seventy days in all, in staying in London on the aforesaid business and in coming from there to Lincoln and staying there at the time of the parliament, taking 2s. a day, by the accounting done with him at Lincoln on 27 February.

fo.31

To Hugh Bussey, sheriff of Lincoln, for money paid by him for transporting grain and meat, purveyed by him within his bailiwick for the expenses of the king's household in his parliament of Lincoln.

---

[12] A controlment roll of the wardrobe, 1300–01.

[13] 30 November 1300.

[14] 21 December 1300–28 February 1301.

fo.36

To John of Droxford, sent by the king from Northampton to London for certain business relating to the king's parliament at Lincoln: for his expenses for 31 days from 29 December to 28 January,[15] on which day he came to the court at Nettleham, the first day being allowed but not the last, £45.

fo.39b

The expenses of the clerks transcribing memoranda relating to the perambulations of the forests

To the four clerks transcribing various items of the book called Domesday at the exchequer, which relate to the perambulations made in various forests of England, to be sent to the king at the parliament of Lincoln: on the tenth day of December 13s.8d. Again, to the five clerks transcribing similar items of the said book for transmission to the aforesaid parliament: on the nineteenth day of January 5 marks. Again, for canvas, wax, hempen cord and panniers bought for packing the rolls of justices and other books and various memoranda concerning the said perambulations in readiness for the aforesaid parliament on the said day: 6s.11d. in money paid by the exchequer for which the wardrobe is charged. Sum total: 116s.3d. (*sic*).

fo.66b

The masters of the university of Oxford

To four masters of the university of Oxford coming at the king's command to his parliament held at Lincoln in the present year, as a gift from the king on account of the expenses they incurred in coming to Lincoln as aforesaid, staying there and returning – by their own hands at Nettleham in the month of February – 24 marks.

The masters of the university of Cambridge

To two masters of the university of Cambridge similarly coming to that parliament, as a gift from the king on account of similar expenses – by their own hands there in the same month – 12 marks.[16]

---

[15] 29 December 1300–28 January 1301.
[16] See Prynne, *Records*, III, 884–5, for the returns of the chancellors of Oxford and Cambridge.

vii

King's Bench Roll, no.164 (Easter 1301), m.61d

[Sayles, *King's Bench*, iii. 111 f.]

Although the Cinque Ports were ordered to send representatives to the mid-summer parliament of 1265 (which in the event did not meet), no returns survive before 1361, though they were being summoned long before then.

Kent

Cinque Ports

John of Hoo, mayor of Sandwich, [and sixteen others] were attached to answer the king of this plea: whereas the king had sent his beloved and faithful Ralph of Sandwich, Roger Chegham and John Abel, his justices, to the county of Kent to make certain inquisitions, the said John [and many others] assaulted the king's justices with force and arms at Ash and ill-treated them, not permitting them to enter the king's town of Sandwich or to do the duties enjoined upon them by the king, and they cut open the pouch with the king's rolls and broke the bows and arrows of the justices' men and inflicted other outrages upon them, in contempt of the king and manifest injury to his royal crown and dignity. And they were also attached to show why they were not at the king's parliament at Lincoln on the Octave of Hilary last, as they were adjourned there by the warden of the Cinque Ports . . . And John of Hoo, the mayor, and the others come and deny force and wrong . . . And as for the adjournment before the king, they say that by letters sealed with their common seal they sent three barons of the town to the king's parliament to hear and do the king's will, as they were accustomed to do at the king's other parliaments, and they say that they believed that they had done what was required in this matter. But if it seems to the king that they have in any way been at fault therein, they submit themselves to the king's grace. And the king reserves this matter to himself etc.

viii

L.T.R. Memoranda Roll No.72 (29 Edward I), m.31, Easter Communia

Devon

Petition of the sisters and heirs of Thomas Peveril

Note that, among the petitions returned here to the exchequer from the king's parliament of Lincoln in the twenty-ninth year of his reign, there is a certain petition in these words:

To the council of our lord the king show Margery Peveril, Joan Peveril and Denise Peveril, sisters and heirs of Thomas Peveril, that, whereas they were all of full age at the time of Thomas's death and they received their inheritance from him at the hand of our lord the king and did him homage and found security for paying their relief, they are now distrained for a fine for their marriages, and they pray grace and redress of this distress inasmuch as they ought by law to be free to make their own marriages.

And this petition is endorsed thus: Let inquiry be made in the exchequer about what is customary and in the meanwhile let them have respite.

And now, at a Fortnight after Easter,[17] a certain John de la Ryvere, knight, comes here and prays on behalf of Margaret, Joan and Denise that the treasurer and barons give answer and judgement upon the aforesaid matter. And after full discussion had taken place thereon among the treasurer and barons and others of the king's council, because some justices of the bench and others of the king's council are now absent, it is agreed that Margery, Joan and Denise are to be further adjourned to parliament so that it can be conclusively discussed then in the full council of the king whether their marriage ought of right to pertain to the king therein. And let them have respite in the meantime from the distraint made upon them for their marriages, and also in the meantime let the rolls of chancery and the rolls and memoranda of the exchequer be examined, provided they find the king security for their marriages if it should be agreed in the said parliament that the king ought of right to have them. And John asks to be allowed on behalf of Margery, Joan and Denise to find the king security in this form, namely, that Margery, Joan and Denise can get married in the meanwhile to whomsoever they will, provided they are in the king's fealty, notwithstanding the oath they had made to the king at another time that they would not get married without the king's leave, and that they will answer to the king for the value of their marriages if the king ought to have them, as is said. And this is granted him. And the said John of the county of Gloucester, Ralph of Shirley, knight, of the county of Shropshire, William Russell, knight, of the county of Gloucester, and Robert de Vere, knight, of the county of Northampton undertook on behalf of Margery, Joan and Denise that they would render satisfaction to the king for their marriages if it be decided he ought to have them for the aforesaid reason. And John acknowledges that he is bound to keep

---

[17] 16 April 1301.

Ralph, William and Robert indemnified with respect to the mainprise undertaken. And to this end he binds himself and his heirs etc.[18]

ix
Register of Robert Winchelsey, f. 1b
[Powicke and Cheney, Councils and Synods, ii. 1210]

The reply to one of the petitions of the clergy complained of abuses in royal writs, prohibiting litigation in ecclesiastical courts.

From parliament to parliament let the prelates bring with them all such improper prohibitions proffered to any judges, to show them to the king and his council.

x
K.R. Memoranda Roll No.75 (30 Edward I), m.52, Trinity Communia

Note that the form of taxation of the ninth, lately granted to the king (which is written out below), was sent to the king, who was then on his war in Scotland, by Walter, bishop of Coventry and Lichfield, the treasurer, so that the king by his council there, and also by the counsel of the earls, barons and other magnates there staying, may ordain how the fifteenth granted to the present king in the parliament of Lincoln should be levied . . . And the treasurer had the said form read out before the king and the earls, barons and others in the king's army at Glasgow, and later before the king's son Edward, prince of Wales, and the earls, barons and others in his army at Newcastle in Ayr; and after the said form and the grant of a fifteenth, made to the king in the parliament of Lincoln, had been heard, it was agreed by general advice of the said earls, barons and others that the fifteenth should be levied in the aforesaid form. And the treasurer delivered the document to the exchequer on the eighth day of October in the twenty-ninth year.[19]

---

[18] See also m.28, which almost wholly consists of writs to the barons, consequent upon petitions in the Lincoln parliament; and ms. 22d, 27d, 31d, 32d, 34, 36, 40d, 41, 71. And notice in particular m.32; 'and when the rolls of petitions delivered in the parliament and thence returned here were examined, it was discovered that Roger Brabazon, chief justice of the king's bench, had handed in a petition relating to the church of East Bridgford, Nottingham'. No such rolls have survived. Many petitions of this parliament, despite the regrettable break-up of parliament files in modern times, are still found in close proximity with one another: see Ancient Petitions, E.107-E.248. Petitions are also sent from this parliament to be determined before the king's council at York on the Morrow of Ascension Day (11 May 1301) (Exchequer Parliament and Council Proceedings, file 1, no.4).

[19] 8 October 1301. The form of taxation is set out on m.8, Michaelmas Communia.

PARLIAMENT AT WESTMINSTER: Midsummer 1302

i

K.R. Memoranda Roll, no.75 (30 Edward I), m.33, Trinity Communia

Concerning the petitions sent to the parliament of London

Note that on the twenty-fourth day of July in this year[1] all the petitions, returned to the exchequer from the king's parliament at Lincoln in the Octave of Hilary in the twenty-ninth year [of the reign],[2] were sent to the king's parliament at London by the hands of Henry of Cobham, sheriff of Kent. And they were all put in a canvas bag, sealed with the exchequer seal etc.

ii

K.R. Memoranda Roll, no.75 (30 Edward I), m.33, Trinity Communia

Concerning the business relating to the chapel of Hastings, sent to the parliament of Westminster

Note that on the thirteenth day of July in the thirtieth year of King Edward's reign[3] the underwritten documents were sent under the king's exchequer seal from York to the parliament of Westminster by the hand of William of Wickerford, clerk of William Sutton, namely, two petitions recently shown in the parliament of Lincoln in the Octave of Hilary in the twenty-ninth year of the aforesaid king's reign, that is to say, one on the king's behalf and the other on behalf of Gilbert, bishop of Chichester, relating to the exemption and jurisdiction of the chapel and prebends of Hastings,[4] and the inquisition made thereon by Robert of Burwash by virtue of two writs from the king under the great seal, addressed to Robert thereon, and these writs were likewise sent there, and also the record of the king's chancery rolls, which had been handed in in the parliament of Lincoln on the aforesaid business.

---

[1] 24 July 1302.

[2] 20 January 1301. It is quite clear that no parliaments were held between Hilary 1301 and Midsummer 1302 (*Parl. Writs*, i. 108).

[3] 13 July 1302.

[4] For this petition and the proceedings upon it until the matter came up at the parliament of Carlisle in 1307 and was eventually settled, see Sayles, *King's Bench*, iii. 180-190.

iii

L.T.R. Memoranda Roll, no.73 (31 Edward I), m.13d, Michaelmas Communia

Petition for the abbot of Vale Royal

The abbot of Vale Royal on behalf of himself and his convent presented to the king's parliament at Westminster at the Octave of St. John the Baptist in the thirtieth year[5] a petition in these words:

> Concerning the arrears of payments by the king for work on the abbey.

And this petition was endorsed before the king in the aforesaid parliament thus:

Let the treasurer and barons of the exchequer scrutinise the account of Reginald [de Grey] and the allowance made to the abbot and let the abbot be summoned thereupon and let them inform the king thereon.

And this petition, endorsed as aforesaid, together with various other petitions, was sent from the parliament to the exchequer here.

And by reason of this petition and the reply given to it, the abbot is summoned here thereon, and he comes now by his attorney.

> The treasurer and barons examined the account of Reginald de Grey while he was justice of Chester in and after 1282 and reported their findings to the king on 7 November 1302.[6]

iv

Close Roll, no.119 (30 Edward I), m.3, schedule
[*Parl. Writs*, i. 131-32; *Cal. Close Rolls, 1296-1302*, pp.564-65]

Note that, after the death of Sir John Tregoz, tenant-in-chief of the king, his lands were taken into the king's hands and valued. And after the valuation had been returned into chancery, John la Warre, son of Sir John's elder daughter, and William Grandison, who had married the other daughter, did homage to the king for the portions belonging to them of the aforesaid lands and tenements. And they had a writ to Walter

---

[5] 1 July 1302.

[6] For other petitions, some said to be presented 'to the parliament' (*ad parliamentum*) at Midsummer 1302 and transmitted to the exchequer, see ms. 12d, 13d, 15, 18, 30d, 40. And note K.R. Memoranda Roll, no.75 (30 Edward I), m.47d (Dies date): a matter was postponed from Midsummer to Michaelmas 'on account of the absence of some of the barons who were at parliament'.

of Gloucester, the escheator, ordering him to apportion the lands and tenements in the presence of the said heirs and co-sharers in accordance with the valuation. And after this apportionment had been made by the escheator in the presence of the heirs and co-sharers and with their agreement and had been returned and enrolled in the chancery, a writ issued, as is customary, for valuing the fees and advowsons of the said inheritance. And after the said valuation had been returned, William came into court and asked for his portion of the aforesaid fees and avowsons. And inasmuch as his co-sharer did not come, he was therefore informed that he should come at a certain day to receive his portion thereof. On that day John came into the chancery at Westminster before John Langton, then chancellor, in the presence of Roger Brabazon, Ralph Hengham, Gilbert Rothbury, William Bereford, William Haward and other good men of the council and said that no apportionment ought to be made of fees and advowsons by reason of the fact that the castle of Ewyas Harold with its appurtenances was assigned to him as his portion and most of the fees were appurtenant to it and cannot be severed from it since the tenants owed corporal service. And when he accepted his portion, he understood that he had received it with the fees and advowsons appurtenant to the castle. And William said that the apportionment, made before the escheator, was made only in respect of lands and tenements and accepted in no other form and he could not receive his portion because the escheator had no warrant save for the lands. And he vouched the escheator to warranty thereof, who was then present, as also was [a copy of] the apportionment enrolled in the chancery. And the escheator was at once questioned about it and replied that he made no apportionment other than of lands and tenements, and for this he had a writ. Therefore a hearing of the writ and of the apportionment was asked for, and when they had been read out and heard, no mention was made of anything but the apportionment of lands and tenements. And inasmuch as this was found to be the case and it is the custom that one apportionment should be made of the lands by themselves and another apportionment of the fees by themselves, therefore it was agreed by the whole council that the apportionment of fees and advowsons should be made in accordance with the law and custom of the realm. And John was not satisfied with this, and so he went to the king and delivered into his hands before his council at his parliament at Westminster at Midsummer in the thirtieth year [of his reign] a petition, requesting that right be done him in these matters. And the king received it into his own hands and delivered it at once to the receiver of petitions. And when it was read out and heard immediately before the king, Roger Brabazon replied to the king that the parties had been before his council and had spoken their arguments on one side and the other and that it was agreed before the council that apportionment should be made. Thereupon the king commanded that there should be done what ought to be done according to the custom of the realm. And then, because William's wife was not in court to agree to accept her portion, authority was given to John Havering to receive the lady's attorneys. And day was given to the parties to receive their portions at the next parliament. At that parliament William came in his own person and his wife by her attorney, and they asked for their portion as before. And John did not come, but since he was present in and about the court, he was therefore warned to come before the third day. At that day he came and said as before that no other apportionment ought to be made than was previously made for the abovesaid reasons. And inasmuch as the parties could not agree and no apportionment was made thereof save of the lands, it was therefore awarded and granted as before that apportionment should be made of fees and advowsons. And after it had been made into two parts, they were delivered in the chancery at Westminster by the hand of the earl of Lincoln in the presence of William of Greenfield, chancellor, Roger Brabazon, Gilbert Rothbury, the escheator and others of the council, by lot: one part to William and the other part to John. And John did not wish to sue out a writ to obtain his portion. Therefore it was awarded that he who wished to sue out a writ to have his portion should have it, and that the portion of the one who did not wish to sue out a writ should remain in the king's hands until he wished to sue one out.

PARLIAMENT AT WESTMINSTER: Michaelmas 1302

i

Close Roll, no.119 (30 Edward I), m.9d

[*Parl. Writs*, i. 114; *Cal. Close Rolls 1296-1302*, p.592]

The king to the reverend father in Christ Robert, archbishop of Canterbury, primate of all England, greeting. Although you are well aware how it was arranged in our parliament held just now in London that, in order to make wiser provision and sounder decisions on the things that were discussed in that parliament and on other matters which should be discussed for the benefit and security of our realm and its inhabitants, parliament was to be held again at London at the next feast of Michaelmas, yet as a precaution we command and firmly charge you by the fealty and love by which you are bound to us that you are to lay aside all other business whatsoever and be present at that future parliament in person. Witness the king at Westminster on the twenty-fourth day of July.[1]

ii

Ancient Correspondence, vol. XIII, no.105

The king to the earls of Lincoln and of Savoy, greeting. We have well understood the letters you lately sent us by the bearer of this letter. And as regards changing the agreement reached at Hesdin or postponing the day thereof, know that we do not wish it to be changed or postponed in any way. For we have no intention of doing this, because for the change we made from the place of Montreuil, at which place the treaty was lately agreed on, we have since been greatly censured by our people, inasmuch as this place was agreed on by us and our good people in our common parliament. Therefore we do not give our consent to make henceforth any alteration therein. And know well that already before this time the king of France has seven or eight times postponed the days agreed on between him and us. And inasmuch as we do indeed think that you will now have further hindrance and that the business before you will not be accomplished without some delay, therefore we have had our parliament adjourned, which it was agreed should be at Westminster at this Michaelmas, until the Morrow of the Feast of St. Edward[2] at Westminster as previously agreed. Therefore we pray you to carry out what you can with respect to our business for which you have gone there

[1] 24 July 1302.
[2] 14 October 1302.

and to be at the said parliament at all costs with what you have been able to do therein. And we pray God that He give you grace to do well. And know that we are on our way to Bradsole[3] near Dover where we will stay until this next Michaelmas to hear news from you. And on the Morrow of Michaelmas we shall depart on our way to our parliament of Westminster, for we will not be able to remain any longer there on account of our said parliament and other business we have to do elsewhere.

Endorsed: At Battle Abbey on the sixteenth day of September.[4]

iii
Ancient Correspondence, vol. XII, no.59

The king to Sir Roger Brabazon, greeting. Whereas there is a plea between Lady Joan de Valence, our aunt, on the one hand and our faithful and loyal Hugh de Vere and Denise, his wife, on the other, and the day for hearing it is on Monday after Michaelmas[5] at Gloucester before our faithful and loyal William Inge and Roger de Beaufeu, so we have understood, and we have now had our parliament, which was to have been held at Westminster at this coming Michaelmas, postponed until the Morrow of the Feast of St. Edward next, we command and charge you to be at Gloucester on the day of the plea and to advise us skilfully about the business and so to act that right is done on one side and the other.

Battle Abbey, the sixteenth day of September.[6]

iv
Ancient Correspondence, vol. XIII, no.109
[Stevenson, *Documents, Scotland*, ii. 446 f.]

The king to the bishop of Chester etc., greeting. Whereas we have ordered you to be at our next parliament, which will be held at Westminster on the Morrow of the Feast of St. Edward next, notwithstanding this, we order and charge you not to depart from our exchequer for any business touching us or anyone else unless it is for your own business which you must do. But you are to stay there and give to our business in the exchequer the best arrangement and the best advice

---

3 Alias St. Radegund's [in Poulton], co. Kent.
4 Edward I was then at Battle Abbey in 1302.
5 30 September 1302.
6 16 September 1302.

you can.[7] And you are to think about our Scottish business so that our interests may prosper there. And wages are to be well and promptly paid to our men who stay in those parts. And you are to have the castles of Scotland, the fortresses and the other places which concern us there to be well surveyed and they are to have plenty of stores so that there are no shortages. For if they have good stores everywhere it will be a great security in all our business in those parts. And if our business prospers there, we hope that it will prosper everywhere, with our Lord's help. And the new castles we are having constructed there are to have the best they can have in order to finish the work.

Bradsole, the twenty-fourth day of September.[8]

v

Ancient Correspondence, vol. XIII, no. 110

The king to the bishop of Chester, greeting. With regard to the lands and wardships we have assigned to Sir John de St. John for the term of his life, about which you have now advised us by your letter, know that recently, when the news of his death reached us, for the good service John had done us and because he had maintained his estate so honourably and because of the debts he had incurred on behalf of our service, we ordered our escheators not to meddle with anything we had assigned to John for the term of his life until our next parliament. And truly when we made that order, we had no thought to undertake so much and did it more to save the goods of the dead man and to profit his soul than to advantage the heir or for any other reason, and we did not do it with the intention of making such grace to another. And consequently we will that this order shall hold good as long as we have previously instructed until some of John's people have come to us or at least until our next parliament, and then we will decide what seems appropriate to be done. And as to your advice to us that Sir John Botetourte will be suitable, so it seems to you, to have the guardianship that John had in the parts of Scotland, know that we hold Sir John Botetourt to be a good man, wise and competent, and we understand that he would always do his duty there and anywhere else he happened to be, but in truth we do not wish to do or decide anything about the guardianship until our next parliament and until we have spoken with the wise men of our council.

Bradsole, the twenty-fifth day of September.

[7] The exchequer was stationed at York during 1298–1304. Walter Langton, bishop of Chester, was the treasurer.

[8] 24 September 1302.

1303 and 1304

No parliaments were held during these years when the king was fully occupied with the war in Scotland. But, though no opportunity was provided for hearing petitions at large, the administration of the country continued in the normal way when the king was absent from his kingdom. Two illustrations are given here.

i

Exchequer Parliament and Council Proceedings, file 1, no. 12.

The king's business to be expedited before the king's council at York after Easter[1]

Concerning the writs that have to be made under the great seal following the Fortnight after Easter in order to have the fifteenth levied from the temporalities of the prelates and clergy, which the king postponed at the instance of the prelates until the said Fortnight. And that certain clerks or others be appointed to hasten that levy.

     Let it be done.

The mayor and sheriff of London are ordered by a writ under the great seal to arrange for all the merchants of every company of merchants in London to come to the exchequer a Month after Easter, that is to say, three or two from each company who are to have full authority for themselves and the whole company.

     Let the writs be made in chancery.[2]

Concerning the writs to be addressed to the archbishops, bishops, abbots and other prelates with respect to doing their service or sending money for their fines to the exchequer at a specified day, and to every sheriff to certify who wishes to do service or to make fine etc.

     Let the writs be made in chancery.

To ordain how the aid for marrying the king's daughter can be fully levied with haste.

     Let writs thereon be made under the exchequer seal to make all collectors of the said aid come to the exchequer on various days to notify etc.[3]

---

[1] 7 April 1303.
[2] *Parl. Writs*, i. 134 (16 April 1303).
[3] *Ibid.*, i. 132 (7 November 1302).

Concerning forfeited wool.
Let there be discussion [with the king].

Concerning the scrutiny of the extent of the lands of Ralph Pipard in
Ireland and the value of the lands assigned to him in England.

It is agreed by the council that Ralph Pipard is to be ordered by a writ
of chancery to be at the exchequer and before others of the king's
council at York on the Morrow of the Ascension[4] in order to inform
the king and his council about the aforesaid extent and to hear and do
further in this matter what the king shall see fit to ordain by his
council. And the extents are delivered to the exchequer so that the
king's council can be more fully informed thereof. And in the
meantime let the valuation of the lands which the king granted to
Ralph in England be scrutinised.[5]

ii
Ancient Correspondence, vol. XXXI, no.99

Greeting as to himself.[6] Inasmuch as the merchants of the good towns of
England have requested and expressed their good will to pay customs for
cloth in the same way as foreign merchants do in order that they may be
free from prises on the king's part, and this has been shown to Philip
Willoughby, to me and to the barons of the exchequer, it is good that you
should bring this business to the king's notice and that he should have the
chancellor quickly instructed to make writs to summon two or three
men from every good town of England so that they will be at York on
the Morrow of Trinity[7] or the Morrow of St. John [the Baptist][8] and that
he should order his council to be there to discuss this business with these
men. For I hope that it will be to the great benefit and profit of the king if
he so acts. And with regard to his boroughs, if he wishes to tallage them
in accordance with what was previously done, he will be able to do it
conveniently then all at once. May God preserve you. Send me your
reply as soon as possible.

---

[4] 17 May 1303.
[5] *Ibid.*, i. 134 (16 April 1303). See also Chancery Warrants, Series I, file 49, no.4878
(*Cal. Chancery Warrants*, i. 232) for the reference of Irish business to the king's 'next
parliament', a request that it should be settled before then, and an order to the council at
York on 28 August 1304 to deal with the matter, 'without waiting for the parliament'.
And for petitions heard at York at the exchequer by the king's council, see Exchequer
Parliament and Council Proceedings, file 1, no.17.
[6] Presumably the treasurer.
[7] 25 May 1304.
[8] 25 June 1304.

PARLIAMENT AT WESTMINSTER: Lent 1305

i

Chancery Warrants, file 53, no.5274

[*Cal. Chancery Warrants*, i. 246]

Edward by the grace of God king of England, lord of Ireland and duke of Aquitaine, to our dear clerk William Hamilton, our chancellor, greeting. We command you that, in co-operation with the bishop of Chester, our treasurer, to whom we have sent similar instructions, you are to have it speedily proclaimed that all those who wish to deliver petitions to us and our council in our next parliament are to hand them day by day to those who are assigned to receive them between this day and the first Sunday of Lent[1] at the latest. And furthermore you and the others of our council at London are to answer these petitions as far as possible before we come there so that no petitions come before us ourselves save only those which cannot in any way be answered without us, and these you are to have well inspected and examined and put in good array. And we order you to arrange for the proclamation to be made in the Great Hall of Westminster, in the chancery, before the justices of the bench, at the exchequer, in the Guildhall of London and in West Cheap and in all other places where you think it should be done. And in making this proclamation you are to name those who are assigned to receive the petitions. And let us know without delay by your letter and by the bearer of this letter quite how and in what manner you have complied with this order and how you have arranged the business in all its details. And send us also the names of those you have appointed to receive the petitions. Given under our privy seal at Swaffham on the fifth day of February in the thirty-third year of our reign.[2]

ii

Exchequer Parliament Roll, no.12, m.1

[*Rot. Parl.* i. 159; *Parl. Writs*, i. 155; Maitland,

Memoranda de Parliamento, pp.3-4]

The ordinance for receiving petitions

It was ordained by the king that Gilbert Rothbury, master John de Caen, John Kirkby and master John Bush were to receive all the petitions of those who wished to hand in petitions to this parliament of Westminster.

---

[1] 7 March 1305.

[2] 5 February 1305.

And a proclamation thereon was made on the king's orders in the Great Hall of Westminster, in the chancery, before the justices of the bench, at the exchequer, in the London Guildhall and in West Cheap in these words:

All those who wish to hand in petitions at this approaching parliament shall deliver them day by day between now and the first Sunday in Lent[3] at the latest to Gilbert Rothbury, master John de Caen, John Kirkby and master John Bush, or to one of them, who are appointed to receive them between now and the first Sunday in Lent at the latest. And they by virtue of this ordinance and this proclamation are to deal with all the petitions in the way aforesaid.

Then the king afterwards appointed William Inge, master Richard Havering, Henry Guildford, James Dawley, and master John Weston to receive all the petitions which concern the kingdom of Scotland.

And he also appointed the bishop of Chester, the earl of Lincoln, Aymer de Valence, John of Brittany, John of Havering, Arnold de Caupenne, the prior of Le Mas, master Peter Arnold de Vico, master Peter Amaury and John Sandall to receive and answer all the petitions, put forward by the people of Gascony, which can be answered without the king.

And the king also appointed John Berwick, Hervey Stanton, William Dean, William Mortimer and Roger Beaufeu to receive all the petitions of those of Ireland and of the Isle of Guernsey and to answer all those which can be answered without the king.

And all the petitions which concern the said lands of Scotland, of Gascony, of Ireland and of Guernsey were at once handed over by the aforesaid Gilbert Rothbury, master John de Caen, John Kirkby and master John Bush to those there assigned in the way aforesaid.

Proclamation

Then after the twenty-first day of March a proclamation was made on the king's orders in these words:

Archbishops, bishops and other prelates, earls, barons, knights of the shires, citizens and burgesses and other people of the community who have come to this parliament at our lord the king's behest: the king thanks them greatly for coming and wishes that, whereas they are now going back to their homes, they may return immediately and without delay whenever they are again summoned: the exception being the bishops, earls and barons who are members of our lord the king's council, for these may not go away without special leave from the king.

[3] 7 March 1305.

And those who have business to do, let them remain to carry out their business. And let the knights who have come on behalf of the shires and the others who have come on behalf of the cities and boroughs make request to John Kirkby and he will arrange for them to have writs to obtain their expenses at their homes. And the aforesaid John Kirkby, by virtue of the aforesaid proclamation, shall deliver to the chancellor the names of the knights who came on behalf of the shires and the names of others who came on behalf of the cities and boroughs and he shall have it proclaimed that all who wished to sue out writs for their expenses, as aforesaid, are to sue there [in the chancery] for their writs.

iii
Chancery Parliament and Council Proceedings, file 53, no.17

Warwick

On behalf of Peter of Wolverton, knight, of the county of Warwick, for having a writ for his expenses at the instance of Robert de la Warde, the king's steward, and John of Broughton.

Endorsed: Let him have expenses like the others whose names are contained in a schedule delivered into the chancery.[4]

iv
Liberate Roll, no.81 (33 Edward I), m.5

On behalf of various men with respect to various sums of money due to them in the wardrobe

John Mowbray with respect to twenty pounds for his expenses in coming to the king's last parliament and returning to the parts of Scotland: as a gift from the king.

v
Close Roll, no.122 (33 Edward I), m.18d
[*Cal. Close Rolls, 1302-1307*, p.321]

Of the marriage of John de Warenne

Note that on Monday before the Feast of St. Edward, king and martyr, namely, on the fifteenth day of March in the thirty-third year of his reign,[5] the king offered John de Warenne, grandson and heir of John de

---

[4] Cf. *Parl. Writs*, i. 145; Peter Wolverton's name is almost obliterated and unrecognisable on the original return, made by the sheriff to the writ of summons.
[5] 15 March 1305.

Warenne, late earl of Surrey, deceased, tenant-in-chief of the king, in the king's chamber at Westminster in his parliament the marriage of Joan, daughter of Henry, late count of Bar, and John willingly accepted the marriage.

vi

Chancery Warrants, file 52, no.5234

[*Cal. Chancery Warrants*, i. 244]

Edward by the grace of God king of England, lord of Ireland and duke of Aquitaine, to his dear and faithful clerk, William of Greenfield, our chancellor, greeting. We have sent you enclosed herein some plaints[6] which Geoffrey of Morton, the bearer of this letter, has made to us against Richard of Bereford, our treasurer of Ireland, by which it seems to us that he should be summoned before us at our parliament to answer Geoffrey on these plaints. And we command you thereon that you are to examine these plaints and, if it seems to you as it seems to us, then you are to let Geoffrey have a writ under our great seal in proper form to cause our treasurer to come before us in our next parliament to answer Geoffrey on the aforesaid plaints and to do therein what our court shall award. Given under our privy seal at Thornton on Humber the fourteenth day of December in the thirty-third year of our reign.[7]

vii

Chancery Warrants, file 53, no.5263

[*Cal. Chancery Warrants*, i. 246]

Edward by the grace of God king of England, lord of Ireland and duke of Aquitaine, to our dear clerk, William Hamilton, our chancellor, greeting. Because we have heard that the archbishop of Canterbury has arranged to summon bishops, abbots, priors and other clergy of his province in order to hold his council at Lambeth on Saturday or Sunday after the Octave of Candlemas next,[8] we order you that, in cooperation with the bishop of Chester, our treasurer, to whom we have sent similar instructions, you are to have assembled at London those of our council whom you consider should be summoned there and so to do and arrange that appeals are made by certain men at the said council on behalf of us and ours, just as has been done at the council[s] and assemblies the archbishop has held before now, so that our estate may not be diminished

---

[6] Ancient Petition, no.8773.

[7] 14 December 1304.

[8] 6-7 February 1305.

and we can be saved from harm. Moreover, because we understand that the archbishop and others of the clergy may perchance wish to debate with us at our next parliament some matters concerning their estate, we instruct you that you are as diligently as possible to have all the memoranda that can be found in our chancery scrutinised with respect to the articles which have been exhibited by those of the clergy, along with the answers made to them, in the time of our father and of ourselves so that whatever you can find thereon we can have it quickly at our parliament. And we order you to let us know by your letter and by the bearer of this letter your answer on these matters and what you have done thereon. Given under our privy seal at Wisbech on the twenty-sixth day of January in the thirty-third year of our reign.[9]

viii
B.L., Harleian MS., no.696
[*Record of Carnarvon*, p.212]

It is interesting to see so soon the presentation of 'common petitions' before the prince of Wales and his council at Kennington during the parliament held at Westminster at the same time.[10] The formula for enrolling the 'common petitions' is: 'To the common petition made . . . it is replied . . .' But it should be observed that they are not always from the whole of North Wales but from individual counties and cantreds, or the prince's villeins of the commote of Menai, or single individuals. The list of 'common petitions' ends with the provision (as below) to secure that petitions and complaints were first made to the Justice of North Wales. The following 'Petitions of individual people of North Wales' appear to be in two groups, first the petitions of the Welsh and then the petitions of 'the English boroughs of North Wales', where the overall distinction seems to be between petitions touching 'the law and custom of those parts', that is Welsh law, and those touching the common law of England.

The petitions of the men of North Wales, made on behalf of the communities of the counties as well as individual persons and shown to the prince and his council at Kennington outside London in the time of the king's parliament held at Westminster on the First Sunday of Lent in the thirty-third year of the reign of King Edward; and the replies made to these petitions, which were delivered to the Justice of North Wales under

[9] 26 January 1305.
[10] Cf. *Rot. Parl.*, i. 308-9, no.83, for the 'common petitions of North Wales' and the 'ordinances made at Kennington'.

the prince's privy seal so that he could implement the replies as mentioned below and have them firmly observed and kept etc.

In order henceforward to spare the men of these parts labour and expense the Justice is told to inform all who are concerned in making complaints or petitioning in cases similar to those included in these rolls that they are to come before him and show their petitions and they would receive from him like replies in like case. Indeed, all who wish to complain about sheriffs, ringilds[11] or other ministers, with the exception of the Justice, are to go before the Justice and receive justice before him, with the consequence that no one shall come to the prince's court with petitions or complaints, unless he has first shown them to the Justice, except where the Justice has failed to give him justice.

[11] I.e. Welsh bailiffs. The 'Ordinances of Kennington' were ordered to be observed in the parliament of Lincoln in 1316 (*Foedera*, II. i. 283).

PARLIAMENT AT WESTMINSTER: 15 September 1305

i

Chancery Warrants, file 54, no.5344

[*Cal. Chancery Warrants*, i. 250]

Edward by the grace of God king of England, lord of Ireland and duke of Aquitaine, to our dear clerk William Hamilton, our chancellor, greeting. With regard to postponing our parliament, which we arranged to be summoned and held at Three Weeks after Midsummer next,[1] until the Feast of our Lady in the following mid-August,[2] and to increasing the power of our justices, appointed to hear and determine the trespasses committed in breach of our peace within the counties of England,[3] and to postponing their arrival to us, we order you to trust our dear clerk Robert of Cottingham and do what he says on our behalf. Given under our privy seal at Stoke d'Abernon on the twenty-ninth day of May in the thirty-third year of our reign.[4]

ii

Exchequer Parliament and Council Proceedings, file 1, no.20

Edward by the grace of God etc. to the reverend father in God William, by the same grace bishop of Worcester, and to our dear abbots in God of Westminster and of Waverley and to Brother Hugh of Manchester, and to our faithful and loyal subject Henry of Lacy, earl of Lincoln, our dear cousin Humphrey de Bohun, earl of Hereford and Essex, our dear loyal subjects Hugh Despenser, Henry Percy, John Hastings, John Botetourte, William Martin, Roger Brabazon, Ralph Hengham, William Bereford, Roger Hegham, John de Lisle, and to our dear clerks master Philip Martel, Reynold of Brandon and John Sandall, our chamberlain of Scotland, greeting. Inasmuch as for certain reasons we are not able to be at Westminster at the Octave of this approaching Feast of the Nativity of our Lady[5] for the beginning of our parliament, as we recently arranged, therefore we are sending to you the reverend father in God Walter, bishop of Chester, and we request and instruct you to trust him faithfully

---

[1] 15 July 1305.

[2] 15 August 1305. The parliament was again postponed to 15 September (*Parl. Writs*, i. 158–60).

[3] See Sayles, *King's Bench*, ii. pp.cxlix ff.

[4] 29 May 1305.

[5] 15 September 1305.

with respect to the things that he will tell you on our behalf. Given under our privy seal at Lambourn the fourteenth day of September in the thirty-third year of our reign.[6]

iii
L.T.R. Memoranda Roll, no.75 (33 Edward I), m.61, Trinity Communia

Norfolk

With respect to a day given

Day is given to Thomas Bardolf, son and heir of Hugh Bardolf, that he is to be here at the Octave of the Nativity of the Blessed Mary next[7] to acknowledge how much his father held on the day he died of John earl of Surrey, deceased . . . And if it should happen that the king's parliament is postponed until after Michaelmas, Thomas is told by the king's council that he is to be here on the Morrow of Michaelmas to do what is aforesaid etc.

iv
Exchequer Miscellanea, 5/2, m.14
[Johnstone, *Letters of Prince Edward*, p.115]

To the noble lady, my lady Mary, his dearest sister, from Edward, her brother, greeting and dear love. Most dear sister, we have indeed heard how you have asked our lord the king, our father, to be so good as to give us leave to come to you at Amesbury. And he has given it to us at your request, for which we thank you kindly. But inasmuch as the time of parliament is already approaching and we do not know at what time our lord and father will wish to send for us to come to him, so we dare not for the present go away from where we are. Wherefore we pray you, dearest sister, to kindly hold us excused for not coming to you at this time. Most dear sister, may our Lord have you in His keeping. Given under etc. at Bray the fourteenth day of September.[8]

---

[6] 14 September 1305: a draft letter.
[7] 15 September 1305.
[8] 14 September 1305.

v

Exchequer Miscellanea, 5/2, m.14

[Johnstone, *Letters of Prince Edward*, p.113]

To the earl of Lincoln

To the noble man, his dear cousin Henry of Lacy, earl of Lincoln, greeting and dear love. We pray you specially that you will kindly be solicitous about the business which will concern us at this approaching parliament, and particularly with respect to Gower so that our jurisdiction and our right is there preserved. And kindly give your help and advice to our dear friend, William Langton, who will prosecute business before you in that parliament in order to preserve and maintain our rights. May our Lord etc. Given under etc.[9]

vi

Vetus Codex, fo.118

[*Parl. Writs*, i. 160]

Memoranda of the king's parliament at Westminster at the Octave of the Nativity of the Blessed Mary at the close of the thirty-third year

The king sent his writ to John Kirkby, clerk, in these words:

Edward by the grace of God etc. to his beloved clerk, John Kirkby, greeting. Because we have arranged that you and our beloved clerks Gilbert Rothbury, master John of Caen and master John Bush are to receive all the petitions which may be delivered in our approaching parliament, which will begin at Westminster at the Octave of the Nativity of the Blessed Virgin Mary next,[10] we command and firmly charge you to put aside all other business and to come in person to London with all the haste you can and to receive there, along with our aforesaid clerks, such petitions day by day from now until the third day after Michaelmas next[11] and no longer, and you shall in no wise fail to do

[9] Written apparently at Windsor Park on 11 September 1305. Other letters to the same effect were sent to William Hamilton the chancellor, and to Henry Spigurnel and John of Benstead.

[10] 15 September 1305.

[11] 2 October 1305.

this. Witness myself at Laver on the fourth day of September in the thirty-third year of our reign.[12]

By writ of privy seal

And similar writs were addressed to Gilbert Rothbury, master John de Caen, and master John Bush.

Afterwards, on Monday before Michaelmas,[13] a proclamation was made in the city of London by the king's orders in these words:

We would have you know on behalf of our lord the king that he has willed and commanded that all manner of people who have petitions to hand in at this parliament are to deliver their petitions to Gilbert Rothbury, master John of Caen, John Kirkby and master John Bush, or to one of them, between now and Sunday next after Michaelmas at the hour of sunset, for he has forbidden petitions to be received from anyone after that hour.

This proclamation was made in London on Monday before Michaelmas.[14]

vii

L.T.R. Memoranda Roll, no. 76 (34 Edward I), m.8d (14d), Michaelmas Communia

Norfolk

On behalf of Ralph of Roding

Note that now, namely, on Saturday after the Octave of Michaelmas[15] John Kirkby, the king's clerk appointed to receive petitions presented in parliament, handed in here a petition to be enrolled, which Ralph of Roding, son and heir of William of Roding, presented to the king's parliament at Westminster at the Octave of the Nativity of the Blessed Mary in the thirty-third year of the reign in these words:

> A petition regarding the debts owed to the king by William of Roding, late sheriff of Norfolk and Suffolk, at his death.

[12] 4 September 1305.
[13] 27 September 1305.
[14] 27 September 1305.
[15] 9 October 1305.

viii
Ancient Petition, no.495
[*Rot. Parl.*, i. 479]

To our lord the king and his council shows Robert de Vere, earl of Oxford, that the manor of Roding Aythorp has been always held of the earl and his ancestors by the service of two knights' fees. This manor came into the king's hand by acquisition of Queen Eleanor, formerly queen of England. And in consequence of her seisin she enfeoffed Sir Guy Ferre with the manor by her charter, to hold of her and her heirs and not of the chief lordships of the fee. By that enfeoffment the earl and his heirs wouild lose wardships, reliefs, escheats and other profits if the said charter were not corrected and changed. Wherefore the earl prays our lord the king that, if it please him, the charter may be corrected and that he may not wish to allow the earl to be disinherited of his fee or of the services which are due to him from the manor.

Endorsed: Let the answer, made to this petition in another parliament, be looked at and let the earl seek that answer from John Bush, in whose possession his petition, then put forward, remains.[16]

ix
Dean and Chapter, Canterbury, Letters, ii. 219
[Hist. MSS. Commission, *Reports on Various Collections*, App., p.447]

Greeting, grace and good. As to the fact that you have taken the trouble to tell us the news heard by you, we are well pleased and gratified by that kindness. And know that it is not necessary for you to think about your coming to the parliament at London because the parliament is ended, and there was nothing save a discussion in the king's most secret council upon an ordinance for the state of the realm of Scotland, and what the ordinance did was published on Thursday before the Feast of St. Edward[17] in the king's chamber at Sheen in our presence and that of many others. And it would be more troublesome than exact to recount the series of articles . . .[18] Farewell. Given at Lambeth on the fifteenth of October in the twelfth year of our consecration.[19]

To the prior of our Christ Church, Canterbury

[16] The earl's petition was granted on 5 November 1305 (*Cal. Patent Rolls, 1301-1307*, p.393).

[17] 7 October 1305.

[18] Illegible.

[19] 15 October. The twelfth year of Archbishop Robert Winchelsey's consecration apparently began on 12 September 1305.

x
B.L., Harleian MS. no.6806, fo.346d

This manuscript contains abstracts in English of nearly sixty petitions presented at this parliament (fos.335-361), and many of them are from Scottish petitioners. They may be those which came before the council for consideration. The folios of the manuscript are manifestly jumbled.

Scotland

To our lord the king Eymer de Haddon humbly prayeth the king to command the sheriff of Roxburgh to see him paid 22m. per annum due to him out of certain land in the field of Haddon granted unto him, and accordingly ever paid by the late King Alexander and by the King also during the time he was guardian of that land and sovereign lord of Scotland. And if the King desire to be discharged of this demand he desireth to have a letter of perambulation between the Prior and Canons of Kirkham and of Carham and himself of the said land,[20] out of which the said rent of 22 marks issueth, and that he may have justices assigned to hear and determine the said perambulation, which will be to the profit of the king and the petitioner's relief.

Reply on back: Let him sue before the king's lieutenant in Scotland and show King Alexander's charter or any other document if he has it concerning the said 22 marks, and justice is to be done him.

xi
King's Bench Roll, no.178 (Michaelmas 1304), ms 52d-53
[Sayles, *King's Bench*, iii. 138-144]

Gloucester

Litigation between the prior of St. Oswald's, Gloucester, plaintiff, and the archbishop of Canterbury defendant, concerning the archbishop's claim to exercise jurisdiction over St. Oswald's church, which the prior alleged was a free chapel, founded by the king's predecessors.

---

[20] See *Memoranda de Parliamento*, p.166, for a petition from the prior of Kirkham in the previous Lent parliament. Carham was a manor in Northumbria and on the Scottish border.

While the aforesaid plea was pending here in court in the form aforesaid at the suit of the prior, who is suing in this matter for the king as well as for himself, the archbishop came before the king and his council, specially convoked for this purpose at Kennington on Thames[21] on the day etc. in the thirty-third year of the present king's reign, and he spoke and propounded certain arguments on behalf of his right and that of his church of Canterbury. And afterwards, for the information and instruction of the council, he put forward in writing and delivered with his own hand a petition containing the arguments, together with certain evidences on which he was relying, to make clear the right as well as the possession of his own church with respect to the jurisdiction of the church. By that petition he asked that the king would be graciously pleased to hear his evidence and to speak his will to him thereon without prosecuting any further plea against him.

> The parties set out in detail historical evidence, going back to the reign of King Athelstan, in support of their claims. Thereupon the council proceeded to judgement.

And when the charters of the kings, along with the other apparently trustworthy evidences put foward by the prior, had been seen and understood, it is quite plain that the priory had been founded as a free chapel by the king's predecessors and defended and protected at the royal command by their sheriffs. And it is no objection that the archbishop says that the contrary can be found in chronicles, which are not admitted in this court in place of proof and particularly against the aforesaid charters . . . And so it seemed to the court that the priory should henceforth be held and kept as a free chapel of the king, whereupon the archbishop at once submitted his person to the king's grace . . . And because the king wished to proceed by greater deliberation of his council upon these and all other matters in which a plea is pending before him in his court between himself and the archbishop, a day was given thereon to the archbishop at the next parliament etc.

Afterwards, at the next Fortnight after Michaelmas, the archbishop came into parliament at Westminster by his attorney. And he was given a day on the Morrow of the Ascension of the Lord[22] wherever etc. to hear the king's grace and pleasure etc.

> Judgement against the archbishop was confirmed in the Michaelmas term of 1306.

[21] Note the activities of the council of the prince of Wales at Kennington during the parliament at Westminster at Lent 1305 (above p.265).
[22] 13 May 1306.

PARLIAMENT AT WESTMINSTER: Trinity 1306

It was taken for granted at Michaelmas 1305 that the next parliament would be held at Easter 1306. An inquisition, resulting from a petition in the Michaelmas parliament of 1305, was to be sent 'before the king in the king's next parliament after Easter' (L.T.R. Memoranda Roll, no.76 (34 Edward I), m.15, Michaelmas Communia). Still more specific was an adjournment from the Octave of Michaelmas 1305 'until the next parliament after Easter in the thirty-fourth year of the reign' so that the king could then speak his will (L.T.R. Memoranda Roll, no.75 (33 Edward I), m.35, Hilary Communia; no.76, m.23d, Hilary Communia). Information relating to Scotland was also to be reported to the king 'at his next parliament Three Weeks after Easter', apparently postponed until Ascension Day on 12 May (Parl. Writs, i. 160-163; Cal. Close Rolls, 1302-1307, p.335). The writs of summons to the assembly in May 1306 appear to be styled as 'the king's letters regarding an aid' and were sent on 20 April to a large number of magnates and others (Exchequer, Various Accounts, 369/11, fos.142a, 142b). A good many Scottish petitions were considered and answered after 12 May (Parl. Writs, i. 162a). The knights and burgesses who were summoned to attend on 30 May had their writs of expenses authorised apparently on the same day (Parl. Writs, i. 177) but they were in attendance for many days. The conflicting evidence is fully discussed in Richardson and Sayles, Parliaments and Great Councils in Medieval England, *pp.24-30 (reprinted in* The English Parliament in the Middle Ages*). It is a pity that there should be doubt about the nature of this assembly because, if it was a parliament, it was the first occasion that women – four abbesses – were summoned to be present.*

L.T.R. Memoranda Roll, no.76 (34 Edward I), m.43, Trinity Recorda
[Pasquet, *Origins of House of Commons*, pp.234-36]

England

Concerning the aid granted for making the king's son a knight

Note that, whereas the king has recently arranged that Edward, his eldest son, was to be honoured with the belt of knighthood at the Feast of Pentecost in the thirty-fourth year of his reign,[1] archbishops, bishops, abbots, priors, earls, barons and other magnates of the realm had been ordered to be before the king and his council at Westminster on the Morrow of Trinity next[2] to discuss and settle the making of an aid to the

---

[1] 22 May 1306.
[2] 30 May 1306.

king for the aforesaid knighting and to consent to those matters which might be further ordained in this respect, or else to send there at that time their proxies or attorneys, sufficiently informed to carry out the aforesaid things in their place. And an order was also given to all the sheriffs of England that every one of them was to arrange for two knights from his shire to come at the aforesaid day and place, and two citizens from every city of his bailiwick and two burgesses (or one etc.) from every borough of his said bailiwick, to discuss, arrange and consent as aforesaid.

There follows a list of those present in person or by attorney

And all the aforesaid men assembled before the king's council, and the king's council showed them on the king's behalf that an aid ought to be made to the king in this case by right of his royal crown and also that manifold expenses and many other burdens lay upon the king in repressing the rebellion and wrongdoing of Robert Bruce, the king's traitor, and his adherents in the parts of Scotland who now presumed to wage war against the king in those parts. And the prelates, earls, barons and other magnates as well as the knights of the shires had a conference and discussion about it and, considering an aid was due, as aforesaid, and the many burdens that befell the king on account of the war, they at last unanimously granted the king on behalf of themselves and the whole community of the realm a thirtieth of all their secular and movable goods . . . And the citizens and burgesses of the aforesaid cities and boroughs and others of the king's demesne were assembled and had discussion on the aforesaid matters and considered the burdens lying upon the king, as aforesaid, and unanimously granted the king a twentieth of their movable goods for the aforesaid reasons.

PARLIAMENT AT CARLISLE: Hilary 1307

i
Close Roll, no.124, m.7d
[*Foedera*, i. 1009; *Cal. Close Rolls, 1302-7*, p.537]

The form of oath for those of the king's council

Ralph, bishop of London, whom the king wishes to be a member of his council, took oath in full parliament at Carlisle on Thursday,[1] the Morrow of the Conversion of St. Paul, in accordance with the articles of the oath contained in this schedule.

That you shall counsel the king well and truly according to your knowledge and ability.

That you will well and truly conceal his counsel.

That you will not accuse anyone for what he shall say in the council.

That you will give and apply your effort, aid and counsel and all your ability to keep and maintain the rights of the king and of the crown and to preserve and restore them wherever you can without doing wrong.

That where you know that matters affecting the crown and the king's rights have been concealed or wrongly alienated or withdrawn, you shall make it known to the king.

That you shall uphold the crown so far as you can and in a lawful way.

That you shall not be in a court or at a council where the king deprives himself of anything that belongs to the crown, if it is not something you can properly do.

That you shall not fail for any reason, for love or for hate, for good will or for ill will, in causing right and equity to be done according to your ability and your knowledge to everyone, no matter his estate or condition, and that you will take nothing from anyone for doing wrong or delaying right.

That in doing judgement or right where you are appointed, you will spare no one for his eminence or for poverty or for riches so that right is not done.

That, if you have made a contract with a lord or anyone else whereby you are not able to do these things or sustain them without a breach of that contract, you shall tell it to the king or cause him to be informed.

That henceforth a sworn contract shall be made with no one without the king's leave.

---

[1] 26 January 1307. The treasurer, Walter Langton, and the earl of Lincoln were appointed to open parliament on the king's behalf (*Rot. Parl.*, i. 189).

That you shall take no gift from anyone, except it be food and drink for the day, for any plea or other matter that he has to conduct before you.[2]

ii

Exchequer Parliament and Council Proceedings, file 1, no.21, m.9d

Edward by the grace of God king of England, lord of Ireland and duke of Aquitaine, to the sheriff of Nottingham, greeting. Whereas we had lately appointed a day to Ralph of Crophill, John Fleming [and forty others], burgesses of Nottingham – who were accused of various acts of confederacy and conspiracy before our beloved and faithful Peter Maulay and his fellows, our justices appointed to hear and determine various trespasses – that they should be at our next parliament to hear their judgement thereon, and we have now caused this parliament to be summoned at Carlisle at the Octave of Hilary next, we command you to inform Ralph, John and the others that they are to be at our said parliament at the aforesaid day and place to hear their judgement, as aforesaid. And you are then to have this writ before the reverend father Walter, bishop of Coventry and Lichfield, our treasurer. Witness William Carleton at Westminster on the fifth day of December in the thirty-fifth year of our reign.[3]

> By record and process of the said justices,
> delivered to the exchequer

iii

King's Bench Roll, no.189 (Trinity 1307), m.1
[Sayles, *King's Bench*, iii, 175-78]

Record sent from the parliament at Carlisle etc.

Pleas before Henry de Lacy, earl of Lincoln, appointed by the king on the information of the king's son, the prince of Wales, to hear and determine the petitions of John de Ferrers, put forward in the king's parliament at Carlisle at the Octave of Hilary in the thirty-fifth year of the reign of King Edward son of King Henry.

---

[2] The last article was to be sworn only by justices.
[3] 5 December 1306.

Northampton

John de Ferrers comes by John of Annesley, his attorney, before Henry de Lacy, earl of Lincoln, whom the king has appointed on the information of the prince of Wales to hear and determine certain petitions which John put forward before him against the bishop of Chester, the king's treasurer.

> A complaint that the treasurer had contravened the statute of Westminster of 1285 which forbade the king's ministers and judges to maintain pleas.

And the treasurer comes and says that he ought not to answer John's petition in this respect etc., because he says that, deputising for the king, he is occupied with all and sundry business connected with this present parliament, and he prays judgement whether he ought to answer so suddenly without previous warning etc. And John says that the treasurer is the king's minister and present in court and, inasmuch as the king's statute is binding upon the treasurer first and foremost among other ministers of the king etc., he prays judgement whether the treasurer ought not to answer his petition.

> Both litigants agreed to accept a jury.

And because this petition was put forward here before the king's council at the end of the present parliament and for that reason, on account of the shortness of time and the closing of parliament, the truth of the aforesaid matters cannot here be inquired into by a local jury of the county of Northampton on which both the parties had put themselves, day is given them in the king's bench on the Morrow of the Ascension next wherever etc.

> In Trinity term the treasurer informed the court by a chancery writ, dated 24 May 1307 at Carlisle, that the king had pardoned him the statutory offence, 'inasmuch as such punishment appertains to the king and no one else'.

iv
Placita in Cancellaria, file 2, no.9, m.1

The king by the grace of God king of England and France and lord of Ireland to the treasurer and barons of his exchequer, greeting. As we wish for certain reasons to be informed about the record and process in the parliament of Edward, former king of England, our grandfather, at Carlisle in the thirty-fifth year of his reign with respect to the ordinance and form of peace made between our grandfather and the people of Scotland, we command you to scrutinise the relevant rolls and memoranda of the exchequer, the rolls of parliament as well as other rolls, and to send us to our chancery, openly and clearly under our exchequer seal, the tenor of the record and process which may happen to be found in the exchequer, and this writ. Witness myself at Westminster on the twelfth day of May in the twenty-ninth year of our reign and the sixteenth year of our reign in France.[4]

Endorsed: A certification regarding the contents of this writ appears in a schedule attached to this writ.

ibid., m.5

The rolls and memoranda of the exchequer having been scrutinised by virtue of the writ sewn to this schedule, there was found in a roll of parliament, held at Carlisle:
The form of the peace of Scotland on the arrival of John Comyn and others.

The rest follows as in *Rot. Parl.*, i. 212b.

v
Assize Roll, no.1344, m.1d
[Beardwood, *Trial of Walter Langton*, p.252 f.]

Plaints heard at Windsor before justices of oyer and terminer against Walter Langton, late treasurer of Edward I, on the Morrow of St. Andrew the Apostle in 1307.[5]

Warwick

Robert de Herle put forward a plaint against Walter Langton, bishop of Coventry and Lichfield, late treasurer of England, in these words:

To our lord the king complains Robert de Herle against Walter Langton, bishop of Chester, that, whereas Robert came to Coventry with his lord, Sir John Hastings, the said bishop, who was then the treasurer of the king, recently deceased, because he coveted Robert's manor of Caldecote

---

[4] 12 May 1355.
[5] 1 December 1307.

in Warwickshire, trumped up a false excuse on the morrow[6] of his enthronement and by colour of his office and without warrant he had Robert arrested there and imprisoned, and he delivered him into the custody of John of Broughton, the then sheriff of Warwick, and he had him kept in prison until at the request of great lords who then were there he released him by mainprise, undertaking that he would be at the next parliament of the king to answer the things he would speak against him. Robert came to that parliament as a prisoner under mainprise as well as to two other parliaments following, always as a prisoner under the same mainprise. And at each parliament he was given the answer that, if he wished to lease the manor to the bishop, he would be free of everything alleged against him and he had no other answer, to his serious loss of a thousand marks, for which he prays redress.

And the bishop, having heard the plaint, denied all trespass, imprisonment and whatever etc. And he flatly denies that he ever arrested and imprisoned Robert or caused him to be kept in custody or prison by John of Broughton, the sheriff etc. Furthermore, he did not adjourn Robert from parliament to parliament as he alleges against him. And as to this he puts himself on the country. And Robert does likewise. Therefore the sheriff is ordered to arrange for twelve etc. to come here on the Morrow of Hilary, by whom etc. and who neither etc. to declare etc. Because etc.

Afterwards the process thereon between them was continued until the Octave of Trinity in the first year of the present king.[7] Then Robert came to the Tower of London. And the jurors did likewise. And in the bishop's presence and having been chosen with the consent of the parties, they said on their oath that the bishop took, arrested and imprisoned Robert on the aforesaid day and year at Coventry and handed him over as a prisoner to John of Broughton, the then sheriff of the county. And they say that the bishop on the same day, at the urgent request of friends, released Robert to bail in these terms, that his guarantors should undertake to have Robert in person at the next parliament of the king, that is to say, body for body. And from that parliament he further released him to the same bail in the same way to another parliament. And so from parliament to parliament up to three subsequent parliaments. And they say that the bishop imprisoned and harassed him, as said, on account of the fact that the bishop coveted John's manor of Caldecote, which he intended to acquire by such harassment and oppression. And so it is awarded that Robert is to recover damages against the bishop, which are assessed by the jurors at two hundred marks. And the bishop is to be committed to gaol etc.

[6] 24 December 1296.
[7] 28 May 1308.

vi

Ancient Petition, File 322, no. E.537

To our lord the king and his council prays Blasco Lopez, valet of Aragon, that, whereas our lord the king is under obligation to him for a quantity of money for the Gascon war, and for it I have sealed letters from Sir Henry Lacy, earl of Lincoln, and I have stayed in England since the first truce between the king of France and our lord the king in order to get paid this money. And I have put forward a petition at every parliament there has since been held to get payment of the money. And at every parliament the council gave me a specific day on the dorse of my petitions for having my payment. And still I was not paid. And the bishop of Chester, our lord the king's treasurer, ordered me at Langley in the presence of my lord the prince that I should come to the parliament at Carlisle and that I should show my letters to Sir John Sandall, and he would have me paid. And I am ready to show my letters. And I have spent two thirds of what the king owed me since I stayed to get my pay. Wherefore the said Blasco claims pity and prays our lord the king and his council that he may be paid so that he may return with honour to his own country.

vii

Vetus Codex, ff.124–151

[Ryley, *Placita Parliamentaria*, pp.372 f.; *Rot. Parl.*, i. 214]

Joan de Besilles

Note that in the parliament held in the thirty-third year of our present king at Westminster Joan, widow of Edward de Besilles, prayed the king and his council by her petition that the king would be pleased to remove his hand from the manor of Woodhill in the county of Wiltshire, the custody of which ought to belong to her as nearest heir of Edward, her former husband. Answer was given to this petition, and the council told her to sue before the treasurer who would convoke the justices and the king's council and do speedy justice to her.

> An examination of chancery and exchequer enrolments was made as well as a local inquisition, and the results were sent to the parliament at Carlisle in 1307.

A discussion thereon was held with all the magnates in full parliament, and they acknowledged that the service [of rendering four barbed arrows every year to the exchequer] is simply a service of petty serjeanty . . . on account of which petty sergeanty the king ought of right to have the wardship or marriage of any heir who now holds of him the custody of the said heir's lands, and it is found that in similar cases, as appears from the rolls of chancery, the king removed his hand from such custodies. Therefore in the presence of the reverend Walter, by the grace of God bishop of Coventry and Lichfield, the keeper and treasurer of England, Henry de Lacy, earl of Lincoln, John of Brittany, earl of Richmond, Guy, earl of Warwick, Otto de Grandison, Hugh Despenser and other justices and loyal subjects of the king, then and there present, it was adjudged that the king should remove his hand from the custody and that Joan should have the said custody as the mother and nearest relative, to be kept for the heir, in accordance with the law and custom of the realm, and that she should have a chancery writ to John of Droxford, to whom the king had demised the said custody, to the effect that he should remove his hand and let Joan have seisin thereof without delay.[8]

viii

Chancery Parliament and Council Proceedings, file 3, no.18

[*English Historical Review* LIII, 436-7]

News of the parliament

It is to be noted that the king of England and the prince, archbishops and bishops, abbots and priors, earls and barons, and all the king's council in general and all the community of the land have assented to the marriage between the prince and the daughter of the king of France with the result that the king of France has granted to the prince and to his daughter all the lands which then pertained to the crown of England in such fashion that he has reserved nothing for himself except the homages for the said lands. And to enforce everything regarding this peace, each article will be put in writing so that one copy under the seal of the king of England will remain in the possession of the king of France and the third copy[9] will remain in the possession of the pope under the seals of the king of England and the king of France so that the pope will have power to provide redress by Holy Church against the one who so offends therein that the form [of peace] does not hold force as ordained in writing by the two kings.

Again, the cardinal has given a guarantee, together with the earls and

---

[8] See Ancient Petition, file 33, no.1633, which is endorsed: 'Let this petition be discussed in the presence of earls, barons and chancery clerks, and let the Great Charter be there inspected'.

[9] The 'foot' of the trifold chirograph.

barons of the land of Spain, to the prince of England with regard to the suzerainty of Spain that, whereas the king of Spain died without direct heirs and the prince of England is nearest in blood on his mother's side, for that reason the suzerainty of the land has been granted to him.

Again, the cardinal has power to provide redress against the clergy of Scotland, who have rebelled against the king of England and against his peace. Therefore he has pronounced sentence of excommunication upon Robert Bruce and upon all those, no matter their estate, who have given him help, whether in deed or in word or in anything that can assist him in maintaining the war in Scotland against the king of England. Therefore you will see great hardship to have been imposed upon the clergy of Scotland through the pronouncement of this sentence.

Again, all the lands of the bishop of Durham for which homage is due to the king have been taken into the king's hands, and the king is making grants of his rents everywhere, because he has been accused before the king and his council of being an accomplice of Robert Bruce and, if the bishop had not been such, Robert would not now have succeeded in maintaining the war of Scotland.

Again, the bishop is charged with aiding the archbishop of Canterbury against the king, whereby he has fallen ill both of the pope and the king.

Again, the cardinal has received an answer from the king and from all his council with regard to his demand and his payment from churches: the king will not let him have it except as other cardinals have previously had it. And in this matter the archbishops, bishops and the proctors of churches have made their appeal to prohibit the sentence of excommunication. And thereon the king has ordered each bishop to arrange for the money from his diocese to come to his treasury at London, and the cardinal will find it there whenever it suits him, provided that the cardinal shall have no power to receive any money or take any money abroad.

The sum of his demand and of his payment from churches in England and Wales amounts to four hundred thousand pounds and sixty five shillings. And because his demand was so outrageous and so much to the great destruction of the land, the king and his council have ordained that he shall by way of courtesy be found his expenses so long as he remains in England but no other concession is to be given him.

EDWARD II

PARLIAMENT AT NORTHAMPTON: Michaelmas 1307

i
Close Roll, no.125, m.19d
[*Parl. Writs*, II. ii. 1]

Of coming to the king's parliament

The king to the reverend father in Christ William by the grace of God archbishop of York, primate of England, greeting. Because we wish to have a conference and discussion specially with you and the other prelates and magnates of the realm upon some business relating to us ourselves who have recently undertaken the governance of our realm, namely, not only upon the burial of the body of Edward, famous in renown, former king of England, our father (upon whose soul may God look in mercy) but also upon celebrating the formalities of our betrothal and our coronation under the Lord's dispensation and upon other important business touching the state of the realm, we order and firmly charge you in the fealty and love which bind you to us that, putting all else aside, you are to be in person with us and with the other prelates and magnates of the realm at Northampton a Fortnight after Michaelmas next, there to discuss the said business and to give your advice and help. And you are to premonish the dean and chapter of your church, the archdeacons and the whole clergy of your diocese, that the dean and archdeacons are to be present with you in their own persons, and the chapter by one suitable proctor and the clergy by two who shall have full and sufficient power from the chapter and clergy to do and consent then and there in every way to what may be decided then by common counsel, God willing, upon the aforesaid business. And this in no way you are to neglect. Witness the king at Cumnock on the twenty-sixth day of August.[1]

---

[1] 26 August 1307.

ii

Registrum Henrici Woodlock, 1305-1316, fo.66-67
[Canterbury and York Society, XLIII, pp.206-207]

A letter addressed at another time to the archdeacon of Winchester or his official for the wages of the proctors of the clergy of his archdeaconry, summoned to the parliaments of Carlisle and Northampton

Brother Henry etc. to the archdeacon of Winchester or his official etc. Whereas at another time, at the instance of the proctors of the clergy of the archdeaconry of Winchester, appointed by them in a certain form to the parliament lately held at Carlisle by the lord Edward of famous renown, formerly the illustrious king of England, we have addressed our letters to you for levying their wages, as is more fully mentioned in our said letters made thereon, we have nevertheless heard that some ecclesiastics of your archdeaconry have stated that they are most oppressed by such a levy and murmur and utter disreputable things for the aforesaid reason against us and ours among the clergy as well as the people, however unmerited this is, and they pretend that the aforesaid taxation and collection can reach, so it is said, a sum of forty pounds at least, and this has so far escaped our notice and still does so. Being therefore desirous of bringing to the notice of everyone that we have no intention of oppressing any of our subjects in any way but rather of preserving to each his rights, so far as we can, we instruct and command you that, if this be the case, in the next congregation of the clergy summoned by you in your archdeaconry for now appointing a new proctor to appear for them in the parliament at Northampton a Fortnight after Michaelmas next, you are to persuade them that, should the aforesaid sum amount to so much, as is aforesaid, they are to appoint such-and-such a man as a suitable proctor who regards the money previously collected as fully adequate for himself and for the previous proctors appointed by the clergy and, so far as we are concerned, it is our pleasure that his costs, labours and expenses therein be properly provided for him out of the aforesaid sum. And if there are any who have been and may be placed under excommunication for not paying the aforesaid levy at their appointed term we commend them to you and command you to absolve them on our authority in form of law when they have done what they ought to do. Given at Farnham on the fourteenth kalends of October in the abovesaid year.[2]

----

[2] 18 September 1307. A previous letter had authorised an increase in payments to clerical proctors on account of their long delay in the previous parliament at Carlisle and of the high cost of living (*ibid.*, p.194f).

PARLIAMENT AT WESTMINSTER: Lent 1308

Close Roll, no.125, m.11d
[*Parl. Writs*, II, ii. 18; *Cal. Close Rolls, 1307-13*, p.51]

Summons of parliament

The king to the reverend father in Christ William, by the same grace archbishop of York, primate of England. Because we wish to have conference and discussion with you and with other prelates, magnates and other loyal subjects of ours on various important matters concerning us and the state of our realm, and we propose, God willing, to hold a parliament, we command you in the faith and love in which you are bound to us, firmly charging you to put all else aside and to be with us and with the other prelates and magnates of our realm at Westminster on the first Sunday of Lent next,[1] to discuss these matters and to give your counsel. And you shall in no wise neglect this. Witness the king at Dover on the nineteenth day of January.[2]

[1] 3 March 1308.
[2] 19 January 1308.

PARLIAMENT AT WESTMINSTER: Easter 1308

L.T.R. Memoranda Roll, no.78 (1 Edward II), m.97 (98)
[Madox, *Baronia Anglica*, p.117f]

Devon

To the assessors and collectors of the fifteenth

The king to the assessors and collectors of the twentieth[1] and fifteenth in the county of Devon, greeting. Master Walter of Stapleton, bishop-elect of Exeter, an executor of the will of the late bishop of Exeter of happy memory,[2] has shown us on behalf of himself and his fellow executors that, although the said deceased had died before the earls, barons and the communities of the shires of our realm had kindly granted to us as a subsidy a twentieth of their movable goods, and the citizens and burgesses of our realm and the tenants of the ancient demesne of the crown in England a fifteenth of their movable goods,[3] and the deceased was never in his lifetime required to pay such a subsidy to us and had not given consent to the grant made to us, yet you do not hesitate to assess the goods and chattels which the deceased had on the day of his death in the aforesaid county at the twentieth or fifteenth and to levy the twentieth or fifteenth thereon unjustly. Wherefore the bishop-elect has besought us on behalf of himself and his fellow executors to kindly show them redress therein. And because we wish the fullness of justice to be done therein, we command you to supersede altogether the levying of the twentieth or fifteenth on those goods and chattels which it is quite clear to you belonged wholly to the deceased on the day he died and after that up to the time that the grant was made to us by the community of our realm, as aforesaid (provided that no one other than the executors had at that time on any pretext any right or property in those goods and chattels or any part of them, and even the executors only by reason of the execution to be made of the will) until a Fortnight after Easter next, so that then in our parliament,[4] or elsewhere where the king shall see fit to ordain, there may be finally discussed what ought to be done of right in the aforesaid matter. And if you have levied anything from the aforesaid

[1] By error the MS. reads 'thirtieth'.
[2] Thomas Bitton, 1292-1307. He died on 26 September 1307.
[3] The subsidy was granted in the Michaelmas parliament of 1307.
[4] Summoned to meet on 25 April 1308 (*Parl. Writs*, II. ii. 20).

goods on this account, you are to restore it to the executors in the meantime. And you are to let the treasurer and barons of our exchequer at Westminster know on that day what you have done therein, returning there this writ then. Witness the treasurer on the thirtieth day of March.[5]

By the council

---

[5] 30 March 1308.

PARLIAMENT AT WESTMINSTER: Michaelmas 1308

i

Chancery Miscellanea, Bundle 22, file 6, no.1
[*Cal. Documents Scotland*, III, p.9]

Minutes of a meeting in June 1308.

It is agreed, if it please our lord the king, that the king should have a parliament at Westminster at Three Weeks after Michaelmas.[1]

ii

L.T.R. Memoranda Roll, no.79 (2 Edward II), Michaelmas Recorda, m.41
[Davies, *Baronial Opposition*, p.547f]

Devon

Ordinance on behalf of the king's mines

Note that it has been ordained by the honourable father in God Walter, by the grace of God bishop of Worcester, our lord the king's treasurer, in the presence of John Sandall, chancellor, William Carleton, Thomas of Cambridge, Roger Hegham, master Richard of Abingdon, Master John of Everdon, barons of the exchequer, and several others of our lord the king's council in his parliament at Michaelmas term in the second year of his reign that Robert Thorp, clerk, was to be the keeper of the king's mines in Byreland in Devon and of other mines he shall manage to find in the parts of Devon where he believes a profit can be made for the king, and that John of Repple, clerk, is to keep the counter-roll of the mines . . . This indenture was made at Westminster on the twelfth day of December in the aforesaid year.[2]

---

[1] *Register of Walter Stapleton*, p.414: summons on 16 August 1308 to this parliament to complete business begun in the parliament of Lent 1308.

[2] 12 December 1308. See also *ibid.*, m.58: a petition of Peter Flory and his fellows, merchants of Ireland, at the Michaelmas parliament of 1308 for the payment of debts the king owed them.

PARLIAMENT AT WESTMINSTER: Easter 1309

i
Close Roll, no.127, m.22d (schedule)
[*Rot. Parl.*, i. 443f; *Cal. Close Rolls, 1307-13*, p.175]

The articles written below[1] were presented to our lord the king by the community of his realm at his parliament, which he held at Westminster a Month after Easter in the second year of his reign.[2] And at this parliament the king asked to have an aid from his land. And the laity granted the king a twenty-fifth on condition that he would give counsel and redress with regard to the aforesaid articles. And at his parliament at Stamford, beginning on the Sunday after St. James's Day in the third year of his reign,[3] the king provided an answer and redress to the said articles. And he had this answer and redress made known to his people at his said parliament at Stamford, and they are here written below, that is to say, after each article there is the redress which has been provided for it.

The good people of the realm, who have come here to parliament, pray our lord the king that, if it please him, he will have regard for his poor people who feel themselves much aggrieved inasmuch as they are not governed as they ought to be, especially in respect of the articles of the Great Charter, and they pray redress therein, if it please him. Furthermore, they pray our lord the king that, if it please him, he will kindly hear the things that have much aggrieved his people, and still aggrieve them afresh from day to day, through those who call themselves his ministers, and that, if it please him, he will provide redress therein.

> There follows a list of grievances relating to prisage, customs duties, the coinage, the jurisdiction of the court of the steward and marshal.

Sixthly, whereas the knights and the men of the cities and boroughs and other townships, who have come to his parliament at his command on behalf of themselves and of the people and who have petitions to deliver concerning wrongs and grievances done to them, which cannot be redressed by the common law or in any other way without special

---

[1] The copy of these articles with their replies, which was sent to the chancellor, still survives (Ancient Petition, no.14698:4 below, p.293). Cf. the similar substance of the *Articuli Super Cartas* of 1300 (*Statutes of the Realm*, i. 136f).

[2] 27 April 1309.

[3] 27 July 1309. See the Statute of Stamford (*Statutes of the Realm*, i. 154-6).

warrant, do not find anyone to receive their petitions, as used to be the case at parliament in the time of their lord the king's father (to whom God be merciful), they pray his grace and redress thereon.

The king wills that henceforth in his parliaments men are to be appointed to receive petitions, and that these petitions are to be answered by their counsel, as they used to be in his father's time.

> There follows a further list of grievances relating to prisage at fairs; the indiscriminate grant of royal protections in litigation and charters of pardon; constables of castles and escheators.

And it is ordained and commanded by our lord the king that to those who wish to complain to the chancellor that someone has contravened any of the said articles, the chancellor shall by writ under the great seal provide such remedy therein as he shall think ought to be done of right. And the king has also charged the chancellor and his other ministers that each should as regards himself keep the aforesaid articles.

PARLIAMENT AT STAMFORD: 27 July 1309

i

Chancery Warrants, file 63, no.576

[*Cal. Chancery Warrants*, i. 291]

Edward by the grace of God king of England, lord of Ireland and duke of Aquitaine, to the reverend father in God John, by the same grace bishop of Chichester, our chancellor, greeting. Whereas we had caused the archbishop of Canterbury to be summoned by writ of our great seal, together with other prelates and nobles of our realm, to be at our parliament at Stamford, which will begin on Sunday before the Gules of August,[1] where we wish with God's help to settle much important business touching the honour and profit of ourselves and of our crown and of our realm by the counsel of the said nobles, and we have understood that, since the summons made to him by our writ, the archbishop has caused to be summoned by his own letters the prelates of his province and some nobles to be present at a consecration at Canterbury on the Feast of St. Lawrence next,[2] a Feast which will be within the time of our parliament, so we believe, or so soon afterwards that the prelates will not be able to come there without being too much harassed and without deserting our parliament and thwarting the great affairs of our realm, to our hurt and the peril of the kingdom. And we do not wish and ought not to suffer such a thing. We command you that on this matter, of which you can be more fully informed by the bearer of this letter, you are to have framed a prohibition in proper form under our great seal that the archbishop is not to make any such assembly of prelates and others of our realm in our prejudice and in hindrance or disturbance of our parliament or of the great affairs which we have to discuss and settle there, and that, if any assembly should be summoned, he is to have it repealed at once. And you are to have the prohibition made in such a way that, if the archbishop does not obey it, we can have him attached to answer for it to us in our court, as is fitting. Given under our privy seal at Towcester on the eighth day of July at the beginning of the third year of our reign.[3]

---

[1] I.e. Sunday before 1 August, namely, 27 July 1309.

[2] 10 August 1309.

[3] 8 July 1309. And note *Cal. Patent Rolls, 1307-13*, p.180; on 6 August 1309 all earls and barons were ordered to put their seals on a letter to the pope in protest against papal aggressions, in accordance with an agreement reached in the parliament of Stamford.

ii
Chancery Warrants, file 64, no.655
[*Cal. Chancery Warrants*, i. 295–96]

Edward by the grace of God king of England, lord of Ireland and duke of Aquitaine, to the reverend father in God John, by the same grace the bishop of Chichester, our chancellor, greeting. We send you under our privy seal the articles which were presented to us at our last parliament at Westminster on behalf of the good people of our realm, in which they besought us to give advice and redress, together with the answers and redress we have already ordained for the said articles at our last parliament at Stamford. And we command you that you have it made known by letters of our great seal in appropriate form in every county that the redress ordained in the aforesaid articles is to be firmly kept and maintained throughout our kingdom. And because we have ordered our treasurer and several others of our council to be at London on Sunday or Monday after this Feast of the Assumption of our Lady[4] to settle how the aid, which has been granted to us by the laymen of our realm, and the tenth of the clergy, granted to us by the pope, can be quickly levied for our use, we instruct you to be at London on the said Monday or the following Tuesday[5] at the latest to decide in these matters with our treasurer and the others of our council concerning how they can be quickly levied. Given under our privy seal at Langley on the fourteenth day of August in the third year of our reign.[6]

iii
Ancient Correspondence, vol. XLV, no.146

Edward by the grace of God king of England, lord of Ireland and duke of Aquitaine, to the sheriff of Somerset, greeting. Because we have by our letters instructed our dear cousin and loyal subject Henry de Lacy, earl of Lincoln, that, with respect to the suit he is bringing against our dear bachelor, Richard Lovel, for a debt of five hundred marks – for which our said bachelor and some others offered themselves to the earl as guarantors on behalf of the steward of Scotland – he should bear with our bachelor until our next parliament after this St. James's day,[7] and we

---

[4] 17–18 August 1309.
[5] 19 August 1309.
[6] 14 August 1309.
[7] 25 July 1309.

understand for certain that the earl will freely comply with our request thereon, we order you not to make any distraint upon our bachelor for this debt between now and our aforesaid parliament. Given under our privy seal at Chester the twenty-seventh day of June in the second year of our reign.[8]

[8] 27 June 1309.

PARLIAMENT AT WESTMINSTER: Candlemas 1310

i

K.R. Memoranda Roll, no.83 (3 Edward II), Michaelmas Brevia, m.10d
[Davies, *Baronial Opposition*, p.548 f.]

To Henry de Lacy, earl of Lincoln, from the king

Edward, by the grace of God etc., to our very dear cousin and loyal subject Henry de Lacy, earl of Lincoln, greeting. Know that by our council whom we have at York we have arranged to have our great parliament summoned to be at York on the Morrow of Candlemas[1] to deal with the business of Scotland and with various other matters in accordance with the advice we shall get from you and from other good men of our council. For that reason we command you that, as soon as you can conveniently manage it, you are to summon to you our treasurer and others of our council whom you think should be summoned and get advice on how and where it will be suitable for us to hold this parliament, and all arrangements are to be made before you and the calendar of our parliament set down in writing so that there is no need for us to stay there for discussion more than ten days or twelve at the most.[2] And you are to let us know by your letter as soon as you conveniently can how you have arranged the business. Given under our privy seal at Ribston the fourth day of November in the third year of our reign.[3]

ii

Patent Roll, no.133, m.25d
[*Parl. Writs*, II. ii. Appendix p.24; *Cal. Patent Rolls, 1307-1313*, pp.248-249]

The king to his beloved and faithful Henry Cobham the younger, John of Northwood and Roger of Tuckton, greeting.

> The regulations laid down at the Stamford parliament in 1309 concerning the taking of prises has been broken by the king's servants as well as others. Commissioners were appointed in every county to make inquiries and to attach all offenders

So that they may be before us and our council in our parliament, which we will hold at Westminster at the Octave of the Purification of the

---

[1]   3 February 1310.
[2]   This was written before it was decided to hold the parliament at Westminster instead of York.
[3]   4 November 1309.

Blessed Mary next[4] to do and receive what our court may adjudicate in these matters. And should it happen that some who are guilty of taking such prises are not to be found within the county, then you are to inform us and our council clearly and openly in the aforesaid parliament of their names and of all you have done in this respect. And so we command you to carry out the aforesaid matters within the county at the specified days and places you have provided and to let us know in that parliament in the aforesaid manner what you have discovered thereon, returning this writ to us then and there . . . Witness the king at Westminster on the eighteenth day of December.[5]

iii

B.L., Additional MS. 25459, fo.43

All reverence and honour. Know, sir, that my lord the king and my lady the queen and all their company are in good health, thank God, and will stay this winter at Berwick, and the earl of Gloucester at Norham, and the earl of Cornwall at Roxburgh, and the earl of Warenne at Wark. Other news, sir, has not come our way save that my lord has ordered all the courts to be congregated up at York so that they be there at the close of Easter,[6] and I am to go to him with all his chancery by his instructions. And the prelates and the earls ordainers who are at London are bitterly dismayed at this and greatly vexed, and each of them has gone to his own estates, and they have secretly arranged to re-assemble. But no one yet knows where or when, for which reason many people fear the worst. And so the earl of Lincoln is greatly annoyed at this congregating the courts together and has informed the lord our king that it is neither to his advantage nor his honour that the courts should be congregated in such fashion and especially at a time like the present, and that he will not have the authority to be his lieutenant or to keep his peace for him after the courts are joined in this way. But indeed, sir, I really believe that, inasmuch as the earl of Lincoln has informed my lord of the dangers that may befall through such congregation, the business will be put off.[7] . . . Sir, may our Lord by His power preserve you. Written at York on St. Catherine's Day.[8]

---

[4] 9 February 1310.
[5] 18 December 1309.
[6] 18 April 1311 (*Cal. Chancery Warrants, 1244-1326*, p.329).
[7] In the event the courts did not move to York and remained in London.
[8] 25 November 1310.

iv

It is strange that the Lords Ordainers did not summon a parliament before August 1311. The French king evidently believed that there would be one at Easter 1311, though it apparently did not meet. The previous document indicates the turmoil and disagreement that made the normal routine of government well-nigh impossible.

Ancient Correspondence, vol. XXXV, no.53
[Richardson and Sayles, *English Parliament in Middle Ages*, XVI, 81*n*]

Philip, by the grace of God king of the French, to the wise men beloved of us, the chancellor and other people of our most dear and faithful Edward, illustrious king of England and duke of Aquitaine, who have been deputed by the said king to hold the parliament of England at London after the approaching Easter, greeting and affection. Whereas our beloved and faithful bishop of Avranches, a member of our council, has been summoned, so he says, to the aforesaid parliament on account of some rents and goods which he is said to have in the islands of Jersey, Guernsey and Herm, we request and pray you that, having the bishop and his business commended to you by love for us, you should be so good as to receive the said bishop's men and his business in friendly and kindly manner and deal with it and quickly and happily despatch it as hitherto has been the custom. Given at Paris the sixth day of April in the year of our Lord 1310.[9]

---

[9] 6 April 1311, the dominical year being dated from Easter. Easter Day in 1311 fell on 11 April.

PARLIAMENT AT LONDON: 8 August 1311

i

Chancery Warrants, file 79, no.2138

[*Cal. Chancery Warrants*, i. 369]

Edward by the grace of God king of England, lord of Ireland and duke of
Aquitaine, to our dear nephew and loyal subject Gilbert de Clare, earl of
Gloucester, our lieutenant and keeper of the realm, the reverend father in
God Walter, by the same grace bishop of Worcester, our chancellor, and
to our dear clerk John de Sandall, our treasurer, greeting. Because we
have to deal in parliament with some important business concerning us
in relation to the general council,[1] the king of France[2]. . . and the articles
upon which the prelates of our realm have asked us to give them a
definite answer, we order you to have the members of our council
assembled without delay wherever you think suitable and to examine the
points of each piece of business and discuss them and put them in such
good array that we can expedite them well and speedily as soon as we
have come to London to our parliament. Given under our privy seal at
Berwick-on-Tweed on the eighteenth day of June in the fourth year of
our reign.[3]

ii

Treaty Rolls, 4 Edward II, m.2d

[*Foedera*, II. i. 138]

To the most excellent prince Philip, by the grace of God the illustrious
king of France, his most dear father, Edward etc., greeting and a
happy and prosperous outcome of your desires. We have received your
letters, addressed to us on behalf of the merchants of your realm, and
especially those of Amiens, who come into our land with their goods and
merchandise, and among other matters they mention that we ought to
refrain from the exaction of three-pence which your merchants pay
within our kingdom out of every pounds-worth of their merchandise in
contravention of the customs-duty hitherto obtaining therein. But
because the grant of the customs-duty was made some time ago to

---

[1] Before going to the General Council of Vienna in October 1311 the archbishop of
York was ordered on 26 July 1311 to attend parliament where the business to be
transacted at that Council would be discussed (*Foedera*, II. i. 141).

[2] The next few words are lost by reason of a hole in the MS.

[3] 18 June 1311.

Edward, our father, of distinguished memory by the merchants of your kingdom and other lands abroad in a certain general parliament of his in return for some privileges and special immunities, given them by our father, which are to obtain henceforth within his realm and jurisdiction (and by use of them the merchants derive no small profit every day), we cannot at the moment make you a certain and definitive answer in this matter without common counsel of our realm. But in the next parliament which we have already arranged to be summoned, we will cause to be ordained and done therein what it seems to us and our council most advisable to do. Given at Berwick-on-Tweed on the twentieth day of June.[4]

iii
Close Roll, no.129, m.27d
[*Parl. Writs*, II. ii. 56; *Cal. Close Rolls, 1307-13*, p.437]

The king to his beloved and faithful Robert Retford, greeting. It was lately enjoined upon you on our behalf that you were to remain continually with the rest of our council in our present parliament at London to deal there with various important business concerning us and the state of our realm until we gave you other instructions thereon. And incorrectly understanding our instructions in this matter, you have departed elsewhere from the parliament while the rest of our council were there dealing with our said business, whereat we are no little astonished and properly disturbed. Therefore we order you in the faith which binds you to us and firmly charge you that, as soon as you see this letter, you are to put everything else aside and return with all haste to the said city, there to deal with the said business with the rest of our council and to lend your advice, and you are by no means to depart thence while parliament is going on without our special leave. And you shall in no wise neglect this as you wish to avoid our wrath. Witness the king at Hadleigh the twelfth day of September.[5]

[4] 20 June 1311.
[5] 12 September 1311. There must have been serious confusion at the time, for this letter was sent to sixteen others, including many judges. Parliament, assembled on 8 August, was to be prorogued on 8 October for a month.

iv
Guildhall, London: Letter Book D, fo.139*b*
[*Parl. Writs*, II. ii. 58]

Proclamation made concerning the continuation of parliament at London in the fifth year of King Edward

It is agreed by our lord the king and his council that the parliament which was lately summoned to London is to be continued at Westminster on Friday after the next Feast of All Saints,[6] and that the continuation is to be made by certain men appointed by the king for this purpose, and that all other people who have come here for the said parliament may go to their homes or stay elsewhere as they please until the said Friday, always provided that the knights of the shires, citizens, burgesses and others who were summoned to the said parliament at Westminster may be there on the Morrow of Martinmas[7] to continue the same parliament in accordance with the summons previously made. And those of the clergy are to be there at the Octave of Martinmas[8] for the same parliament.

v
Registrum Simonis de Gandavo, fo.140
[Canterbury and York Society (1934), i. 417 f.]

And a certificate was made in this form:[9]

To the venerable father in Christ and the reverend lord Robert, by the grace of God archbishop of Canterbury, primate of all England, his beloved Simon, minister of the church of Salisbury, obedience and the respectful reverence due to so great a father. This mandate and the letters of certification of the vicar of the lord bishop of London concerning the aforesaid convocation, which we have sent you, sealed with that vicar's seal, along with this letter, were read by us to the prelates and clergy appearing in the chapter-house at Westminster on Thursday, and it was said by those who thus came on summons that, although we could in no

[6] 5 November 1311.
[7] 12 November 1311.
[8] 18 November 1311.
[9] The previous document, dated 27 November 1311, is a commission from the archbishop of Canterbury to the bishops of Salisbury and Chichester to examine proxies and excuses for absence in the present parliament, which is also referred to as 'convocation'.

way fulfil the instructions thus entrusted to us at Westminster which was, so it seemed to them, a truly exempt place, yet in reverence for your commands they were prepared to obey your instructions in the aforesaid parliament, if any should then be held, and it was permitted them both to attend the parliament and to consent to what was ordained therein in accordance with what is right. But, because there seemed to them at that time no sign of a parliament and the said clergy were in no wise admitted to some other discussions which certain prelates and nobles held in secret there with the king's ministers for two days, and afterwards at St. Paul's for ten days, and again at Westminster for two days, nor did anyone tell them throughout that time anything about the matters which seemed to concern parliament, some of them departed out of boredom and others departed complaining that they had run out of funds and that the business for which they had come was not being done. And they humbly pray that your lordship will be so good as to hold them excused in these matters. May the Most High keep you for ever and ever to rule and honour His holy Church.

Given at London on the fourteenth kalends of January in the aforesaid year of the Lord.[10]

vi
Ancient Correspondence, vol. XLV, no.165
[Davies, *Baronial Opposition*, p.592]

Edward, by the grace of God king of England, lord of Ireland and duke of Aquitaine, to our dear and faithful, the good people of our council at London, greeting. We send you word that you are not to sell the wardship of the lands and the marriage of the heir of Sir John ap Adam or of his widow to Sir Hugh Despenser or to anyone else until our next parliament after this Feast of All Saints[11] and, if you have sold them to Sir Hugh or any other, you are to revoke the sale at once so that nothing new is done until our aforesaid parliament. Given under our privy seal at Westminster the twenty-seventh day of October in the fifth year of our reign.[12]

[10] 19 December 1311.
[11] 1 November 1311.
[12] 27 October 1311.

vii
Ancient Correspondence, vol. XLV, no.221

Edward, by the grace of God king of England, lord of Ireland and duke of Aquitaine, to our dear and faithful Sir Robert de Holland. We will have you know that we are very joyful and pleased about the good news we have heard concerning the improvement in our dear cousin and loyal subject Thomas, earl of Lancaster, and that he will soon be able to ride in comfort. And we send you word and dearly pray that, as soon as he is comfortable and able to ride without hurt to his body, you should ask him to be so good as to hasten to us at our parliament and that you yourself should kindly come in his company to our said parliament if you can for love of us. Given under our privy seal at Westminster on the twentieth day of November in the fifth year of our reign.[13]

viii
B.L., Additional MS. 35116 and other MSS
[*Year Book, 5 Edward II*, Michaelmas 1311, pp.46, 122, 171]

Chief Justice Bereford's remarks in the court of common pleas.

We will record your arguments. Keep a day a Fortnight after Hilary, and meanwhile we will show this matter to our fellows in parliament.

Parliament is at hand, and we will send the matter into parliament to know whether a man can arrive at his law etc.[14] concerning such a high and heinous matter.

The judgement is much vexed. Therefore we wish to act in accordance with the ordinances.[15] And let him who sees his advantage sue to have the record and process in full parliament.

---

[13] 20 November 1311.

[14] Wager of law: the use of neighbours to authenticate a plea by their oaths.

[15] Ordinances of 1311, c.29: where justices disagreed, the case was to be sent to parliament for decision.

ix
B.L. Cotton Charter 43D 18
Canterbury Cathedral MS. K.11
[*Statutes of the Realm*, i. 157-67]

The Ordinances of 1311,[16] forty-one in number, included the following:

c.7. Moreover, because the crown is so much abased and fragmented by various grants, we ordain that all gifts made to the king's harm and the impoverishment of the crown since the commission given to us, of castles, towns, lands and tenements, bailiwicks, wardships and marriages, escheats and discharges of whatsoever kind, in Gascony, Ireland, Wales and Scotland as well as in England, are to be revoked, and we revoke them completely so that they shall not be regranted to the same persons without common assent in parliament; and that, if any such kinds of gifts or discharges be henceforward made in contravention of the aforesaid ruling without the assent of his baronage and this in parliament, and before his debts are settled and his estate unburdened for the future, they shall be considered void, and he who accepts them is to be punished in parliament by judgement of the baronage.

c.9. Inasmuch as the king ought not to undertake an act of war against anyone or to go outside his kingdom without the common assent of his baronage on account of the many dangers that may befall him and his realm, we ordain that henceforward the king is not to go outside his kingdom or to undertake any act of war against another without the common assent of his baronage, and this in parliament. And should he act otherwise and cause his armed service to be summoned for such an undertaking, the summons is to be regarded as void. And should it happen that, with the assent of his baronage, the king undertakes an act of war against anyone or goes outside the land, and it is necessary for him to appoint a keeper in his kingdom, he is to appoint him as keeper of it by common assent of his baronage and this in parliament.

c.14. And inasmuch as many evils have been incurred through bad advisers and ministers, we ordain that the king is to appoint the chancellor, the chief justice of the king's bench and the common bench, the treasurer, the chancellor, the chief baron of the exchequer, the steward of his household, the keeper and the controller of the wardrobe

---

[16] A draft version has been found in the Dean and Chapter Muniments at Durham and printed by M. Prestwich in *Bull. Inst. Hist. Research*, LVII, 194-203.

and one competent clerk to keep his privy seal, one chief keeper of his forests below the river Trent and another beyond the river Trent, and also one escheator below the river Trent and another beyond the river Trent, and the king's chief clerk in the common bench, with the advice and assent of his baronage, and this in parliament.[17] And if by some chance it happens to be necessary for him to appoint any of the said ministers before parliament meets, then the king is to make the appointment by the best advice he has at hand until the time of parliament. And henceforward let it thus be done in the case of such ministers when necessary.

c.24. And inasmuch as the people feel themselves greatly harassed by sundry debts demanded from them for the king's profit by summonses of the exchequer, and these debts have been paid and the people have various discharges for them, some by tallies and writs and some by various franchises granted to them by royal deeds, for which allowance should be made, we ordain that henceforward in the accounting of all sheriffs and of other royal ministers who have to render account at the exchequer such kinds of tallies, writs and franchises as are allowable in the accounting are to be allowed, provided the said discharges are shown to the court so that they do not fail to be demanded through negligence in seeking allowances. And if the treasurer and the barons of the exchequer do not act in the aforesaid manner, let the plaintiffs have their recovery against them by petitions in parliament.

c.25. Inasmuch as merchants in general and many others of the people are admitted to plead pleas of debt and of trespass at the exchequer much sooner than they ought to be because these are favoured [in being heard] by the officers of the exchequer and thereby the accounts and other matters concerning the king are all the more delayed and, in addition, many people are harassed, for that reason we ordain that henceforward no pleas may be held in the said court of the exchequer except pleas that concern the king and his ministers who are answerable in the exchequer on account of their duties, and the officers of the exchequer and their households and their servants who generally stay with them in the places where the exchequer is stationed. And if anyone should be admitted by favour of the said court to plead in the exchequer in contravention of the aforesaid ruling, let those impleaded have their recovery in parliament.

---

[17] This part of the Ordinances was deliberately repeated in a common petition in 1341 (*Rot. Parl.*, ii. 128, no.15).

c.29. Because many people are delayed in their claims in the king's court inasmuch as defendants allege that demandants ought not to be answered without consultation with the king and thus many people are harassed by the king's ministers against what is right, and no one can recover his right with regard to these grievances without a common parliament, we ordain that the king is to hold parliament once a year, or twice if need be, and this in a convenient place, and that the pleas which are delayed in the aforesaid manner and the pleas where the justices hold different opinions are to be heard and determined in the said parliaments; and likewise the petitions, which shall be handed in at parliament, are to be determined as before, as law and justice require.

c.30. Forasmuch as at all times when an exchange of money[18] is established in the realm, the whole people are harassed in many ways, we order that, when it is appropriate and the king wishes to establish an exchange, he is to do it by common assent of his baronage, and this in parliament.

c.38. We also ordain that the Great Charter of Liberties and the Charter of the Forest made by King Henry, son of King John, are to be kept in all their articles, and that the articles which are ambiguous in the said Charters of Liberties are to be clarified in the next parliament after this by the advice of the baronage and the justices and other learned men of law. And let this be done [then] because we are not empowered to do it during our term of office.

c.39. We also ordain that the chancellor, the treasurer, the chief justices of both benches, the chancellor of the exchequer, the treasurer of the wardrobe, the steward of the king's household, all justices, sheriffs, escheators, constables, officials who hold inquests of whatever kind, and all other bailiffs and servants of the king are to be sworn, whenever they receive their bailiwicks and offices, to hold and keep all the ordinances, made by the prelates, earls and barons chosen and appointed for this purpose, and each one of them without contravening any of their articles.

c.40. We also ordain that one bishop, two earls and two barons are to be appointed in each parliament to hear and determine all the plaints of those who wish to complain against the king's ministers, whoever they may be, who shall contravene the aforesaid ordinances. And if the said bishop, earls and barons cannot hear them all or are prevented from

[18] Where an exchange, usually of foreign money, into pounds sterling could be made.

hearing and determining these plaints, then three or two of them may act, and those who shall be found to have contravened the said ordinances are to be punished both in respect of the king and in respect of the complainants, at the discretion of those appointed.

c.41. We also ordain that the aforesaid ordinances are to be maintained and kept in all their articles, and that our lord the king is to have them put under his great seal and sent into every shire in England, as well within franchises as outside them, to be published, held and firmly kept. And the keeper of the Cinque Ports is similarly ordered to have them published, held and kept in the aforesaid form throughout his whole bailiwick.

We agree, accept and confirm these ordinances, shown to us and published on Monday before Michaelmas last,[19] and we will and grant, on behalf of ourselves and our heirs, that all and every one of the said ordinances, made in accordance with the form of our aforesaid letters, are to be published throughout our realm and henceforth to be firmly held and kept. In witness thereof we have caused these our letters patent to be made. Given at London the fifth day of October in the fifth year of our reign.[20]

[19] 27 September 1311.
[20] 5 October 1311.

PARLIAMENT AT WESTMINSTER: 20 August 1312

i

Ancient Correspondence, vol. XLIX, no.104

Sire. The bishop of Salisbury, the bishop of Norwich, Roger Brabazon, William Bereford, Guy Ferre, William Inge, master Thomas of Cobham and master Walter of Thorp have been at Westminster, as you commanded them by your letters, to discuss, advise and ordain concerning Gascon affairs as well as matters concerning the peace like extortions, acts of trespass and heinous offences. And because your letters mentioned that they should be there to hold discussions with you and with prelates and great lords and others of your council and, sire, you have not appointed anyone to deputise for you there, and the other prelates and great lords and members of your council are not there, it seemed to them that the business was so important, so heavy and so dangerous that they dared not and could not take it upon themselves to decide anything thereon without your presence and that of the council of the greatest of your realm. And they understand that these will assemble together by your orders on the First Sunday of Lent[1] at your parliament at Westminster if matters may be suffered to wait until then. And, sire, it seems to them that there is great need for you to have this business much at heart and expedited as soon as possible because the time is short before the parliament of France and your adjournment there at Mid-Lent,[2] as the messengers of the king of France informed you at London when you were last there, and because the danger is great.

ii

Exchequer, Various Accounts 375/8, fo.7 (6 Edward II)

The expenses of John of Benstead

To John of Benstead, knight, sent by the king from Dover to the earls of Lancaster, Hereford and Warwick to summon them to come to the

---

[1] 13 February 1312. This parliament was abandoned (*Register Walter Reynolds*, p.34: on 20 January 1312 the king told the bishop of Worcester not to come to the parliament summoned for 13 February 1312). The next parliament was summoned to meet at Lincoln on 23 July, but this was changed to Westminster on 20 August. Knights and burgesses were sent home on 28 August and re-summoned for 30 September and received writs of expenses dated 16 December.

[2] 5 March 1312.

king's parliament, to be held at Westminster or London on the Sunday[3] after the Feast of St. Bartholomew the Apostle with the prelates and other magnates of the realm, summoned to it to discuss there certain ordinances promulgated by them to the damage and prejudice of the king: for his expenses and those of his men and his horses from 9 August, when he started his journey from London, until 30 August, when he returned to London, that is 22 days inclusive . . .

To the same for similar expenses of his in coming from London to Dover to the king at his command for the business the king ordered him to do (as above), in staying at the court and returning to London: for 6 days before the said 9 August . . .

iii
Ancient Petition, File 327, no. E. 843

John of Fressingfield who came by the king's orders to this parliament[4] is attached by the bailiff of the Liberty of the abbot of Westminster in Tothill by his horses and harness on the complaint of Adam of Ely for debt. And he prays redress therein.[5]

[3] 27 August.

[4] *Parl. Writs*, II. ii. 76.

[5] John was not a knight of the shire but summoned among justices and other members of the king's council. See *ibid.*, II. ii. 195a, for litigation over the expenses of a Dorset knight of the shire from 20 August to 16 December 1312, and *Rot. Parl. Ined.*, pp. 58-9 for petitions presented in this parliament.

PARLIAMENT AT WESTMINSTER: 18 March 1313

i

Vatican MS: Instrumenta Miscellanea, no.5947
[*Camden Miscellany*, vol. XV, pp.15 ff.]

*The arguments of the barons by which they say that the security
found for them by the justices is not sufficient*

First, because the king says in that passage, among other things, that in his parliament he is providing this security on the ground of necessity, and it can be understood from these words that the earls and barons had coerced the king and placed him under that necessity, which is not true, and this method of expression does not please them.

The second argument, because the said passage suggests that the security should be provided in parliament. But parliament cannot be held without them and they would never come to parliament if they had not first of all been given good security. Therefore this passage seems meaningless.

Again, let it be noted that it has been discussed and decided[1] that in the next parliament, which is to be on the third Sunday of this approaching Lent at Westminster,[2] security ought to be provided at the beginning of that parliament for the said earls and barons, their adherents and their households and their staff.

Again, they certainly agree that, if the said security pleases the earls and barons and they do not wish to come to parliament in person, they may send proxies with sufficient power to agree to the security and accept it on their behalf and, in addition to this, with sufficient power to agree to the security which is to be provided in the said parliament for the adherents and harbourers of Peter of Gaveston.

Again, the negotiators [for the earls and barons] well agree that an ordinance should be made in the next parliament by the king and the common assent of prelates, earls and barons that people may for ever come to all parliaments, councils and other assemblies, that shall in

---

[1] For the agreement between king and the barons just before Christmas 1312, see *Foedera*, ii. 191f; *Cal. Close Rolls, 1307-13*, p.574.

[2] 18 March 1313. The archbishop of Canterbury had summoned a convocation at St. Paul's, London, on 20 March and steps had to be taken to make sure that it did not prevent their presence in parliament (*Registrum Simonis de Gandavo*, pp.444-5).

future be held within the realm of England, without any bodyguard and without arms but properly and peacefully to the honour of the king and the peace of himself and his realm.

And it is to be well understood that no other business shall be done in the said parliament, except for the said securities and the ordinance that no one is to come with arms, until [certain specified earls and barons] have made their submission, and once this has been done, the rest of parliament's business shall be dealt with in reasonable manner.

Again, the negotiators firmly promise that, when the said reconciliation has been made, they will do all they possibly can, when they shall be in open parliament with their peers, to see that the king has a satisfactory aid from all his kingdom for his war in Scotland.

ii
Ancient Petition, file 42, no.2062

May it please our lord the king to grant leave to his chaplain, the bishop of St. David's, to give a church, lands and tenements to the value of thirty pounds, whether they be of his inheritance or of his own acquisition, to six poor chaplains, to be held by them and their successors for ever, as a chantry for the souls of the ancestors of the king and of the bishop and of all Christians in accordance with the bishop's arrangements.

Endorsed:
Before the king and the great council.[3]
It pleases the king for a fine.
Let him come before the chancellor and the treasurer and make a fine.[4]

iii
B.L., Harleian MS. no.3763 (Register of Evesham Abbey), fo.45*b*

A writ to free a man kept in prison for a trespass committed in the forest, who had not been indicted in accordance with the terms of the new Statute of the Forest[5]

The king to his coroners in the county of Worcester, greeting. We have received a plaint from Robert de Sumery, stating that he had brought an assize of novel disseisin against Malcolm Musard, the steward of our forest of Feckenham, before our beloved and faithful Henry Spigurnel

---

[3] This is an early reference to the existence of that 'great council in parliament' which came into existence as a result of the Ordinances of 1311.

[4] *Cal. Patent Rolls, 1307-13*, p.563 (25 March 1313).

[5] *Statutes of the Realm*, i. 147-9 (1306).

and his fellows, our justices assigned to hold assizes in the said county, and he, Robert, had alleged before the justices that Robert of Warwick, the sheriff of the county,[6] had wickedly stolen our original writ of assize sent and delivered on Robert de Sumery's behalf, and he publicly stated that he wished to prosecute a plaint thereon against the sheriff in our present parliament. And Malcolm and the sheriff, by a pre-conceived conspiracy between them at Worcester to harass Robert de Sumery and prevent him from prosecuting such a plaint in the said parliament, declared that Robert was indicted of a trespass committed in our aforesaid forest, and they had him arrested and imprisoned in our prison of Feckenham, in impairment of the common law and of our realm and to Robert de Sumery's no slight loss and injury. But because it is stated in our court before us by trustworthy men that Robert de Sumery had not been indicted of any trespass committed in our forest by the oath of twelve jurors in accordance with the terms of the statute promulgated by Edward, formerly king of England, our father, famous in renown, and we are not willing that this statute, which our father promulgated for the welfare of his people and granted on behalf of himself and his heirs to last for ever, should be destroyed, violated or in any way weakened or that the aforesaid trespass and conspiracy, if such have been committed, should be left unpunished, we command you that, if Robert de Sumery finds you a guarantee that he will prosecute his action, then you are to put Malcolm and Robert of Warwick on gage and safe pledges to be before us a Month after Easter wherever we may then be in England to answer Robert de Sumery on the aforesaid trespass and conspiracy, and you are in the meantime to have him released on security from the aforesaid prison, provided he is detained in it for this and no other reason. And you are to have there the names of the sureties and this writ. Witness myself at Westminster on the third day of April in the sixth year of our reign.[7]

---

[6] He acted as sheriff from Michaelmas 1310 to 25 August 1315.
[7] 3 April 1313.

PARLIAMENT AT WESTMINSTER: 8 July 1313

i

Chancery Warrants, file 85, no.2746

[*Cal. Chancery Warrants*, i. 391]

Edward by the grace of God king of England, lord of Ireland and duke of Aquitaine, to the reverend father in God. Walter, by the same grace bishop of Worcester, keeper of our great seal, greeting. Because our dear one in God, the abbot of St. Augustine's of Canterbury, is summoned to be at this our parliament at Westminster, and we do not wish him to be absent from it, we order you to let our justices in eyre in the county of Kent know by letters of our great seal that they are to hold up the business before them concerning the abbot completely as long as the abbot remains at our parliament, provided that that business is finished before the end of the eyre in accordance with the law and custom of our realm. Given under our privy seal at Sturry the nineteenth day of July in the seventh year of our reign.[1]

ii

Ancient Correspondence, vol. XXXV, no.84

To the reverend father in Christ, Walter, by the grace of God bishop of Worcester, the chancellor of our illustrious lord Edward, by the grace of God king of England, Ralph by Divine permission bishop of London, greeting in the Saviour of us all. We have lately received the king's letters as follows:

> a writ, dated at London on 16 June 1313, pointing out that the convocation of Canterbury, meeting at London, had agreed to levy a subsidy from spiritualities and to hold the proceeds in reserve in case of foreign invasion and that an imminent attack by Scotland now justified the request that the money be sent to London by Midsummer.

But because such business concerns the prelates and clergy of the whole province of Canterbury, and we hope to be able to meet them in the next parliament at Westminster, summoned, so we understand, for a

---

[1] 19 July 1313. The king appointed two bishops and two earls as his commissioners to open parliament in case he was hindered for a few days from being present (*Cal. Patent Rolls, 1307-13*, p.594).

Fortnight after St. John the Baptist's Day,[2] and now the time is too short and our means inadequate to execute the business or to notify clearly and openly at present what we mean to do therein, we implore you to be kindly forebearing until what is to be done can be discussed at the aforesaid parliament and a fuller reply be made thereon. Given at Stepney on the Vigil of the Nativity of St. John the Baptist in the year of the Lord one thousand three hundred and thirteen.[3]

iii
Ancient Correspondence, vol. XXVIII, no.39

To the highly respected and, if it pleases you, a most dear friend in Christ, Adam of Osgodby, clerk of Edward, by God's grace the most illustrious king of England, Richard by that same God's permission the bishop of Hereford, all possible friendship and greeting with the Saviour's blessing and grace. Because we have been given to understand that the king's justices in eyre will be sitting at Canterbury at the Octave of the Nativity of the Blessed John the Baptist,[4] and we have some lands belonging to us in those parts by hereditary right and some (though little) by acquisition, therefore we earnestly implore you of your accustomed and kindly friendship to be so good as to sue out and obtain for us the king's writ, addressed to William of Mortimer, formerly the king's justice, who is staying these days in Hereford, so that he can receive on our behalf before the aforesaid justices two attorneys whom we shall arrange to be nominated before him and assigned, jointly and separately, in all pleas and plaints, brought or to be brought against us there. And we earnestly beg this of you, not because we know that any plaint has already been brought or is to be brought against us there, but so that we may be kept completely protected before the aforesaid justices by your kindly wisdom. And please send that writ to us by Roger of Wallington as soon as it can be made, along with any others it pleases you to send.

And trusting always in your customary goodwill we ask and pray you, now as always, to be so good as to make our excuses to your aforesaid lord and ours for our absence in the approaching parliament to be held at Westminster, and please take upon yourself the burden of being our proxy, and we are sending you by the bearer of this letter the

---

[2] 8 July 1313.

[3] 23 June 1313. The parliament was to be adjourned until September on account of the absence of prelates and magnates (*Foedera*, II. i. 223, 225; *Register Richard of Swinfield*, pp.489-90).

[4] 1 July 1313.

letter of proxy, in which we have appointed you, along with others in case it should sometimes happen that you are absent. And please apply such diligence in these matters that we may be indebted to you for this most special grace and favour.

We also send you our certificate regarding the receipt of the king's writ addressed to us for the aforesaid parliament, which you may wish to show in appropriate times and places in accordance with what you think in your wisdom will be most expedient. May the Most High preserve you and ever guide your doings. Given at Bosbury on the twenty-second day of June in the thirteen hundred and thirteenth year of the Lord.[5]

Endorsed: To the highly respected Adam of Osgodby, clerk of the king of England.

---

[5] 22 June 1313.

PARLIAMENT AT WESTMINSTER: 23 September 1313

i

Ancient Correspondence, vol. XLIX, no.23
[Davies, *Baronial Opposition*, p.595]

Edward, by the grace of God king of England, lord of Ireland and duke of Aquitaine, to our dear cousin and loyal subject, Aymer de Valence, earl of Pembroke, greeting. Dearest cousin, because we wish to have counsel and advice from you and from some other intimate members of our council before our next parliament[1] on the business which has to be discussed and done at our said parliament, we pray and charge you, as we put our trust in you, to be with us at Chertsey on Monday after the Feast of the Exaltation of Holy Cross next[2] in order to talk over and deal with the aforesaid business. And you are in no way to neglect this. Given under our privy seal at Windsor the twenty-eighth day of August in the seventh year of our reign.[3]

ii

Ancient Deeds, C. 10541

To all the faithful in Christ to whom the present letter shall come, John Giffard of Twyford [and eleven others], greeting in the Lord. Because Geoffrey of Bradden, sheriff of Northampton, committed to us in custody the person of Nicholas Turville, attached by the king's writ of privy seal to answer the king in his next parliament to be held after this letter is written for the disobedience and trespass committed by Nicholas against the king, we bind ourselves and each one of us jointly and severally, our heirs and executors, our lands, tenements, goods and chattels, our movable and immovable property, wherever they may be found, to have Nicholas in person before the king in his aforesaid parliament to do well and faithfully all the aforesaid things and to keep Geoffrey, the sheriff, indemnified therein as against the king and any others. In witness whereof our seals are appended to this letter. Given at Northampton on Saturday,[4] the Morrow of St. Bartholomew the

---

[1] For the writs of summons, see *Parl. Writs*, II. i. 100–19.

[2] 17 September 1313.

[3] 28 August 1313.

[4] 25 August 1313. The abbot of Battle was told in the Common Bench at Trinity 1313 to sue in parliament and ask the king and his council to indicate the king's will to the court 'because the justices refuse to adjudicate upon numerous royal charters or to admit any proof in contradiction of any one of them without the king's advice and wishes' (B.L., Harleian MS., no.3586, fo.3–5*b*).

Apostle, in the seventh year of the reign of King Edward son of King Edward.

iii
Treaty Rolls, no.9, m.5d
[*Foedera*, II. i. 226]

To the most excellent prince Philip, by the grace of God the illustrious king of France and his most dear father, Edward by the same grace king of England etc., greeting and a happy and prosperous issue to your desires. We are hoping that the business concerning ourselves and certain magnates of our realm would be very happily expedited by the noble men, Louis count of Evreux, your brother, and Ingelram de Maregny, and by the ripeness of their counsel and their wise provision in the parliament summoned at London on Sunday after the approaching Feast of St. Matthew the Apostle,[5] to the honour and profit of ourselves and of our whole realm. For the business has already been discussed before your brother and certain cardinals who were then in the kingdom and before other magnates of the realm, and we regard the count and Ingelram as men of peace and eager to find agreement. We request and implore you, most dear father, with loving prayers that you should be pleased to send your brother and Ingelram to our aforesaid parliament, as our beloved and faithful Edward de Maulay, our steward, whom we are sending to your presence for this reason, shall deem it proper to request of you on our behalf, and to show him faith and trust in those matters which he will propound to you by word of mouth in our name. Given at Windsor on the twenty-eighth day of August.[6]

[5]   23 September 1313.
[6]   28 August 1313.

PARLIAMENT AT YORK: 9 September 1314

It had been intended to hold a parliament at Westminster at Easter 1314 and writs were issued. But the parliament was cancelled as a consequence of disturbances in Scotland which required the king's presence at Newcastle upon Tyne.

i

Patent Rolls, no.142, m.26

[Ryley, *Placita*, p.552: *Cal. Patent Rolls, 1313-1317*, p.169]

Of a commission of power to begin parliament

The king to the reverend father in Christ Walter, by the same grace bishop of Exeter, and his kinsmen and loyal subjects Aymer de Valence, earl of Pembroke, and Henry de Beaumont, greeting. Because on account of some important and special business concerning us we are not able to be present in person at York on the first day of our parliament which we have caused to be summoned there, namely, on this instant Monday, the Morrow of the Nativity of the Blessed Virgin Mary,[1] possessing complete confidence in the Lord as regards your loyalty and wise discretion, we by the tenor of this letter commit full power to you three, or to two of you, to do in our name those things which appertain to beginning and holding our parliament until our arrival there. Moreover, we will hold right and acceptable those things which happen to be done by you three, or two of you, in our name therein. In testimony whereof etc. Witness the king at Oulston on the seventh day of September.[2]

By writ of privy seal

ii

Chancery Warrants, file 90, no.3202

[*Cal. Chancery Warrants*, i. 407]

Edward, by the grace of God king of England, lord of Ireland and duke of Aquitaine, to our dear and faithful John de Sandall, our chancellor, and Walter of Norwich, our treasurer, greeting. Because the prelates, earls and barons of our realm have requested us lately at our parliament at York to be so good as to repeal all the gifts and discharges we have made of lands, tenements, bailiwicks, wardships, marriages, debts and services since the time we gave authority to some of the prelates, earls

[1] 9 September 1314.
[2] 7 September 1314.

and barons to ordain about the state of our realm and of our household, therefore we wish to be informed and advised about these gifts and discharges. We order you to search the rolls and memoranda of our chancery and of our exchequer and to inform us clearly and openly as soon as you can about all the gifts and discharges we have made, since the time when the said authority was granted, of lands, tenements, bailiwicks, wardships, marriages, debts and services, and to whom and of what and in what form, so that we can be advised before our next parliament about what has to be done. Given under our privy seal at Berkhamsted on the fourth day of December in the eighth year of our reign.[3]

---

[3] 4 December 1314. Cf. above, p.303.

PARLIAMENT AT WESTMINSTER: Hilary 1315

ia
Exchequer Parliament and Council Proceedings, file 2, no. 4

In this interesting document protests are made against royal encroachments upon ecclesiastical jurisdiction by the issue of writs. They are recited and then criticised. Among the comments are the following:

This writ seems to be in breach of ecclesiastical liberty and contrary to the usual chancery style, since such a general prohibition was not wont to be made in cases still to be begun, but the prohibition should be specific and between specified persons and in cases already begun. And it does not seem that it was in the power of those who answer petitions to order and authorise such an unusual and prejudicial writ without consulting the king or the great council. And although it is stated in the petition to which the said answer was made that such a petition was made at the request of the community of Devon, this is not true, as can be ascertained from the knights sent to parliament for the said shire, one of whom is in town. But the petition was made in the name of the community by some individual persons who mean thereby to harass the bishop and clergy. And if the petition thus put forward is carefully examined as well as the answer to it, the writ of prohibition does not agree with them.

And it seems that it does not pertain to those who answer common petitions in parliament to appoint specified and nominated justices of oyer and terminer without greater advice or special instructions from the king.[1]

Endorsed: Before the great council.

ib
Exchequer Parliament Roll, no. 18, m. 7
[*Rot. Parl.*, i. 297]

The bishop of Chichester brings a petition, complaining of a royal writ of prohibition obtained by the bishop of Exeter, who was contesting his jurisdiction over Bosham chapel.

It seems to the council that the form of the writ is not conceived in accordance with the usages and custom of the chancery inasmuch as the

---

[1] Cf. Ancient Correspondence, vol. XLV, no. 187: the king informed the archbishop of Canterbury on 18 May 1315 of the names of four justices of oyer and terminer in Norfolk and Suffolk who were appointed 'by common assent of our parliament'.

king asserts that Bosham chapel, which is not in his hands but in the hands of another, is and ought to be and has of old been free, immune and exempt from all jurisdiction of the ordinary.[2] But the council does not know for what reason or on what grounds the king makes such a statement and therefore there should be consultation with the king thereon.

Afterwards, after a discussion had been held with the king at the instance of the great council concerning the revocation of the aforesaid writ, the king ordered full justice to be done therein. Therefore, after there had been deliberation on the matter before the council, it was agreed that the writ should be revoked and annulled because it was conceived against the accustomed practice of the chancery. And let the bishop of Chichester have a writ in chancery thereon so that, notwithstanding the aforesaid prohibition, he may sue for his rights etc.

iia
Ancient Petition, no.102
[Sayles, *King's Bench*, II. cxxvi f.]

To our lord the king and his council shows Maud, the widow of Ellis de Rabayn, that Sir Stephen de Baiuse, the said Maud's father, at the request of King Henry, the grandfather of the present king, granted and gave all the barony of Baiuse with appurtenances to Ellis and Maud in frank-marriage. By virtue of that gift they held this barony for a long time without anyone disturbing them until, after Ellis's death, one Peter Baudrant of Poitou, saying that he was one of Stephen de Baiuse's heirs, put forward a petition before the king and his council, claiming that half the barony was his heritage on the ground that Stephen had two daughters, one Maud, the elder, and another Joan, the younger, whose son he was, so he said, and he claimed the said half as his heritage from his mother's apportionment. And Sir Ralph Hengham, then a royal justice, gave an arbitrary judgement on this petition in favour of Peter, without Maud being summoned and without any regard to the deed and the estate that Stephen bestowed upon Maud and her husband. Then afterwards Sir Peter Malorre, who had married Maud, came to court and arranged for the record and process of the said plea to come before Sir Gilbert Thornton and his fellows, then the justices of our late lord king, and asked for the errors found in the record to be redressed. And then the errors were so much argued and disputed among the aforesaid justices that at last it was decided that he should speak to the king about the said

---

[2] An ecclesiastic exercising the judicial authority of a bishop.

business. And it was in this way held up until now. Wherefore Maud prays our lord the king that he may of his grace be good enough to order the record and process to come before his council and justice to be done after Maud's arguments had been heard.

Endorsed: Let her have a writ at common law against the tenant and, when the point is reached where the tenant says that he cannot answer thereon without the king, then let the record and process, mentioned in the petition, be brought and justice be done.

Before the great council.

Afterwards, when the petition had been read and heard before the great council and the arguments, contained in the bill sewn to this petition,[3] had been understood, inasmuch as it seems that Maud cannot prosecute by common law, therefore let her have a writ to have the record and process of the whole of the aforesaid business come before Roger Brabazon and his fellows etc. And they are ordered to examine these matters in the fullest way and do her the full complement of justice.

It is enrolled.

iib
Chancery Parliament and Council Proceedings, file 3, no.24
[Sayles, *King's Bench*, II. cxl f.]

To this petition answer was made at the last parliament in this fashion: let her have a writ at common law against the tenant and, when the point has been reached where the tenant says that he cannot answer thereon without the king, then let the record and process, mentioned in the petition, be brought and justice be done. But because a writ at common law cannot serve in this case, neither a writ of right on account of the frank-marriage where there is only an entail, nor a writ of formedon because she was a party to the gift and it serves the issue only, nor does a writ of entry lie as for a mixed right[4] inasmuch as the tenant has had entry by our lord the king, for this entry cannot be taken from him as from an ordinary person, nor can an assize of novel disseisin serve because of our lord the king's seisin which must not be termed disseisin, may it please our lord the king to advise on the petition and on the answer and, in order to avoid the great mischief of disinheritance, to ordain that right should be done by some other way since a writ [at common law] cannot serve.

---

[3] For this note, see below, no. iib and *Rot. Parl.* i. 337.
[4] See Fleta, book V, c.2.

iii
King's Bench Roll, no.210 (Michaelmas 1312), m.59
[Sayles, *King's Bench*, IV. 37-43]

Litigation over a fine made in 1257 concerning lands in Wiltshire.

Edward by the grace of God king of England, lord of Ireland and duke of Aquitaine, to his beloved and faithful Roger Brabazon and his fellows, justices assigned to hold pleas before us, greeting. For some certain causes we order you to do nothing further concerning old fines, levied before the promulgation of the Statute of Fines[5] and pending undecided before you, until our next parliament so that there may then be done in the matter what may be ordained by common counsel. Witness myself at York the twenty-fifth day of September in the eighth year of our reign.[6]

Edward by the grace of God king of England, lord of Ireland and duke of Aquitaine, to his beloved and faithful Roger Brabazon and his fellows, our justices assigned to hold pleas before us, greeting. Although for some certain causes we have lately commanded you to do nothing further concerning old fines, pending undecided before us, until our next parliament, because it is agreed by the prelates, earls and barons and others of our council in our present parliament assembled at Westminster that the execution of fines, such as were levied before the Statute of Fines was lately promulgated by the counsel of our realm as well as of fines levied afterwards, should be proceeded with in accordance with the terms of the statute, we order you to cause due execution to be made with respect to such old fines pending at present before us and justice to be done thereon to the parties in accordance with the law and custom of our realm and the terms of the statute, notwithstanding our said order. Witness myself at Westminster the first day of May in the eighth year of our reign.[7]

---

[5] In 1300.

[6] 25 September 1314.

[7] 1 May 1315.

iv
Exchequer Parliament Roll, no.18
[*Rot. Parl.*, i. 287-333]

m.3 (p.290)

The king and the whole council had ordained that, in an action for
ravishing a wife and taking away property, the defendant was to be
released from prison on bail if he was of good character and the
plaintiff was to go to prison for a year if he lost his case.

Because the petition on which the preceding ordinance was based was
delivered, not to Robert Ashby but to Master William Maldon, the said
Robert did not insert the ordinance in his parliament roll in the proper
place, wherefore he has had the said ordinance put on the preceding
schedule and sewn and fastened here for future remembrance.

m.4d (p.292)

A petition, complaining of loss of rent and property as well as theft,
and requesting the appointment of justices of oyer and terminer in
Cornwall because no jury would wish to set off from a place so far
from the court.

It seems to the auditors of petitions that, because the county is so remote
that jurors will never come to the king's court from those parts, the writ
of oyer and terminer, mentioned in the petition, should be granted to the
petitioner, and some trustworthy men are to be appointed for this
purpose.[8]

m.7d (p.298b)

A petition of the abbot of Rufford.

It seems to the council that the said abbot of Rufford and his monks . . .
are not in the case where they may have the writ called *supersedeas* from
the chancery. Therefore the chancellor told those who sued for the abbot
that they could not have that writ. Those then present at the house of the
Dominicans: the archbishop of Canterbury, the earl of Hereford and
Essex and the earl of Warwick, Bartholomew of Badlesmere, John
Sandall, the king's chancellor, Walter of Norwich, the treasurer, Master
John Walwayn and Richard of Burton, Adam of Osgodby, Robert of
Barlby, William of Airmyn and others.

[8] Cf. above, p.319 *n*.1.

m.9d (p.302a)

A petition of Queen Margaret, complaining that, while the city of Hereford had been committed to her in dower with all the issues therefrom, the citizens had obtained a charter from the king, dated 16 September 1314, giving them certain jurisdictional rights which would be to the queen's loss.

Answer is made by the great council: let the citizens of Hereford be ordered by writ to send the charter, made for them by the king, before the council by two of their citizens so as to have it there on the Morrow of St. John the Baptist's Day next.[9] And let the queen come before the council, or someone with instructions on her behalf, on the aforesaid day so that, after the business has been further examined, there may be done what then ought of right to be done.

m.11 (p.305b)

Petition of Roger Mortimer for the restoration of land.

Answer is made: because the lands mentioned in the petition have been taken into the king's hands on account of the Ordinances [of 1311], and the Ordinances state that such lands are not to be handed back to those who formerly held them without the common assent of the magnates in parliament, and there are not here at present as many as are requisite, therefore let him await the next parliament.

m.11 (pp.305b–306a)

Petition of Gruffydd de la Pole regarding his ejection from Powys in Wales.

Answer is made etc.: Inasmuch as many of the great lords, prelates and others are not now at this parliament, and those who are here do not wish to undertake judging a matter concerning the agreement [previously made] without the assent of all, it is decided that this business is to stay until the next parliament and that there should then be done with the assent of all what ought to be done therein.

[9] 25 June 1315.

m.20d (p.326b)

Petition of Eleanor de Percy regarding the custody of the manor of Pocklington, which her husband, Henry de Percy, held of the king by socage.

Answer is made: let the petition be delivered to the treasurer and barons of the exchequer and let them examine the inquisitions returned into chancery after Henry de Percy's death, and let these inquisitions be shown in the exchequer; and let the books and memoranda of the exchequer be likewise examined to find out what was wont to be done in the case of the said petition; and let John of Doncaster, who now holds the manor, be summoned and be put to answer on the matters contained in the petition. And after discussion there on the petition, let the whole business be brought back before the great council.

m.21d (p.327b)

Petition of the burgesses of St. Albans: they hold the town directly from the king and, like other burgesses of the realm, they ought to come as in times past to the king's parliaments, when these happen to be summoned, to do all their services to the king. The names of the burgesses who come on behalf of St. Albans to the king's parliaments are always enrolled in the rolls of chancery. Nevertheless the sheriff of Hertfordshire, at the instigation of the abbot of St. Albans, has refused to return the names of the burgesses as he is in duty bound.

Answer is made by the council: let the rolls etc. of chancery be examined as to whether or not the aforesaid burgesses were accustomed to come in the time of the king's ancestors, and then, after summoning those who should be summoned if necessary, let justice thereon be done them.

v

Duchy of Lancaster, Royal Charters, 10/217

Edward by the grace of God king of England, lord of Ireland and duke of Aquitaine, to our dear and faithful Sir Hugh de Neville, greeting. Whereas by assent of the prelates, earls and barons of our realm we have had this our parliament continued until Three Weeks after Easter next[10] for the answering of petitions and other business concerning our said parliament, for these could not be accomplished before the said Feast on account of the shortness of time and because we and the good people of

---

[10] 13 April 1315.

our council were greatly occupied with the ordering of our affairs regarding Scotland, we command and charge you, firmly enjoining you that you are to be with us at Westminster at Three Weeks after Easter in order to accomplish the aforesaid business. And you shall in no way neglect this as you love us and the welfare of our whole realm. Given under our privy seal at Westminster on the fourteenth day of March in the eighth year of our reign.[11]

vi

Ancient Correspondence, vol. LXI, no. 46

Edward by the grace of God king of England, lord of Ireland and duke of Aquitaine, to our dear clerk, Robert of Clitheroe, our escheator beyond the river Trent, greeting. Inasmuch as the prelates of our realm have, among other things, requested us at this last parliament of ours that we should be kind enough to grant on behalf of ourselves and our heirs to the chapters and convents of cathedral churches and houses of religion of our realm and to their successors, whose temporalities are in your custody in the time of vacancies, the custody of the said temporalities for as long as they remain in our hands and in the hands of our heirs by reason of the aforesaid vacancies in return for a certain payment to us and our heirs at every vacancy in the aforesaid churches and houses, reserving to us and our heirs fees and advowsons during the said vacancies, and we have a great desire to do for the said prelates whatever we can in due manner, we order you to arrange without delay to summon the bishops, deans and chapters, abbots and priors, of all the cathedral churches and houses of religion within your bailiwick, whose custody pertains to you in the time of vacancies, that they should send proxies with sufficient authority to Westminster at Three Weeks of Easter now approaching, to which day we have for certain reasons adjourned our parliament, in order to speak finally on this business with us and with the good men of our council on whether they consider it should be done. And inform us then distinctly and openly which bishops, deans, chapters, abbots and priors you have caused to be summoned thereon. And have this letter there at the said Three Weeks. Given under our privy seal at Westminster on the fourteenth day of March in the eighth year of our reign.

Endorsed: The archbishop and the dean and chapter of York, the bishops and priors of Durham and Carlisle, the abbots of St. Mary's of York, of Selby and Whitby, and the priors of Repton, Lenton near Nottingham and of Newstead Abbey in Sherwood have been notified in accordance with the terms of this writ.

[11] 14 March 1315.

vii

Ancient Correspondence, vol. XLII, no.36

To Walter of Norwich, baron of the exchequer of our lord the king, John of Enfield shows his complaint against Walter Crepyn, the late sheriff of Middlesex[12] on this ground: whereas the said John was chosen on behalf of the whole county of Middlesex to go to the lord king's parliament at York in the eighth year of his reign[13] so that, allowing for going and staying and returning, there was a period of twenty-eight days and, at four shillings a day, the sum involved came to £5. 12s. And the sheriff received instructions from our lord the king to levy this money for his expenses. And he has levied it and withheld it, and for this John prays grace and redress.

And furthermore, whereas the said John was chosen on behalf of the whole county of Middlesex to be in our lord the king's parliament at Westminster in the same year,[14] and for his stay, allowing four shillings a day, the sum amounts to £8. 8s.[15] And the aforesaid Walter Crepyn, the then sheriff, had a writ from our lord the king to levy this money. And he has levied it and withheld it, and for this John prays grace and remedy.

viii

Exchequer Parliament Roll, no.20, m.4d

[*Rot. Parl.*, i. 353-55]

A difficult case concerning the inheritance of the late earl of Gloucester. There was no doubt that his estate ought to be divided among his three sisters, provided it was not true, as had been suggested, that the countess of Gloucester was pregnant and the earl was the father of the unborn child.

And the chancellor and the justices, having examined the inquisitions and having had careful discussion thereon with others of the council summoned there, wrote back to the king that they dared not settle the business and could not give the king advice about it without the

---

[12] He is not among the sheriffs of Middlesex given in the *List of Sheriffs*, p.201, but John of Enfield and Walter Crepyn were elected as knights for Middlesex for the parliament of 9 September 1314, and John of Enfield and Richard of Batchworth for the parliament of Hilary 1315.

[13] 9 September 1314.

[14] Hilary 1315.

[15] This covers 42 days. The official dates for this parliament are 20 January-9 March 1315, i.e. 49 days. It was adjourned until 13 April (above, p.325) and was still in session on 30 April (Sayles, *King's Bench*, IV. 64).

agreement of the magnates of the realm because the matter was difficult and rarely encountered . . . . And at last, after the business had been discussed, because those present dared not for these reasons settle it, it was agreed that the lands and tenements should be committed to reputable men, to be kept in the aforesaid form until the Octave of Trinity next, unless in the meantime a parliament or an assembly of the magnates of the realm should be held . . . . Afterwards, at a Fortnight after Easter in the tenth year etc.[16] in an assembly of prelates and magnates of the realm, at the king's command the reverend father Walter, archbishop of Canterbury, primate of all England, recorded before the king's council at Westminster that the king had instructed him that he, in the place and with the authority of the king, was to summon prelates, nobles and others of the king's council in London and that they were to examine the matter carefully among themselves and let the king know what he ought to do further for the heirs and co-sharers on their petition thereon by the principles of justice and in accordance with the law and custom of his kingdom. For that reason, before the archbishop and other prelates, earls, barons, the chancellor, the treasurer, the justices of both benches, the chancellor and barons of the exchequer, the clerks of chancery and others of the king's council, the whole process was recited and scrutinised and the fullest disputation and discussion was held thereon. And some inquisitions, taken and returned into chancery a full year after the day of the earl's death concerning some defects contained in previous inquisitions, were also inspected and examined. And it was found from them that Eleanor, Margaret and Elizabeth were the earl's nearest heirs and of full age.

ix

Exchequer Parliament and Council Proceedings, file 2, no.5

To those entering upon this mighty sea may God order the beginning, manage the middle and see to the end. For truly the Gascon business is like a mighty sea, full of shipwrecks, and has no port of safety. Therefore be it known that on the Morrow of All Souls in the thirteen hundred and fourteenth year of the lord,[17] when some of the council of our lord the king were assembled by writ at Westminster, what had been done and accomplished in the previous parliament of Paris last held was there expounded by J. and H. and R.[18] the deputies for Gascon business, and after some grievances relating to the decrees of the French court had been recounted, it seemed to several of the council that such grievances ought

[16] 17 April 1317.
[17] 3 November 1314
[18] John Abel, Henry of Canterbury and Richard Burton.

to have been discussed in parliament and before the great council and by the greatest and wisest men because the business seemed to be of the greatest importance. Moreover, after the acts of the French court had been rehearsed with respect to the audience of judgement relating to the processes held concerning Périgord, it seemed as it were to all that this item ought to be dealt with in the presence of those who were present during the processes and initiated them because these men knew more about what was done. And so the matter was continued and delayed until the next parliament. And when the day for calling the parliament arrived, a petition from Richard Burton, a deputy for the Gascon business, was shown to our lord the archbishop and the lord chancellor containing the underwritten statement:

Because the day for the business of the duchy of Aquitaine in the present parliament of Paris is the Morrow of St. Matthew the Apostle,[19] as is shown by the statement and certification of the council of Gascony, and the said day is at hand, and our lord the king has been given an adjournment to that day to hear the sentences of condemnation on various processes as well as many grievances which were inflicted upon our lord the king in the last parliament against the liberties of the duchy, therefore the deputies for the Gascon business pray that the council will quickly come to a decision on these matters, for the nature of the business and the shortness of time do not brook delay.

And they said in their reply that, because such business is pressing and ought to be discussed in the presence of the earls, therefore from fear of offending them the business was delayed.

Afterwards on the arrival of the earls, which was on the Eve of the Purification,[20] after a few days had gone by, another document was put forward to the lord chancellor, and its tenor is contained in the schedule sewn hereto. And because the days thus passed by without anything being done and it is impossible that any deputies from England could arrive on the day for the business of the duchy, it therefore seems that, saving a better judgement, what appears below should be sent.

> A detailed list of instructions and interesting guide-lines for further action, with attached documents.

It is expedient that some notification should be given to the earls about the deliberations on the said business, once they have been reached, because the matter is one of the greatest importance to the king and business is now directed and carried through by their advice, and already on account of their absence the said matter has been frequently delayed through excuses made by the great men of the king's council.

[19] 22 September 1314.
[20] 1 February 1315.

PARLIAMENT AT LINCOLN: Hilary 1316

i

Exchequer, Various Accounts 376/7, fo.14

To John of Carlford

To John of Carlford, sent by the king from Clipston to Lincoln to repair and put right various houses and chambers there in readiness for the arrival of the king and queen in his parliament and others of their household lodging in them: for money paid by him for the purchase of timber, boards, nails, different kinds of laths and other things and for the wages of various carpenters, masons and others working to repair and clean up these houses before parliament began in January in the present year, as is shown by the detailed statement handed in by John to the wardrobe at Westminster on 10 March[1] . . . £10. 2s. 4d.

ii

Ancient Correspondence, vol. XXXV, no.143

To his very dear and honourable friend, Sir John Sandall, the chancellor of our lord the king, Hugh de Courtnay if it please him, greetings and friendly regards. Dear Sir, because we have been depressed since last Christmas onwards and thus still remain so that I am not able to travel, as Sir Stephen de Haccombe can tell you by word of mouth, may it please you, Sir, when you see it to be convenient, to be so good as to make my excuses to our lord the king for not coming to this parliament of Lincoln. And, Sir, as soon as I can travel, I will come at his pleasure where he pleases. May God, dear Sir, have you in His keeping.

iii

Exchequer Miscellanea, King's Remembrancer, Bundle 3
[Richardson and Sayles, *English Parliament in the Middle Ages*, XVIII. 107]

To his dear colleagues Hervey Stanton and other barons of our lord the king's exchequer, Walter of Norwich, greeting as to himself. My dear colleagues, inasmuch as Sir William Trussel, sheriff of Warwick and

---

[1] This is a Wardrobe Account for 1315–1316.

Leicester, is in attendance on my lord, the earl of Lancaster, who has now come to this parliament of Lincoln, and for that reason he cannot be in person at Westminster before you at this Fortnight after Candlemas to render his account for his bailiwick, I therefore pray you, sirs, that in place of Sir William you may receive to render that account William le Falconer, his attorney, whom I have accepted for this purpose for the time being, and that you should have this account audited graciously and as quickly as you can for my sake. And if I should owe something on this account, then suffer it until my arrival. Sirs, be with God. Written at Lincoln the tenth day of February.[2]

iv

Exchequer Miscellanea, King's Remembrancer, Bundle 3
[Richardson and Sayles, *loc. cit.*]

To his very dear friend Sir Walter of Norwich, our lord the king's treasurer, Richard Lovel, honour and reverence. Dear sir, I pray you, please, to be good enough to give special instructions that the business relating to me is to be finished before you go off to the parliament, both the account of the land of the Templars and the debts I owe the king and the king owes me, for which you received Reynold of Frome, my attorney, for which thank you very much, and that you should be kind enough to be helpful, gracious and well-disposed to me in the aforesaid business in making reasonable allowances as you promised me, and that you should kindly give me a respite for the debt which I shall be found owing as regards our lord the king until I have spoken to you at the parliament, so that my attorney may not be challenged concerning it but that he may come to me to notify me about how much I shall be in the king's debt, and I will free myself from it and pay part at Easter, God willing, without delay. Kindly do so much, dear sir, for my sake, and know that you have my thanks for it. To God, dear sir, that He may have you in His keeping.

---

[2] 10 February 1316. The king had on 8 January 1316 informed the exchequer that Trussel could not be present to render his accounts and ordered an adjournment (L.T.R. Memoranda Roll, no.86 (9 Edward II), m.52, Hilary Recorda).

v
Exchequer Parliament Roll, no.20, m.1
[*Rot. Parl.*, i. 350-55]

Memoranda of the parliament of Edward II, summoned and held at Lincoln a Fortnight after Hilary[3] in the ninth year of the king's reign, made by William Airmyn, clerk of the king's chancery, nominated and specially deputed for this purpose by the king.

On Wednesday, that is on the Morrow of the Fortnight after Hilary, the king entered a chamber in the house of the dean of Lincoln, where he was then lodging, among the prelates, earls and others who were there and he caused it to be announced in public by William Inge, one of the king's justices of the common bench, that the king greatly desired that the aforesaid parliament, summoned on account of various important business concerning him and the state of his realm, and particularly his land of Scotland, as mentioned in the summons of parliament, should be held with all the haste that could be conveniently made, and that the aforesaid business and other matters to be dealt with in the parliament should be similarly speeded up, adding that the king had great consideration for the fact that the prelates, earls and others had come there from distant parts and that their stay there, if it were long, would become tiring and burdensome to them on account of the lack of food which was more serious these days than it used to be previously.[4] Nevertheless, because Thomas, earl of Lancaster, and some other magnates of the realm, by whose counsel the king wished to proceed in the said important business, had not yet arrived, the king wished to postpone setting forth that business until these nobles had come. Yet despite this he charged the prelates, earls and others who were then and there present to meet there every day and continue the parliament and deal with other business until, as is said, the absent nobles came. And John Sandall, the chancellor, was told that he was to receive the proxies and excuses of prelates and others who had been summoned to the parliament and had not come, and that he and others whom the king would associate with him were to examine them and to allow adequate excuses provided those excused had proctors with sufficient authority, and that the names of those who neither came nor sent excuses nor appointed proctors were to be reported to the king so that he could act thereon as he ought to do. And the king associated with the chancellor for this purpose Walter of Norwich, the treasurer of England, and the

---

[3] 27 January 1316.
[4] A reference to the great famine throughout Western Europe.

aforesaid William Inge.

It was agreed the same day that petitions should be received and expedited, as was wont to be done previously at other parliaments, and that they should be received up to the Morrow of the Purification of the Blessed Mary next and on that Morrow.[5] And Robert of Ashby, clerk of chancery, and Adam of Limber, one of the remembrancers of the exchequer, were nominated to receive the petitions relating to England; and master Edward of London, clerk of chancery, and master William of Maldon, one of the king's chamberlains of his exchequer, to receive the petitions relating to Gascony, Wales, Ireland and Scotland. And a proclamation was made to that effect. Afterwards the chancellor and the treasurer and the justices of both benches were charged that they should cause the business, which was pending before them in their courts and which they could not determine outside parliament, to be set down briefly in writing and referred to the parliament so that what ought to be done could there be done.

On the Thursday following it was agreed to proceed with petitions until the arrival of the earl of Lancaster and other nobles similarly absent, and John, bishop of Norwich, John bishop of Chichester, and Roger bishop of Salisbury, Edward Deyncourt, Philip de Kyme, John de Lisle, one of the barons of the exchequer, Henry le Scrope, one of the justices of the bench, and Robert of Barlby, clerk of chancery, were nominated to hear and expedite the petitions relating to England. And Henry, bishop of Winchester, Walter, bishop of Exeter, and John, bishop of Bath and Wells, the aforesaid William Inge, master Roger of Rothwell, Richard of Plumstock, Thomas of Charlton, and Henry of Canterbury, clerks, the petitions relating to Gascony and the Channel Isles. And Ralph fitz William, master William of Birston, archdeacon of Gloucester, master John Walwayn, escheator below the river Trent, John Bush, Philip de Turville and John de Lisle, clerks, and John of Mutford, one of the justices of assize, the petitions relating to Wales, Ireland and Scotland.

On the Saturday following Humphrey de Bohun, earl of Hereford, in the presence of the king and on his behalf, told the prelates then and there present that, with regard to the petitions that the prelates had presented to the king at another time on behalf of the state of the Church, those which had been adequately answered were to be observed and, where the answers were inadequate, they were to be corrected, and that an answer was to be given to those petitions to which there was as yet no answer, in accordance with what it seemed among the prelates and earls and the king's council should be done on behalf of the state of the king and of his realm and of the Church.

---

[5] 3 February 1316.

On the Friday following[6] the magnates and the community of the realm granted the king in aid of his war in Scotland one footman, sound and physically fit, from every township in the realm save cities, boroughs and the king's demesne.

The citizens, burgesses, and the knights of the shires who came to the parliament granted the king, in aid of carrying out his war in Scotland, a fifteenth of the movables of the citizens, burgesses, and men of the cities, boroughs and demesne of the king within his realm.

vi

Chancery Parliament and Council Proceedings, file 5, nos.19, 20

The prelates, chapters, abbots and priors who are present at this parliament and the proctors of those absent, in the firm hope that Holy Church may have its liberties as it ought to have them without blemish, will grant our lord the king, in order to defend Holy Church and the realm against the Scots, enemies of Holy Church and the realm, an aid from their temporalities which are assessed for the tenth, such as the laity of the community will grant from their goods and chattels, to be paid after next Michaelmas at convenient terms, not by making a new assessment of their goods and chattels but in accordance with the assessment by which the tenth is paid and on the following conditions: that is to say, if our lord the king undertakes in person the journey in going to Scotland and remaining there as agreed in parliament; and if our holy father the pope has imposed or does impose anew any subsidy or tax on them and on the clergy of England, to be paid between now and next Michaelmas or thence for a year following, this grant is to be annulled; and if any of it is paid, it is to be allowed to those who have paid it in the said subsidy of the pope, whenever it shall be demanded; and also, if our lord the king does not go and remain in the defence of his land, as aforesaid, this grant is to be annulled; and the levy of this grant is to be made by each bishop within his diocese or by his commissaries, and what they cannot levy is to be levied by the king. And for doing these things and observing them in the abovesaid form and conditions, each bishop is to have on behalf of himself and those of his diocese letters patent under the king's great seal.[7]

---

[6] 20 February 1316. See *Parl. Writs*, II. ii. 195 b, for an action by a Dorset knight of the shire against the sheriff for not paying his expenses from 27 January to 20 February 1316.

[7] *Cal. Patent Rolls. 1313-17*, p.649.

vii
Ancient Correspondence, vol. XXXVII, no.33

From a letter from the king's envoy to the king of France.

And moreover, sire, my lord is so strongly pressed by his enemies of Scotland as well as in his land of Ireland and his marches of England that as yet he cannot well dispatch such important persons as he would like to assign to these matters and such as those who have been nominated for you. But, sire, he will, God willing, hold his parliament a Fortnight after Hilary next and there he will appoint the persons whom he wishes to act for him in this business.

viii
B.L., Cotton MS, Claud. E. VIII, fo.256-256b

Selected passages of this letter are given in Latin by Bridlington (*Chronicles of Edward I and Edward II*, ii. p.50), who stated that he had the letter in French before him but because it was long he had contented himself with giving excerpts. Stubbs failed to find the 'original of this important letter'.

A letter sent to King Edward the second after the Conquest by the earl of Lancaster

Dearest sire, we received two letters under your great seal from the hands of Master William Dean at Ashbourne in the Peak District on 21 July.[8] The tenor of one letter was that you had been given to understand that we and ours had made two assemblies and confederations in defiance of your prohibition and that we and ours had retained many people and seem likely to retain them without number and we are said to have made bonds thereon in disturbance of your peace and the destruction of your people. Dearest sire, please understand that we have made no assemblies in disturbance of your peace and in no way retained men against you or against your peace and, God helping us, the retinue we are forming is to maintain your peace and you, sire, and your suzerainty, and we shall keep the retinue every day for the said reason, for, sire, you have of late ordered us by your letter to be with you in your service at Newcastle upon Tyne on the Morrow of St. Lawrence,[9] and when that day comes we shall be constrained to come in the most powerful way we can, ready

---

[8] 21 July 1317.
[9] 11 August 1317.

to go to war with you in person, should we have life and health, against our enemies to the utmost of our ability. And, dearest sire, it seems to us most astonishing that you should reproach us for the retinue we are forming, inasmuch as you have ordered us to come to you with your service and, furthermore, with your service as powerfully as we can, for it seems to us that, after you youself, we ought to be more strongly equipped than any other for the common welfare of the realm and for your own honour, and we ought to maintain ourselves to the utmost of our ability.

And, dearest sire, as for the other letter by which you have ordered us to be with you this Thursday on 21 July at Nottingham to discuss with you and some prelates and magnates and others of your council, who will there be found, the following matter: that the Scots, our enemies, have once more entered your kingdom, committing homicides, robberies, arsons and other damages without number, please have us excused for not coming on that day, for we are in no state to travel.

And furthermore, sire, you must remember that at your last parliament held at Lincoln,[10] inasmuch as the governance of your realm was in the hands of incompetent men, you agreed that the archbishop of Canterbury, the bishops of Llandaff, Chichester, Norwich, and Salisbury, the earls of Pembroke, Hereford, Arundel, Richmond and we, along with Sir Bartholomew Badlesmere, should ordain, by the advice of wise men sworn of your council, how your estate ought to be amended and the governance of your realm and of your household be better ordered and that incompetent men might be removed from you for ever and in no fashion kept in your service and that arrangements should be held firm and established. And thereupon we came to London where the wisest of your council were, and by their advice made[11] the most suitable arrangements for your household and the governance of your realm. And we sent you the articles thereof in writing by Sir Bartholomew Badlesmere and Master William Inge, and you have so far complied with none of these articles.

And, sire, it was found in the Ordinances made in the time of Archbishop Robert[12] whom God assoil, that some men who are with you were not suitable to stay beside you or in your service, wherefore it was ordained that you should have them removed from you and ousted from your service, and, sire, nothing has been done about it but you have held them dearer than they ever were before, and you have since taken others in addition to you who are of the same disposition, and every day

[10] Hilary 1316.
[11] Some words are missing in the original.
[12] Robert Winchelsey died 11 May 1313.

you give them of your substance so that little or nothing remains to you, and, sire, if you had kept these grants in your hands instead of thus wasting them, they would have placed you in a much better position in the business you have now to do; and the ordinances made in the time of Archbishop Robert you have in no way kept, and thereby the people are much grieved. And you made the prelates, earls and barons and all your ministers swear to keep the said Ordinances, and thereafter you confirmed by your letters that they were to be kept in all their articles, and these we and several others of your kingdom have in our possession, and nothing is kept. And, sire, you ought not to be surprised that we are not coming on that day, for the matters on which you wish to have our counsel, advice and assent, according to what you have told us, ought to be dealt with in full parliament and in the presence of the peers of the realm. To do this, sire, we are sworn. So, sire, you ought not to wish us to come in any way to discuss out of parliament the things which ought to be discussed in parliament, for this is against our oath and against your own doing. And, sire, inasmuch as you have informed us by your last command that the Scots have once again entered your land and thereupon you would like to have our counsel and our assent, we understand, sire, that you have made up your mind thereon at the time you sent your writs to us and to all the others of your kingdom who owe you service to be with you at Newcastle upon Tyne on the specified day. On that day we shall be there, God helping us, if we are alive and you are there. And, sire, if going to those parts requires greater haste, then move there, sire, when you please and we will follow you in honour of you and for the salvation of your land and your person and of your people. And, for God's sake, sire, make haste to do it. Written etc.

PARLIAMENT AT YORK: Michaelmas 1318

Writs had been issued for a parliament at Lincoln at Hilary, then on 12 March, then on 19 June 1318 but an attack from Scotland forced it to be abandoned (Ryley, Placita, 545; Cal. Close Rolls, 1313-18, p.619).

i
Exchequer Parliament Roll, no.21
[Cole, *Documents*, pp.1-46]

m.1d (page 4)

Of summoning the army

It is granted and agreed by the prelates, earls and barons that the king should have his army fully at Newcastle upon Tyne at the Octave of Trinity.

Of parliament

It is granted and in the same way agreed that the next parliament should be a Month after Easter at York or at Lincoln in accordance with the best possible advice between now and the time when it will be necessary to have the writs issued for summoning the said parliament and in accordance with the way affairs turn out between now and then.

m.3d (page 13)

The names of those who are appointed to hear the bills and petitions of England, Ireland and Wales, put forward in the parliament, and to answer the same, namely, the bishop of Winchester, the bishop of Worcester, the bishop of Carlisle, and Hugh de Courtnay, William Martin, John Botetourte, Robert of Barlby, Henry of Cliff, Gilbert of Tothby, Geoffrey Scrope, Roger de Beler. And to these Walter of Norwich and Henry Scrope shall be summoned when they can conveniently find time for this purpose.

For the petitions of Gascony are appointed the bishop of Coventry and Lichfield, the bishop of Exeter, and the bishop of Bath and Wells. And they shall summon master Richard of Burton to them when it please them.

m.4d (page 16)

Petition of Matthew of Crowthorne

On the petition of Matthew of Crowthorne it is shown the king that, whereas he was lately elected by the community of the county of Devon to come here to this parliament on behalf of that county, the sheriff of that county has now returned here the names of other knights, for which he prays redress.

Answer is made thus: Let him have a writ to the treasurer and barons of the exchequer to cause the under-sheriff to come to answer for his false return etc:

[1]To the council of our lord the king shows Matthew of Crowthorne that, whereas a writ had arrived in the county of Devon for having two knights come here at this parliament on behalf of the community of that county, the said Matthew was chosen by the bishop of Exeter and Sir William Martin with the assent of the other good people of the county, and presented to the sheriff in full county court and admonished to be at this parliament, and he was thereupon summoned by the sheriff for this purpose. But now, in deceit of him, Robert Bendyn, sheriff of the said county, has returned others in his place, against the will of the community, in order to do him this damage. And Matthew prays due redress thereon in order to have his expenses.[2]

Endorsed: As regards this petition let him have a writ to the treasurer and barons of the exchequer to have the under-sheriff come to answer for the aforesaid false return.[1]

m.5 (page 17)

Walter of Langton, bishop of Coventry and Lichfield, presented a written petition in this parliament, requesting that it should be read before the prelates, earls and barons in open parliament, and its tenor is as follows:

To our lord the king and his council shows Walter of Langton, bishop of Chester, that, whereas he was the chief executor of Edward, formerly

---

[1] This document was found by Madox in a bundle of petitions of 1317–18 in the Tower of London (B.L., Add. MS. 4492, fos.161–62).

[2] Crowthorne had been returned to represent Exeter and was present at this parliament and in this capacity paid two shillings a day. As a knight of a shire he would have got four shillings a day.

king of England of blessed memory, father of our present lord king, immediately after his death the present king had the bishop suddenly arrested and imprisoned and kept in prison for a year and a quarter without his being judicially indicted or appealed in contravention of the forms of law of the land and of the articles of the Great Charter, and he was a long time in that prison where none of his own people could come near him and where he knew nothing and could know nothing of what was being done outside it. And he was guarded by strangers of evil type and the guard was changed frequently. And in the meantime all his lands were seized and kept in our lord the king's hand, as well those belonging to his bishopric as those belonging to his lay fee, and all his movable property found within his said lands and elsewhere within and outside sanctuary was seized and destroyed by the servants of our present lord king to the sum of £20,000 and much more. And these matters are known and notorious throughout the realm of England and in various parts of the world. Wherefore he prays that the violence done to his body may be redressed in the eyes of God and the law and that proper restitution of the property taken from him may be made to his church and to himself.

This petition, immediately after it had been read before the prelates, earls and barons, was by their orders taken to the king and shown to him. And when the king had had discussion with some of his council on the matters contained in the petition, because the petition seemed obscure to the king and to some of the prelates, earls and barons and others of his council then attending him, the king ordered the bishop to be summoned before him, the magnates and others of his council to clarify his petition. And being thus summoned he came. And he was asked by the council whether or not the petition, which was then read before the bishop, had been presented by him, and he says that he well remembers handing that petition in to this parliament. And the council added that the bishop should further clarify the petition, especially since it seemed somewhat obscure to the king and all attending him, and if he thought anyone to be guilty of the charges contained in his petition he should have said so and given a precise basis to his action and he should not have neglected to do this, especially as the king was ready to dispense justice to him and to any others whomsoever who brought plaints in his court. He says that he cannot and will not mention anyone by name as guilty of those charges. For he says that in drawing up that petition he had the advice of some of his people who are not now in these parts. On being required further to say precisely whether he meant by that petition to burden the king or any other specific person with what is contained in the petition, he says that he has no idea whom to charge therewith. Therefore it is awarded that the bishop is to take nothing by that petition and the king is to go quit thereof. And as for the things which appear from the terms of the petition to redound to the king's dishonour, he is to go to the judgement of his peers.

m.8 (page 27)

Note that the undernoted petitions are handed over to William of Airmyn, clerk, appointed with others to deal with the business concerning Flemings and Englishmen.

m.9 (page 33)

Bathley

To the petition of William of Bathley, praying redress on this matter: whereas he had prosecuted on behalf of the king against the bishop of Norwich a certain writ called 'why he did not admit' (*quare non admisit*) for seven years or more, first before the justices of the bench and later in the king's bench, the justices say that they cannot proceed to judgement without the assent of the earls and barons in parliament, and this process is prolonged in contravention of the Ordinances.[3]

Reply is thus made: Let him have a writ to the justices that they are to proceed to render judgement as quickly as they can in accordance with the law etc., and if difficulty should arise whereby they cannot do so without more information, let them bring the record thereof into parliament according to the terms of the Ordinances etc.

ii

Exchequer Parliament and Council Proceedings, file 1, no.22, ms. 2, 3
[Richardson and Sayles, *Rotuli Parliamentorum Inediti*, 70-80]

This document stands quite unique among the parliamentary miscellanea that still survive. It contains lists of petitions presented at the Michaelmas parliament according to different categories: (a) those for the great council; (b) those for the king's personal consideration; (c) those concerning the king's debts; (d) those not fully expedited or 'sped' because of various difficulties; (e) those that had been expedited.

[3] Ordinances of 1311, c.29.

Before the great council

A list of twenty-four petitions, including:

Of the clerks of the king's chancery.
Of the lords of liberties and burgesses and citizens with respect to the maintenance of their liberties.
Two petitions on behalf of the clergy of the realm with respect to prohibitions.
Another petition regarding the extortions of the court of Rome.
Of Robert de Umfraville, earl of Angus.
Of Hugh Audley and Margaret, his wife.
Petition for ordaining greater certainty about the custody of the mints of London and Canterbury.
Petition concerning the corrodies granted by the king in various places and abbeys which ought not to be charged with them etc.

Before the king

A list of seventy or more petitions, including three from Scotland and four from Wales.

Petitions concerning debts demanded from the king

A list of nineteen petitions, including:

Of the merchants of England with respect to giving a loan on sacks of wool.

Petitions not fully expedited on account of various difficulties

A list of twenty-seven petitions, including:

Three petitions concerning the clerk of the market in the king's household.

A petition of the community of the county of Nottingham, asking for a perambulation to be made.

A petition concerning the merchants of Germany relating to a royal charter.

A petition of the archbishop of York with respect to having a port at Hull.

Two petitions of the clergy of England concerning prohibitions presented during judicial proceedings.

A petition of Hugh Audley and Margaret, his wife.

A petition of the merchants of England with respect to half a mark on a sack of wool.

The advice of the people concerning an ordinance against provisors etc.

A petition of the merchants of Germany, written to the earl of Lancaster.

Petitions expedited

Petitions handed to Robert of Ashby.
    118 petitions.
Handed to Henry of Edwinstowe
    Eleven petitions.
To Geoffrey of Welford
    Ten petitions, including the petition of Matthew of Crowthorne.
Handed to William de Cliff
    Four petitions.
To [Thomas of] Tinton
    Eight petitions.
To [Hugh de] Burgh
    Twelve petitions.
To [John of] Norton.
    Three petitions.
To [Thomas of] Bamborough
    Three petitions.
To William of Airmyn
    Two petitions.
To Richard of Nassington
    Eight petitions.
To William de Harlaston
    Two petitions.
To William of Barton
    Two petitions.

iiia
Exchequer Parliament and Council Proceedings, Roll 20
[Richardson and Sayles, *Rotuli Parliamentorum Inediti*, 66–68]

Process held before the council of King Edward, father of King Edward etc., on the petition which Hugh de Courtnay presented in the king's parliament at Westminster after the Octave of Hilary in the eighth year

> There follows the petition, as recorded on the parliament roll (*Rot. Parl.*, i. 334-6), seeking the Isle of Wight as his inheritance. What follows is not on the parliament roll.

Note that Robert of Ashby, clerk of chancery, who was appointed in the last parliament at Lincoln[4] to receive, read and enrol the petitions and plaints presented in the aforesaid parliament, sent this process under his seal into this parliament, held at York at Three Weeks after Michaelmas in the twelfth year,[5] at the instance of Hugh de Courtnay, and this process is continued in its present state until the next parliament because a final discussion of it could not be proceeded with in this parliament without more advice etc. And Hugh is adjourned there. And note that the said Robert sent this process into this parliament at York[6] by virtue of an answer made to a petition from Hugh, sewn to this roll, which was handed in in the present parliament.

iiib
Ancient Petition, no. E.712

The petition of Hugh de Courtnay

Endorsed: Let this petition be sent to Robert of Ashby, whose duty it was to receive bills and petitions presented in the parliament of Lincoln, which is referred to in this petition, so that he may inform himself about this business, and if the process thereon should lie in his possession, then he is to send back the whole of that process to the present parliament. Afterwards, after the petition with that process had been sent back, answer was made to it as appears below:
Because our lord the king cannot profitably proceed to a final discussion of the business herein contained without more deliberation and advice, the business is continued in its present state until the next parliament, and Hugh is thereon adjourned there.

[4] Hilary 1316.
[5] Michaelmas 1318.
[6] Easter 1319.

iiic
Chancery Warrants, file 316, no.18100

Edward by the grace of God king of England and of France and lord of Ireland to his dear clerk, David of Wooler, clerk of our rolls of chancery. We command you to have the rolls of parliament which were in the time of our grandfather and of our most dear lord and father (whom God assoil), searched for the petitions presented in the said parliaments by our dear and faithful Hugh de Courtnay, cousin and heir of Isabella de Forz, formerly countess of Devon, in connexion with the hereditary right he claims to have in the Isle of Wight and in the manor of Christchurch with the appurtenances in Hampshire. And after you have found the petitions you are to send us copies of them under your seal, together with the endorsements of them just as they were endorsed in the abovesaid parliaments. And do not neglect this. Given under our privy seal before Calais on the sixteenth day of February in the twenty-first year of our reign in England and eighth in France.[7]

iv
Ancient Petition, file 83, no.4106

Robert of Holywell, a chancery clerk, had been appointed at Midsummer 1307 to go to North Wales to pay the Welsh, who went on the king's service to Scotland, their wages. He asked for allowances when he presented his account and stated:

And this petition, and the other one which follows it,[8] were approved at the parliament of York after Michaelmas in the twelfth year[9] and endorsed by the hand of Sir Robert of Ashby, whom God assoil, as you will see later.

Dear Sirs, answer was made at another time to the abovesaid petitions and they were endorsed in the following manner:

Let the treasurer and the barons of the exchequer be instructed by writ in accordance with Robert's proposal to have someone of the exchequer appointed to hear his account for the whole of his time, and after seeing the letters Robert possesses, let justice be done him and reasonable allowances given according to what is contained in the first petition.

---

[7] 16 February 1347.
[8] A second petition relating to his visit to Ireland to solicit help against the Scots in 1310-11.
[9] Michaelmas 1318.

[10-]William de Harlaston saw the other petitions, previously answered, and the answer endorsed on them in the hand of Robert of Ashby in the aforesaid manner.[-10]

All this business, to which answer had been made at another time, is lost through Robert's illness and through the long stay of the chancery in the north.

Endorsed: Let it be done according to his petition and according to the answers made to his petitions at another time.

It is enrolled.

v

B.L., Additional MS. no.41612 (Cartulary of Ely Priory), fo.53
[Richardson and Sayles, *Rotuli Parliamentorum Inediti*, pp.68-70]

The petition made to the king by the bishop of Ely, that is John Hotham,
for a confirmation of the charters of Ely in his parliament at York
in the twelfth year of his reign

To our lord the king prays the bishop of Ely that it may please him that the charters of liberties, granted by his ancestors to the bishop's predecessors, may be rehearsed, granted and confirmed, with the clause that, if any article has fallen into disuse, it can be used from this time forward. And that the franchises which he and his predecessors have had and used in the past and claimed and been allowed in the eyre can be affirmed by charter and confirmed in the aforesaid form.

Again, whereas the bishop and his predecessors have had the chattels of felons and of fugitives in their lands and their fees wherever they may be, that it may please our lord the king to grant to the bishop that he and his successors, by themselves or through their bailiffs, can seize, hold and have the said chattels so that no sheriff, bailiff or any other minister may meddle as soon as the felons are indicted and the chattels of fugitives forfeited.

Again, whereas the bishop and his predecessors have for all time had the return of writs and all the aforesaid franchises in their half-hundred of Mitford in the county of Norfolk, that it may please our lord the king to grant that the bishop and his successors may have a coroner chosen in the said half-hundred by the king's writ as usual.

Let there be appointed the justices, the king's serjeants, and two of the wisest and best informed clerks of the chancery to view the charters mentioned in the petition, and let them consider the articles contained in

[10-10] This is a note scribbled in another hand on the petition.

them and which clauses have been enjoyed and which not, and let them consider whether a confirmation of these charters is to be granted or not, and whether or not the clauses not in use can be granted to be properly used henceforth without causing prejudice to the crown, and let them report their advice thereon to the king. And as for the second and the third petition let them discuss them and likewise report their opinion. And as for the coroner, let an inquiry be made in due manner etc. and returned into the chancery and, if it is found that this will not harm the king or anyone else, let it be granted and done by grace of the king.[11]

It seems to the justices, clerks and serjeants that the first point asked for may well be granted, with the clause that the items in disuse may henceforth be in use.

As for the articles claimed and allowed in any eyre, it seems to them that what has been recorded as allowed can be put in the charter.

It pleases the king that these things be done by fine.[12] And that, if it pleases the king and the magnates, this should be done on behalf of the king and the lords who have such franchises and that it would be greatly profitable to him and to them if they could seize and have such chattels soon. For through the delays arising in an eyre great damage results to the king and to them in many ways, and a petition in parliament was lately presented thereon on the people's behalf.

Then the king,[13] by the advice of the aforesaid justices, serjeants and clerks who have diligently looked at and examined the details of the said charters and furthermore the clauses affecting these petitions in every detail as they have been charged to do, and with the assent and advice of the magnates and others of his council, agrees to grant of his grace that the bishop may have confirmation of his charters with the clause that, if there has been neglect in the use of any of the items contained therein, he can have them in use henceforward etc. As for his franchises, claimed and allowed in an eyre, the king agrees that what is recorded as allowed may be put in a charter for him. As for the chattels of fugitives and felons he is in agreement with the said assent and advice and it pleases him that the bishop and his successors should have them seized and have and hold them in accordance with the terms of his petition. And as for having a coroner etc., it pleases the king that there should be an inquiry made in the above-written manner, and if it is found that it is not to the damage etc., that he may have one as requested.

[11] This is the advice given by the committee to which the petition was referred and it is to be found on Ancient Petition, no. E.459, where it is cancelled as an indication that it was not to be enrolled.
[12] An interpolated decision.
[13] These are the decisions made on the advice given.

vi

Coram Rege Roll, no.240 (Easter 1320), m.88

[Sayles, *King's Bench*, IV, 94–95]

An action brought against the mayor and bailiffs of Lincoln for failure to pay the expenses at two shillings a day of the two citizens who attended the parliament at York at Michaelmas 1318. The defendants made the following statement:

It was agreed between the community of the city and Thomas Gamel and Henry Stoil in the hall of pleas at Lincoln, before they left the city on the aforesaid business, that the community should pay them two shillings a day, that is to say, twelve pence to each of them for their expenses, and, when they came back, twenty shillings for their work, and they have received full payment of that money, as well for expenses as for their work, except for sixteen shillings, and the community is ready to pay them the sixteen shillings.[14]

---

[14] The parliament lasted from 20 October to 9 December, i.e. 51 days.

PARLIAMENT AT YORK: Easter 1319

i

Register of Abbey of St. James, Northampton, fos. 222, 223
[*Parl. Writs*, II. ii. 199 f.]

The abbot of St. James without Northampton was summoned to parliament at York a Month after Easter, 1319.[1] Because he was ill he appointed a proctor on 2 May 1319.

And because neither the abbot nor his predecessors had ever before been summoned to parliament, the proctor asked in chancery whether he had been summoned through a single writ or by a register. And the rolls of chancery were examined and the name of the abbot was found enrolled among those to be summoned to parliament, and by that enrolment he will always be summoned among the others to every parliament. And the proctor in effect requested William of Airmyn, the then keeper of the rolls, that the abbot's name should be deleted inasmuch as it had never been enrolled before, and the abbot holds nothing of the king in chief nor by barony but holds only in pure and perpetual alms. And the keeper replied that he had no power or wish to make cancellations in any way in the rolls of chancery, and this seemed to the proctor harsh and unjust. Nor did the proctor in his capacity as a proctor wish to appear at all because in consequence the abbot would ever afterwards have to appear in person or by proxy; nor did he wish to excuse his absence on the grounds of illness because it would then seem that he would have appeared there if he could; nor yet could he have him excused in parliament that he should not have come on the ground that he had never been summoned or that he does not hold by barony or hold of the king in chief etc., because he would then be held to be contumacious since all people in the kingdom, no matter from whom or how they hold their lands, must come at the king's summons. But he drew up thereon a bill to be delivered to Thomas, then earl of Lancaster, and to be expounded by that earl in common council in order to obtain redress. And the tenor of that bill follows.

The bill recapitulates the proctor's arguments.

Afterwards it seemed to the proctor that, if he had pursued such a bill in common council, he would have slandered the chancellor and the

---

[1] 6 May 1319.

keeper of the rolls for making such an enrolment, and the chancellor and the others, in order to favour their own side and avow their deed, would say that the abbot had been properly summoned and that it was right that he should be summoned, and inquisitions, losses, expenses, and many other perils could arise therefrom. For that reason the proctor did not deliver that bill but drew up and handed another bill to the chancellor and his clerks. And the tenor of that bill is as follows:

The abbot of St. James without Northampton is newly enrolled in the king's chancery among those who are to be summoned to parliament, and he does not hold by barony or of the king in chief but only in pure and perpetual alms, and that abbot or his predecessors were never enrolled in chancery or summoned up till now to parliament, wherefore the abbot prays redress.

To deal with this bill the chancellor, along with his chancery council, decided that the abbot's name was to be removed from the chancery register, and so the abbot was excused in the sight of many onlookers. But because the abbot or his successors could at another time at the instigation of ill-disposed persons be perchance enrolled and in consequence summoned, the proctor set down the tenor of the decision in writing by way of evidence.

This decision was made under the eye of John of Hotham, bishop of Ely, the king's chancellor, William of Airmyn, the then keeper of the rolls, Robert of Barlby, master Henry of Cliff, Roger of Sutton, master Edmund of London, Geoffrey of Welford, Robert of Ashby, Adam of Broom, William of Leicester, and other clerks of chancery and other clerks of sundry courts of the king and his realm etc.

ii

Ancient Correspondence, vol. LV. no. 46

To the most excellent prince, the lord Edward, by the grace of God the illustrious king of England, lord of Ireland and duke of Aquitaine, John by the same grace bishop of Winchester, brother Peter, abbot of Beaulieu, and John de St. John, submission and honour. We have recently received with due respect the orders of your Excellency in these words:

The Scots had invaded the country and it had been decided in the last parliament that the king was to summon his army to Newcastle upon Tyne to defeat them. The king had now come to the conclusion that he required assistance at sea, both to cut off supplies to the enemy and to protect supplies from abroad to his own forces. The bishop and the others were therefore to ask the communities of the cities, boroughs, townships and ports of Hampshire to provide ships, adequately equipped with men-at-arms, foodstuffs and other necessities for three or four months at their expense and afterwards at the king's expense. The letter was dated 20 March 1319. The king's commissioners accordingly summoned the aforesaid communities before them from 27 April 1319 onwards and received separate answers to their demands but very little satisfaction. The following extract from a long report, sent to the king on 2 May 1319, is of particular interest.

On the Feast of the Apostles Philip and James[2] we caused to come before us at Winchester the mayor and community of Winchester and twelve upright and law-worthy men from every borough and township of the whole county of Hampshire who can reply on behalf of those boroughs and townships upon the matters expounded to them by us on your Serene Highness's part and required of them and do what ought to be done to the honour and profit of your realm. And on that day the mayor and community of your city of Winchester handed us this answer by indenture to the request made to them by us: The mayor and citizens of Winchester offer the king forty quarters of corn for victualling ships. And because some boroughs and townships of the county are part of your ancient demesne and liable to tallage at your will, whilst some of the county territory are liable to taxation, we have by the advice of distinguished men present with us separated the latter from the former and asked each of them to pay the aforesaid subsidy for themselves.

And the whole community of the county thus replied by Richard Fromund that the greatest and ablest men of the county had been summoned to your parliament at York,[3] in which, as they firmly believed, it was necessary for a common tax to be arranged and granted throughout the whole of your kingdom in aid of your war, and they were prepared to pay this subsidy along with the others of the kingdom, and nothing else. Furthermore, they said that the county of Hampshire was near to places by the sea and bordered on them and, if by the menaces of the enemies of you and your realm these places should happen to be molested by enemy attacks, it would be necessary for them in defence of that region to risk not only their goods but their bodies.

And the rest of your boroughs of the county gave individual answers.

Alton, Andover and Basingstoke by Nicholas of Holt, William of Rotherfield, John Chamberlain and John Pipwit. They answer that, when the king wishes to tallage his boroughs and demesnes, they will

---

[2] 1 May 1319.
[3] Summoned on 20 March for 6 May 1319.

readily pay the subsidy due, but as for the aforesaid request they have not the wherewithal to do anything. They also say that the boroughs of the most serene lady, Queen Isabella, your consort, are mentioned, and her advice would be required in the case of such requests.

The borough of Alresford answers by Robert le Arblaster the same way as those of Alton had done, and they say that they are the men of the bishop of Winchester and were never accustomed to pay any such subsidy.

The borough of Stockbridge answers by Robert le Marshal and Thomas le Chapman that they are the men of Henry of Lancaster and, as often as the king tallages his demesne lands throughout the realm, they should be tallaged by their lord and, because they are few and poor, as is there testified, they can pay no subsidy.

The borough of Odiham refused to appear before us, although summoned by the sheriff, or to make any answer.

In witness thereof we have caused this letter to be sent to your Excellency. Given at Winchester the second day of May.[4]

---

[4] 2 May 1319.

PARLIAMENT AT YORK: Hilary 1320

Exchequer Parliament Roll, no.20, m.3
[*Rot. Parl.* i. 352]

Hugh le Despenser

Hugh le Despenser the younger was accused by Gilbert Tothby and Geoffrey Scrope, the king's serjeants, in the king's bench, of this: that on Sunday before Lent[1] in the king's presence and in the then parliament he assaulted John de Ros, knight, in the cathedral church of St. Mary's, Lincoln, and beat him, that is to say, striking him with his fist until he fetched blood, and inflicted other outrages upon him in contempt of the king of a thousand pounds and in breach of the peace and the terror of the people then in the parliament. And if Hugh wishes to deny it, they are ready to prove it on the king's behalf etc. And Hugh first of all says that he did not essay anything to the king's contempt or the breach of the peace or the terror of his people in the said parliament, and he is ready to prove etc. Afterwards Hugh acknowledged before the king that in the aforesaid church on the said Sunday he had accused John of arranging for Ingelram Berenger, one of Hugh's knights, to be arrested, and he asked him to deal more gently with Ingelram in the matter of this arrest. And John took offence at Hugh's words, charging him with outrageous insults, and he taunted him with scandalous words and, putting his hand on his dagger, he threatened him and shouted at him as if he meant to strike him with his dagger. And lest John should strike him, Hugh stretched out his hand between himself and John, and in doing so he touched John on his face, but he does not believe that he did anything in contempt of the king etc. or the terror of the people. And as regards this he puts himself on the king's grace. And because what was done seemed to be in breach of the peace etc., therefore he is committed to the marshal's custody until etc. Afterwards Robert de Umfraville, the earl of Angus [and five others] undertook to have Hugh in person before the king at the king's command to do therein what the king should decide in this matter with the advice of his council, and John was released on this undertaking.[2]

Afterwards at his parliament summoned at York in the Octave of Hilary in the thirteenth year of his reign the king of his special grace pardoned Hugh le Despenser the aforesaid trespass and ordered the process, set out above, to be annulled. And it was so annulled.[3]

[1] 22 February 1316.
[2] John de Ros was similarly charged and released on bail.
[3] Note the wrapper on a file of petitions: 'Petitions before the king and the great council, to which no answer was given in the parliament assembled at York in 1320' (Ancient Petition, no.E.1389).

PARLIAMENT AT WESTMINSTER: Michaelmas 1320

i

Chancery Parliament and Council Proceedings, file 43, no.20
[Richardson and Sayles, *Rot. Parl. Inediti*, p.87]

Our lord the king, at his last parliament at York after the Octave of Hilary last,[1] showed to the magnates of his realm who were there assembled how he had earlier fixed a day with the king of France to be at next Mid-Lent[2] in the parts of France to do him homage for the land he holds of him overseas and, because time went by so quickly and the road was long, he was not able to remain there to complete all the business relating to the said parliament if he wished to get on his way, and with the assent of the magnates he appointed parliament to meet at Westminster at the Octave of Trinity following[3] to complete the business which remained over at the said parliament of York and to accomplish the other business of the realm concerning parliament. And afterwards, on account of various hindrances and excuses on the part of the king of France, the day of Mid-Lent was useless and there was a continuation from time to time until the Nativity of St. John the Baptist,[4] and at that time he was at Amiens and did his homage and his other business well and faithfully, thank God, and consequently for these reasons he could not hold the parliament at Westminster at the Octave of Trinity. Therefore our lord the king, on his return to England, having a great desire and longing to do all the things that pertain to a good lord to the profit of his realm and of his people, arranged to hold his parliament here at Westminster at this Octave of Michaelmas[5] to the greater welfare of his realm and at the most suitable time for his people after the August season, and our lord the king wishes and charges you all, prelates, earls and barons and others who are here assembled at this parliament, to proceed with the business of this parliament as is fitting.

ii

Exchequer Parliament Roll, no.23
[*Rot. Parl.*, i. 365]

First of all, on Monday the king, attended by Walter, archbishop of Canterbury, John bishop of Norwich, chancellor of England, Walter

[1] 20 January 1320.
[2] 9 March 1320.
[3] 1 June 1320.
[4] 24 June 1320.
[5] 6 October 1320.

bishop of Exeter, the king's treasurer, and Stephen bishop of London, John bishop of Ely and Walter bishop of Coventry and Lichfield, Aymer of Valence, earl of Pembroke, Edmund of Woodstock, the king's brother, and some other magnates and nobles of his realm, decided how the petitions to be presented in parliament were to be received and expedited. And in the presence of the said prelates, magnates, nobles and others the king ordained and commanded that Adam of Limber and William of Harlaston, clerks, were to receive all the petitions of England and Wales to be handed in at the parliament.

And the prelates and others, given below, were to answer these petitions namely:

The bishop of London	William de Herle
The bishop of Coventry and Lichfield	John of Stonor
The bishop of Chichester	Robert of Barlby
The abbot of St. Albans	Master Henry of Cliff
John de Sumery	Geoffrey le Scrope
Richard de Grey	

It was likewise agreed that master Edmund of London and master Henry of Canterbury, clerks, were to receive all the petitions of Gascony, Ireland and the Channel Isles to be handed in at the parliament.

And the prelates and others, given below, were to answer these petitions, namely,

The bishop of Bath and Wells	Guy Ferre
The bishop of Worcester	Walter of Friskney
The bishop of Hereford	Master Jordan Morant
The abbot of Ramsey	Master Richard of Burton
Hugh de Courtnay	Gilbert of Tothby
William Martin	

The complaint of the whole community of the realm upon the trespasses and felonies committed in the realm[6]

In this parliament, among the other petitions presented to the king, there was handed in a petition from the knights, citizens and burgesses, who were there on behalf of the counties, cities and boroughs of his realm, whereby they alleged that outrageous felonies and trespasses had been done and unlawful leagues and confederacies formed in every county of the realm by trespassers and disturbers of his peace in breach of his peace to the terror of his people, and they prayed that proper redress should be shown therein. Whereupon our lord the king, at the supplication of the

[6] *Rot. Parl.*, i. 371.

knights, citizens and burgesses, ordained the form to be observed by the king's justices, appointed by his council to inquire into such felonies, trespasses, leagues and confederacies and to hear and determine them, as below:

The details of the arrangements follow.

And it is agreed by the king, with the counsel of the prelates, earls, barons and other learned men in the parliament, that the justices are to receive the plaints of all and sundry who wish to complain before them with respect to trespasses committed against them in breach of the king's peace, and they are to hear and determine them, and they are to do them justice by procedure by bill just as they would by the king's original writs, in accordance with the law and custom of the realm.

The men of Holderness[7]

To the petition of the men of Holderness, complaining that John Goldney and Robert Romayn, appointed by the king to make various purveyances for the king's household in the parts of Holderness during the king's stay at his parliament in the twelfth year of his reign,[8] took various prises from various people in the aforesaid parts for the king's use up to the sum of eighty-three pounds, taken from persons specifically named in the bill handed in thereon, and for this they claimed an allowance in the wardrobe and they paid them nothing, whereof they pray redress.

Answer is made thus: let the steward of the king's household and the keeper of the wardrobe come etc. and let the business, mentioned in the petition, be expounded to them so that they can apply such redress in this matter as is appropriate and fitting on behalf of the complainants.

Afterwards, when what had been done was explained to the king, master Robert of Baldock informed the auditors of petitions on his behalf that it pleased the king that these petitions, and others like them, should be handed to Roger of Northburgh, so that, when the parties had been summoned before the steward of the household and himself, they should cause such redress to be made in this respect as ought of right to be done etc.

---

[7] *Rot. Parl.*, i. 377.
[8] The parliament at York at Hilary 1320.

John of Eriswell[9]

To the petition of John of Eriswell, complaining that the justices, before whom a plea of trespass is pending between him and the prior of Ely, are causing too great delay in rendering justice etc., and furthermore they are putting men of the household who bear the prior's robes on the inquisition pending between the prior and John. And he prays redress thereof. Answer is made thus: As regards not rendering a judgement in the case still pending before the justices, let them be stimulated by a writ to proceed to judgement etc. And if such a difficulty is found in the process that they cannot proceed to render etc., then let them have the record and process before the king and his council in this parliament according to what was ordained at another time in such a case.[10] And as for his asking for a writ to the coroners etc., let him speak his challenges before the justices in the event of an inquisition and let justice be done him there according to the discretion of the justices.[11]

iii
Chancery Parliament and Council Proceedings, file 5, no. 4

This is a label which has become detached from a file of petitions in chancery.

William of Harlaston's petitions of the king's parliament at Westminster at the Octave of Michaelmas in the fourteenth year, which were answered by the auditors of petitions: delivered into chancery to be expedited.

iva
Ancient Petition, no. 4273

A petition of the bishop of London and the dean and chapter of St. Paul's, requesting that the exchequer should make allowance for amercements of their tenants, the chattels of felons and fugitives, and other franchises of theirs.

Endorsed: The treasurer and barons of the exchequer are ordered by a chancery writ on behalf of the bishop and the dean and chapter named

---

[9] *Rot. Parl.*, i. 383a
[10] Ordinances of 1311, c.29 (above p.305).
[11] It is of interest to notice that the petition in 1320 (Ancient Petition, no.174), addressed 'to our lord the king and to his council' by the past and present sheriffs of Devon, is enrolled in the parliament roll (*Rot. Parl.*, i. 381*b*) with the rubric 'The community of Devon', while a petition enrolled as from 'the community of Kent' is addressed 'to the lords of the council of our lord the king' (Ancient Petition, no.147).

herein that, as regards what is contained in the petition, they should cause them to be dealt with in accordance with the terms of the charters and as was wont to be done hitherto.[12]

ivb
Ancient Petition, no.169

This is an exact duplicate of the petition referred to above, save for variations in spelling.

Endorsed: There is another general petition in common on behalf of the community of the realm.

ivc
Ancient Petition, no.3926

A petition to the king and council from the archbishops, bishops, abbot, priors, earls, barons and all others who claim to have fines and amercements and the profits and chattels of felons by virtue of charters of the king's ancestors: they ask that such may be allowed in the exchequer and that their tenants be acquitted of any demands made by sheriffs in connection with them.

Endorsed: Before the king.
Answer has been made in common in a petition, presented before the king and council, which contains the substance of this petition and several other articles concerning the community of the realm.
And the petition remains in the custody of William de Harlaston.

v
King's Bench Roll, no.242 (Michaelmas 1320), m.8, crown

A petition in the parliament at Westminster at Michaelmas 1320 of the men of Bury St. Edmunds: it states that Henry II had obtained a papal bull to permit him to have his own confessor and he had appointed Abbot Sampson of Bury St. Edmunds. And the abbot ordered him as a penance to found the Hospital of St. Saviour. The king made an endowment in support of twelve chaplains, six clerks, twelve poor gentle men (*gentils hommes*) and twelve women to pray

---

[12] This is the endorsement entered on the parliament roll (*Rot. Parl.*, i. 380, no.86).

for him and his children. But he had reserved the nomination of a warden to the crown, and the last man appointed, Geoffrey Beaufeu, had after some years gone on pilgrimage to the Holy Land, entrusted his charter of appointment by the king to the sacristan and monks of Bury St. Edmunds for a sum of money until his return, and never returned. Ever since the abbey had kept the wardenship to itself.

This petition was read before our lord the king in his full parliament where the abbot of Bury St. Edmunds was present and heard the petition read out, and he readily answered before our lord the king that the hospital of St. Saviour, mentioned in the petition, was never the foundation of our lord the king or of any of his ancestors and that no land or tenement was ever given by our lord the king's ancestors to the hospital. But this hospital was founded by the abbots of Bury St. Edmunds and has been the foundation of the abbots, his predecessors. And one of their monks was keeper of the hospital from time immemorial. And the abbot said that he had muniments and other satisfactory evidence on this matter. And because his muniments were not there available, the king gave the abbot a day on the Morrow of All Souls[13] next before the king or wherever he was within his realm to have his muniments there and to do further what shall be decided.

This petition was handed by our lord the king in full parliament to Henry le Scrope, the chief justice for his pleas, to do in this business on the aforesaid day what pertains to it. And the sheriff of Suffolk was ordered to notify the bailiff and four of the most worthy men of Bury St. Edmunds to be before the king on that day to advise him on his right in the matter.[14]

vi

Ibid., m.19, crown

Lincoln

The king in his parliament at Westminster at a Fortnight after Michaelmas in the fourteenth year of his reign delivered to Henry le Scrope some petitions, handed in at the parliament, against Richard Sampson of Stamford and he ordered Henry to have justice done thereon.

The petitions are given in full.

And thereupon Richard was attached in the parliament and brought before the king's council to answer upon the aforesaid matters etc. And

---

[13] 3 November 1320.
[14] Eventually the action against the abbot was dropped.

on being asked before the king's council how he wishes to clear himself of these trespasses at the king's prosecution, he says that he is in no way guilty thereof. And as to this he puts himself on the country etc. Therefore let a jury thereon come before the king a Fortnight after Hilary wherever he may be etc. And Richard is in the meantime committed to the marshal.

PARLIAMENT AT WESTMINSTER: Midsummer 1321

The arrangements for receiving and hearing petitions, made in the previous parliament (above p.355) seem to have been repeated: see Richardson and Sayles, Rot. Parl. Ined., pp.92-93 and Cal. Close Rolls, 1315-23, p.545

Ancient Petition, no.13840

To our lord the king pray the archbishops, bishops and other prelates that, as the canonisation of St. Thomas Cantilupe, late bishop of Hereford, is to be solemnly made in the court of Rome at the suit begun by your father and brought to a worthy conclusion by God's aid and yours, and as it would be greatly to the honour of God and Holy Church, and particularly of you and your kingdom, that the translation of the holy body should be made in your presence, please, sire, take advice on this matter and do your good will.

Endorsed: It pleases the king to be there. And our lord the king, the prelates and all the magnates assembled at the parliament have assented and agreed about a precise date for the translation, that is to say, ten days before the Feast of the Nativity of St. John the Baptist next, and this is the Sunday after the Feast of St. Barnabas the Apostle, which is Trinity Sunday.[1]

---

[1] 14 June 1321.

PARLIAMENT AT YORK: Easter 1322

i

Close Roll, no.139, m.13d

[Ryley, *Placita*, p.570; *Cal. Close Rolls, 1318-1323*, p.539]

On behalf of the king

Concerning the summons of Welshmen to the parliament at York

The king to his beloved and faithful Edmund, earl of Arundel, his justice of Wales, greeting. The pleasing and laudable services of our beloved and faithful men, as well knights as others, in our aforesaid land, by which we feel ourselves to have been frequently strengthened in our affairs, move and induce us to have the counsel and consent of the said our loyal subjects in those matters which specially concern us and the state of our kingdom and the said land and the peace and quiet of the people entrusted to our governance. We therefore command and firmly charge you to cause twenty-four of the most distinguished, law-worthy and able-bodied men of the parts of South Wales, who have full and sufficient authority on behalf of the whole community of those parts, and twenty-four of the most distinguished, law-worthy and able-bodied men from the parts of North Wales, who similarly have full and sufficient authority on behalf of the whole community of those parts, to come to us at York in our next parliament to be held there to discuss our business there with us and with the prelates and nobles of our realm and to give us their counsel. And you shall in no wise neglect this as you love us and our honour and the profit of our aforesaid kingdom and land and the peace and quiet of our people. And you are to have there the names of the aforesaid men and this writ. Witness the king at Rothwell on the eighteenth day of April.[1]

By the king himself

ii

Ancient Correspondence, vol. XXXIII, no.57

To the most noble and honourable prince and his most dear lord, if it please him, Edward, by the grace of God king of England, lord of Ireland and duke of Aquitaine, his loyal subject William de Braose, if it please

---

[1] 18 April 1322. The king apologised on 10 June 1322 because their petitions in this parliament had not been answered, for he had been fully occupied with preparations for his Scottish campaign (*Cal. Patent Rolls, 1321-24*, p.136).

him, in all the honour and allegiance he can show. Most dear lord, in that you have commanded me by your writ to be at your parliament at York at Three Weeks after Easter,[2] may your noble Highness understand that I have become so feeble and have so little use of my body that I cannot mount a horse or travel in any way. And, dear sir, I request your Highness to be so good as to have me excused for not coming, if it please you. Most dear lord, may God grant you an honourable life.

iii

Chancery Warrants, file 119, no.6121

[*Cal. Chancery Warrants*, i. 531]

Edward by the grace of God king of England, lord of Ireland and duke of Aquitaine, to the reverend father in God John, by the same grace bishop of Norwich, our chancellor, greeting. We order you to summon to you our justices of the one Bench and the other and cause them to be charged on our behalf to take good advice among themselves and have ready and speedy process made against the fugitives from our realm who go slandering us at the court of Rome and elsewhere in foreign lands, in accordance with what was ordained by common counsel. Furthermore, they are to have the points of the Ordinances put in a statute as well as the other things that were established in our last parliament and agreed should be put into a statute. And also they are to enrol and publish the process made and the judgement given against the earl of Lancaster and our other enemies and rebels.[3] And you are to inform us plainly and openly of what has been done as soon as you can. Given under our privy seal at Darlington on the twenty-seventh day of July in the sixteenth year of our reign.[4]

iv

Statute Roll, no.1, m.31

[*Statutes of the Realm*, i. 189-190]

Our lord the king, at his parliament at York at Three Weeks after Easter in the fifteenth year of his reign, caused the Ordinances [of 1311] to be rehearsed and examined by the prelates, earls and barons, among whom

---

[2] 2 May 1322. For £42 as the expenses of master John of Shoreditch in going at the king's command from London to the parliament at York, i.e. 36 days from 24 April to 29 May, to cover the journey both ways and daily sustenance, see B.L. Stowe MS. 553, fo.29 (Wardrobe Account).

[3] For the enrolment in the king's bench in the Easter term of 1322, see King's Bench Roll, no.248, m.69.

[4] 27 July 1322.

were most of the Ordainers who were still alive, and by the community of the realm assembled there on his orders. And inasmuch as by that examination it was found in the said parliament that the royal power of our lord the king had been in many things restricted by what was thus ordained, in contravention of what is proper, in derogation of his royal sovereignty and against the estate of the crown, and inasmuch as in times past dissensions and wars have come about in the realm by such ordinances and provisions, made by subjects regarding the royal power of our lord the king's ancestors, whereby the land has been in danger, it is agreed and established at the said parliament by our lord the king and by the said prelates, earls and barons and the whole community of the realm, assembled at this parliament, that everything ordained by the said Ordainers and contained in the said Ordinances is to cease immediately and for ever and lose title, force, virtue and effect at all times, whilst the statutes and ordinances, made in due form by our lord the king and his ancestors prior to the said Ordinances, are to remain in force, and that every kind of ordinance or provision, made by the subjects of our lord the king or his heirs by whatever authority or commission it may be, regarding the royal power of our lord the king or his heirs or against the estate of our lord the king or his heirs or against the estate of the crown, shall henceforth for all time be annulled and shall in no wise have validity or force. But the things which are to be provided for the estate of our lord the king and of his heirs and for the estate of the realm and the people, are to be discussed, agreed and ordained in parliaments by our lord the king and with the assent of the prelates, earls and barons and the community of the realm, as has been the custom in times past.

The king to the sheriff of York, greeting. Whereas in our parliament summoned at York at Three Weeks after Easter in the fifteenth year of our reign we have caused some ordinances, lately made by certain prelates, earls and barons of our realm chosen for this purpose, to be rehearsed and examined by the prelates, earls, barons, nobles and the community of the realm there assembled, and for certain causes revealed by that examination it has been agreed and ordained at our said parliament by us and the said prelates, earls, barons, nobles and the community that everything ordained by the aforesaid Ordainers and contained in the Ordinances is to cease in future and for ever lose title, virtue, force and effect, while the statutes and ordinances made in due form by us or our ancestors before the said Ordinances were made are to remain in force, as is more fully contained in the statute promulgated thereon in our said parliament, which we are sending to you sealed under our seal in patent form: we command and firmly charge you that you are to have this statute read and published in your full county court and each and all the matters contained in it are to be observed, so far as you can, whilst the aforesaid statutes and ordinances, published previously, are to remain in their force as stated. Witness the king at York the nineteenth day of May.[5]

By the king himself
Every sheriff throughout England is written to in this way.

v
Close Roll, no.139, m.8d (schedule)
[*in extenso* in *Cal. Close Rolls, 1318-23*,
pp.557-8, and *Rot. Parl.*, i. 456-7, Appendix no.35]

Though the revocation of the Ordinances of 1311 is on the statute roll, the supplementary statute which re-enacted some of the ordinances in the original or a modified form is not enrolled there. Cf. Historia Roffensis, fo.38b: the Ordinances 'made by archbishop Robert of Winchelsey, prelates, earls, barons, justices, citizens, burgesses are annulled except six, from which were made six statutes, the name of "ordinance" being altered to "statute".'

Our lord the king Edward, son of King Edward, at his parliament at York at Three Weeks after Easter in the fifteenth year of his reign, desirous of ordaining, constituting and establishing what would be to the honour of God and of Holy Church, the profit of himself and of his realm, the good keeping of his peace, and the tranquillity of his people, has by the assent of the archbishops, bishops, abbots, priors and other prelates, earls, barons and the community of his realm there established made the provisions written below.

There follow nine clauses, taken from the Ordinances of 1311, and now after some redrafting re-enacted. They relate to:
the liberties of the Church
the peace of the realm
the taking of prises
the appointment of sheriffs and keepers of hundreds
the trespasses of the Forest
the court of the marshalsea
the statutes merchant
false appeals and indictments
appeals of felony and mayhem

[5] 19 May 1322.

vi
Ancient Petition, no.3955
[Davies, *Baronial Opposition*, p.597]

To our lord the king pray the knights of the shires and all the community
of his land that it may please him of his grace to appoint some justices to
take fines from all adherents to his rebels and enemies who wish to come
voluntarily and confess their adherence and make fine with the king for
their trespass in accordance with their power and the amount of their
lands, and the king in this way will be able to have a great profit quickly
and the community of his land will be put at ease.

Endorsed: Before the king.
   It is the council's opinion that, if it please the king, this should be done.

vii
Register of Walter de Stapleton, fo.216
[Ed. F.C. Hingeston – Randolph, p.443 f.]

Hugh Despenser had petitioned that the sentence of disinheritance
and exile passed against him was invalid, and in consequence the
king was seeking advice on the matter.

But as regards the advice which is sought from us in the aforesaid
matters, it seems to us, without prejudice to wiser counsel, that the
definitive revocation of the judgement which had been made in time of
parliament, without the presence or consent of the prelates, could be
more honourably, usefully and securely made in parliament than
anywhere else if time permits it and it pleases your highness to convoke
parliament – would that it be peaceful and act in peace – in a suitable place
for these and other matters. And if it should seem advisable to wiser men
and those more expert in the laws of England that he should stand trial on
suitable security in the next parliament, the said judgement could maybe
be revoked or suspended in the interim, for if it be that the judgement
was made unjustly and erroneously, yet it does not seem proper that any
injustice or error should occur in whatever way it is revoked.[6]

---

[6] Cf. Historia Roffensis, fo.37-37*b*: in December 1321 the convocation of Canterbury
declared that it would be good and conciliatory to revoke the exile of the Despensers.

viii
L.T.R. Memoranda Roll, no.93 (15 Edward II), m.55*d*, Easter Writs

To the barons from the king

We are sending you under the foot of our seal the process of certain judicial proceedings which have taken place in our present full parliament assembled at York with regard to the annulment of a certain judgement, wrongly made in our parliament summoned at Midsummer last at Westminster by the peers of our realm against our beloved and faithful Hugh Despenser the younger and Hugh Despenser the elder, to the prejudice of us and our crown, and we order you under the foot of our seal to have the process published before you in the exchequer and enrolled in the exchequer rolls and to have the judgement, which we recently sent you under the foot of our seal for publication in the exchequer, annulled and cancelled. Witness myself at York the tenth day of May in the fifteenth year of our reign.[7]

---

[7] 10 May 1322. The statute against the Despensers is enrolled on King's Bench Roll, no.246 (Michaelmas 1321), m.40, and the statute in their favour on no.248 (Easter 1322), m.67, no.249, m.33.

PARLIAMENT AT YORK: 14 November 1322

This assembly was first summoned to Ripon and then to York. As the king could not be present the chancellor and treasurer were empowered to open and continue the 'discussion' (Cal. Patent Rolls, 1317-21, p.217). For doubts whether it should be regarded as a parliament, see Bull. Inst. Hist. Research, vi. 83-84. We have been unable to find references to the business transacted: the decisions concerning the administration of Gascony resulted from discussions by the council at the Octave of Martinmas (Foedera, ii. 505 f.), but there is no mention of parliament.

King's Bench Roll, no.262 (Michaelmas 1325), m.61d

Middlesex

A writ to the sheriff of Middlesex, ordering him to pay Richard Duraunt and William le Rous, knights of the shire, 108 shillings for their expenses (at two shillings a day for twelve days' travel and fifteen days' stay) in coming to York on Sunday after Martinmas 1322 'to discuss there sundry important business concerning the king and the state of his realm'. The sheriff had continually disobeyed.

And now came the aforesaid William le Rous, Richard de Hayle[1] and Richard Duraunt. And they say that the sheriff, namely Richard Pountz, received the aforesaid writs from the hands of William le Rous on Sunday,[2] the Vigil of Martinmas, this year so that he could execute them properly. And they tendered a bill under Richard Pountz's seal, as they assert, which testifies to this. Therefore the coroners of the county are ordered to have the sheriff come before the king's bench at a Fortnight after Hilary wherever etc. to answer to us as well as to the aforesaid Richard de Hayle, William le Rous and Richard Duraunt regarding his aforesaid false return. And further etc. And the sheriff is ordered, as often, to let Richard and William as well as Richard Duraunt have their expenses in accordance with the terms of the king's instructions etc. And how etc. he is to let the king know at the aforesaid term etc.[3]

---

[1] He represented Middlesex with William le Rous at the parliament in February 1324 and was also suing for his expenses.

[2] 10 November 1325.

[3] For further process see King's Bench Rolls, nos.263, m.142; 264, ms.107, 131. The sheriff informed the court that he took twelve marks' worth of goods from the community of Middlesex but could find no buyers.

PARLIAMENT AT WESTMINSTER: 23 February 1324

There was no parliament summoned in 1323, though in a letter, dated 6 June 1323, the king had announced his intention of convening a parliament soon after Michaelmas (Cal. Close Rolls, 1318-22, pp. 713-14). *In the event this parliament was summoned on 20 November 1323 to meet on 20 January 1324 but was postponed on 26 December 1323 until 23 February 1324 to await the arrival of the king's agents from Paris* (Cal. Chancery Warrants, i. 548).

i

King's Bench Roll, no.254 (Michaelmas 1323), m.38
[Sayles, *King's Bench*, IV. 122-132]

John of Stratford, archdeacon of Lincoln, was brought under severe examination in the king's bench for the conduct of a mission he conducted to the papal court in 1323. He submitted an indenture which listed the many items of business he was to transact there and the answers given by the pope. The fifth is of particular interest.

Let supplication be made that the oaths taken to observe the Ordinances [of 1311], which had recently been taken by some prelates and magnates of the land in derogation of the rights of the king and his crown, be revoked.

To the fifth article [as above] the pope replied that many were in peril on account of these Ordinances in England, and he raised a great deal of difficulty in granting this article, stating that, although the king could change and revoke his statutes, yet it was not for him to annul the oaths taken in such matters. Still, in the long run he granted this article, addressing his bulls thereon in precise terms to the archbishop of Canterbury, who has to do therein what seems to him expedient for the profit and honour of the king and his realm.

Edward by the grace of God king of England, lord of Ireland and duke of Aquitaine, to his beloved and faithful Hervey of Stanton and his fellows, our justices appointed to hold pleas before us, greeting. We command you to postpone all business concerning us, which is pending before you in regard to master John of Stratford, to our next parliament convened at Westminster at Three Weeks after the Purification of the Blessed Virgin Mary next,[1] adjourning John to that parliament so that he

---

[1] 23 February 1324.

may then be there to do and receive what shall be decided therein in that parliament. Witness myself at Worcester the fifteenth day of January in the seventeenth year of our reign.[2]

ii

King's Bench Roll, no.255 (Hilary 1324), m.87d

[Sayles, *King's Bench*, IV. 143–46]

> The bishop of Hereford was charged by a presentment in the king's bench in the Hilary term of 1324 with complicity in the treason of Roger Mortimer in 1322–23.

Afterwards the bishop came. And on being asked by the justices how he wishes to clear himself therein, he says that he is the bishop of Hereford by the will of God and of the supreme pontiff and that the substance of the aforesaid articles alleged against him is so serious that he ought not to answer here in court on the matters imputed to him, nor can he answer thereon without offence to God and Holy Church. Therefore the bishop is told to be in person from day to day before the justices etc. to hear judgement upon him in this respect etc.

Afterwards, on Friday after the Feast of St. Peter in Cathedra,[3] the bishop came to Westminster before the king in full parliament. And after the aforesaid presentment had been recited in the presence of the king, earls, barons and other loyal subjects of the king then assembled in parliament and, furthermore, after it had been recorded that Roger traitorously levied war against the king, committing many evil and atrocious deeds within his realm to the king as well as to others whereof Roger stands adjudged as a traitor to the king and the realm, and that Gilbert atte Nashe of the bishop's household, sent at the bishop's expense to strengthen Roger's army against the king, was found guilty thereof by a jury . . . the bishop is asked whether he wishes to say anything more in the matter than he has already said. And the bishop says, as before, that he is the bishop of Hereford and that he cannot answer here in court to the things alleged against him without offence to God and Holy Church.

> He was given into the charge of the archbishop of Canterbury, who brought him again before the king's bench on 19 March 1324. And a jury was ordered to be empanelled to ascertain whether it was as a convicted clerk that the bishop should be handed over into the archbishop's custody. A jury later found him guilty and his property was accordingly confiscated.

[2] 15 January 1324.
[3] 19 March 1324.

iii
King's Bench Roll, no.255 (Hilary 1324), m.66
[Sayles, *King's Bench*, IV. 135-43]

Walter of Bourton was successful in an action of trespass against
Robert of Bourton before Henry le Scrope and his fellows, justices of
the king's bench. Robert alleged error in the proceedings, and the
king's bench, now under Hervey of Stanton as chief justice, was
ordered to examine the record and to amend it if necessary. The
court did in fact find error and annulled the judgement. Then it was
Walter's turn to allege error as follows:

Afterwards, in the king's parliament at Westminster at Three Weeks
after the Purification of the Blessed Mary in the seventeeth year of the
king's reign, on the petition of Walter son of William le Grant,
submitting that error had occurred in the record and process before
Hervey of Stanton and his fellows over the annulment of the judgement
rendered before Henry le Scrope and his fellows . . . the rolls relating to
these matters were brought into the parliament for inspection and
examination etc. so that, if error were found in them, it might be
corrected in accordance with what is lawful etc. And after the records and
processes have been looked at, inspected and examined in the said
parliament in Walter's presence, it is agreed and adjudged there in that
parliament that the judgement rendered therein before Hervey and his
fellows is just and lawful according to the law and custom of the realm
and that no errors occurred in the record and process held therein before
Hervey and his fellows.

iv
Chancery Inquisitions, Miscellaneous, file 92, no.23

Petition of Joan Colepeper,[4] praying restitution of lands which had
been taken into the king's hands.

She also prays our lord the king that he will of his grace command that
her charters and muniments be delivered to her, which are in Tonbridge
Castle in a sealed hamper among her other goods in the custody of Sir
Henry Cobham.

---

[4] This petition is accompanied by a writ, dated 26 May 1324 and warranted 'by
petition of the council', and by the consequent inquisition, taken at Tonbridge on 7
August following.

Answer: Let her come to chancery and, if the charters mentioned in her petition are in the castle etc., let Henry Cobham be ordered to arrange for those charters to come into chancery, and, if it should appear from those charters that Walter Colepeper and his wife did acquire in the way the petition alleges, let the truth be investigated and justice be further done in the chancery.

Endorsed: Because the petition was extracted from the files and accidentally lost, this petition has been made anew from the roll of William de Harlaston, as he has acknowledged.[5]

---

[5] This roll does not survive.

[PARLIAMENT AT WESTMINSTER: Michaelmas 1324]

This assembly was originally summoned on 13 September to meet at Salisbury on 20 October but the place was on 24 September changed to London on 20 October (Parl. Writs, II. ii. 317-25: Cal. Close Rolls, 1323-27, p.311). The writs of summons, as enrolled on the Close Rolls, and the marginal notes refer to a conference (colloquium), as do the writs of expenses (Parl. Writs, II. ii. 319-325), and a writ of protection for the archbishop of York speaks of 'a certain conference at London' on 20 October (Parl. Writs, II. ii. 318 f.). Only knights of the shire were required to be present and they were paid the unusual rate of 2s.6d. a day. Citizens and burgesses were not summoned to attend with the knights. The clergy sent letters of proxy but only two have survived: those of the abbot of St. Augustine's Canterbury, and the abbot of Peterborough (S.C.10/ 10/452-3).

PARLIAMENT AT WESTMINSTER: Midsummer 1325

i

Diplomatic Documents, Exchequer, E.30/1582

[Richardson and Sayles, *Rot. Parl. Inediti*, 95–96]

A speech by or on behalf of the king.

Lords, some things pertaining to the crown which fall to be discussed I have shown you as one who is your leader and has the supreme responsibility and is prepared to maintain the crown in all its rights with your advice and assistance and to defend it as far as possible with the support of all your strength. And on this matter I have always requested your counsel and have done nothing in the said business without counsel and thereby I believe that I have done my part. And therein I have asked for your counsel, aid and support which you must at your peril offer, give and show me as you would wish to avow it now and in time to come, and each one of you separately and individually should give his counsel and advice about what I ought to do. Which said, I will that it be entered in the parliament roll in perpetual remembrance. Wherefore I again ask you by your faith and allegiance that you should still tell me [your advice] by word of mouth, each one of you separately and individually. For although it may be that you have shown me all your opinions and arguments in general in a bill, something that can be arranged and put in a bill by the advice and counsel of one or two of you who know best how to attract and lead you to agree with them, nevertheless I wish to have your answers separately and from each one of you on his own and that each should say by his own mouth what he feels so that I can be completely advised about the said business and all its circumstances, point by point, and I wish to be answered in such a way by clergy as well as laity so that in future each one can answer for what he has said without a general covering-up, and that your answers should be put in writing, both what I have shown you and what you shall answer. For I do not wish that in so important a matter there should be between us any covering-up or any subtle evasion but that you should make your answers plainly and distinctly by word of mouth in the way in which the matters have been plainly and distinctly shown to you.

Then follows the advice given in reply to the king's request. The parliament had been specially convened to consider the affairs of Gascony and the thirteen replies mainly relate to them.[1]

ii
Ancient Petition, File 77, no.3840

The proxy of Master William de Weston was acting on behalf of his lord who was abroad on the king's service.

He put forward a petition in this parliament, which is still pending before the auditors of petitions, as they well knew.[2] And while the petition was pending before them, the sheriff of Bedford came with a great press of men, that is to say, knights and other men of the county who had been chosen to go to Gascony, with a warrant as follows:

> A writ, dated 15 June 1325, to the sheriff of Bedford, ordering him to oust any lay force within the church of Leighton Buzzard which was preventing the bishop of Lincoln from exercising his spiritual authority there.

And this writ was afterwards executed by the sheriff of the county. And whereas the bishop of Lincoln or any of his men did not come there to exercise any spiritual office as the warrant implied and no judge or executor was appointed on behalf of our Holy Father the pope for this purpose, they exceeded their warrant and ejected his lord from his possession of the prebend, in despite of the king and of all his parliament. Wherefore the said proxy prays for the sake of God and his soul and the maintenance of the king's right and estate and the right and possession of his aforesaid lord that redress may be provided him in this parliament so that the condition of his lord may not be so seriously worsened through his absence in foreign lands on the business of the king and his realm that he lose his said possession and especially that no bad example be shown to others who have to go as the king's messengers in times to come.

Endorsed: Because the instructions our lord the king gave to the sheriff to oust lay force were made on the signification of the bishop and this is

---

[1] Dr. Chaplais prefers to ascribe this document to the assembly of October 1324 (*War of St. Sandos*, pp.95-98) but there are many difficulties: for example, Edward II did not cancel the military muster arranged for August 1325 until 10 July, and in France the subsidy for a war in Gascony continued to be collected in the south until September. And if the assembly in 1324 was not a parliament, it would hardly have a 'parliament roll'.

[2] For the date of this petition, which is badly mutilated, see *Cal. Patent Rolls, 1324-27*, p.90.

customary, let him sue to regain his possession as he shall think it best to do by law and the principles of justice. And if he believes himself to be disseised or if another trespass is done him, let him come to the chancery and sue there at common law.

Before the king, because it concerns the king.

iii

Lincoln's Inn: Hales MSS

[*Rot. Parl.*, i. 437a]

To the chancellor of our lord the king Emma, the wife of Roger de Plat, prays grace and remedy for God's sake: that you may be good enough to look at the petition which was handed in at the common parliament at Midsummer and answered by the common council and delivered to you, and that you should order a writ to be sent to William de Herle to have the record and process sent before you. And this record has now arrived and been delivered into chancery by William de Herle's hand. And the said petition was in the custody of William of Harlaston.

iv

Lincoln's Inn: Hales MSS

[*Rot. Parl.*, i. 439]

To our lord the king and his council shows the prior of St. Frideswyde's of Oxford that he had at another time sued by petition, presented at his parliament at Westminster in the ninth year of his reign, showing that he had the right to the advowson of Oakley church in the county of Buckingham and to hold it to his own profit as the right of his church of St. Frideswyde of Oxford, and thereby a writ, within which the petition was enclosed, was sent to William Inge and his fellows, the then justices appointed to hold the pleas of our lord the king,[3] ordering them to hold a final discussion of the matters contained in the petition and not to proceed to judgement before our lord the king had been notified thereon. And now before Geoffrey le Scrope and his fellows the business contained in the petition has been given a final discussion up to the point of rendering judgement, as shown by the record and process pending before them. And Geoffrey and his fellows do not wish in any way to proceed to rendering judgement without specific instructions.

---

[3] William Inge was appointed chief justice of the king's bench on 18 April 1316 and the parliament mentioned must be that which met at Hilary 1316 at Lincoln, the only parliament to meet in 9 Edward II. Therefore 'Westminster', where parliament met at Hilary 1315, is presumably an error for 'Lincoln'.

Wherefore the prior sued by petition, presented in the recent parliament of our lord the king, that is to say, at Midsummer in the eighteenth year of his reign.[4] And this petition was endorsed by the council thus: It seems to the council that what is asked for should be granted, yet because it concerns the king, let it go before the king. And the prior has sued day after day before our lord the king and his council that Geoffrey and his fellows should proceed to render judgement and to do what is right, and the prior can get no answer in this matter. Wherefore the prior prays our lord the king and his council that they will be good enough to command the said judgement to be rendered in accordance with what is found in the record and process, and right be done him, and to send his writ thereon to Geoffrey and his fellows.

Before the king.
It pleases the king that a writ should be sent to Geoffrey le Scrope and his fellows that, having looked at the process before them, they should proceed to render judgement in the said business according to law and the principles of justice, notwithstanding that the business touches himself.

[4] 1325.

PARLIAMENT AT WESTMINSTER: Martinmas 1325

i

Chancery Warrants, file 130, no.7247

[*Cal. Chancery Warrants*, i. 571]

Edward by the grace of God king of England, lord of Ireland and duke of Aquitaine, to the reverend father in God William, by the same grace, archbishop of York, primate of England, our treasurer, and to our dear clerk, Master Robert of Baldock, archdeacon of Middlesex, our chancellor, greeting. Whereas we have caused our parliament to be summoned at Westminster on this Monday, the Octave of Martinmas,[1] and we are coming as straight and quickly as we can and we are trying to be there, with God's help, on Monday evening, we will that you hold our place on the first day of parliament to do what pertains to that day, letting the prelates, earls, barons, and other magnates who will be there know that we shall be at the aforesaid time, ready to discuss and deal with the business for which we have had our parliament summoned. Given under our privy seal at Isleworth on the eighteenth day of November in the nineteenth year of our reign.[2]

ii

Close Roll, no.143, m.15d

[*Rot. Parl.*, i. 430; *Cal. Close Rolls, 1323-27*, p.539 f.]

Note that the petitions written below were granted in the parliament, summoned at Westminster at the Octave of Martinmas in the nineteenth year of the reign of Edward II, by the king with the assent of the prelates, earls, barons and others, then present in the said parliament, in the following form:

> Six petitions concerning breaches of the Great Charter and the Charter of the Forest, wrongful imprisonment, delays of justice and London franchises are presented to the king by his loyal subjects, who are twice described as acting on behalf of the whole community of the realm.

And also, sire, your loyal subjects pray that, whereas they have put forward their petitions in various parliaments as regards various grievances, and some have been adjourned before the king's bench and some before the chancellor and none of them have reached a conclusion, that it may please your highness to order redress.

It pleases the king.

[1] 18 November 1325.
[2] 18 November 1325.

EDWARD III

PARLIAMENT AT WESTMINSTER: Epiphany and Candlemas 1327

This parliament was first summoned on 28 October to meet on 14 December 1326 and was postponed on 3 December until the Morrow of the Epiphany, that is 7 January 1327.[1] *Little official evidence exists to tell us in detail what happened. Some petitions survive which were presented at this Epiphany parliament. But in these troubled times this last parliament of Edward II's reign was adjourned until the Morrow of Candlemas, that is 3 February, two days after Edward III was crowned king, and it is called by one petitioner 'the parliament of the coronation'.*[2] *Technically there were two parliaments but no further summons was made and for all practical purposes they were treated as two successive sessions of one parliament, petitions presented at the Epiphany parliament under Edward II being dealt with and answered at the Candlemas session under Edward III.*

i

B.L., Royal MS. 20 A III, fo.200 f.

This little known chronicle describes the deposition of Edward II and stresses the character of parliament as a feudal court.

How King Edward was deprived of his royal powers

Queen Isabella and her son Edward and all the great men of England sent John Hotham, bishop of Ely, and Henry Percy, baron, to Edward at Kenilworth Castle where he was imprisoned to ask him to arrange for his parliament to meet at a certain place in England to make provision for the state of his realm. And he answered them: 'Lords, see here my seal, so I give you authority to summon the parliament wherever you wish.' So they took their leave of him and, as soon as they had thereon the king's letter patent, they went back to the baronage and showed it to them.

---

[1] The writ of summons of 28 October 1326 is entered in the register of the abbot of Peterborough with the marginal note: 'A writ for coming to parliament and of an unusual character regarding the king himself' (B.L., Cotton MS., Vespasian E. XX1, fo.57). One contemporary observer styled it 'the parliament of the queen-regent' (Historia Roffensis, fo.48) and speaks about the proceedings during the first two days. For the expenses of 40s. of the prior of Christ Church, Canterbury, in attending the Epiphany parliament at London, see Lambeth MS., 242, fo.365. The long list of expenses of knights of the shire for Shropshire describes this parliament as that 'held at Westminster on the Morrow of the Epiphany' (Writs and Returns of Members of Parliament, 6/13A).

[2] Ancient Petition, no.12839.

Thereby it was agreed that the parliament should be held at Westminster at the Octave of Hilary [20 January 1327]. And all the great men of England made their preparations at London in readiness for this parliament. The king would in no way come on that day as he had himself agreed. Nevertheless the barons asked him time after time to come to the parliament they had set up. But the king swore by the soul of God that he would not set foot there. Therefore all the great men of England agreed that he should not be king but wished to crown Edward, duke of Aquitaine, his son. And so the barons sent to King Edward by common assent John de Warenne, earl [of Surrey], John Hotham, bishop of Ely, Henry Percy, baron, and Sir William Trussel, knight, to give him back their homage for themselves and all those in England. And Sir William Trussel spoke the words and said: 'Sir Edward, because you have ill-treated your people of England in despoiling several of the great men of England without reason, though lately, thank God, you have been restrained, and because you refuse to come to your parliament which you have established at Westminster, as stated very fully in your letter patent, in order to have discussions with your liege people as a king must do, I speak to you the following words by the common assent of all England: "Know that the barons of England do not assent to your reigning any longer but have ousted you from your royal powers for ever".' To these words the bishop of Ely said: 'Sir Edward, I give you back fealty and homage on behalf of all the archbishops and bishops and all the clergy of England.' Then earl John de Warenne said: 'Sir Edward, I give you back fealty and homage for myself and all the earls of England.' Then Henry Percy said: 'Sir Edward, I give you back homage and fealty for myself and all knights and for all those who hold by serjeanty or any other way of you, so that from this day forward you shall not be styled king or held to be king but considered henceforth as just one of the people.'[3] And then they took themselves away to go to London where the baronage awaited them. And Sir Edward went back to prison in safe custody. And this was before the Day of the Conversion of St. Paul in the twentieth year of his reign [25 January 1327].[4]

ii

Chancery Parliament and Council Proceedings, roll no.11
[Richardson and Sayles, *Rot. Parl. Inediti*, pp.121, 125]

Item, the commons pray that good and suitable and wise men be placed around the king to give him good counsel and that they be chosen by the

---

[3] According to B.L., Cotton MS., Cleopatra D III, fo.166, Percy spoke simply for the barons and Trussel for the knights and those who held by serjeanty and in other ways.

[4] This was the day of Edward III's accession to the throne.

magnates with the assent of the commons so that none of them nor any other magnate of the land nor anyone, great or small, of the king's household nor any minister serving the king may maintain a suit or plea, either himself or through anyone else or by written instructions, whereby the common law is disturbed, and if it be found that anyone has done so, let it be shown at the next parliament and let him be ousted from the king's council and let the injured party have recovery of damages against him.

Item, the commons pray the king and his council that all the above articles, together with other articles which our lord the king and his council may wish to agree and grant for the profit of the community and of the realm, may be put in writing and that the writing be sealed with the great seal and delivered to the knights of the shire, to each of them individually for each shire, and that the sheriffs be ordered to make proclamation throughout all the shires, as well within liberties as outside them, that everything contained in the said grant may be held firm and established by all men for all time, and that the community in each shire may be made to swear as we have sworn to uphold the undertaking now begun. And let the bishops also be ordered to make the clergy swear in the same manner.

iii
Chancery Parliament Roll, no. 1, m. 1
[*Rot. Parl.*, ii. 10-12]

And to make the commons swear, as we are sworn, to maintain the cause (*querela*), writs are to be issued throughout the land, as well to bishops for the clergy as to sheriffs for the commons. And if any other bill be presented in the name of the commons, we disavow it save for this indentured bill.

And the commons beseech our lord the king and his council that all the aforesaid points, together with any other points that our lord the king and his council may wish to grant and to accept, should be put in writing, and this writing should be sealed with his great seal and delivered to the knights of the shires for each individual county, to be delivered to the sheriffs for proclamation throughout their bailiwicks, within liberties as well as outside them, and that all the things contained in the said warrant may be regarded as statutes and hold good and established for all time.

Responses

As for the petition on the point that the matters should be put into statutes and that those that need to be put into a statute be put into a statute and the others be enrolled in chancery, it pleases the king etc.

As for the point concerning the oath of the commons, the oath of the magnates is sufficient.

iv

Chancery Parliament and Council Proceedings, roll no.1
[Richardson and Sayles, *Rot. Parl. Inediti*, p.134]

Again, the citizens of London pray that our lord the king may hold his parliament at Westminster every year until he comes of full age, and those who shall be appointed to be near him may be removed at the beginning of parliament and that everyone who can rightly complain about them should be heard.[5]

v

B.L., Cotton MS., Titus E. I. fos.2-24
[Richardson and Sayles, *Rot. Parl. Inediti*, pp.169, 173]

Yorkshire

To our lord the king and to his council prays the abbot of York that, whereas he is held to account in the exchequer for various tenths, granted to the king by his clergy, the said tenths may be paid in instalments at a hundred marks a year on account of the great devastation done by the Scots.

Answer is made thus:

It seems to the council that, having regard to the devastation the abbot has suffered, it is necessary to grant him suitable payment by instalments, if it please the king.

It is agreed by the great council that he should pay instalments for what is owing at a hundred pounds a year.

---

[5] This article has been crossed out.

Winchester

The bishop of Winchester complains of the unlawful levies on spiritualities by the keepers of the bishopric during a vacancy.

Answer is made thus:

It seems to the council that the seizure of the profits of such churches is wrongful on account of the [nature of the] possession held therein.

Let this petition be put before the king.

Afterwards, after this petition had been discussed again before the king and the great council, it is agreed and granted that the keepers of the temporalities of the bishopric are no longer to meddle in times of vacancies with the profits of such churches.

vi
Ancient Petition, no.2148
[Sayles, *King's Bench*, II. clxv f.]

The bishop of Durham in his petition to the king and council pointed out that, when royal eyres were frequent, the men of his franchise of Durham were able to obtain speedy justice but now that eyres were seldom held, he asked permission to be able to issue writs from his own chancery within his Liberty similar to those issued by the king's chancery.

Endorsement: Before the king and the great council.

This request concerns a change in the law which should not be made except at the request of the bishop of Durham and the community of the bishopric and with the assent of the king and of the prelates, earls, barons and other nobles of the land and, if anything ought to be done, it must be in parliament. Therefore nothing can be done at present.[6]

vii
Chancery Warrants, file 136, no.79

Edward by the grace of God king of England, lord of Ireland and duke of Aquitaine, to the reverend father in God John, by the same grace bishop of Ely, our chancellor, greeting. We send you enclosed herein a bill which was presented in our parliament by the sons of Llewellyn Bren with regard to some requests they made to us, and these we have granted

---

[6] Cf. *Cal. Close Rolls, 1327-30*, p.55 and *Cal. Patent Rolls, 1330-34*, p.360.

in accordance with the endorsement of the bill made by the auditors of bills in the said parliament. And we instruct you that, having looked at the bill and its endorsement, you are to let them have such letters under our great seal as are appropriate according to the aforesaid endorsement.[7] Given under our privy seal at Westminster on the eleventh day of February in the first year of our reign.[8]

viii

King's Bench Roll, no.269 (Trinity 1327), m.84

[Sayles, *King's Bench*, V. 8-12]

This action concerned the right of the archbishop of York from time immemorial to the prise[9] of wine from ships in the river Humber, which had been confirmed by royal letters dated 4 June 1327 after consideration of the matter in the parliament of 1327. The king's butler, Richard de la Pole, refused to obey the king's orders and was summoned before the king's bench for contempt. He there sought to put forward arguments against the archbishop's claim.

And the archbishop says that the butler has day here on this day to answer the king for contempt only etc. and not for doing anything else, and inasmuch as the aforesaid judgement had been made in so solemn a place as the parliament etc. by the king, prelates, earls, barons and the community of the realm, assembled in that parliament, there had issued as a result of that judgement the writ, addressed to the butler as a minister of the king, to execute the judgement. And that judgement cannot be revoked elsewhere than in parliament, and the king's right, if he has any, to the prise etc. cannot be determined in court here by virtue of the aforesaid writ, and the archbishop ought not to answer thereon to the king until he is put back in possession of the prise by reason of that judgement. And he asks that the butler should be ordered, as before, to remove the king's hand from such prise etc. and that he should be punished for contempt etc.

And because the justices here wish to be more fully advised thereon, day is given to the parties from day to day etc.

---

[7] Chancery Warrants 136/80 is the petition, happily still attached to the warrant, complaining of disseisin by Hugh Despenser (for which see *Cal. Close Rolls, 1327-30*, p.121). The petition is endorsed: 'It seems to the council that it should be granted, if it please the king, because a confirmation will not be prejudicial to him.'

[8] 11 February 1327.

[9] That is, taken by way of customs-dues.

A writ of privy seal, dated 24 June 1327, ordering the justices of the king's bench, if in doubt, to send the business before the king and his council.

And because it seemed to the justices here to be doubtful whether further proceedings could be held in this court on that business, the record and process of the business held here were dispatched to the king by reason of that writ etc. And the king handed them to the chancellor, instructing him that he was to convene the whole of the king's council in chancery and that, after the record and process had been read over and the arguments on the king's behalf as well as the archibishop's had been heard etc., justice was to be done further in these matters.

And afterwards the archbishop and Richard de la Pole came before the chancellor and treasurer, the justices and others of the council convened in chancery. . . . And because the judgement was made in the aforesaid parliament and the writ for executing it, addressed to the butler, issued as a result of that judgement . . . it seems to the whole council etc. that execution in accordance with the form of the judgement made in parliament should not be stayed in this respect.[10]

ix

Exchequer Plea Roll, no.54 (1 Edward III), m.9d

A petition of the abbess of Elstow to the king and council in parliament. Malcolm, king of Scotland and lord of the town of Bedford, had, long before the town came into the hands of the king's ancestors, granted the then abbess the third penny (i.e. £4-10s-0d) of his revenue from the town in perpetuity by a charter which the king's ancestors had confirmed.[11] Though the abbess and her predecessors had received the proceeds of this grant, the mayor and bailiffs of Bedford had since 1320-1321 deprived the abbess of them. The treasurer and barons of the exchequer were ordered by a writ, dated 4 February 1327, to hear her petition and give her redress. At Trinity term 1327 the mayor and bailiffs challenged the jurisdiction of the court on the ground that the rent in question was a freehold and a plea relating to freehold must be determined elsewhere at common law. The abbess replied that the grant from the profits of the town was given as alms.

And she prayed the court to decide whether, inasmuch as it is ordained and specially laid down on her behalf by the king's council in his

---

[10] Cf. *Rot. Parl.*, ii. 24: 'it is awarded and adjudged in parliament, which is the highest and most solemn judgement in this land.'

[11] *Regesta Regum Scottorum*, ed. G.W.Barrow, ii. 158.

parliament that she was to sue for redress and that justice would be done her in the exchequer court regarding the detention of the money, the mayor and bailiffs can in any wise say that the rent was a freehold and thereby escape answering the abbess thereon in that court. The mayor and bailiffs likewise pray judgement as before. And because the barons wished to deliberate fully in this matter before proceeding to judgement, the parties were given a day to hear judgement at a Fortnight after Michaelmas.

Exchequer Plea Roll, no.56 (3 Edward III), m.22d

In a writ dated 3 July 1329 the king noted that the treasurer and barons had postponed proceedings 'against the decision made in our parliament'.

And because it is not consonant with what is right that pleas and processes, begun on writs authorised in our parliament by us and our council, should be thus hindered, we order you to proceed further with this plea and let the abbess have speedy justice therein.

The abbess asked that the mayor and bailiffs should answer.

And the mayor and bailiffs say that, whatever instructions the king had given that proceedings were to continue and speedy justice be done therein to the abbess, nevertheless it is and ought to be the king's intention that such justice should be done in this matter in such a way that it does not subvert the law and custom of the realm or prejudice the parties. And inasmuch as it has been the practice for a long time in accordance with the law and custom of the realm that pleas concerning freehold should not be tried or determined in that court, they pray judgement, as before, if they ought to answer here with respect to the aforesaid freehold.

In the Trinity term of 1330 the treasurer and barons were ordered to send the record of the plea to chancery.[12]

---

[12] Nevertheless, the court of the exchequer of pleas was still being ordered in 1336 to give judgement (Exchequer Plea Roll, no.63, m.31: writs dated 3 April and 8 November).

PARLIAMENT AT YORK: Candlemas 1328

Exchequer Plea Roll, no.56 (Hilary 1329), m.8d

Kent

John of Bourne comes here in connection with the account of William of Orlaston, sheriff of Kent, and complains that, whereas John had been one of the knights elected by the community of the shire to be on behalf of the community at various parliaments of the king, namely, at the king's parliament held at Lincoln on the Morrow of the Exaltation of Holy Cross in the first year of the said king's reign, and at two parliaments at York in the second year, and at the parliament held at Northampton and the parliament held at Salisbury in the said second year, and thereupon he had brought and delivered to the sheriff sundry writs at various times at Canterbury to levy from the community for the benefit of John and his fellows sundry sums of money for his expenses in staying at these parliaments, namely, on the first day of October in the first year one writ to levy £7. 12s. for the parliament at Lincoln, and on the twenty-eighth day of March in the second year another writ to levy £16. 16s. for one of the parliaments at York and on the thirtieth day of August in the second year a third writ for £8 for the other parliament there, and on the thirtieth day of May in the second year a fourth writ of £10. 8s. for the parliament at Northampton, and on the eleventh day of November in the said year a fifth writ to levy £10. 8s. for the parliament at Salisbury, and the sheriff had levied all the sums of money and paid John none of it and took no pains so far to pay anything, in contempt of the king etc. and to John's loss of 40 marks. And thereof he produces suit etc.

And William readily agrees that he received the aforesaid writs but says that he levied none of the money for the aforesaid expenses. For he says that, because neither he nor his servants could attend to levying the money on account of the king's business, he appointed Robert of Folking and Eustace of Bourne at the instance and special request of John, and with John's assent he made commission for them, namely, one commission to Robert and another commission to Eustace, to levy the money and to pay it to John and his fellows. And whether or not they levied any of it is not known and cannot be known to him because he has not so far meddled further therein. And he prays judgement.

And John does not deny that a commission had been made for Eustace to levy the money, but he says that, before that commission had been made, the sheriff himself and his servants had levied or caused to be levied all the sums of money from the community, namely, from the men of the last of St. Augustine, from the men of the bailiwick of Aylesford, from the men of the bailiwick of Scray, from the men of the seven hundreds, and from the men of the bailiwick of Sutton. And he is ready to prove this etc.

And William says that he levied and caused to be levied not a penny of the aforesaid sums of money before the said commission was made. And he is ready for this to be inquired into etc. And John likewise. Therefore the coroner is ordered to arrange for twelve etc. to come here a Fortnight after Easter to acknowledge etc. And the same day is given to the parties.[1]

[1] For a discussion of these meetings, see Introduction, p.40, *n*.127. It may be observed here that an eyre in Kent that should have been held in the Hilary term of 1328 was cancelled because it conflicted with the Candlemas parliament of 1328 and, while the eyre could not proceed without the nobles summoned to parliament, the parliament could not proceed without the presence and counsel of the eyre justice (*Cal. Close Rolls, 1327-1330*, p.224).

PARLIAMENT AT NORTHAMPTON: 24 April 1328

i

King's Bench Roll, no.285 (Trinity 1331), m.4, crown
[Sayles, *King's Bench*, III. p.cxviii]

John Kirketon, indicted and arrested for two murders, had produced
in the king's bench a royal charter of pardon, dated 10 March 1329.

And in the full parliament held at Northampton in the second year of the
present king's reign[1] it was enacted and ordained that no such charter
with respect to a man's death was henceforth to be granted except in full
parliament and for a specific and reasonable cause. And it does not seem
to the court that it can allow or disallow the aforesaid charter without
parliament etc.

> Kirketon, released on the undertaking of eight men that they would
> have him in person before the king's bench in the Michaelmas term
> of 1329, then appeared.

And after consultation with the king and his council with regard to
allowing the charter after the statute forbidding the grant of charters
outside parliament, it is not the king's wish that such charters, granted
thus in times past by the king's ministers, should be disallowed to the
prejudice of those to whom they were granted. So John is discharged
thereof for the present.

ii

King's Bench Roll, no.275 (Hilary 1329), m.8, crown

Kent

The sheriff was ordered, as before, to distrain the prior of Holy Trinity,
Canterbury, by all the lands etc. and the issues etc. so as to have him in
person before the king on this day, that is to say, a Fortnight after Hilary
wherever etc. to answer the king and the prior of St. Martin, Dover, on
this matter: certain petitions and other memoranda had come before the
king and his council in his parliament convened at Northampton, and
they concerned the prior of St. Martin, Dover, as well as the prior of

---

[1] This parliament was summoned by agreement with the prelates and other magnates
of the king's council to deal with business of the previous parliament at York, which had
been unfinished because of the absence of some of the prelates and magnates (*Foedera*, II.
ii. 733; *Cal. Patent Rolls, 1327-30*, p.248: which omits this point completely).

Holy Trinity, Canterbury with respect to certain grievances and demands made by the prior of Holy Trinity on the prior of Dover, to the prejudice of the king and his crown, and in breach of the immunity of the prior of Dover and in contravention of the judgement lately made in the court of Edward, former king of England, father of the present king. And the king had caused the prior of Holy Trinity to come before the justices of the king's bench to hear the aforesaid petitions and memoranda and to hear his judgement etc. And he did not come.

The defendant was to be distrained to appear in the Easter term.

iii
Chancery Warrants, file 155, no. 1918
[Sayles, *King's Bench*, V. p. cxxxiiif]

Edward, by the grace of God king of England, lord of Ireland and duke of Aquitaine, to the reverend father in God, Henry, by the same grace bishop of Lincoln, our chancellor, greeting. Inasmuch as it was shown to us in our last parliament convened at Northampton that several royal charters of liberties, granted to the communities of great towns and to others, have been issued under our great seal since we received the governance of our realm, to the diminishment of our crown and the obvious disheritance of us and of our crown, it was thereon agreed in our said parliament that instructions should be given to the treasurer and barons of our exchequer, our justices of both benches, and other ministers where appropriate that they were to stop allowing charters, made by us since our coronation, concerning royal franchises granted or interpreted on the basis of ancient words, until our next parliament so that they can then be looked at, examined and judged according to what is right, with the exception of the things granted to our most dear lady and mother for the term of her life, and the charters which have been granted in parliament and with the assent of parliament to the people of London and others. We order you to make thereon such writs as you think necessary under our great seal in accordance with the aforesaid agreement. Given under our privy seal at Credenhill the twenty-eighth day of May in the second year of our reign.[2]

---

[2] 28 May 1328.

iv

King's Bench Roll, no.282 (Michaelmas 1330), m.141

Yorkshire

The parsons and vicars of churches inside the Forest of Galtres had presented a petition before the king and his council in his late parliament at Northampton, complaining that the forest officials were demanding payments from them although their lands were church property only. John of Godley, prebendary of Stillington in St. Peter's, York, who held lands within the Forest, had obtained writs from the king to forbid these exactions but no heed was paid to them. The action by John of Godley against John de Crumwell, the keeper of the Forest beyond the river Trent, and others, was heard in the king's bench in the Hilary term of 1330.

On that day John came by his attorney as well as John de Crumwell and the others by their attorney. And thereupon John de Crumwell and the others prayed judgement of the writ in that the said writ was founded on the petition presented before the king and his council in his parliament at Northampton at the suit of the parsons and vicars of churches within the Forest of Galtres, who made supplication to the king that they should be quit of payments for lands and tenements which are the endowments of their churches within the Forest, and it is contained in the writ that the king ordered the keepers not to molest or in any way harass the parsons and vicars for payments to them on account of their lands and tenements which are the endowments of their churches, but he makes no mention in his order about the prebendary or the lands and tenements of his prebend. Therefore the writ purports that redress had been arranged by the petition for the parsons and vicars only and not for the prebendary etc. And as to this they pray judgement of the writ etc.

And John of Godley says that his writ ought not in this particular to be quashed for the aforesaid reason, because he says that he believes that redress was arranged on the aforesaid petition for prebendaries, with respect to the lands and tenements within the Forest which are the endowments of their prebends, as well as for parsons and vicars within the Forest etc.

And because the court wishes to be certified concerning the contents of the petition and the answer made to it, therefore the king's chancellor is ordered to certify the king about the contents of the petition and the answer made to it at Three Weeks after Easter wherever etc. The same day is given to the parties by their attorneys etc.[3]

---

[3] For another petition in 1334 on this subject from these petitioners, see *Rot. Parl.*, ii. 75.

v

King's Bench Roll, no.275 (Hilary 1329), m.108

Rutland

Writ, dated 17 June 1328, to the sheriff of Rutland. Justices of oyer
and terminer are to send the record of a plea before them to the king,
and the sheriff is to send prisoners before the king's bench:

Inasmuch as it was agreed by us and our council[4] in our parliament
recently convened at Northampton that all writs of oyer and terminer,
adjourned by us in contravention of the terms of the statute published in
the time of our grandfather Edward, the late king of England, are to be
re-summoned, and that the processes of any other such writs of oyer and
terminer, which have been adjourned, are to be placed before the king's
bench, with the exception of two writs of oyer and terminer in the case of
the abbot of Bury St. Edmunds and the abbot of Abingdon as well as
writs of oyer and terminer affecting those involved in the rebellion.

vi

Cambridge University Library, MS. Hh. 2. 4, fo.265
[Cam, *Liberties and Communities of Medieval England*, p.160 f.]

A speech made by William Herle, chief justice of the eyre at
Nottingham, at its opening in 1329.

And then Herle said that the reason for this eyre was that the community
of the realm had put forward a petition at the king's parliament held at
Northamptom to the effect that the peace of his land could not be kept or
maintained as it ought to be. Whereupon the king and his council
ordained that certain justices were to be appointed in each county to
inquire into every kind of felony etc. and trespass at the prosecution of
the king and of others and to hear and determine etc. And then
afterwards at the king's council held at Windsor another petition was put
forward on behalf of the community[5] on the ground that their former

---

[4] In the pleadings this is stated to be 'by the king, prelates, earls, barons and the
community of the realm'. See King's Bench Roll, no.279, m.126: the record of oyer and
terminer proceedings regarding the abbot of Abingdon is sent to the king's bench for
further action.

[5] The council was summoned for 23 July 1329 (*Cal. Close Rolls, 1327-30*, p.550). It
should be observed that popular representatives had not been summoned to this council
and that the 'community' cannot be identified with them.

request did not seem to have been implemented, and this petition was there shown to the great men of the realm and it was there agreed by all that, in order to preserve the peace of the land, justices should be appointed to go on eyre throughout the land. And so the king has heard your petition, so far as he can, and has appointed us to hold this eyre and to show that our powers are such-and-such and that we have authority to hold all manner of pleas.

PARLIAMENT AT SALISBURY: Michaelmas 1328

i

Patent Roll, no.170, m.19

[*Foedera*, II. ii. 752; *Cal. Patent Rolls, 1327-30*, p.323]

The king to the archbishops, bishops, abbots, priors, earls, barons, knights and all others, about to meet at our immediate parliament, summoned at Salisbury. Since we are at the moment hindered by certain business that has befallen us so that we cannot come in person to this place this Sunday,[1] and as we repose the fullest confidence in the great discretion and diligence of the reverend father Henry, bishop of Lincoln, our chancellor, and of our wise Master Walter Harvey, archdeacon of Salisbury, we appoint and depute them to begin the parliament in our name and to do the things which should be done for us and by us until we arrive there. And so we instruct you to be obedient to the bishop and the archdeacon in the aforesaid matters in the aforesaid way. In witness whereof etc. Witness the king at Marlborough on the fifteenth day of October.[2]

By the king himself.

ii

King's Bench, Controlment Roll, no.1 (3 Edward III), m.1

Hampshire

John, bishop of Winchester, amerced for several defaults. The said Bishop John was attached to answer the king on this matter: whereas in the king's parliament lately held at Salisbury the king had forbidden anyone who was summoned to the parliament to depart from it without the king's leave, the bishop during the parliament departed from it without the king's leave, in manifest contempt of the king and against the king's prohibition. And the king by Adam of Fincham, his attorney, says that Bishop John committed the aforesaid trespass against him and to the king's contempt of a thousand pounds. And he offers to prove it etc. And the bishop comes in person and denies all contempt and trespass and whatever etc. And he says that he is one of the peers of the realm and a prelate of Holy Church and it is for them to come to the king's parliament by summons and at the king's will when it pleases him. And

---

[1] 16 October 1328.
[2] 15 October 1328.

he says that if any one of them should offend against the king in parliament, it ought to be redressed and amended in parliament and not elsewhere in a lesser court than parliament, wherefore he does not believe that the king would wish to be answered here in this court with respect to trespass and contempt committed in parliament etc. And day is given them thereon in the king's bench a Fortnight after Trinity wherever etc., reserving the arguments etc. On that day Adam, the king's attorney, comes. And likewise the bishop in his own person. And he is asked if he wishes to say anything as his answer other than he had before, and he says that it seems to him he answers quite adequately. And if etc., he will be ready to answer further etc. And day is given them thereon in the king's bench a Fortnight after Michaelmas wherever etc. reserving to the parties the arguments etc. On that day Adam, the king's attorney, comes etc. And likewise the bishop in his own person. And Adam says on the king's behalf that, when it pleases him to hold his parliament for the welfare of his realm, he has it summoned by his royal authority where and when etc. at his will, and he also sees to it that those who are then at the parliament etc. are all of them forbidden from departing thence against his prohibition etc. in contempt of the king etc., so it is quite lawful for the king to begin his prosecution against such offenders in which court he pleases. And inasmuch as the king holds his parliament at his pleasure etc., he prays judgement for the king whether he ought to be persuaded or compelled to prosecute in this matter elsewhere against his will etc. And the bishop says as before that, when anyone commits an offence in parliament, it ought to be redressed and amended there etc. And, should anyone have been summoned to come to parliament and did not come, he ought to be punished there. Wherefore he does not believe that the king would wish to be answered elsewhere than in parliament etc. And day is given thereon on the Morrow of All Souls wherever etc. in the same state as at present etc.[3]

> Further adjournments were given until the Hilary term of 1330 when process was ended by the king's writ.

---

[3] Cf. *Cal. Close Rolls, 1327-30*, p.420, *1330-33*, p.171.

ADJOURNMENT TO WESTMINSTER: Candlemas 1328

This was not a new parliament but an adjournment of the parliament at Salisbury to Westminster, as the writs of expenses clearly state (Cal. Close Rolls, 1327-30, p.527f.). This is not the only instance of adjournments from one place to another but they are rare. It is evident that it was not easy to accommodate prelates and nobles, with their accompanying retinues, at places outside Westminster or York for very long, and the local people found their sustained presence burdensome. (Foedera, II. ii. 752; Cal. Patent Rolls, 1327-30, p.327). *Since the king was prevented from being present on the opening day of parliament (9 February), he appointed the treasurer and master Henry Cliff and master Adam of Herwinton to begin the session on his behalf* (Foedera, II. ii. 756; Cal. Patent Rolls, 1327-30, p.359).

i
Close Roll, no.148, m.33d
[*Foedera, II. ii. 756; Cal. Close Rolls, 1327-30, p.522*]

The king to the sheriffs of London, greeting. We command you to have it publicly proclaimed throughout the city in places you think appropriate that all and sundry archbishops, bishops, abbots, priors, earls, barons, knights of shires, citizens and burgesses of cities and boroughs, and all others who come or are bound to come to our parliament, continued and adjourned from the city of Salisbury to Westminster at the immediate Octave of the Purification of the Blessed Mary,[1] are to come to Westminster to do what is enjoined upon them on our behalf. And on seeing this letter you are to do this at once. Witness the king at the Tower of London on the eighth day of February.

By the king himself and the council

ii
Chancery Warrants, file 161, no.2574

Edward by the grace of God king of England, lord of Ireland and duke of Aquitaine to the reverend father in God, Henry, by the same grace bishop of Lincoln, our chancellor, greeting. For the good and kindly services that our dear and faithful Sir John de Mohun has done us and our predecessors and because he is now so very much fatigued and of such an age that he cannot labour to good purpose, we will that henceforth he may take his ease on his lands wherever he pleases and that he is not to be

[1] 9 February 1329.

harassed by reason of any service he owes us for the lands he holds of us, neither by summons to the army nor to parliament, always provided that our dear and faithful Robert de Mohun, his son, does us the said services for him. We order you to let John have thereon letters under our great seal in due form.[2] Given under our privy seal at Wallingford the nineteenth day of April in the third year of our reign.[3]

iii

Dean and Chapter, Canterbury, Register I, fo.427, 427*b*
[*Litterae Cantuarienses*, iii. 415, App.68]

The supplication of the prelates, earls and barons and of the whole community of London, made to the king on the Feast of St. Thomas the Apostle in the year of the Lord 1328[4] on behalf of themselves and the community of the realm of England.

Most honourable lord, your lordship may remember how at your last parliament at Salisbury it was announced by your orders in your presence and the presence of the prelates, earls and barons of the land and by common assent of parliament that the said parliament of Salisbury should be continued at Westminster at the Octave of the Purification of our Lady next, and that all things should remain at peace regarding the magnates of the land until that parliament of Westminster, and thereupon a public proclamation was made immediately to the people, to the great relief of all the land. Furthermore, sire, your counsellors who are around you are well aware of the articles you swore at your coronation, and there is included among them that you shall keep the laws and customs granted to your people of England by your predecessors, and that you shall keep peace and quiet as fully as you can for God's sake and that of Holy Church, the clergy and the people, great and small. And it is well known that it is contained in the Great Charter that you shall not go nor send nor ride against any of your land[5-] except by process of law and the judgement of peers, and sentence of excommunication is thereon given by the archbishops and bishops of your land[-5] and this has since been affirmed by several popes and established as the law of your land and confirmed by you and you are bound to maintain it by your said oath. And besides this, sire, all those who break the peace or instigate, aid and counsel in disturbing it and the quiet of your land, or favour or assent to this, are excommunicated by

---

[2] *Cal. Patent Rolls, 1327-30*, p.383.
[3] 19 April 1329.
[4] 21 December 1328.
[5-5] Omitted in the inaccurate printed version in the *Litt. Cant.*

various councils held by various prelates of your realm, as some who are around you can well inform you.

And, sire, inasmuch as it is commonly rumoured that some of your counsellors have advised and abetted you in riding in strength and haste against some peers and others of your land, in breach of the peace of your land and against the aforesaid articles, in great peril to yourself and the great terror of your people and the ruination of your realm, we pray your most noble lordship devoutly and from the heart and warn you in the name of God and the Holy Spirit that you should please cease from such things and from all other dangerous matters that can turn to the dishonour and hurt of yourself, and particularly from the things touching the magnates of your land, until your said parliament of Westminster, according to what was agreed at another time, as abovesaid, and also that you should keep and maintain the peace and the law of your land as you are bound to do by your said oath. And if there be anyone of your land, be he peer or anyone else, who has trespassed or done anything he ought not to have done to your lordship, let him come to your said parliament of Westminster and make amends and be duly punished in accordance with the laws and customs of your land. And considering the great perils we see in the land, may it please your noble lordship to send back your wishes in the aforesaid matters by the bearers of this supplication so that we can stay the cry of the people and be not compelled to do other than it behoves us.

PARLIAMENT AT WINCHESTER: Mid-Lent 1330

i

Close Roll, no.149, m.38d

[*Foedera*, II. ii. 783; *Cal. Close Rolls, 1330-33*, p.130]

The king to the reverend father in Christ Simon, by the same grace archbishop of Canterbury, primate of all England, greeting. It is not, we hope, absent from your memory how lately at Eltham in your presence and that of other prelates and nobles of our realm, whom we caused to be assembled then and there on account of our great and urgent business, the matter concerning us and the king of France was among other things expounded; and after earnest discussion thereon it seemed both to you and to them that we should endeavour by all the ways and means we can to have peace with that king, short of incurring the peril of disinheritance; and, should that king happen to eschew the reasoned ways of peace and strive for our disinheritance in respect of the duchy of Aquitaine and other lands we hold under his overlordship, we must apply our strength to defend ourselves against him with God's help; and for this purpose both you and the other prelates and magnates then and there present offered advice and promised to lend timely aid and assistance; and it was thereon agreed that we should have our parliament summoned at Winchester on Sunday before the Feast of St. Gregory the Pope last.[1]

When the aforesaid business had been expounded in the said parliament and deliberation had taken place about the means and the method of defence to be applied against the said king's power, should he perchance intend to invade our lands, every prelate and magnate had been asked individually what kind of aid he meant to give us in such event and the earls and barons had expressed their will to us in this matter, wishing us well. But the prelates replied that they could not then make a definite reply on account of your absence, but in a convocation, called by you for this purpose, they would do so in such a manner that we should be satisfied therein.

We therefore, looking with proper consideration upon the perils and dangers which could happen not only to us but also to you and the whole of our realm if the aforesaid king should wish to make war upon us, as aforesaid, and if good and stout resistance be not forthcoming, and mindful that you and other prelates and all the clergy of our realm are bound to give a helping hand thereto, not only from due allegiance but also for the purpose of avoiding such great and such likely perils, require

---

[1]   11 March 1330.

and command you that you should arrange for all the prelates, as well religious as others, and all the clergy of your province of Canterbury to be assembled before you on Monday after the Feast of St. Tiburtius and St. Valerian,[2] and you should endeavour to explain most earnestly to them the said business and the imminent dangers and induce them by ways and means you think advisable to make us in so great an emergency such a subsidy in avoidance of so great perils that by the assistance of you and of them we may be able to preserve the rights and the honour of ourselves and the whole of our realm and to defend and protect them and all our people from enemy invasions, God helping us. So we send to you some of our trusted men on the day and at the place aforesaid to follow these matters up and secure their accomplishment, as is then enjoined upon them on our behalf. Witness the king at Winchester on the eighteenth day of March.[3]

ii
Liberate Roll, no.108 (5 Edward III), m.5

Allowance to the sheriff of Hampshire of £104. 14s. 7d. in his account at the exchequer.

For mending and repairing the dilapidated buildings within the castle of Winchester for our stay in that castle on account of our parliament summoned there in the fourth year of our reign.

iii
King's Bench Roll, no.280 (Easter 1330), m.53

Middlesex

At the last parliament of the present king at Winchester on Monday after the Feast of St. Gregory the Pope in the fourth year of his reign[4] Stephen, bishop of London, came among the prelates, earls, barons and other magnates of the realm,[5] and the bishop was interrogated by the king's council in the presence of the king himself on this matter: that the king was given to understand that a certain John of Wimborne was said to have come to the bishop at Stepney in Middlesex on Sunday after

---

[2] 16 April 1330.
[3] 18 March 1330.
[4] 19 March 1330.
[5] The same charge against the archbishop of York is on m.38 (Sayles, *King's Bench*, V. 43).

Michaelmas in the third year of the present king's reign,[6] reporting to him and positively stating that Edward, late king of England, father of the present king, was alive and in good health in the prison of Corfe Castle and asking him if he wished to provide any advice or help for his release. And to this the bishop was said to have replied that he would loyally act and provide all his counsel and aid, not only his own goods and chattels but also a force of men and, if necessary, his own person, to release him as best he could. Therefore he was asked in the king's presence how he might see fit to acquit himself thereof just as the king's court should decide etc. Therefore a day was given him to be before the king and his council at Woodstock on Sunday, a Fortnight after Easter.[7] On that day the bishop came before the king and his council at Woodstock.

> He was then given a day to come before the king's bench at Banbury in Oxfordshire on the Wednesday following the Three Weeks after Easter,[8] where the charge against him was repeated by the king's attorney.

And because such alliances and conferences against the king's estate and such an assembly of armed men, if made within the realm without the king's assent, greatly yield and redound to the king's shame and the harm and impoverishment of his people and the disturbance of his peace and the infringement of the estate of his crown and the king's loss of £10,000, the bishop is asked by the justices how he wishes to acquit himself thereof.

> Eventually on 12 December 1330 the king ordered the charge of adhering to Edmund, late earl of Kent, to be dropped.

iv
Chancery Parliament Roll, no.2, m.7
[*Rot. Parl.* ii. 52-3]

The judgement of Roger Mortimer

These are the acts of treason . . . committed by Roger Mortimer . . . The said Roger in deceitful manner caused the knights of the shire to grant to the king at the parliament of Winchester one man-at-arms from every township in England that answers in an eyre by the reeve and four

---

[6] 1 October 1329.
[7] 22 April 1330.
[8] 2 May 1330.

men, to be at their expense in his war in Gascony for a year . . .
Whereupon our lord the king charges you, earls and barons, the peers of
his realm, that, inasmuch as these things principally concern him and you
and all the people of his kingdom, you are to render just and lawful
judgement upon Roger such as such a one ought to have who is so truly
guilty of all the abovesaid charges, as he understands, and these things are
notorious and known to be true to you and to all the people of the
kingdom. And the earls, barons and peers, having examined the charges,
came back before the king in the said parliament, and they all said
through one of the peers that everything contained in the charges was
notorious and known to them and to the people, and particularly the
charge concerning the death of Edward, father of our present king.
Therefore the earls, barons and peers, as judges of parliament, awarded
and adjudged in the said parliament by assent of the king that Roger was
to be drawn and hanged as a traitor and enemy of the king and his realm.[9]

v

Chancery Parliament Roll, no.2, m.6d
[Rot. Parl. ii. 59b]

A petition of John Clavering concerning a wardship

And after this petition had been read and understood before the council in
this parliament, because the magnates and other men of wisdom therein
were not able to wait there to have a final discussion on the matter, it was
replied that this same petition and all other petitions presented in this
parliament, together with the inquests returned into the chancery by the
escheator . . . should be sent into the chancery and that the chancellor,
having there convened the wise men of the king's council, should do
right therein. And then, after these petitions, inquests, certifications and
other memoranda had been examined before the chancellor, the
treasurer, the justices of both benches, the barons of the exchequer and
other wise men of the king's council, it seems to them that [the petition
should be granted].

---

[9] When the earls, barons and peers were asked to pass a similar judgement on Sir
Simon Bereford for aiding and abetting Roger, 'they all said with one voice that Simon
was not their peer and therefore they were not bound to judge him as a peer of the land',
but as 'judges of parliament' they passed a similar sentence on him (cf. *Rot. Parl.*, ii. 54,
no.6).

PARLIAMENT AT WESTMINSTER: 26 November 1330

i
Close Roll, no.149, m.16d
[*Cal. Close Rolls, 1330-33*, p.166]

That justices in eyre may proceed, notwithstanding the absence of the chief justice

The king to his beloved and faithful Robert of Mablethorpe, Robert of Thorp and Robert of Scarborough, greeting. Whereas we have lately appointed our beloved and faithful William de Herle and you as our justices in eyre for common pleas to be held in the county of Derby and to do other things, as mentioned more fully in our letters patent made thereon, and we have now ordered William to be present in person at our parliament summoned at Westminster on Monday after the Feast of St. Katherine next[1] to discuss with others of our council the business concerning ourselves and our realm. We, being unwilling to delay the said pleas on account of William's absence, order you to proceed to hold those pleas and to do justice to the parties, notwithstanding William's absence for the aforesaid reason. Witness the king at Leicester on the thirteenth day of October.[2]

ii
Ancient Petition, no.8223
[*Rot. Parl.*, ii. 37a, no.32]

To our lord the king and his council show the people of his community that, whereas our lord the king and his ancestors have granted to many towns within their realm that they should not be sued anywhere outside the borders of their Liberties for anything done within their Liberties, and thereby, by colour of these Liberties, they oppress the people there, that is to say, they beat and kill the folk coming there because they have the assurance that they themselves will have jurisdiction over their own

---

[1] 26 November 1330. The parliament was summoned on 23 October and the king had, with the assent of his prelates and magnates, shortened the period between summons and assembly (i.e. 34 days) and promised that this should not constitute a precedent (*Cal. Close Rolls, 1330-33*, p.160). Though writs of expenses were issued on 9 December to popular representatives, the parliament was still in session on 20 January 1331 (*ibid.*, pp.179, 280 f., 553; cf. p.175). The abbot of Dore was given £20 for expenses in expediting the king's affairs at this parliament (*Cal. Close Rolls*, 1330–1333, p.189).

[2] 13 October 1330.

acts and will give themselves an acquittal. Therefore these Liberties are granted in prejudice of the crown, for thereby the law cannot be provided, and to the people's harm, and we pray redress thereof.

Let those who feel themselves aggrieved sue at common law, and if they cannot be assisted by it, the king will apply another remedy.

iii
Close Roll, no.149, m.18d
[*Foedera*, II. ii. 800; *Cal. Close Rolls, 1330-33*, p.161 f.]

The king to the sheriff of Lancaster, greeting. Inasmuch as we have heard that sundry oppressions and hardships have been inflicted upon many men of our kingdom by some who have been our ministers in various offices and also by some magnates of our realm, as well our councillors as others, so that our business has, by reason of our tender age, been conducted by some to our loss and dishonour, which we would not wish to suffer any longer, and we have a very great desire for everything to be put in proper order and the wrongs and misprisions redressed, we command and charge you in the fealty you owe us that you should immediately and without delay cause it to be proclaimed within your bailiwick, within Liberties as well as outside them, that all those who wish to make a complaint about oppressions, hardships and other grievances inflicted upon them in contravention of right and the laws and customs of our realm, are to come to Westminster to this next parliament of ours and there show their plaints to us or to those whom we shall appoint as our deputies for this purpose, and we shall cause appropriate and immediate redress to be done them, by which they ought to be rightly satisfied.

And inasmuch as before this time some of the knights, who have come to parliament on behalf of the communities of the shires, have been members of unlawful associations and the maintainers of false plaints and have prevented the good men [of the shires] from being able to show the grievances of the common people or the things which should have been redressed in parliament, to the great injury of us and of our people, we order and charge you to cause to be elected, by common assent of your county court, two of the most loyal and most respected knights or serjeants in the said shire, who are not under suspicion of unlawful associations or of being common maintainers of any parties, to be at our said parliament according to the form of our command which you have thereon. And you are not to neglect this as you wish to avoid our vexation and indignation. Given at Woodstock the third day of November.[3]

By the king himself.

The same order is sent to every sheriff throughout England.

iv

Exchequer Plea Roll, no.59 (5 and 6 Edward III), m.30

Yorkshire

Whereas William archbishop of York and Richard de la Pole now had a day here a Fortnight after Easter with regard to certain customary prises of wine in the port of Hull which belonged to the archbishop and were collected by Richard, the king's late butler, to the amount of forty pounds within the time of the king's parliament convoked at Winchester[4] and the time of the parliament convoked at Westminster on the Morrow of St. Catherine the Virgin in the same year,[5] the said archbishop and Richard have appeared. And at their request they had a further day a Fortnight after Midsummer.[6]

v

King's Bench Roll, no.282 (Michaelmas 1330), m.125 (6 B)

The long drawn-out contest between the two Yarmouths, Great and Little, and Gorleston, ports on the Norfolk coast, concerning their respective privileges. It was not settled until 3 June 1331 (*Cal. Patent Rolls, 1330-1334*, p.124). The proceedings before the king's bench in the Michaelmas term of 1330 ended thus:

And because the whole business relating to the claims made by the aforesaid ports and their charters pends undiscussed before the king and his council in his parliament, and therefore, if further proceedings were to be taken on this plea and judgement rendered thereon, the said judgement might happen to be in disagreement with or contrary to the

[3] 3 November 1330.
[4] 11 March 1330.
[5] 26 November 1330.
[6] 8 July 1331. Four commissioners, appointed to examine the evidence in this dispute, were ordered by the council on 21 July to incorporate into an agreement all the points accepted by both parties and to refer all doubtful and controversial matters to the king in the next parliament for decision there (*Cal. Patent Rolls, 1330-34*, p.200).

judgement which still remains to be pronounced before the king and his council on the aforesaid business, for this reason the court here is not yet advised whether or not it ought to proceed further in this plea. Therefore a day is given to the parties in the king's bench a Fortnight after Hilary.

vi

King's Bench Roll, no.283 (Hilary 1331), m.149

Writ, addressed on 20 January 1331 to the king's bench, sending the petition presented before the king and his council, with relevant documents, and ordering an investigation in the presence of the king's serjeants, though no judgement was to be reached without consulting the king.

To our lord the king and his council show his chaplains, the Empress's abbot and convent of Stanley,[7] that, by petition in the parliaments of Westminster, York, Northampton, Salisbury, and further at Westminster and at Winchester, they have sued for the right of their church in the manor of Berwick Basset in Wiltshire, whereof the abbot's predecessors were in peaceful seisin by leave of Sir Philip Basset until they were ousted and disseised by Sir Hugh Despenser the elder against the law of the land, and he then had their charters and muniments of the manor within their abbey burned so as to deprive them of their right. And though this disseisin was proved by an inquisition, taken by the good men of the neighbourhood on a writ of our lord the king, authorised at his first parliament of Westminster, and though the inquisition was returned into the chancery and asked for and shown at his parliament of Northampton and at this parliament the treasurer and chamberlains were ordered to search Sir Hugh's muniments and found nothing, and though they were ordered several times by writ to make a search and they found nothing that would be able to exclude the abbot and his house from their right in the manor, the treasurer, the chancellor, the triers of bills, and the justices have not yet wished to give an answer to the abbot and convent on this petition. They pray that it may please our lord the king and his council to order what is proper and right to be done them with regard to their petition.

The endorsement of this petition is as follows:

Let this inquisition and the other memoranda be sent by writ to the king's bench and, after the king's serjeants have been summoned and

---

[7] The abbey was founded by the Empress Matilda.

their arguments on behalf of the king have been heard as well as the arguments of the party, let right be done, provided that there is no proceeding to judgement without consulting the king.

There was then copied on to the roll the inquisition and the writ to the treasurer and chamberlains, dated 10 November 1327. The abbot was still petitioning in parliament 'for justice for the wrong done him' in 1334. The argument centred on whether the abbot's predecessor had the right to have the manor without first obtaining leave from the king, even though he had it before the Statute of Mortmain of 1279. At last in the parliament at Westminster on the Morrow of the Purification in 1338 the complete record was read before the archbishop of Canterbury and the chancellor, treasurer, justices and others and examined with great care, and each and all agreed that the abbot and convent should regain seisin of the manor after a fine had been made with the king. The fine was later fixed at ten marks.

PARLIAMENT AT WESTMINSTER: Michaelmas 1331

*It had been intended to hold a parliament at Easter 1331 but it was cancelled on 23 March (*Cal. Close Rolls, 1330-33, p.298).

Chancery Parliament Roll, no.2, m.4
[*Rot. Parl.*, ii. 60]

These are the memoranda of what was done in the parliament held at Westminster on the Morrow of Michaelmas in the fifth year of the reign of King Edward the Third.[1]

First of all, it was announced by the bishop of Winchester, the king's chancellor, that the parliament had been summoned for the business concerning the duchy of Aquitaine and the king's lands overseas in order to make peace or other conclusion in the disagreements arising between the kings of England and of France by reason of the said lands; and also for the business of Ireland in connection with the departure of the king to those parts, as he was advised by his loyal subjects there; and also to arrange how the peace [of the land] can best be kept.

And it was also agreed there that the king's business should first of all be accomplished before anything was done about any other business, and that the business concerning the lands overseas, that is to say, between the two kings, should first be dealt with, as aforesaid.

[1] 30 September 1331,

PARLIAMENT AT WESTMINSTER: 16 March 1332

Chancery Parliament Roll, no.2, m.3
[*Rot. Parl.*, ii. 64–66]

These are the memoranda of the parliament summoned to Westminster on Monday after the Feast of St. Gregory in the sixth year of King Edward the Third.[1]

On that Monday the following two articles were read before our lord the king and all the prelates and other great men who had then come to the parliament, and they were then proclaimed in Westminster Hall as well as in the city of London. And because the archbishop of Canterbury and many other magnates of the realm, summoned to this parliament, had not yet arrived, nothing more was done during this day.

Because quarrelling, rioting and fighting have arisen and been set going before this time at parliaments and councils of our lord the king because people have gone to the places, where parliaments and councils have been summoned and assembled, armed with hatchets and iron bars, swords, long knives and other kinds of arms, and for that reason the business of our lord the king and of his realm has been hindered and the magnates and others who have come to him at his command have been terrified.

> The carrying of arms is forbidden, under total forfeiture of property, in the city of London or its suburbs or between the city and the palace of Westminster, or within the palace.

And it is not our lord the king's intention that any earl and baron may not be accompanied by his sword, except in the king's presence and in the place where the council meets.

Our lord the king forbids under pain of imprisonment that any children or others shall play in any part of Westminster Palace during the parliament summoned there at bars,[2] or at other games or at knocking off people's hats or laying hands on them or causing any other hindrance by which no one can peacefully pursue his business.

And then in full parliament the said archbishop announced in the form of a sermon, in the presence of our lord the king and of all the prelates and other magnates, the cause for which the parliament was summoned; and also it was announced by the bishop of Winchester, the chancellor, in the

---

[1] 16 March 1332.
[2] The pitching of iron or wooden bars to see who had the ability to throw them farthest.

form of a sermon, how the king of France had decided that he would go
to the Holy Land two years from this March, and that it would greatly
please him to have the company of our lord the king of England on this
journey, believing thereby to make a better onslaught on the enemies of
God. And he has by his letters as well as by his messengers requested our
lord the king of England to do this, and this was the reason why the
parliament was summoned, and on behalf of our lord the king he asked
for the counsel and advice of the prelates, earls, barons and all other
magnates in full parliament on this matter.

> Arrangements were then made for keeping the peace throughout the
> country while the king was away in the Holy Land.

And these things, thus ordained by the earls, barons and other
magnates, were read before our lord the king and the prelates, knights of
the shire and the people of the community, and were pleasing to them all,
and they received full assent and agreement from our lord the king, the
prelates, earls, barons and other great men as well as from the knights of
the shires and the people of the community.

Note that on the Saturday after the first day of parliament the knights
of the shires, the citizens and burgesses summoned to this parliament, as
well as the clergy, have leave to go to their own homes, provided the
prelates, earls, barons and the members of the king's council remained
there. And it was announced on the same day that, because parliament
had been summoned for the aforesaid reasons and the petitions of the
people were neither received nor answered at the said parliament, our
lord the king meant to have another parliament soon.

PARLIAMENT AT WESTMINSTER: 9 September 1332

i

Chancery Warrants, file 192, no.5687
[Sayles, *King's Bench*, V. p.cxlvii f.]

Edward, by the grace of God king of England, lord of Ireland and duke of Aquitaine, to the reverend father in God John, by the same grace bishop of Winchester, our chancellor, greeting. Because we have adjourned our dear ones in God the abbot of St. Mary's York, the dean and chapter of York and the master of St. Leonard's, York, and others to be before you and our council at Westminster on the Morrow of St. Peter's Day[1] with respect to the customary allowances from our forests beyond Trent, and we wish you to adjourn them further to our next parliament, so we order and enjoin you to have them adjourned on this business in the aforesaid manner. Given under our privy seal at Woodstock the twenty-sixth day of July in the sixth year of our reign.[2]

ii

Chancery Parliament Roll, no.2, m.2
[*Rot. Parl.*, ii. 66-67]

The third day of parliament, that is to say, on Friday,[3] Geoffrey le Scrope on behalf of our lord the king asked all the magnates of the parliament as well as the knights of the shire to give their counsel and advice whether our lord the king should stay until the business of the parliament was finished or go his way quickly to the north, as aforesaid. And the magnates and the knights advised him that it would be better for him to take his way to the north without waiting any longer for the business. And they further prayed the king that, when the time was suitable, it would please him to give instructions that the affairs of the people, whose petitions were put forward at this parliament, should be completed. And the king graciously granted their request.

---

[1] 2 August 1332.
[2] 26 July 1332. The archbishop of York wrote on 14 August to Edward III to say that he had received a writ under the great seal, summoning him to parliament on 9 September 1332, and he asked for a protection for himself, his cross, and his company against the archbishop of Canterbury (Ancient Correspondence, vol. XXXVIII, no.104; *Cal. Close Rolls, 1330-33*, p.598).
[3] 11 September 1332. See also *Cal. Close Rolls, 1330-33*, p.604, for a decision made in parliament concerning proceedings against Philip Turville and others, indicted for harbouring felons: the enrolment is dated 10 September.

PARLIAMENT AT YORK: 4 December 1332 and 20 January 1333

i

King's Bench Roll, no.290 (Michaelmas 1332), m.30d
[Sayles, *King's Bench*, V. 71-72]

Yorkshire

A plaint of contempt and trespass concerning an assault on the steps outside the door of the hall in which the king's bench was sitting. A jury returned a verdict in the plaintiff's favour.

And because the trespass and contempt were done in the presence of the justices within the summons of parliament, that is to say, on the day before parliament began, and also within the king's verge and in obstruction of the law of the land and of the plaintiff's suit in the king's court, the defendant is committed to the marshal, to be kept securely in prison until the king shall decree his will thereon in his parliament etc.

ii

B.L., Cotton MS., Vespasian E. xxi., f. 97

To the revered man of discretion and our special friend, Henry of Edwinstowe,[1] Adam by divine permission abbot of Peterborough, with a full embrace of love and devoted greetings. We have sent you our letter of proxy for parliament by the bearer of this letter, Adam Cliff, your servant, together with a letter for your pension, as you requested, and we pray you to be good enough of your grace to excuse our absence from the said parliament, as before this time you have done. And, indeed, dearest one, the benefice you thought acceptable is not included, though we diligently urged its acceptance upon our brethren, who refused to give their assent to it because it should not be granted from our house to anyone with any such letter of pension. Yet you must know for certain that, as soon as any of those churches you have already named in your letter happens to be void and we learn of the vacancy, we will confer it upon you, and furthermore, if a better one in our patronage perchance falls in, we will present it to you by our letters without delay. May you flourish happily in the Lord. Written at Peterborough on the Morrow of St. Clement.[2]

---

[1] He was clerk of parliament.
[2] 24 November 1332. The proctorial letter, dated 29 November, precedes this letter.

iii
Chancery Parliament Roll, no.2, m.1
[*Rot. Parl.*, ii. 67]

These are the memoranda of the parliament summoned at York on Friday before the Feast of St. Nicholas in the sixth year of the reign of king Edward III.

On Friday[3] the king did not come but he was near by, awaiting the arrival of the magnates who were summoned to the parliament, and so the parliament was continued until the following Monday. And on that Monday, in the presence of our lord the king, the parliament was continued until the next day, Tuesday, on account of the non-arrival of the magnates as aforesaid. And on Tuesday Geoffrey le Scrope, in the presence of the king and all the magnates, announced in open parliament how the previous parliament had been summoned to Westminster for business concerning the land of Ireland, whither the king had arranged to go to restrain the wrongdoing of his rebels there; and how the prelates, earls, barons and other magnates of the parliament and the knights of the shires were charged to give advice upon the security of the land of England; and how the prelates by themselves, the earls and barons by themselves, and the knights of the shires by themselves, had a discussion and answered and advised that it would be better if the king were to remain in England. And on account of the news which then came from the parts of Scotland the king made his way to the region of the north by reason of the dangers which could befall his people and his realm if the Scots should purpose to enter there to do mischief; and how the king, agreeing with their advice, had thus arrived there; and how then, because of other news which came to him at York from the parts of Scotland to the effect that Edward Balliol had had himself crowned king of Scotland, by the authority of the king and of his council then and there convened[4] he had caused his parliament to be summoned at once to York, and that the cause of the summons was that our lord the king wished to have the counsel of his good people and the loyal subjects of his realm, prelates and others, whether he ought to make his way to Scotland, demanding the lordship of that land. . . . And the prelates with the clergy by themselves, and the earls and barons by themselves, and the knights and people of the counties and the people of the community by themselves,

---

[3] 4 December 1332. Since the king could not be present on the opening day he appointed the archbishop of York, master Robert Stratford and Geoffrey Scrope to begin parliament in his name (*Foedera*, II. ii. 848; *Cal. Patent Rolls, 1330-34*, p.371).

[4] For this council see *Rot. Parl.*, ii. 69c.

discussed and deliberated until the following Friday . . . And they replied that they dared not and knew not how to advise on such great and urgent business, so closely affecting the king, his people and his realm, without the advice of the prelates (of whom only three, that is to say, the archbishop of York and the bishops of Lincoln and of Carlisle, with the abbots of York and Selby, have come) and of other magnates of the realm who had not come there. And they requested our lord the king thereon that he would be good enough to continue this parliament until the Octave of Hilary next, to be still at the same place of York, and to order and charge the prelates and the other magnates, who were absent, to be there then at the said day and place so that the business would be no longer delayed by their non-arrival. And our lord the king granted this request. And thereupon all the prelates, earls and barons, knights of the shire, and people of the community, then present, were ordered to be there at the said Octave at the said parliament without having any further instructions . . . And so the parliament ended on the Friday before the Feast of St. Lucy.[5]

And the reason why petitions were not received and answered in the parliament was because prelates and other magnates as well as men of the law, who could try them and answer them, had not come to the parliament, and also because Christmas was so near that no one would have been able to get a good hearing. And thereon it was agreed that petitions should be received at the next parliament.

Note that John de Crumwell, by word of mouth in the presence of our lord the king and of all the magnates in full parliament on the said Friday when the parliament ended, showed what is contained in the following petition, but because his request cannot be met without new law being ordained in such a case, therefore it was adjourned until the next parliament.[6]

[5] 11 December 1332.

[6] For the precise answer to the petition see the transcripts of parliamentary petitions in B.L., Cotton MS., Titus E. 1, fo. 26b: a statute of 1327 annulled acquisitions of land made by the Despensers under duress after their return from exile in 1321, and it was now requested that the statute should be extended to cover such acquisitions made before their exile. The petition was endorsed: 'Let the petition be put among the petitions on which new law is to be made'.

iv
King's Bench Roll, no.293 (Trinity 1333), m.24, crown

The officials and servants of the sheriffs of Lincoln were indicted in
the Easter week of 1333 of serious wrongdoing, including the
following:

They present that, whereas the knights of the shire are elected to
parliament for the community of the county at the county court and have
their expenses specified, all the bailiffs of that county came there and
levied the aforesaid expenses at double or treble the rate at least, to the
very serious loss of the community of the county etc.

They present that, whereas the king's writ came to the sheriff of
Lincoln, ordering him to elect and send two knights to the king's
parliament in the fourth year and likewise in the sixth year on behalf of
the whole county of Lincoln, Thomas of Carleton, the then sub-sheriff,
returned the names of the said Thomas of Carleton and of a certain John
de Trehampton as being the knights of the shire,[7] and afterwards,
whereas their expenses did not exceed ten marks, the said Thomas and
John had twenty pounds levied by extortion as their expenses from the
county, to the no slight loss and grievance of the men of that county.

m.25

And as for the third article to the effect that Thomas on his own
authority without the assent of the community of the county of Lincoln
returned his own name and that of a certain John de Trehampton as being
the knights about to set off to the king's parliament and was said to have
levied twenty pounds, which was more than their expenses came to etc.,
he says that such election was made by the community of the men of the
whole county, and the expenses of the knights are always assessed by the
king's court, and their expenses were levied by the king's writ in
accordance with that assessment etc., without his imposing anything
extra or levying or causing to be levied any money beyond their expenses
thus assessed etc. . . . .

---

[7] *Parl. Returns*, pp.92, 100.

Chancery Parliament Roll, no.2, m.1
[*Rot. Parl.*, ii. 68–69]

These are the memoranda of the parliament summoned at York on Wednesday in the Octave of Hilary in the sixth year of the reign of King Edward the Third.[9]

On this Wednesday it is granted by our lord the king and his council that petitions are to be received, as was granted at another time in the previous parliament last summoned there, and that all those who wish to hand in petitions at this parliament are to hand them in between now and Sunday next, including this Sunday, and beyond that Sunday no petition is to be received by an auditor of petitions or anyone else, and that the petitions are to be handed in to Henry of Edwinstowe, clerk of the parliament, Thomas of Bamborough and Thomas of Evesham for England and to master John of Blyborough and Thomas of Brayton for Gascony, Ireland, Wales and the Channel Isles.

It is also granted that the archbishop of York, the bishop of Ely and the bishop of Chester, Hugh de Courtnay, William la Zuche of Ashby, barons, Henry le Scrope, John of Stonor, William of Deanham and Richard of Aldborough, justices, are to try and to determine the petitions for England; the bishops of Lincoln, Norwich and Exeter, Ralph Basset of Drayton, Richard de Grey, barons, Thomas Bacon and Geoffrey of Edenham, justices, are to try and to determine the petitions of Gascony, Ireland, Wales and the Channel Islands; and that the said prelates, barons and justices, the triers and auditors of the petitions, are to summon to them the bishop of Winchester, chancellor, Geoffrey le Scrope, chief justice, and the treasurer, or any of them when trying and determining the aforesaid petitions, when necessary or when they think it should be done.

It is also granted that the petitions which shall be tried and determined by the said prelates, barons and justices, thus appointed triers, are to be sent into chancery under their seals, or the seals of two of them, or the seal of one of them at least, and that the rest of the petitions are to remain under the seals of the triers in the custody of the clerks until the next day, and so from day to day, and that the petitions which are to be tried and determined before the king should be tried before him, summoning to him such as he pleases, and that the said petitions are to remain under the seals of the auditors, or of one of them, until they are brought before the king.

[9] 20 January 1333.

And in open parliament at the said Octave Geoffrey le Scrope on behalf of our lord the king, charged all the prelates, earls, barons and other magnates who were there as well as the knights of the shire that, in the allegiance and fealty they owe our lord the king and having regard only to the honour of the king and of the realm, they were to advise him what he ought to do in respect of the business of Scotland. And it was agreed thereon by our lord the king and by all in open parliament that the archbishop of York, the bishops of Ely, Winchester, Lincoln, Chester and Norwich, the earl Warenne and the earl of Warwick, the lord Percy, Henry de Beaumont, Hugh de Courtnay, and William de Clinton, barons, were to deal with the said business by themselves; and the other prelates, earls and barons, and the proctors by themselves; and the knights of the shires and the people of the community by themselves.

And on Tuesday[10] the knights of the shires and the people of the community had leave to depart to their homes, and the prelates, earls and barons were told to remain until the next day. And thus the parliament ended.

vi

Parliament and Council Proceedings file 6, no.20

[Richardson and Sayles, *Rot. Parl.Inediti*, pp.224–230]

The commons pray that all the bills, presented by the commons at various parliaments in the time of our present lord king and not answered, may be duly answered and expedited at this parliament, especially concerning the goods transported by aliens, both men of religious orders and other natives and foreigners.

The commons pray that, whereas petitions are put forward in parliament and answered by the justices, in a case where instructions are given to search in the treasury or elsewhere to see if any evidence can be found in favour of the king, the treasurer and the chamberlains reply that they have searched in part and not everything, and so it goes on day after day to every writ that comes to them, and the parties are all the time delayed by such replies and may lose their action because they make no answer to the writs, it may please our lord the king and his council to ordain that, after the party has sued out three writs and nothing has been found, even though they make such a reply, the justices may proceed to

---

[10] 26 January 1333.

do justice to the parties, or else the people will be more oppressed through submitting petitions than they were before.[11]

To this thirteenth petition concerning scrutiny:

The king wills that his justices and his other ministers do justice fully to the parties in accordance with law and right.

vii

Chancery Warrants, file 199, nos.6341-2

[Sayles, *King's Bench*, III, p.cxix]

Edward by the grace of God king of England, lord of Ireland and duke of Aquitaine to the reverend father in God, John, by the same grace bishop of Winchester, our chancellor, greeting. We are sending you, enclosed within this letter, a petition which was presented to us on behalf of the community of our realm, and instruct you to inspect the petition with regard to the matters mentioned in it and to have such redress ordained on the advice of our council that justice and what is right be done to all. Given under our privy seal at Newcastle upon Tyne the twentieth day of April in the seventh year of our reign.[12]

Endorsed: Let it wait until the next parliament.[13]

To our lord the king prays the community of his land that it may please him to order redress in the case where, when a man brings a writ of debt against several executors and [only] one of the executors appears in court and the others ought to lose their issues, the appearance of one of the executors saves the issues of the others so that the plaintiffs will never be able to bring the executors to answer, to the great loss and the great damage of the plaintiffs, wherefore they ask for a remedy to be formed on the case in accordance with what they requested by petition in parliament, that is to say, that at the term day following the appearance [of one of the executors] the executors are to come to plead and, if they do not, the plaintiffs are to have judgement in their favour for the debt.

---

[11] Cf. *Cal. Close Rolls, 1333-37*, p.60, for the countermanding on 20 June 1333 of arrangements made in this parliament.

[12] 20 April 1333.

[13] Statute 9 Edward III, c.3 (*Statutes of the Realm*, i. 271).

PARLIAMENT AT YORK: Lent 1334

Chancery Parliament Roll, no.4
[Richardson and Sayles, *Rot. Parl. Inediti*, 232-39]

Roll of parliament of the eighth year of the reign of king Edward the Third.

Note that, whereas at the parliament of Edward the Third, king of England, summoned at York on Monday before the Feast of St. Peter *in cathedra* in the eighth year of his reign,[1] sundry petitions were handed in and presented in the parliament by the people of the community. And some of them were granted in the parliament to be put in a statute, and some to be enrolled, along with the answers to them, and stay in the chancery, and some received no answers in order to get better information and advice about them. And the following petitions with the answers were delivered to Michael of Wath, keeper of the rolls of chancery, by Henry of Edwinstowe, clerk of the parliament, to be kept in the chancery and enrolled and to have writs made on them when it is appropriate.

To our lord the king pray the good people of the community that the Great Charter and the Charter of the Forest, all the statutes and laws of the land, be kept in every particular.

Answered: Let the Great Charter, the Charter of the Forest, and the other statutes be kept in every particular, and let the statutes which are obscure be clarified on good advice.[2]

---

[1] 21 February 1334.
[2] This parliament was 'continued' at Three Weeks after Easter (Ancient Correspondence, LXI. 46): a fact unknown from other sources.

PARLIAMENT AT WESTMINSTER: 19 September 1334

i
Ancient Petition, file 32, no. 1564

To our lord the king and to his council pray his poor people of Bamborough that they had before this time taken the demesne lands of Bamborough Castle to farm for a specific time – some for six or seven years, others for ten years, and sometimes for longer terms, sometimes for lesser terms, one acre for two shillings a year, another for two shillings and sixpence, another for three shillings. And each time the constables of the castle have been changed, they have ousted the said people from their lease and have taken fines from them, that is to say, from one 20s. from another 30s., from another 40s., for allowing them to have their lease, to the great loss of the said people, and this money does not profit our lord the king at all but only the constable. And the said men sued thereon by petition in the parliament last held at Westminster in order to get redress of such extortions, praying the king and his council that they might have letters patent under the great seal with respect to their aforesaid lease. And answer was made to this petition that certain men would be appointed to inquire about whether it would be to the loss of the king or to his profit if our lord the king should grant them the said lands on lease and about the value of the land and about other essential points. And the petition is now in the memoranda of chancery in the Tower of London. And nothing has been done in connection with this business. Wherefore they pray the king that it may please him to appoint again some specific person to make inquiry in the aforesaid manner and that, when the results have been returned, they may have his letters patent of a specific lease so that they may no longer be aggrieved and the king without profit.

Endorsed: Let certain men be appointed to inquire about whether it is to the king's loss or to his profit if he should grant the said lands to the said people for a certain term and about the number of acres and about the value in the presence of the constable, and let the results of the inquiry be returned into the chancery, and if it be found from the inquiry that it would not be to the king's loss, then let them have letters patent under the great seal for some specific term, paying the value of the land.

ii

Register of John de Grandisson, fo.184

[ed. F.C. Hingeston-Randolph, ii. 760]

Edward by the grace of God king of England, lord of Ireland and duke of Aquitaine, to the reverend father in God John, by the same grace bishop of Exeter, greeting. Because we wish for a certain cause to be informed which benefices of Holy Church within your diocese are held by aliens, that is to say, archdeaconries, priories, prebends, churches, chapels, hospitals, portions,[1] pensions and any other benefices, and how and by what title they have attained them, and of the true value of each of the said benefices, and the names of those who possess them, we instruct and charge you, in the faith and allegiance you owe to us, to inquire fully into this business and let us be informed clearly and openly about it in our next parliament. And in no way are you to neglect this. Given under our privy seal at Windsor the third day of August in the eighth year of our reign.[2]

[1] That is, parts of divided benefices.

[2] 3 August 1334. The bishop replied with the names on 12 September (*op. cit.*, ii. 763).

PARLIAMENT AT YORK: 26 May 1335

Ancient Correspondence, vol. XXXVII, no.152

The king to his beloved clerk John Piers, greeting. Whereas we have appointed you to the office of proctor and envoy and prosecutor and defender of the rights of us and ours in all processes between us and our ancestors and the king of France and his people in the court of France and elsewhere, and these pend undecided before commissaries . . . And you are to inform us in writing about matters too difficult and in need of speedy redress, together with the details and doubtful points you have found in the aforesaid business so that on these matters we can have counsel and discussion with the prelates and nobles of our realm and other councillors of ours assembled in our present parliament at York in order to provide redress in the said affairs . . . Witness me myself at York on the seventh day of June in the ninth year of our reign.[1]

[1] This is a draft letter, much altered and difficult to read. The date 7 June 1335 has been substituted for 28 May. For writs of expenses, issued on 3 June, see *Cal. Close Rolls, 1333-1337*, p.500).

PARLIAMENT AT WESTMINSTER: Lent 1336

i

King's Bench Roll, no.305 (Trinity), m.33

A writ, dated 6 May 1336, to the king's bench, enclosing a petition presented before the king and his council in parliament on 11 March 1336.

May it please our lord the king and his good council to understand that Sir Hugh Despenser the father, formerly lord of the manor of Parlington in the county of York, gave the manor with its appurtenances to Philip, his son, father of Philip, the present demandant, to have and to hold to him and his heirs, the lawful issue of his body. And Philip, peacefully seised of this manor, took to wife Margaret, daughter and heiress of Ralph de Goushill, and engendered with her the demandant, Philip. And meanwhile the father, Philip, passed away and after his death Sir Hugh Despenser the father re-entered the manor and kept it for years and days until he gave it to Sir John Crumwell. And Philip brought his writ against the said John and before the plea could be determined, Sir John passed away. And after his death the bailiffs of my lady the queen entered the manor as being held of the honour of Pontefract. And Philip had sued against my lady the queen by a petition, and my lady's council answered the petition and said that my lady had only a life-interest in the honour of Pontefract and the reversion belongs to our lord the king and his heirs, and therefore she can do nothing in the aforesaid business without advice from the king. And Philip prays redress thereon.

The endorsement of the petition follows in these words:

If the king's great council approves, let this petition be sent to the king's bench and let it be shown there what Philip has from Hugh's gift of the aforesaid manor, and after summoning the queen's ministers as well as the king's serjeants – should any right pertain to the king – and others who ought to be summoned in this respect and after the justices of the king's bench have been informed of the reason why the manor was taken into the queen's hands and have heard the arguments for the king and the queen as well as for Philip, let them do further what is right, provided they do not go to final judgement in the said business without consulting the king.

It is then agreed by the great council that the petition should be sent as aforesaid.

The proceedings were subjected to constant adjournments and judgement was not given until Easter term 1347.

ii

K.R. Memoranda Roll, no.113 (11 Edward III), m.176, Trinity Recorda

Of the biennial tenth to be collected

Note that the prelates and clergy of the province of York have granted the king a biennial tenth in aid of some important business of his – that is to say, in their convocation at St. Peter's church, York, on the sixth day of May in the tenth year[1] for the first year, and in another convocation there on Monday after the Feast of St. Luke the Evangelist following[2] for the second year – from their ecclesiastical property and benefices, to be paid each year at the Feasts of the Purification of the Blessed Virgin Mary[3] and the Nativity of St. John the Baptist[4] by equal instalments . . .

Of the biennial tenth to be collected

Note that the prelates and clergy of the province of Canterbury have granted the king a biennial tenth – that is to say, in their convocation in St. Paul's church, London, in the king's parliament at Westminster summoned on Monday after the Sunday in Mid-Lent in the tenth year, namely the eleventh day of March in the said year,[5] for the first year of the tenth, and in another convocation at Leicester on Monday after Michaelmas in the said year[6] for the second year of the said tenth.

---

[1] 6 May 1336.
[2] 21 October 1336.
[3] 2 February.
[4] 24 June.
[5] 11 March 1336.
[6] 30 September 1336.

PARLIAMENT AT WESTMINSTER: 3 March 1337

i

Exchequer Accounts 388/2

[cited Tout, *Chapters*, iii. 62n]

The first day of parliament: Sunday, the second day of March.

Sunday, the sixteenth day of March . . . On this day the king made his eldest son duke of Cornwall, six became earls, namely, Gloucester, Salisbury, Derby, Northampton,[1] Huntingdon and Suffolk, and twenty knights. And he held a great court on that day with full ceremonial, and the queen held a little court at the king's expense with two countesses and ladies.

ii

B.L., Additional MS. 41612, Ely Cartulary, fo. 18b (80b)

Proctor to parliament: Let it appear to all men by the present letter that we, the prior and chapter of the cathedral church of Ely, have jointly and severally made, appointed, and constituted our beloved in Christ W. of London and Henry of Thetford, clerks, by the present letter to be our proctors to appear for us and in our name at the approaching parliament of our illustrious lord king of England, to be held at the Octave of the Purification of the Blessed Mary at York,[2] and also to consent to those things which then happen to be ordained there by common counsel of his realm, the Lord being kindly disposed, and we will hold as both right and accepted whatever these our proctors or each of them may think fit to do in our name in the aforesaid affairs. In witness whereof our common seal is appended to this present letter. Given at Ely on the eighth day of January in the year of the Lord 1337.[3]

---

[1] For grants made to enable the earls to maintain their new dignity, see *Cal. Patent Rolls, 1334-38*, pp. 409 f., 414-16, 418, 426; *Cal. Close Rolls, 1337-39*, pp. 48 f., 57, 60 f., 173.

[2] 9 February 1337. This parliament had first been summoned to meet on 13 January at York, then postponed to 9 February at York, and finally assembled on 3 March at Westminster. It was thought advisable to hold the parliament in a place more removed from danger (*Cal. Close Rolls, 1333-37*, p. 736).

[3] 8 January 1337. For an important petition presented in this parliament, charging a justice of oyer and terminer with wrongfully trying a case in which he had an interest, see Ancient Petition, no. 10249 (cf. *Cal. Close Rolls, 1337-1339*, p. 12 f.). The chancery warrant (1538/21) refers to 'the prelates, earls, barons, justices and others of our lord king's council, appointed to do right to all who complain in parliament of wrong and grievances done to them'.

PARLIAMENT AT WESTMINSTER: Candlemas 1338

i
Chancery Warrants, file 240, no.10493

Edward by the grace of God king of England, lord of Ireland and duke of Aquitaine to the reverend father in God Robert, by the same grace bishop of Chichester, our chancellor, greeting. Whereas we have arranged to have and to hold our parliament at Westminster on the Morrow of the Purification next[1] for certain business concerning us and the state of our realm,[2] we order you to have writs made without delay under our great seal as peremptory as you know how to make them,[3] with a suitable date, to be sent to all prelates, earls, barons, commons and others of the clergy of our realm, instructing them to be at Westminster on the said day of parliament to discuss the aforesaid business and to assent to what shall there be decided. Moreover, we order you to set aside all excuses and to be at Oxford this next Saturday morning,[4] to discuss and consult with some of our council whom we shall then send there on the important business touching us, about which they will fully inform you when you arrive. And you are in no way to neglect this as you love us, our honour and our welfare. Given under our privy seal at Westminster the twenty-second day of December in the eleventh year of our reign.[5]

ii
Close Roll, no.159, m.11d
[*Foedera*, II. ii. 1007; *Cal. Close Rolls, 1337-39*, p.279 f.]

The writ of summons to the prelates, including the clause requiring the attendance of proctors. It continues as follows:

And know moreover that, because of the important nature of the aforesaid business and because some other business of ours and of our realm was frequently held up, not without harassment to us and our realm, in sundry parliaments, held before this time, on account of the absence of prelates and magnates of the realm who ought to have been present in

---

[1] 3 February 1338.

[2] The pope's attempt to make peace between England and France was to be discussed 'according to the custom of the realm. Such important business is not dealt with without consulting the prelates, magnates, the wise men of the realm and the king's friends' (*Foedera*, II. ii. 1007; *Cal. Close Rolls, 1337-39*, p.285).

[3] See the next document.

[4] 27 December 1337.

[5] 22 December 1337.

person at those parliaments, along with other nobles of the realm, in accordance with our orders addressed to them thereon, we refuse on this occasion to allow proctors or any excuse for you in the absence of a lawful hindrance. Witness the king at Westminster on the twentieth day of December.[6]

By the king himself.

iii

King's Bench Roll, no.314 (Michaelmas 1338), m.31, crown

Cambridge

Presentments made in the king's bench at Michaelmas 1338.

And whereas before this time the king's writ had arrived to cause two knights of the county of Cambridge to come and stay at the king's parliament in accordance with the law and custom of the king's realm, and the said knights ought to be chosen by the county court of the county, William Muschet, while he was sheriff,[7] chose himself two knights of his faction without the assent of the county court and outside the county court and sent them to the king's parliaments held etc. And afterwards, when they had the king's writ, addressed to the sheriff of the county, for levying a specific sum of money, assigned to them for their stay and expenses in the said parliament, William Muschet and other sheriffs before this time and their bailiffs levied in the said county by extortion for their own use twice as much as the correct sum granted to the knights, to the great oppression of the people. And the sheriffs and bailiffs burdened the body of the county by sparing the men of the Liberty of Ely the full amount, whereas the said Liberty ought by right always until now to have been charged with a third of the aforesaid costs.

---

[6] 20 December 1337.
[7] 20 October 1336 – 16 October 1338 (*List of Sheriffs*, p.12).

PARLIAMENT AT WESTMINSTER: Candlemas 1339

i
King's Bench Roll, no.315 (Hilary 1339), m.116 (schedule)
[Sayles, *King's Bench*, V. 111–12]

In the king's parliament, held at Westminster on the Morrow of the Purification of the Blessed Mary in the thirteenth year of the reign of King Edward the Third,[1] John of Lowtham made a complaint in full parliament before the king's great council.

> While a justice of oyer and terminer in session at Ipswich, he had been given the lie direct, taken by the throat and thrown over the heads of the clerks as they sat in court. His assailant was committed to the Tower.[2]

ii
King's Bench Roll, no.315 (Hilary 1339), m.23 (crown)

Lincoln

> The sheriff was ordered to have Alan Ryngolf of Boston exacted from county court to county court until he was outlawed etc. for trespasses whereof he had been indicted. He appeared at the fifth county court and was sent to the king's bench but escaped from the sheriffs' custody in London and was later arrested by the sheriffs of London and committed to Newgate Gaol on being appealed of robbery. They claimed their ancient franchise which allowed them to keep those charged with offences within Newgate Gaol until they were tried before justices of gaol delivery.

And having had consultation thereon in the king's full parliament convened at the time at Westminster, because the robbery of which Alan is appealed is far more hateful than the trespass of which he is indicted, Alan is remitted to Newgate Gaol in the custody of the sheriffs to be kept safely until etc., always reserving the rights of the king, this court and the earl marshal.

---

[1] 3 February 1339.

[2] See also m.22d, crown roll: Richard de Crues was charged with assaulting the chancellor's chamberlain with a drawn dagger in the chancellor's presence in the bishop of Ely's house at Holborn. Richard was brought before the king's council in open parliament at Westminster, asked for grace, was imprisoned and later released on bail.

iii
Ancient Petitions, nos.13584, 13587
[Richardson and Sayles, *Rot. Parl. Inediti.*, 268-272]

This petition was presented on the eighth day of the parliament.

The said commons pray that, whereas it has been ordained by final award of parliament and often reduced to statute form and affirmed as law that nothing, no matter its condition, should be taken within the realm against the will of him to whom the thing belongs, certain people in contravention of this award, statute and ordinance take by means of their commission, and cause to be taken by others under them and acting for them, on the coast land as well as inland country, wheat, barley, hay, peas, oxen and pigs, money and armour without making payment, and they assess and levy upon the people of the countryside a certain sum of money at their will, and thereby the people feel themselves to be outrageously aggrieved, and they pray that such commissions may be repealed inasmuch as no free man should be liable to taxation or taxed without common assent of parliament.

As for the article concerning the point that men appointed by commissions to take corn, make their prises on the coast land as well as elsewhere, our lord the king wishes that no prises should be taken otherwise than was ordained by the statutes, and that the justices who are now appointed in the counties by commissions should have power to hear and determine the complaints and to do right, as well at the prosecution of our lord the king as of the party.

The commons pray that, whereas several petitions have been put forward in parliament and have not yet been fully answered, it may please our lord the king that all the petitions put forward in parliament by the commons may all be answered before parliament rises.

As for the article concerning the point that the petitions of the commons should be answered, all the petitions presented up until now by the commons in parliament have been fully answered before the end of the said parliaments.[3] And as for individual petitions now presented at this parliament, our lord the king wills that the auditors now appointed to try them are to try and determine them before they depart from this parliament.

[3] MS. *sic.*

PARLIAMENT AT WESTMINSTER: Michaelmas 1339

i

K.R. Exchequer Accounts 311/36

The expenses of Richard, bishop of Durham.

And also in returning to the parts of England and staying there, that is to say, in the king's parliament held and assembled at Westminster a Fortnight after Michaelmas in the thirteenth year of the king's reign[1] and on 3 November he departed from the parliament of London to his bishopric of Durham.

ii

Close Roll, no.164, m.1d
[*Foedera*, II. ii. 1098; *Cal. Close Rolls, 1339-41*, p.277 f.]

The king to the reverend father in Christ John, by the same grace archbishop of Canterbury, primate of all England, greeting. Whereas certain important and urgent business concerning us and our honour and the state of our realm has been expounded to the prelates, nobles and commons of the realm, assembled in our parliament summoned at Westminster a Fortnight after Michaelmas last, and the said commons asked for time to deliberate on these matters and requested that another parliament should be held at once and quickly so that, such deliberation having been held, a more speedy answer could be made to what has been expounded. Therefore, by advice of the prelates and nobles as well as at this request of the commons, we have ordained that a parliament is to be held at Westminster at the Octave of Hilary next on these and other most urgent matters concerning us and the conduct of our war and the rights of us and of our crown overseas as well as the defence of the realm and our other lands, and a discussion and conference is to be held there with you and with the other prelates, magnates and nobles of the realm . . . Witness the keeper of England at Langley on the sixteenth day of November.[2]

---

[1] 13 October 1339. This reference is cited in the *Chronological Handbook*, p.521.
[2] 16 November 1339. Cf. *Cal. Close Rolls, 1339-41*, p.332.

Chancery Parliament Roll, no.5, m.1d
[*Rot. Parl.* ii. 103-105]

And those of the community gave their answer in another schedule in the underwritten form:

Lords, the men who are here at this parliament on behalf of the community have well understood the position of our lord the king and the great need he has of help from his people . . . But in order to get agreement for the aid to be granted in this case, they will not venture to give assent until they have consulted and advised the common people of their local districts. Therefore the said men who are here for the communities pray my lord the duke[3] and the other lords who are present that it may please him to summon another parliament on a certain suitable day, and in the meantime each of them would withdraw to his own local district and loyally promise by the loyalty they owe our lord the king that they will take all the trouble they can, each within his own local district, to obtain a good and suitable aid for our lord the king, and they think that, with God's help, they will well accomplish it. And furthermore they pray that a writ may be sent to every sheriff in England so that two of the better-off knights of the counties be chosen and sent to the next parliament on behalf of the community, provided that none of them be a sheriff or other minister. And those of the community also put forward two bills, one containing their reply to the things they were charged to discuss, that is to say, the peace of the land, the safe-keeping of the Scottish March and of the sea, and another bill containing the graces they requested from the king.

---

[3] Edward, duke of Cornwall, regent 1338-1340.

PARLIAMENT AT WESTMINSTER: Hilary 1340

i

Chancery Warrants, file 1534, no.14

Edward, the eldest son of the noble king of England, duke of Cornwall, earl of Chester, and keeper of England, to our dear clerk, Sir John of St. Pol, keeper of the great seal of our dear lord and father, the king. We are sending you herewith enclosed a bill which has been delivered to us by our dear ones in God, the dean and chapter, provost, canons and vicars of the church of Wells at this parliament, held at Westminster at the Octave of Hilary last,[1] and which was endorsed by the magnates and the others of the council assembled at the said parliament. We so instruct you that, in accordance with the purport and effect of the said endorsement, you are to let the dean and chapter, provost, canons and vicars have appropriate letters under the great seal in proper form. Given under our privy seal at our manor of Kennington on the seventeenth day of February in the fourteenth year of the reign of our dear lord and father, the king.[2]

ii

Ancient Petition, no.12124 B

[Sayles, *King's Bench*, V. p.cl f.]

To our lord the king and to his council. Whereas after the death of Robert of Tuddenham it was found by the routine writ of inquisition[3] that he held part of his lands from the earl of Nottingham and from Robert de Scales and from other lordships and nothing in chief from the king, and afterwards another unauthorised inquisition was taken,[4] by which it was found that Robert of Tuddenham held part of his lands in chief from the king, and these two inquisitions were returned into the chancery, a writ was in consequence issued to seize all the lands whereof Robert of Tuddenham was possessed at his death. Thereupon Robert de Scales came into the chancery and asked for redress to be given him so that he might not be disinherited. And the chancellor would do nothing without

---

[1] 20 January 1340.

[2] 17 February 1340. A writ, dated the same day as the warrant, ordered two manors to be released from the king's custody to the petitioners (*Cal. Close Rolls, 1339-41*, p.359f.). The writ was authorised 'by letter of the keeper and by petition of the council'.

[3] It was issued on 12 January 1337 (*Cal. Inquisitions*, viii, no.69). The technical term for this writ was 'diem clausit extremum', that is, when a man ended his days.

[4] Presumably *op. cit.*, no.151: the writ for this inquisition is said to be missing.

judgement of parliament. And at the parliament of Stamford[5] it was adjudged that the treasurer and the barons of the exchequer should be ordered to search their records of fees to see if they could find whether Robert of Tuddenham held anything in chief from the king. And they made a return into chancery that nothing could be found to show that Robert of Tuddenham held anything in chief from the king on the day he died. And the chancellor would not release the lands from the king's hand without the advice of parliament. And at a parliament at Westminster the whole process was then presented and it was adjudged that an inquisition was to be taken and certain justices were ordered to take it. And it was taken and returned into the chancery. And it was found from it that Robert of Tuddenham held nothing in chief from the king on the day he died. And the chancellor had the whole process shown before all the justices of both benches, and it seemed to them that the inquisition had not been taken in accordance with what was decided in the parliament inasmuch as no knight was on the inquisition and the sheriff was not there in person. Therefore they adjudged that there should be another inquisition and appointed certain justices of the bench and clerks of the chancery to take it. And on that inquisition were eleven knights and seven of the wisest serjeants in the district, and the sheriff was there in his own person and the sub-escheator. And it was found by that inquisition that Robert of Tuddenham held nothing in chief from the king on the day he died. And this inquisition was returned into the chancery. And the late chancellor gave Robert de Scales a day a Fortnight after Hilary last. And John of St. Pol, keeper of the great seal, does not wish to accede to removing the king's hands without judgement of this parliament.[6] To our lord the king and his council prays Robert de Scales that redress be given him so that he be not disinherited.

iii
K.R. Memoranda Roll, no.116 (14 Edward III), Michaelmas Recorda

Of John of Godsfield to the Fleet prison for contempt.[7]

Afterwards, that is to say, on 25 April this year, John of Godsfield is freed for the moment from that prison at the king's command because it is testified before the king that John, at the time when he was arrested and committed to prison etc., was here in the king's parliament on behalf of the men of Bedford in accordance with the summons of the said parliament, to do and receive as the others etc.

[5] A council meeting at Stamford on 30 May 1337.
[6] On 13 February 1340 (*Cal. Close Rolls, 1339-41*, pp.451, 467).
[7] I.e. for failure to appear at the Octave of Hilary to answer the charge brought against him.

PARLIAMENT AT WESTMINSTER: 29 March 1340

i

Chancery Warrants, file 263, no.12716

Edward, by the grace of God king of England and of France and lord of Ireland, to the keeper of our great seal, greeting. Because the merchants of our realm who have come to this our parliament, assembled before us and our council, have requested us most urgently on behalf of themselves and all other merchants of our realm that for the ease and profit of ourselves as well as them we should grant and give them leave that they may choose from among themselves a mayor of the merchants in the same way as it used to be done in time past, and that the said mayor may have and enjoy all the franchises and free customs that others have had and enjoyed before this time in such a case. And we have granted them this request of our special grace. We order you to arrange for letters patent to be made for the merchants with respect to our leave to elect such a mayor in the aforesaid manner. And you are to let the chosen mayor have letters under our seal for the appropriate franchises and customs in proper form. Given under our privy seal at Westminster on the second day of April in the fourteenth year of our reign in England and the first year of our reign in France.[1]

ii

Chancery Miscellanea 19/20/3

Edward, by the grace of God king of England, lord of Ireland and duke of Aquitaine, to the treasurer and chamberlains of the exchequer of Dublin, greeting. Whereas we have lately ordered the venerable father Thomas, bishop of Hereford, keeper of our land of Ireland, by our writ of privy seal to come in person to us in England at the approaching parliament at Westminster, now summoned, in order to inform us and our council in the said parliament about the state of our said land, and we have given the bishop forty pounds for his passage towards England, we order you to pay the bishop forty pounds from our treasury, to be kept for the aforesaid cause. Witness Thomas, bishop of Hereford, keeper of our land of Ireland, the twenty-seventh day of March in the fourteenth year of our reign.[2]

---

[1] 2 April 1340.
[2] 27 March 1340.

iii

Chancery Parliament Roll, no.7, m.2

[*Rot. Parl.*, ii. 114]

Inasmuch as the important matters of business dealt with in this parliament cannot be completed before the Feast of Easter which is so close at hand,[3] so it is agreed by our lord the king and by the magnates to continue this parliament until the Wednesday in Easter Week.[4] Therefore the king commands that no prelate, earl, baron or other great man of the council, or knights of the shires, citizens or burgesses who have come to this parliament, may go away before the said day in case they should not be there on the said day to expedite the business of the king and the communities that still remains to be finished, and that those who wish to follow up their petitions which have not yet received a specific answer are to be there on the same day, and they shall be heard there and duly answered.

And note that the under-written persons have been appointed to consider the petitions [endorsed] 'before the king': that is to say, the bishop of Chester, the earl of Huntingdon, Thomas Wake of Liddel, John of Stonor, William of Shareshill, John of Shardlow, Richard of Willoughby, Robert Parving, and the chancellor and the treasurer are to be associated with them when needed.

iv

Cartulary of Winchester Cathedral

[ed. A.W. Goodman, ff. 131-3[5]]

These were the articles and petitions of the community of the kingdom of England . . .

In the first place the community prays that Holy Church may keep her franchises at all points. And if any extortion or grievance or any other wrong be committed against the franchises of Holy Church, that it be redressed by parliament at the suit of anyone who wishes to make a legitimate complaint. The Great Charter and the Charter of the Forest and all other statutes enacted up to the present shall be kept in all the points that may be amended at this parliament . . .

And execution of all the above points [relating to corrupt practices in the collection of taxation] shall be made and overseen by certain of the

---

[3] 16 April 1340.

[4] 19 April 1340.

[5] A more accurate text has been provided by G.L. Harriss in *Eng. Hist. Review*, lxxviii, pp.635-54.

magnates chosen and appointed in this parliament by all the magnates of the community . . .

And certain peers of the land shall be appointed in this parliament to watch over [the allocation of the king's revenues] and to arrange, receive and deliver them for the benefit of the king and for the defence of his land, and especially in connection with what will now be granted by the community in this parliament, for the said community cannot in future support such charges. All the great business of the land shall be arranged, tried, judged and dispatched by the said peers and by no one else, calling to them judges and others when they please. No part of the aids granted to our lord the king shall be given, assigned or in any way granted save by ordinance of the peers as they will answer in full parliament . . .

Also the community prays that, as our lord the king is, and has been, ever ready to do everything that his good council will ordain, without regard to the strain upon his health or any other inconvenience, such people shall be appointed to counsel him and to govern his realm as are good and loyal men of the land and no other, to be elected in this present parliament and from parliament to parliament, and they shall supervise and maintain the business of the land, as stated above, in such a way that they will be willing to answer in full parliament thereon. Thus the said peers or some of them, or those appointed by their common consent to answer, can continually supervise the business of the king and of the realm in the above manner. So where judgements are pending in any of the courts by reason of difficulty or error of the justices, the case and records shall be brought, together with the judges of the court, before the said peers and the difficulties resolved. What is not disposed of before them shall be completed in the next open parliament by the assent of parliament so that the parties who plead shall not be delayed or indeed disinherited by the plea or the divergent opinions of the judges. The said peers shall have full power, whenever they are in session in the above manner, to call to account all the ministers of the king, justices, barons and clerks of the exchequer and clerks of chancery and all other servants with regard to their conduct, both at the suit of the said party and at the suit of the king, by inquisition taken before them, so that any who are attainted of any offence or have taken any illegal payment for discharging their office shall be duly punished by the judgement of the said peers; and the business not completed before them shall be completed at the next parliament. And let it be ordained by parliament that such ministers have sufficient fees from the king so that they cannot on this account excuse themselves for taking anything to the hurt of the people . . . All the justices, clerks of chancery, barons of the exchequer and all other ministers of all courts shall be sworn to do right to all without delay and without taking anything from the parties for discharging their office, and this oath shall be taken before the peers of the land and a pronouncement shall be decreed in parliament against those who shall be found guilty of such offence. No process of pleading shall be discontinued in any court through default of a letter or of a syllable; no petition shall be granted against the ancient law of the land except by judgement of the said peers, and no grant shall be made in future that is termed 'non obstante'.[6]

v

Statute Roll, no.1, m.23
[*Statutes of the Realm*, i. 282 f.]

Because many mischiefs have arisen from the fact that in various courts – in the chancery, in the king's bench, in the common bench, in the exchequer as well as before justices of commission and other justices appointed to hear and determine – judgements have been so delayed, sometimes on account of difficulty and sometimes through the differing opinions of the justices and sometimes for other reasons, therefore it is agreed, laid down and granted that henceforward one prelate, two earls and two barons are to be chosen at every parliament and they shall have the king's commission and authority to hear, by means of petition presented to them, the plaints of all those who shall see fit to complain of such delays or grievances done to them. And they shall have power to have copies of the records and processes of such judgements as are thus delayed brought before them at Westminster or elsewhere where the courts or any one of them shall be. And they shall have the justices brought before them so that they shall then be present in order to hear the case concerning them and their reasons for such delays. And after the case and the reasons have been heard, they shall proceed to reach good agreement and make good adjudication by good advice from among themselves, the chancellor, the treasurer, the justices of both benches, and others of the king's council (as many and such as they deem appropriate for the business), and in accordance with the agreement thus reached the copy of the record, together with such adjudication as shall be agreed, is to be sent back to the justices before whom the plea is pending, and the justices are to proceed without delay to render judgement in accordance with the said agreement. And in a case where it seems to them that the problem is so great that it cannot be settled properly without the assent of parliament, the copy or copies are to be brought by the said prelate, earls and barons to the next parliament and

[6] I.e. unconditional.

there a definitive agreement is to be reached about what judgement ought to be rendered in such a case, and let the justices, before whom the plea is pending, be instructed to proceed to render judgement without delay in accordance with the said agreement. And in order to begin giving redress in line with this ordinance, it is agreed that a commission and authority be given to the archbishop of Canterbury, the earls of Arundel and Huntingdon, the lord Wake and Ralph Basset, to last until the next parliament.[7]

[7] This ordinance was repeated in a letter from the king on 10 June 1344, appointing one bishop, two earls and two barons to carry out its provisions (*Foedera*, III. i. 13; *Cal. Patent Rolls, 1343-45*, p.319 f.). It should be noted that parliament had assembled three days earlier.

PARLIAMENT AT WESTMINSTER: 12 July 1340

i
Chancery Parliament and Council Proceedings, file 7, no.10

Edward III was in Flanders between 22 June and 30 November 1340 and greatly perturbed by the failure of supplies from England for his military campaign. He was particularly angry because the wool was not being efficiently collected. This document is a much corrected draft of the answers made by the council in London to the king's inquiries under fifteen heads.

7 As for this article, answer is made that those of the council will take great pains to do the best they can, and they consider that, if our lord the king were to send some magnate, bishop or other person, he could point out that he himself was campaigning in the furtherance of their business and [the magnates of his land] would make great haste to make him some suitable aid. And on this point the chancellor and treasurer are advised to cause a parliament or a council of magnates and those of the community to be assembled, if the earls who are appointed to the privy council (privé conseil)[1] should be willing to agree and send them their letters thereon.

ii
Close Roll, no.167, m.54d
[*Lords Reports on Dignity of Peer*, iv. 524 f.; *Cal. Close Rolls, 1339-41*, p.613]

Concerning summoning merchants before the council

The king to the sheriff of York, greeting. Because[2] on some urgent business concerning us and our campaign and the general welfare of ourselves and the merchants of our realm of England we wish to have conference and discussion with those merchants at London or at Westminster on Monday[3] after the Feast of the Assumption of the Blessed Virgin Mary next, we order and firmly require you to arrange for six merchants from the city of York, four from the town of Beverley

---

[1] Cf. Ryley, *Placita Parliamentaria*, p.644: information 'to our lord the king and to his privy council' concerning the forfeiture of the elder Hugh Despenser's property.
[2] A draft is to be found in Chancery Parliament and Council Proceedings, file 46, no.10. Similar orders were sent to the sheriffs of the other counties.
[3] 21 August 1340.

and two from the town of Kingston upon Hull, and eight from the body of your shire of the most distinguished and richest merchants of the aforesaid city, towns and shire to come to the aforesaid place so that they be there on the said Monday at the latest to discuss with certain magnates and others of our council upon the said business, to be expounded more fully to them there, and to give their advice and to do further what shall then and there happen to be ordained by common counsel and assent. And you are to have there the names of the merchants thus elected and this writ, knowing for certain that, if you do not have the said merchants, thus chosen from the most distinguished and wealthiest merchants as aforesaid, at the said day and place, we will have you removed without any hesitation from your office and punished as one who impedes the dispatch of our business and is guilty of such obstruction. Witness the keeper at Kennington on the twenty-seventh day of July.

By the keeper and the council in parliament.[4]

---

[4] For petitions at this parliament see *Rot. Parl.*, ii. 117-25.

PARLIAMENT AT WESTMINSTER: Easter 1341

i

Chancery Parliament Roll, no.9, m.1

[*Rot. Parl.*, ii. 126–33]

A proclamation is made that anyone who wishes to present a petition to our lord the king and his council is to present it between this Monday[1] and the Saturday following. And it is not the king's intention to charge them with making him another aid save what they have already granted him. But on account of the great ills he has suffered and because his important business is too much delayed in that he has not been supplied with the ninths and other aids granted to him at another time, so he has charged and required most earnestly that the magnates and others of the community should hold a discussion together and take advice among themselves, that is to say, the magnates by themselves and the knights of the shires, the citizens and burgesses by themselves, how the king may be best and most supplied with what is in arrears of the said ninths. And it was also openly said to everyone that all who felt themselves aggrieved by the king or his servants or by others should put forward a petition, and they will have good and suitable redress. And let it be noted that, in order to settle some disputations arising out of some matters which the magnates and communities of the land have requested of our lord the king, the parliament was continued day by day from that Thursday[2] until the Thursday following, and on that Thursday the magnates of the land presented in parliament a bill containing some requests which our lord the king graciously granted, as is more fully mentioned below. And because mention is made, among other things contained in the supplication of the magnates, that the peers of the land, whether ministers or not, shall not be bound to answer for any trespass charged against them by the king except in parliament, the king was advised that this would be improper and against his estate. So the magnates besought the king that he should be willing to agree that four bishops, four earls and four barons, together with some experts in law, should be chosen to decide in what case the peers would be bound to answer in parliament and nowhere else, and in what case they would not, and to report their opinion to him.

There follows the names of the twelve chosen.

The twelve reported their opinion in open parliament on the following Monday in a schedule, of which a copy follows in this form:

---

[1] 23 April 1341.

[2] 26 April 1341. The parliament went on until 27–28 May.

Honourable lord, with reverence to you it seems to the prelates, earls and barons, who are in one accord, that the peers of the land ought not to be arraigned or brought to judgement except in parliament and by their peers.

And there has been some new discussion thereon whether any one of the peers, who is or has been chancellor, treasurer or any other officer, ought to enjoy this franchise by reason of their office as well as in any other way. And the peers of the land are advised that all the peers of the land, whether a minister or not, ought not by reason of their office in matters concerning their office or for any other reason to be brought to judgement or to lose their temporalities, lands, tenements, goods or chattels or to be arrested or imprisoned, outlawed or exiled, or to answer or be judged save in open parliament and before the peers . . . in cases where the king becomes a party . . .

And then the archbishop of Canterbury prayed the king that it would please his lordship that, inasmuch as he is notoriously slandered throughout the whole kingdom and elsewhere, he might be arraigned in open parliament before the peers and there reply so that he be openly regarded for what he is. This the king granted.

And that at every parliament on the third day of each parliament, the king shall take into his hand the offices of all the ministers aforesaid, and they shall remain like that for four or five days, except for the offices of the justices of both benches, the justices of commission, and the barons of the exchequer, so that at all times these and all other servants may be required to answer every plaint. And if fault be found by plaint or in any other way in any of these servants and he be convicted of this in parliament, let him be punished by judgement of the peers and removed and another competent man be put in his place. And our lord the king will have this announced and carried out without delay in accordance with the judgement of the peers in parliament.[3]

ii

K.R. Memoranda Roll, no.121 (19 Edward III), m.130d, Michaelmas Recorda

> The abbot of Thornton was charged with failing to pay the tenth granted to the king by the clergy. He claimed that he had paid it and added that he should not have been summoned to the parliament where the grant was made.

Edward, by the grace of God king of England and France and lord of Ireland, to all to whom these letters present may come, greeting. Our

[3] *Rot. Parl.*, ii. 132b–133.

beloved in Christ William, abbot of Thornton, has shown us that, although he does not hold by barony or in any way of us in chief whereby he ought to be specifically summoned to come to our parliaments or councils, and he and his predecessors were not summoned to come to such parliaments and councils of ours before the fifth year of the reign of the late Edward, king of England, our father, nor should they have been. However, in the said fifth year and afterwards they were summoned without compulsion to such parliaments and councils, not continuously but occasionally. Therefore they are aggrieved in having to come afterwards to such parliaments and councils frequently and unwontedly. Wherefore the abbot has besought us to deign to provide him therein with redress. And because the abbot and his predecessors were not summoned to come to such parliaments and councils of ours before the said fifth year of our father's reign, as is evident to us from an examination of the rolls of our chancery, and it is not found from the certification of the treasurer and barons of our exchequer, sent at our command into our chancery, that the abbot holds by barony or in any way of us in chief whereby he may be so summoned, we, not wishing that the abbot should be unduly wearied by such summonses, will and grant on behalf of ourselves and our heirs that the abbot or his successors are henceforth not to be summoned to such parliaments and councils but to be completely discharged from coming to them, provided that they consent to sending clerical proctors to such parliaments and councils and make a contribution to their expenses as usual. In witness whereof we have made these our letters patent. Witness myself at Westminster the eighth day of May in the fifteenth year of our reign in England and the second year of our reign in France.[4]

iii

Close Roll, no.169, m.1d

[*Foedera*, II. ii. 1177; *Cal. Close Rolls, 1341-1343*, p.278]

The king to the sheriff of Lincoln, greeting. Whereas in our parliament, summoned at a Fortnight after Easter last at Westminster, certain articles, clearly contrary to the laws and customs of our realm of England and to our royal rights and prerogatives, are alleged to have been granted by us in the mode of a statute, we, considering how we are bound by the bond of an oath to preserve and defend the said laws, customs, rights and

---

[4] 8 May 1341. See *Register of John de Grandisson*, pp.937-39, *Register of Hamo Hethe*, p.657, for protests that the ninth on wools, granted in the Lent parliament of 1340, should be paid by those clergy only who held by barony and were obliged to attend the king's parliament.

prerogatives and wishing therefore to bring back to their proper state those things that have been thus unwisely done, have had counsel and discussion thereon with the earls and barons and other learned men of our realm. And because we never consented to the publication of this alleged statute but dissimulated as was necessary and allowed the said alleged statute to be sealed on that occasion, for we set aside declarations about revoking the statute if it were in fact proceeded with in order to avoid the dangers which it was then feared would be the consequence of withholding it, since the said parliament would otherwise have been dissolved in discord without doing any business, and so our urgent business would truly have been ruined, which God forbid, it seemed to the said earls, barons and learned men that, since the said alleged statute did not proceed from our free will, it was void and ought not to have the name or the force of a statute. And therefore we have with their counsel and consent decreed that the statute is void and we have decided to annul it as far as it in fact went. And yet we will that the articles contained in the said alleged statute, which have been previously approved by other statutes of ours and of our predecessors, kings of England, are to be observed, as is proper, in accordance with the terms of the said statutes in all respects. And we do this, as we are bound to do, only to preserve and restore the rights of our crown but not to oppress or grieve in any way our subjects, whom we desire to rule with gentleness. And therefore we order you to have all these things publicly proclaimed in the places within your bailiwick where you think it advisable. Witness the king at Westminster on the first day of October.[5]

By the king himself and council.

---

[5] 1 October 1341. See below, p.443.

PARLIAMENT AT WESTMINSTER: Easter 1343

i

Chancery Parliament Roll, no.10, m.1

[*Rot. Parl.*, ii. 135 f.]

The same day[1] a proclamation was made that everyone who wishes to present a petition to our lord the king and his council, is to present it between now and the following Monday, this day being included within the time of the proclamation. And there are appointed to receive the petitions of England [three chancery clerks] and to receive the petitions of Gascony, Wales, Ireland, Scotland, Flanders and the Channel Isles [three chancery clerks]. And there are appointed to hear the petitions of England [two bishops, two earls, two nobles, four judges, with the chancellor and treasurer when necessary], and to hear the petitions of Gascony, Wales, Ireland, Scotland, Flanders and the Channel Isles [two bishops, two earls, two nobles, four judges, with the chancellor and treasurer when necessary].[2]

And the reasons for summoning parliament were propounded by the king's chancellor as follows: First of all it was mentioned that the paramount and principal reason is to discuss and take counsel with the magnates and the communities of the realm upon what it will be best to do on the matters concerning our lord the king with respect to the truces made in Brittany between him and his adversary of France; and then afterwards upon the matters which concern the estate of our lord the king and the governance and safety of his land of England and of his people and the betterment of their estate.

On that Thursday the prelates and magnates, assembled in the White Chamber, replied that they were advised that the truces were honourable and profitable to our lord the king and to all his people . . . And then came the knights of the shires and the communities and replied in the White Chamber through Sir William Trussel, who in the presence of our lord the king and the prelates and magnates propounded on behalf of the knights and communities that they fully agree and consent that the truces should be held in order that a good and honourable peace be achieved.

---

[1] 16 April 1343.

[2] For parliamentary petitions at this time see, for example, K.R. Memoranda Roll, no.119, Trinity Recorda; Exchequer Plea Roll, no.69, m.33, no.70, m.9, no.71, m.7.

Of the statute made at Westminster in the fifteenth year, which is repealed

It is agreed and consented that the statute, made at Westminster a Fortnight after Easter in the fifteenth year of our lord the king's reign,[3] should be utterly repealed and void and lose the name of statute as being prejudicial and contrary to the laws and customs of the realm and to the rights and prerogatives of our lord the king. But since some clauses contained in the said statute are right and in accordance with law and what is right, it is granted by our lord the king and his council that such clauses and some others agreed in this present parliament should be made into a new statute by the advice of the justices and other wise men and maintained for all time.[4]

[3] Easter 1341. For the statute see *Statutes of the Realm*, i. 295 f.

[4] For a letter sent to the pope by the 'community of England' on the question of papal provisions to churches, which was authorized 'at the open parliament at Westminster' on 18 May 1343, see Duchy of Lancaster Recorda 42/8, m.2*b*-3 (printed Murimuth, *Continuatio Chronicarum*, p.138, Avesbury, *De gestis Edwardi Tertii*, p.353 and 'Hemingburgh', *Chronicon*, ii. 401 (a Latin version). The letter arose out of a petition presented in the Easter parliament of 1343 (*Rot. Parl.*, ii. 144a).

PARLIAMENT AT WESTMINSTER: 7 June 1344

i

Chancery Parliament Roll, no.11, m.1

[*Rot. Parl.*, ii. 146-9]

First of all, note that on Monday[1] there assembled in the Painted
Chamber our lord the king and the prelates and magnates written below,
that is to say, the archbishop of Canterbury, the bishops of Chichester,
Bath, and Ely, and the earl of Huntingdon, together with some of the
abbots and barons, and the knights of the shires and [burgesses] and it
was at the king's command [explained] before them by the chancellor
how at another time at the council held at Westminster at a Fortnight
after Easter last[2] it was agreed by all the magnates there present that
parliament should be summoned at this day and place for the various
urgent matters concerning the governance and the safeguarding of the
realm of England, which could not be coped with without parliament, as
was then said.

And note that on Tuesday our lord the king and the said prelates, and the
bishops of London and Carlisle, together with the magnates, assembled a
second time in the Painted Chamber, and there they agreed upon the
names of those who should receive the petitions of parliament as follows,
namely:
First, to receive the petitions of England, there are appointed the persons
written below, namely [three chancery clerks].
    And for the petitions of Gascony, Wales, Ireland, Brittany, Scotland
and the Channel Isles and other foreign lands, the persons written below
[three chancery clerks].
    Again, to try the petitions of England are appointed [two bishops, two
abbots, two earls, four barons, three judges and, if necessary, the
chancellor and the treasurer]. And they shall hold their court in the small
chamber near the door of the Painted Chamber.
    Again, to try the petitions of Gascony, Wales, Ireland, Brittany,
Scotland and the Channel Isles and other foreign lands are appointed
those written below, namely [three bishops, two abbots, two earls, three
judges and, when possible, the chancellor and the treasurer].
    And Thomas of Brayton is appointed clerk of the parliament.
    And let the names of the lords who are summoned to the parliament be
looked at, read out and scrutinised before the king in parliament on this

[1] 7 June 1344.
[2] 18 April 1344.

Tuesday to see the names of the lords who have come and of those who have not come.

And let the names of those who have not come be handed to the king in writing so that he may order such punishment as he pleases.

And the commons pray that the petitions which are now presented on account of sundry grievances committed in various counties should be examined and that redress should be ordained by good counsel before the end of the parliament for the salvation of the people; and this should be looked at and examined by the magnates and the other wise men appointed for this purpose; and that the ordinances and grants made to his people by his charter should be kept; and that it may please you to ordain, with the assent of the prelates and magnates, certain men who will kindly remain until the petitions presented in parliament are determined before their departure, so that the commons may not be without redress.

Reply: It pleases the king that the petitions should be examined and answered. And as for the charters and other grants made by the king to the community, it is agreed that they should be inspected and examined, and those that are right and just are to be held and kept.

ii

Chancery Warrants, file 299, no.16310

Edward, by the grace of God king of England and of France and lord of Ireland, to our dear and faithful Robert of Saddington, our chancellor, greeting. We are sending you, enclosed herein, a petition[3] which was presented and endorsed in our last parliament and which we then also granted by the advice of our great council. So we instruct you that, having seen the petition and its endorsement, you are to cause proper execution to be made thereon in the appropriate manner by letters under our great seal. Given under our privy seal at Westminster on the ninth day of July in the eighteenth year of our reign in England and the fifth year in France.[4]

[3] The enclosure is now Ancient Petition, no. 8478. Cf. *Cal. Fine Rolls, 1337-47*, p.381 f.: the restitution, by advice of the great council, to the prior of Sporle in Norfolk of the custody of the priory. For another petition, 'endorsed with the assent of parliament', see K.R. Memoranda Roll, no.121, Michaelmas Recorda.

[4] 9 July 1344.

iii
King's Bench Roll, no.323 (Hilary 1341), m.41
[Sayles, *King's Bench*, VI. 9 f.]

To our lord the king and his council shows Geoffrey, son of Sir William Stanton, that, whereas he recovered certain tenements in the county of Nottingham from Sir John Stanton of Elston and Amy, his wife, by judgement in the common bench on a writ of formedon, and this judgement was ordained and agreed in two open parliaments by great deliberation of all those learned in the law, and after judgement had been delivered, because Geoffrey did not obtain full execution, he caused the record and process thereof to come by the king's writ into the king's bench in order to obtain execution. And the said John and Amy caused the said record and process to come into the king's bench by a writ of error. And there the record and process have pended since the fourteenth year[5] and are still awaiting confirmation or annulment. Wherefore Geoffrey prays our lord the king and his council that, whereas the aforesaid judgement was reached and agreed with such solemnity in the said two parliaments and in open parliaments and by unanimous advice of all the learned men, and this decision and judgement were ordered to be entered on the roll of parliament and, so he understands, are entered,[6] an order may be sent for God's sake to the justices of the king's bench (before whom the record pends at John and Amy's suit in order to have the judgement reversed on account of the errors propounded by them, and before whom the same record pends at Geoffrey's suit to obtain execution as aforesaid) that they are to proceed without delay to a final discussion of the matter in accordance with the law of the land so that Geoffrey may suffer delay no longer nor be deprived, to his disherison, of the aforesaid execution.

The endorsement of the petition is as follows: Let a writ be sent, together with the petitions,[7] to the justices of the king's bench, ordering them to look at and examine the record and process which the petitions mention and to proceed to a final discussion of the matter without delay in accordance with the law and custom of the realm so that the parties no longer suffer delay.

---

[5] 1340.

[6] *Rot. Parl.*, i. 122b–124b.

[7] Both parties had presented petitions.

PARLIAMENT AT WESTMINSTER: 11 September 1346

i

Chancery Parliament Roll, no.12, ms.2, 3
[*Rot. Parl.*, ii. 160–61]

And then the knights, citizens and burgesses were told that, if they wished to put forward any petition in this parliament that might turn to the common welfare and their own relief, they should deliver it to the clerk of the parliament. And they delivered this petition on the Friday and it was brought before the great men of the council on the Saturday, Sunday and Monday following, and on the said Monday an answer was given to the petition.[1]

Furthermore the commons pray that the great subsidy of forty shillings on the sack of wool be removed and the old custom paid, as was agreed and granted at other times.

Reply: As to this point the prelates and the others saw the necessity that the king was under to be assisted before his passage overseas to recover his rights and defend his realm of England, and they gave their consent, in agreement with the merchants, that our lord the king should have as a subsidy in aid of his war and for the defence of his land forty shillings on every sack of wool that goes overseas, to last for the next two years. And various merchants on the basis of this grant have made loans to our lord the king in aid of his war. Therefore this subsidy cannot be repealed without the assent of the king and of his great men.

ii

Chancery Parliament and Council Proceedings, file 7, no.21
[Sayles, *King's Bench*, V. p.clii f.]

It has been decided by the whole council that the bishop of Norwich should await the next parliament in order to have full deliberation upon the business arising out of his petition, put forward in parliament, with regard to the franchises of Lynn, if he does not wish to show and clarify his rights sooner to expedite his said business.

Endorsed: This decision was made at the Carmelites in the council chamber on Sunday, the fifth day of November in the twentieth year of

---

[1] Bartholomew de Burghersh, John Darcy, chamberlain, and John of Thoresby, keeper of the privy seal, and John Carleton were appointed to explain to parliament the state of the king's affairs and his intentions: as envoys they were to report back to him (*Foedera*, III. i. 90; *Cal. Patent Rolls, 1345–48*, p.474).

the reign of our lord the king in England and the seventh year of his reign in France[2] by our lord the king's council, namely, the bishop of Winchester, the treasurer, the dean of Lincoln, the chancellor, John of Stonor, Robert of Saddington, Richard of Willoughby, William of Shareshill, William of Thorp, William Basset, John of Stowford, Roger of Bakewell, justice, Robert of Thorp and William of Norton, the king's serjeants-at-law.[3]

iii

King's Bench Roll, no.342 (Michaelmas 1345), m.115*d*

Yorkshire

Edward by the grace of God king of England and of France and lord of Ireland, to his beloved and faithful William Scot and his fellows, our justices assigned to hear pleas before us, greeting. Because manifest error has intervened in the record and process of the assize of novel disseisin which was summoned and taken before us at York between the prior of Newburgh and Simon Simeon and others mentioned in our original writ, with respect to tenements in Cundall, Leckby, Thornton Bridge and Kilburn near Coxwold, to the serious loss of the said Simon and the others, as we have learned from Simon, grievously complaining to us by his petition presented before us and our council at Westminster, we, wishing in this matter for the error, if such there be, to be corrected and justice done to the parties, order you to examine and diligently hear the record and process of the said assize and to summon thereon, if need be, the parties and to hear the arguments on both sides and to have the errors, if any should be found in the record and process, corrected and amended without delay. Otherwise we will cause the record and process of the assize to come into our next parliament to correct the said errors there in due manner. Witness myself at Westminster on the sixth day of July in the eighteenth year of our reign in England and the fifth year of or reign in France.[4]

Simeon alleged six grounds of error at Michaelmas term 1346.

And the prior says that the assize was brought in court here and taken in the king's bench and judgement rendered there etc. In that case, even

---

[2] 5 November 1346.

[3] The justices of assize in York and Northumberland had been ordered to postpone proceedings because they had been summoned 'like our other justices', to this parliament at Westminster (*Chancery Parliament and Council Proceedings*, 7/20).

[4] 6 July 1344.

though errors may have intervened in the said record and in the rendering of justice, they ought not to be corrected and amended anywhere else than in the king's parliament before the king and his council. Therefore he does not believe that the justices here, by reason of the aforesaid writ addressed to them thereon, would wish or ought to compel him to answer here upon the said errors etc. And if it should appear to the court that he ought to answer here upon those errors, he is always ready to answer thereon etc.

The prior accepted the jurisdiction of the king's bench and eventually the record was adjudged null and void on the ground of error, and judgement was given in favour of Simeon and the others.

PARLIAMENT AT WESTMINSTER: Hilary 1348

i

Close Roll, no.182, m.9

[*Lords Reports*, iv. 572–3; *Cal. Close Rolls, 1346–49*, p.412 f.]

Concerning the parliament to be held at Westminster

The king to the reverend father in Christ John, by the same grace archbishop of Canterbury, primate of all England, greeting. Because for some important business concerning us and the state of our realm of England as well as the general welfare of its people, we intend to hold our parliament at Westminster on the Morrow of Hilary next and to have discussion and debate with you and the other prelates and magnates of the realm, we order you, charging you firmly in the faith and love by which you are bound to us, to put aside every excuse and to be in person with us at the said day and place to discuss the aforesaid business with the said prelates, magnates and nobles of our realm and to give us your advice. And you shall in no wise neglect to do this as you love us and our honour and the general welfare of the people. And you are to warn the prior and chapter of Christchurch, Canterbury, and the archdeacons and all the clergy of your diocese that the prior and archdeacons are to be in person at the day and place aforesaid and the chapter by one proctor and the clergy by two suitable proctors, having full and sufficient power from the chapter and the clergy, in order to consent to those things which happen to be ordained there and then by common counsel of our realm, God willing. And we wish you to know that we have caused this parliament to be summoned, not to obtain aids or tallages from the people of our realm or to impose other burdens upon the people but only to dispense justice to our people for the ills and oppression done to them[1] and to have discussion upon the said business as aforesaid. Witness the king at Westminster on the thirteenth day of November.[2]

By the king himself.

[1] For petitions presented at this parliament see Exchequer Plea Roll, no.80 (30 Edward III), m.54; K.R. Memoranda Roll, no.127, Easter Recorda: a petition bears the endorsement, 'Let the petition and the inquisition come before the triers of petitions, and after they have been read, answer is made'; *Cal. Close Rolls, 1346–49, passim*.
[2] 13 November 1347.

ii
Chancery Parliament Roll, no.13, m.1
[*Rot. Parl.*, ii. 165]

As regards the war which our lord the king has undertaken against his adversary of France with the common assent of all the magnates and commons of his land . . . and what shall be done about it when the present truce comes to an end. Order was given thereon to the knights of the shire and the others of the commons that they should hold a discussion together and they should show the king and the magnates of his council what they felt in the matter. And the knights and the others of the commons, having had consultations thereon for four days, at last replied to the article concerning the war in the following way: Most respected lord: as regards your war and the arrangements for it, we are so unknowledgeable and unversed that we do not know how to advise you thereon and cannot do so. Wherefore we pray your gracious lordship to hold us excused from the arrangement of affairs and that it may please you to settle this matter with the advice of the magnates and the learned men of your council as it seems best to you for the honour and welfare of you and of your realm. And we fully agree to what shall be decided thereon with the assent and agreement of you and the aforesaid magnates and we will keep it firm and secure. And then the commons handed in their petitions, some concerning the peace as well as other matters whereof they feel themselves aggrieved . . . And the commons pray that all the petitions that follow, presented by the commons for the general welfare and to obtain redress of wrongs, may be answered and endorsed in parliament before the commons so that they can know the endorsements and have redress therein according to the ordinance of the parliament.

[*ibid.*, p.172]

Again, the commons pray as regards the judgements, pending in various courts for a long time and not rendered on account of difficulties in the law, that it may please our lord the king to ordain that the said judgements are to be rendered without further delay, to the profit of his commons.

Answer: It pleases the king that the justices before whom the pleas are pending should render judgements as soon as they properly can. And, if they cannot render the judgements, that copies of the record and process of such pleas are to come into parliament and are to be determined there in accordance with the decisions made thereon.[3]

---

[3] For petitions in this parliament, presumably copied from the originals when they were all filed together, see B.L., Lansdowne MS., no.482, fos.3–14.

PARLIAMENT AT WESTMINSTER: Mid–Lent 1348

i
Chancery Parliament Roll, no.14, m.1
[*Rot. Parl.*, ii. 200 f.]

To their most honoured and respected liege lord his poor commons show that, whereas at his last parliament he sent his noble earls of Lancaster and of Northampton and other magnates to inform his commons that it was not his will to take anything from them or to lay a burden upon his commons . . . they pray that henceforth no levy, tallage or charge by way of loan or in any other way is to be made by the privy council of our lord the king without their assent and grant in parliament. And also that two prelates, two lords, and two justices are to be appointed in this present parliament to hear and determine all the petitions, put forward at another time by the commons in the last parliament, that were not yet answered, and along with them the petitions now to be presented, in the presence of four or six of the commons, chosen by them to do and further this business, so that the said petitions may be satisfactorily answered in this present parliament, and as for those which have already been fully answered, that the answers may be enforced without being changed.

And then the commons were told that all individuals who would like to hand in petitions in this parliament should have them delivered to the chancellor, and that they should have petitions concerning the commons delivered to the clerk of the parliament.
And the commons delivered their petitions to that clerk as follows:

Furthermore, the commons pray that all other petitions put forward at another time at the last parliament should be expedited and appropriately answered at this parliament without further delay and for the common profit of our lord the king and of the commons. Sire, if it please you, what is discussed and done for the welfare of your poor commons will particularly redound to your advantage more than any other thing.

Answered: The shortness of time does not permit this matter to be expedited before Easter and so it pleases the king that it be expedited immediately after Easter.

Again,[1] the commons pray that the petitions delivered in the last parliament by the said commons and fully answered and granted by our

---

[1] *Op. cit.*, page 203*b*.

lord the king, the prelates and magnates of the land, may hold good, and that the answers previously granted may not be changed through any bill presented in this parliament in the name of the commons or by anyone else, for if any such bill be presented in parliament to the contrary effect, the commons do not avow it.[2]

Answered: The king at another time, by the advice of the prelates and magnates of the land, caused answer to be made to the petitions of the commons regarding the law of the land, that the laws prevailing and used in times past and the process upon them used hitherto shall not be able to be changed without making a new statute thereon. And to do this the king could not then and still cannot attend for certain reasons. But as soon as he can attend to it, he will bring the magnates and the learned men of his council before him and he will ordain on these articles and others concerning the amendment of the law by their counsel and advice in such a manner that what is reasonable and right shall be done to each and all his loyal men and subjects.

ii
Ancient Petition, no.15549
[*Rot. Parl.*, ii. 180]

To our lord the king and his council shows John fitz Walter that the law of the land is such that, where a man who holds of different lords forfeits his land in war, the king will have it as his escheat, no matter of whom the land was previously held. And the king later gave that land to someone else in fee simple, and he did not state in his charter of whom it was to be held. Because some men of law say that the land will be held of the lords from whom it was first held, John prays that this law may be clearly expressed so that the king may have what he ought to have and that other lords may have what they ought to have. And furthermore in the case where the king gives the land to be held of him and his heirs, whether the charter can be repudiated or not.

Endorsed: Before the king and his great council.

---

[2] Cf. *op. cit.*, p.230*b*, for a similar protest in the Candlemas parliament of 1351 that no petition from an individual should cause a statute to be altered.

iii

Year Book, 29 Edward III (ed. 1532), f. 3

A writ came to Sir William Thorpe, chief justice of the king's bench, to summon into parliament the record and process of a judgement which was rendered for the king at the suit of Edmund Hadlow and his wife. And note that a petition was made to the king before the writ was granted, by which the roll, in which were the process and the judgement, was brought by the said Sir W. Thorpe into parliament. And the king assigned thereon certain earls and barons and, with them, the justices etc. of [oyer and] terminer for the said business. And before anything was done, the parliament was ended. And the deputies demurred but the king himself had departed. And it was alleged before them that the judgement could not be reversed except in parliament, and since parliament is at an end, nothing further can be done in this matter. And it was said that the king made the laws by the assent of the peers and the commons, and not the peers and the commons, and that he will have no peer in his own land, and that the king ought not to be judged by them, and that in the time of King Henry and before him the king was impleaded as would be any other man of the people, but King Edward, his son, ordained that men should sue against the king by petition.[3] But never will kings be judged save by themselves and their justices.

---

[3] Cf. *Year Book, 33-35 Edward I*, p.470: In old times every writ, whether of right or of the possession, lay well against the king and nothing is now changed except that one must now sue him by bill where formerly one sued by writ.

Index

[Contractions: archbp. *for* archbishop; bp. *for* bishop; bro. *for* brother; dau. *for* daughter; kg. *for* king; qn. *for* queen]

Aaron the Jew 95
—, Cok, son of 95f.
Abel, John 249, 328 and *n*.
Aberconway, co. Caernarvon 221
Abingdon, co. Oxford, abbot of 121, 390 and *n*.
—, Richard of 289
Abraham, jew of Norwich 158
Accursi, Francesco 148
Aconbury, co. Hereford, nuns of 22
Acton Burnell, co. Salop 180, 182
—, statute of 222f.
Adam, John ap 301
—, widow of 301
Adrian, John 129
Agenais, Aquitaine 88
Aguillun, Geoffrey 178
—, Robert 86
Airmyn, William 36*n*., 52*n*., 323, 332, 341, 343, 349f.
Alan, Richard fitz 237
Aldborough, Richard of 414
Alexander III, kg. of Scotland 156, 272
—, homage of 156*n*.
Aliens 415, 419
Almain, Henry of 64*n*., 71, 75, 112, 119, 126
—, Richard of 71
Alresford, co. Hants. 352
Alton, co. Hants. 351
Amaury, Peter 262
Amersham, Walter of 181, 239
Amesbury, co. Wilts. 268
Amiens, France 354
—, merchants of 298
Ancient demesne 81
Andover, co. Hants. 351
Anesty, co. Yorks. 151
Angus, earl of 228, 342, 353
Annesley, John of 278
Appeal, false 82

Aquitaine, France 329, 397, 406
—, duke of 297
Aragon, Spain 281
Arblaster, Robert le 352
Ardicio, papal nuncio 159
Argentein, Giles de 74
Arnold, Peter, de Vico 262
Arundel, earl of 228, 237, 336, 361, 435
Ash, co. Kent 249
Ashbourne, co. Derbs. 335
Ashby, co. Leic. 414
—, Robert of 52*n*., 323, 333, 343, 344-6, 350
—, —, illness of 346
Ashridge, co. Herts. 203, 204*n*.
Aspall, Geoffrey 140
Assize of cloth 157, 180
Astley, James 206*n*.
Athelstan, kg. 273
Auditors: appointed to investigate official misconduct 213, 244
—, —, high authority of 213
—, —, error of 213
Audley, Hugh 342f.
—, —, Margaret wife of 342f.
—, James 30, 73, 87, 104*n*.
Aumale, earl of 73f.
—, countess of 101, 107f., 119, 158
Avranches, Normandy, bp. of 297
Aylesbury, co. Bucks. 182
Aylesford, co. Kent 386
Aythorpe Roding, co. Essex 271

Bacon, Thomas 414
Badlesmere, Bartholomew of 323, 336
—, Jocelin de 177
Bagot, Robert of 170 and *n*.
—, —, seal of 170
Baignard, Robert 180